A Primer on PASCAL

WINTHROP COMPUTER SYSTEMS SERIES
Gerald M. Weinberg, *editor*

CONWAY AND GRIES
An Introduction to Programming: A Structured Approach Using PL/1 and PL/C-7, Second Edition

CONWAY AND GRIES
Primer on Structured Programming Using PL/I, PL/C, and PL/CT

CONWAY, GRIES, AND ZIMMERMAN
A Primer on PASCAL

GELLER AND FREEDMAN
Structured Programming in APL

Future Titles

CONWAY, GRIES, AND WORTMAN
Introduction to Structured Programming Using PL/1 and SP/k

ECKHOUSE AND SPIER
Guide to Programming

FINKENAUR
COBOL for Students: A Functional Approach

GELLER
Structured Programming in FORTRAN

GILB
Software Metrics

GREENFIELD
The Architecture of Microcomputers

WEINBERG AND GILB
Humanized Input: Techniques for Reliable Keyed Input

WEINBERG, GOETZ, WRIGHT, AND KAUFFMAN
High-Level COBOL Programming

WILCOX
Compiler Writing

A Primer on PASCAL

Richard Conway

David Gries

Cornell University

E. C. Zimmerman

The College of Wooster

Foreword by Niklaus Wirth

Winthrop Publishers, Inc.

Cambridge, Massachusetts

Library of Congress Cataloging in Publication Data
Conway, Richard Walter,
A primer on PASCAL.
(Winthrop computer systems series)
Includes index.
1. PASCAL (Computer program language) I. Gries, David, joint author. II. Zimmerman, E. Carl, joint author. III. Title.
QA76.73.P35C66 001.6'424 76-5462
ISBN 0-87626-694-4 (p)
0-87626-693-6 (c)

© 1976 by Winthrop Publishers, Inc.
17 Dunster Street, Cambridge, Massachusetts 02138

All rights reserved. No part of this book may be reproduced in any form or by any means without permission in writing from the publisher. Printed in the United States of America.

10 9 8 7 6 5

Contents

Part III Program Development 207

Part IV Independent Subprograms 285

Part V Program Testing 343

Preface

This book is intended to be a primer on programming -- an introduction for students who have not programmed previously. It does not attempt to cover all of the PASCAL language; just to introduce an elementary subset. When PASCAL is taught as a second language to students who have already learned the elements of programming in another language, then parts of this Primer will be tediously slow. (However, some of the material in Parts II, III and V may still be useful.) But PASCAL should be taught more widely as a first language, and this book is designed for that service.

This book is based on the Conway-Gries Primer on Structured Programming (Winthrop, 1976), which uses the PL/I language. Although in that book we attempted to present the key ideas in a manner that was relatively independent of the language, some of the PL/I-heritage of the material persists in the present book. None of us is a hard-core PASCAL fanatic, and our examples undoubtedly do not exploit the unique features of the language as much as they might. If this makes them less elegant, it also makes them less peculiar to PASCAL.

In many places in the text we contrast PASCAL and PL/I, not always favorably to PASCAL, although on balance we believe it is a stronger language. We are less impressed with the diagnostic facilities of existing PASCAL compilers, but we have been spoiled in this regard by PL/C, the Cornell compiler for PL/I, which emphasizes diagnostic assistance. Similarly, we include a brief section on interactive programming, based on Cornell's PL/CT, under the assumption that eventually there will be a comparable interactive version of PASCAL.

We know of no other book that is really suitable for a textbook for an introductory course using PASCAL, and suspect that this has discouraged some instructors who would prefer to use this very worthwhile language. We hope that this Primer may contribute to the growth and acceptance of PASCAL.

We would like to acknowledge the help received from David Kasik of Battelle Institute, Andy Mickel of the University of Minnesota, Niklaus Wirth of ETH, Zurich, and David Wise of Indiana University. We did not always take their suggestions, but without their efforts there would be many more PASCAL errors and the PL/I influence would surely have been much stronger. We would appreciate receiving any suggestions and corrections from users, to incorporate in future editions.

This _Primer_ was produced by an editing program run on the IBM 370/168 of Cornell's Office of Computer Services. A printer-simulator generated page images on a CRT display, from which photo plates were made.

Ithaca, N. Y.

R. Conway
D. Gries
E. C. Zimmerman

Foreword

The construction of a computer program is an intellectual and creative activity. In general, it encompasses the comprehension and analysis of a given problem, decisions on how the given situation is best abstracted and represented by numbers and symbols, a choice of a method of computation, the careful design of the algorithm representing this computation, and finally the formulation of the data and the algorithm in terms of a programming language. Until recently, only this last part was understood by the term "programming." But the evolution of the computer to a powerful and flexible data processor, and its application to problems of ever growing complexity have led to the recognition that programming is much more than merely coding. The principal difficulties lie in finding the appropriate structures of the data and of the algorithm, in demonstrating that the algorithm is correct and efficient, and that the chosen data representation is suitable and economical. The affair of coding these structures in terms of an available machine seems to be of secondary importance.

The present book clearly reflects this recognition. It is a primer derived from an introductory text on programming--understood in the above general sense. The Primer, however, is dedicated to one particular programming language: PASCAL. The development of PASCAL has been strongly influenced by developments in techniques of program construction. Indeed, the purpose of a high-level language such as PASCAL is to allow the formulation of algorithms <u>and</u> data in a form which clearly exhibits their natural structure. The mundane activity of coding can then be left to an automatic compiler.

The programming language PASCAL is the result of developments over many years, initiated within the Working Group 2.1 of IFIP to define a successor to ALGOL 60. These efforts produced the language ALGOL W in 1965, which can be considered the direct predecessor to PASCAL. The main innovation in PASCAL (1970) was a variety of structuring methods for data, and in particular of programmer definable data types. These data types are, however, restricted to structures that can be represented and manipulated quite effectively on modern computers. The use of PASCAL therefore does not only lead to a decrease in programming effort and an increase of program readability, but also guarantees that the resulting programs are efficient in terms of available computers. PASCAL is a language of comparatively moderate complexity or size. As a result, many compilers have been developed for many different computers, usually based on the initiative of individuals or small research groups. Most of these developments have been oriented to the needs of teaching and the economical handling of many small test programs. They are therefore often based on the interpretive approach. However, the number of high quality genuine compilers is also growing, and this is fortunate, because only they exhibit the true advantages of not only learning but also applying PASCAL.

I am very pleased that a primer based on the excellent book "Introduction to Programming" using PASCAL has been made available. The authors are to be congratulated for an admirably well-done job. The adaptation of a programming text to another language is by no means an easy task. It would have been utterly impossible for most similar textbooks. In the present case, the formal similarity of PASCAL and PL/I (the language used in the original book) is only partially responsible for this success, for the authors have succeeded to eliminate "PL/I-erisms" remarkably well. At the same time, their explanations and examples implicitly exhibit the style and air of PASCAL that is so noticeably different from that of PL/I.

Zurich, Switzerland — Niklaus Wirth

A Primer on PASCAL

Part I
Fundamental Concepts

Section 1 The Computing Process

We are concerned with the process by which a digital computer can be used to solve problems -- or at least aid in the solution of problems. This involves learning to:

1. Choose problems that are appropriate to the computer's abilities, and describe the problem requirements, conditions, and assumptions clearly and precisely.

2. Design a solution to a problem and describe it in a language intelligible to a computer. This description is called a "program", while the process of producing a program is called "programming". Programming is a systematic, level-by-level process in which the original problem description, usually given in a combination of English and mathematics, is translated into a "programming language". This process must also transform a statement of objectives -- what is required -- into a description of an executable procedure -- how the objectives are to be achieved. A third aspect of the transformation is to make explicit and precise those portions of the problem description that are implicit and rely on the intuition, common sense, or technical knowledge of the reader, since the computer is completely lacking in these virtues.

3. Confirm the correctness of the program. This means demonstrating in as convincing a manner as possible that the program precisely satisfies the problem requirements.

The selection of appropriate problems is as difficult and important as the analysis and programming, but it is impossible to discuss this issue until one has some understanding of the nature of computing systems and their special abilities. However, two initial observations might be helpful. Firstly, problems for which computer assistance is sought are generally of substantial magnitude. There is non-trivial effort involved in the mechanics of obtaining computer assistance, and if the problem is simple, not repetitive, and not likely to recur, computer assistance may cost more than it is worth. One must bear this in mind even though the examples that will be used for instruction will necessarily be short and often trivial. They are presumably used to develop a competence which will be useful for subsequent attack on real and substantial problems.

Secondly, the computer can only assist in the solution of problems which can be stated very precisely and for which a detailed and precise method of solution can be given. Roughly speaking, one cannot expect a computer to perform a process that could not be performed by a human--if he lived long enough. The digital computer permits a tremendous increase in the quantity of symbols that may be considered, in the precision and reliability with which they will be manipulated, and above all in the speed with which the process will be carried out. But in principle the computer is only performing operations that could be carried out by a human being. It is true that the orders-of-magnitude differences in volume, speed and reliability combine to produce spectacular capability, but the fundamental process is simple and not unlike what a human could perform.

For example, a computer can "play chess" only because the game of chess has been described to the computer as an elaborate symbol manipulation task. On the other hand, a computer cannot be requested to "solve the vehicle emission problem" because no one has as yet figured out how to describe this problem strictly in terms of symbol manipulation. As another example, a computer is not infrequently asked to "select a date for a person from a set of potential candidates" and sometimes produces rather humorous recommendations. The source of the humor lies not in the computer's execution of the process but in the fact that no one really knows how to precisely describe this complex selection process.

1.1 Examples of Programs

At this point we present a number of simple examples of computer programs. These problems are unrealistically simple but they will give you some idea of what a program looks like. We will give some explanation after each example, but we do not intend these to be complete explanations. This is just to give you a general idea of what the end product of the programming process is going to be. The details will be explained in later sections.

(1.1a)

```
(* ADD  THE INTEGERS 245 AND 73 AND PRINT THEIR SUM *)
PROGRAM ADD2(INPUT,OUTPUT);
VAR SUM: INTEGER;
BEGIN (* ADD2 *)
    SUM := 245 + 73;
    WRITELN(SUM)
END.  (* ADD2 *)
```

The meaning of each line in (1.1a) is the following:

line 1 is a "comment" that describes the purpose of the program. It is ignored by the computer and has no effect on the execution of the program. It is provided solely to make the program easier for a human to read. In PASCAL any text between the symbol pairs (* and *) is a comment.

Line 2 "declares" that the name of this particular program is ADD2 and that the program may use an input device and an output device.

Line 3 "declares" a "variable" named SUM. It causes space to be set aside in the computer to receive integer values. This space is given the name SUM so it can be referred to elsewhere in the program.

Lines 4 and 7 mark the beginning and end of the "body" of the program. Although PASCAL does not require it, we will always give the program name as a comment after these lines to help identify them. (Later we will have other BEGIN,END lines within the body of the program.)

Line 5 causes the two numbers 245 and 73 to be added together and their sum stored in the variable named SUM.

Line 6 causes the value of the variable named SUM to be printed out. This will be the only externally-visible result of executing this program -- a line with the number 318 will be printed.

The program ADDTWO in (1.1b) is a minor variation and improvement upon (1.1a). ADD2 just adds two specific numbers -- 245 and 73 -- that are given as constants in the program. ADDTWO will add <u>any pair of integers</u> that are given as data following the program. It is shown in (1.1b) with the same two numbers that were used in (1.1a), but ADDTWO could be rerun with some other pair of integers as data. ADDTWO requires three different spaces to be set aside in the computer -- two to store the input data, and one to store the answer.

(1.1b)

```
(* READ 2 INTEGERS AND PRINT THEIR SUM *)
PROGRAM ADDTWO(INPUT,OUTPUT);
VAR VALUE1, VALUE2, SUM: INTEGER;
BEGIN (* ADDTWO *)
    READ(VALUE1, VALUE2);
    SUM := VALUE1 + VALUE2;
    WRITELN(SUM)
END.  (* ADDTWO *)
    eor
245 73
```

Line 9 of ADDTWO indicates a special card that separates the PASCAL program preceding it from the program data following it. This card is called an "end-of-record card". We will denote it by the symbol "eor" in our examples.

ADDFIVE in (1.1c) adds five integers, and prints the data as well as the answer with appropriate titling.

(1.1c)

```
(* READ 5 INTEGERS, PRINT THEM AND THEIR SUM *)
PROGRAM ADDFIVE(INPUT,OUTPUT);
VAR VALUE1, VALUE2, VALUE3, VALUE4, VALUE5,
    SUM: INTEGER;
BEGIN (* ADDFIVE *)
    WRITELN('INPUT DATA ARE:');
    READ(VALUE1); WRITELN(VALUE1);
    READ(VALUE2); WRITELN(VALUE2);
    READ(VALUE3); WRITELN(VALUE3);
    READ(VALUE4); WRITELN(VALUE4);
    READ(VALUE5); WRITELN(VALUE5);
    SUM := 0;
    SUM := SUM + VALUE1;
    SUM := SUM + VALUE2;
    SUM := SUM + VALUE3;
    SUM := SUM + VALUE4;
    SUM := SUM + VALUE5;
    WRITELN; WRITELN(' SUM IS:');
    WRITELN(SUM)
END.  (* ADDFIVE *)
    eor
245 73 -62 0 1094
```

ADDN in (1.1d) is a more complicated variation of this adding program, but it is more realistic and more typical of the programs you will soon be writing. Each of the previous examples was designed to accommodate a certain fixed number of input values -- two in (1.1a) and (1.1b), and five in (1.1c). ADDN is designed to accomodate any number of values. In each use of this program the number of values to be given is provided as the first item of data.

(1.1d)

```
(* READ N INTEGERS, PRINT THEIR VALUES AND SUM *)
PROGRAM ADDN(INPUT,OUTPUT);
VAR QTY,       (* QUANTITY OF VALUES *)
    VALUE,     (* INDIVIDUAL DATUM *)
    SUM:       (* SUM OF VALUES *)
         INTEGER;
BEGIN (* ADDN *)
    WRITELN(' INPUT DATA ARE:');
    SUM := 0;
    READ(QTY);
    WHILE QTY > 0 DO
      BEGIN
         READ(VALUE);
         WRITELN(VALUE);
         SUM := SUM + VALUE;
         QTY := QTY - 1
      END;
    WRITELN;
    WRITELN(' SUM IS:');
    WRITELN(SUM)
END.  (* ADDN *)
    eor
5 245 73 -62 0 1094
```

With the data given, (1.1c) and (1.1d) produce exactly the same results. However, (1.1d) is much more useful because it can be run with different amounts of data. That is, the data shown above could be replaced by the following:

```
7 21 56 4 -1 3 106 5
```

(1.1d) could also be run with data that began:

```
2500 23 705 -301 0 521 ...
```

(The three dots indicate that we are showing only the first part of the list.) While a program like (1.1c) could be written to compute the sum of 2500 numbers it would be a very tedious process. On the other hand, (1.1d) is already capable of performing this task with no change at all.

ADDN illustrates the concept of a "loop" -- a sequence of instructions that are repeated on different items of data. This idea is central to the computing process. This is what makes it possible for you to write a program of several dozen or several hundred instructions -- and have the computer execute several thousand or several million instructions in accomplishing the desired task. Stripped to the barest essentials what we are going to try to do is teach you to think of problems in terms of loops, and to describe these loops in a language intelligible to computers.

We will give one further example of the loop concept before proceeding with details. Suppose you have to determine the maximum of a list of non-negative numbers. The program to do this uses a process that is repeated for each of the numbers. It will get the next number on the list and compare it to the greatest number encountered "so far". If the new number is greater than the previous maximum it will be retained as a new maximum. The number of numbers is also counted.

This process is straightforward, once it gets started, but you must be careful in the program to start and stop the loop properly. Starting requires some "initialization" -- analogous to initially setting SUM equal to 0 in (1.1d). In (1.1d) we controlled the number of times the loop was executed by using a count given at the beginning of the data list. Now we don't know how many numbers are on the list, so we cannot use this same technique. Instead, we will add a special recognizable value to the end of the list. In this case, since the numbers are all non-negative, we can use a negative number to indicate the end of the list.

The names of locations in which values are to be stored by this program are:

```
NUMBER -- the current number being processed
MAXNBR -- the maximum number encountered "so far"
COUNT  -- the  number of times the central process has been
          repeated "so far"
```

The complete program for this problem, written in PASCAL, is given in (1.1e). The numbers at the beginning of each line of (1.1e) are not part of the program but have been added so we can readily identify each line for discussion.

The printed "output" produced by executing this program with the data on line 27 is:

```
NUMBER OF VALUES = 5
MAXIMUM VALUE =    12
```

This example will often be referred to in later sections. In particular, Section 1.4 discusses its "correctness".

(1.1e)

```
 1)  (* FIND MAXIMUM OF NON-NEGATIVE INPUT NUMBERS *)
 2)  (* DUMMY -1 ADDED AT END OF INPUT FOR STOPPING TEST *)
 3)  PROGRAM FINDMAX(INPUT,OUTPUT);
 4)
 5)  VAR NUMBER,        (* THE CURRENT NUMBER *)
 6)      MAXNBR,        (* MAXIMUM VALUE SO FAR *)
 7)      COUNT:         (* NBR OF NUMBERS SO FAR *)
 8)           INTEGER;
 9)
10)  BEGIN (* FINDMAX *)
11)      MAXNBR := -10;     (* INITIAL VALUE LESS THAN
12)                              ALL POSSIBLE VALUES *)
13)      COUNT := 0;
14)      READ(NUMBER);
15)      WHILE NUMBER <> -1 DO
16)
17)        BEGIN
18)           COUNT := COUNT + 1;
19)           IF NUMBER > MAXNBR THEN MAXNBR := NUMBER;
20)           READ(NUMBER)
21)        END;
22)
23)      WRITELN(' NUMBER OF VALUES =', COUNT);
24)      WRITELN(' MAXIMUM VALUE =', MAXNBR)
25)  END.  (* FINDMAX *)
26)      eor
27)  3 7 12 2 6 -1
```

The loop that represents the heart of (1.1e) is given in lines 17 through 21. Lines 11 through 14 initialize the loop -- prepare it so it works properly on its first repetition. Line 15 describes the conditions under which the loop is to be repeated -- that is, while the value of NUMBER is not equal to -1. (The symbol "<>" means "not equal" in PASCAL.) Lines 4, 9, 16 are blank and are inserted to visually indicate the separate sections of the program. They have no effect on its execution.

1.2 Analysis of a Problem and Design of a Program

The starting point of the analysis process is a problem statement. For example:

> Find the mode and median of a list of numbers.
>
> Solve the annular heat transfer equation for various different coefficients.
>
> Find the roots of the displacement equation for various given coefficients.
>
> Determine the frequency with which each different word appears in a list of words.
>
> Encrypt the following text using a given letter-substitution table.

Problem statements are usually given in English or in a hybrid combination of English and the symbols used in that problem area (mathematical symbols, for example). They generally deal with things -- temperatures, automobiles, colors, voters, dollars, etc. -- that cannot themselves be stored and manipulated by a computer. They are also usually stated in terms of commands that are not intelligible to a computer -- words like "solve", "find", "choose", etc. Typically a problem statement is at least initially somewhat vague and imprecise. This is partly because of a tacit reliance on the knowledge and common sense of the human reader, but also partly because the originator has often not completely formulated the exact requirements.

The end point of the process is a program -- a procedure that can be executed on a computer and that represents a solution to the initial problem. This process of transforming a problem description into a program has several different aspects:

1. A translation of language -- from English/mathematics to a programming language (PASCAL, PL/I, FORTRAN, etc.)

2. A conversion from a statement of objectives -- <u>what</u> is to be done -- to an executable procedure -- <u>how</u> the task is to be accomplished.

3. The definition of symbols (variables) in a program to represent the real-world objects of the problem. For example, a variable in one problem might represent the status of one of the squares of a chess board; in another problem, the number of dollars in a bank account; in another, the temperature at a particular point on a rocket nozzle.

4. The elimination of all vagueness, imprecision and ambiguity in the description. There is never any vagueness in a computer program -- every program always tells the

computer <u>precisely</u> what to do. The trick is to construct a program whose execution <u>exactly</u> solves the particular problem in question.

Only on very simple problems (such as those found in programming textbooks) is there much chance of success if one starts immediately to write the program -- no matter how experienced one might be at programming. On problems of any size and complexity a systematic analysis of requirements, and design of the overall structure of the program, should precede any attempt to write program statements. It is convenient to view this process as a "top down" or "level by level" analysis of the problem. The top level is the initial problem statement; the bottom level is a complete program; the number of intervening levels depends on the complexity of the problem.

Generally the second level is just an elaboration of the problem statement -- an attempt to make complete and precise exactly what is required. This is often achieved by a dialog between the programmer and the "customer" -- the owner of the problem. This dialog can involve questions like the following:

1. In what form will the data be supplied?

2. Are there reasonable limits on the values of data that may be expected?

3. How will the end of the data be recognized?

4. What errors in the data should be anticipated? What action should be taken?

5. What form should the output take? What labelling and titling should be provided?

6. What precision (number of significant figures) of results is required?

7. What changes in problem statement are likely to occur during the lifetime of the program?

There may also be questions and discussion of alternative strategies of solution. There might be two approaches -- one more costly to design and program, and the other more costly to execute. The customer must provide information to guide such a choice.

While the objective of this dialog is ostensibly to convey information to the programmer, to help him to understand exactly what has to be done, very often the customer discovers that the problem is not yet well-formulated, and that he himself is not sure, in detail, what he wants done.

The levels occurring after this refinement of the problem statement are generally designed to accomplish two tasks:

1. To break up big problems into little problems -- which in turn are attacked by this same approach.

2. To reduce the commands from English to programming terms. That is, "find", "solve", etc. must be reduced to "read", "print", "assign", "repeat", and then eventually to READ, WRITE, BEGIN -- the statements of a programming language.

1.2.1 An Example of Initial Problem Analysis

Suppose a problem statement (level 1) is given in the following way:

1. Given a list of numbers, print the first, second, third numbers, etc., but stop printing when the largest number in the list has been printed.

After some discussion this statement of the problem might be refined to something like the following (level 2):

2. A set of not more than 100 integers, each greater than zero, is given on punched cards. A dummy value of zero will be added to denote the end. The ordering with respect to value is unknown. Print a column of numbers corresponding to these numbers in the order given. Begin printing with the first and terminate when the last number printed is the maximum of the entire set. For example, if 1, 7, 3, 9, 5, 0 are given, the output should be:

```
1
7
3
9
```

It should be evident that it is not known how much printing is to be done until the position of the maximum value is determined, and this cannot be done until the last number of the input data has been examined (since the last could be the maximum). Therefore either the numbers will have to be read twice (once to determine the position of the maximum, and a second time to print the values) or the numbers will have to be read once and stored in the computer memory for later use. Card reading is a relatively slow and expensive operation for a computer, so the second strategy is preferable. This could lead to a third level of description:

3.1 Read a sequence of 100 or fewer positive integers from cards until a zero value is encountered; store these integers in memory, preserving order.

3.2 Find the position of the integer with maximum value in

Gifford

this sequence.

3.3 Print the early values of the sequence, from the first to the maximum value, one per line.

One would then attack each of these subproblems to reduce the commands -- "read from cards" and "store in memory" in the first subproblem -- to the corresponding statements in the target programming language. We have carried this analysis far enough here to give the general idea -- the program is completed in Section 5.4.

1.3 Translation to a Programming Language

The level-by-level transformation of the problem description is complete when the entire description is in a language that is intelligible to a computer. However, there is no single, universal programming language into which all problem descriptions are translated; there are literally hundreds of programming languages in use today. The choice of language will have some influence on the manner in which a problem is solved, and may have considerable influence on the difficulty experienced in obtaining a solution. Some programming languages have been designed to facilitate solution of certain classes of problems; they exchange generality for convenience for a particular type of problem. For example, some languages are designed to favor problems in business data processing; some are oriented toward mathematical computations. Some exist to serve different makes and models of computers, and many exist just because there are wide differences of opinion as to what a programming language should look like. Opinions on the subject are strongly held, and debated with a fervor normally reserved for politics or religion.

Although there are hundreds of languages in use, a relative handful dominate the field. The most widely used programming language today is COBOL, which was designed for business data processing problems. (The name comes from the first letters of the words: COmmon Business-Oriented Language.) The most widely used language for engineering and scientific computation is called FORTRAN (from FORmula TRANslation). Both of these languages were developed in the 1950s -- a long time ago in this field. Another language, called PL/I, was developed in the mid-60s in an attempt to serve both the scientific and data processing areas with a single language. The price of this generality is complexity, and PL/I is a very complicated language. It was also designed in something of a hurry, and in some respects the design is not as nice as it could be. Nevertheless, PL/I is the most "modern" of the programming languages in general use. However, it has not come close to displacing either FORTRAN or COBOL from widespread use. Other important languages are ALGOL, APL, BASIC, LISP, PASCAL, and SNOBOL.

PASCAL, the language used in this Primer, was developed in the early 1970s by Niklaus Wirth, now Professor of Computer Science at the Federal Institute of Technology, Zurich, Switzerland. It is derived from ALGOL, but permits a good deal more ease of expression than that language in many circumstances. Like PL/I, PASCAL can be used for both scientific and data processing problems. PASCAL's advantage is a somewhat cleaner and more logical design. PASCAL's principal drawback as a language for introductory instruction is simply that it is not yet widely used in practice. The use of PASCAL is growing, but it is still not clear how widespread it's use will eventually become.

In some places in this book we are critical of PASCAL (or at least apologetic). However, in our opinion, it is the best general-purpose programming language available today. The other possible choices of language for introductory instruction seem to us to have even more serious flaws. You should try to keep an open mind on the matter and realize that PASCAL represents just one compromise solution to the problem of devising a programming language. Not until you have significant experience in several different languages will you be able to appreciate the relative strengths and weaknesses of PASCAL.

For most students, the first programming language learned will be only the first of several. This is true both because there are many specialized languages available for various different areas of application, and because progress in the field of computer science should eventually lead to languages that will replace all those in use today. There is a distinct advantage in learning to program in a language like PASCAL or PL/I, rather than FORTRAN or COBOL, even though you might sometime have to use one of the latter. PASCAL and PL/I are more recent designs, and as such are more representative of current thinking on the subject. Future languages will be developed from this current base, and will certainly bear more resemblance to PASCAL than to FORTRAN. Secondly, PASCAL and PL/I are more general in their capability. All of the programming concepts present in FORTRAN and COBOL are present in PASCAL and PL/I -- but not conversely. It is easier for a student who initially learned PASCAL to later learn FORTRAN or COBOL on his own than it would be to proceed in the opposite order.

We will not attempt to present all of PASCAL in the Primer, and fortunately one does not have to learn all of the language in order to use part of it. One can learn a subset of the language initially and then add topics as required to meet new and more challenging tasks. The subset we will use is summarized in Appendix A.1; some additional elements of PASCAL are described briefly in Appendix A.2. For a description of the full PASCAL language, see Jensen and Wirth, PASCAL User Manual and Report.

It may seem that teaching PASCAL is the major goal of this book, but this is not really the case. Our primary goal is to teach programming principles; to teach problem solving and programming methodologies which can be used no matter what programming language is being used. The principal concepts in programming are essentially independent of the language used.

1.4 Confirmation of Program Correctness

Confirming correctness of a program requires a convincing demonstration that the program actually satisfies the precise requirements of the problem. This phase of the computing process is typically so badly neglected by writers and teachers that it seems as if they regard the possibility of mistakes as somewhat remote and distinctly embarrassing. In any but the most trivial task many errors will be made in each phase. Anyone who intends to use a computer might as well accept this unfortunate fact and make plans to systematically track down the inevitable errors. Very typically more than half of the total time, effort, and cost of the computing process is devoted to testing and "debugging" the program -- and yet in spite of this effort the process is not often completely successful. An embarrassingly large fraction of programs that are declared to be complete and correct by their authors still contain latent flaws. This situation is so prevalent and serious that a large proportion of society today has diminishing confidence in the computing process. Computers are increasingly thought to be somehow inherently unreliable, but in almost all cases the true fault lies in a program that was ill-designed and/or inadequately tested.

The program given in (1.1e) was deliberately constructed to illustrate this point. It works perfectly for the data given, and also for many other sets of data, but line 8 restricts this program so that it can only successfully handle integer values. However, there is nothing in the problem statement that suggests that the program will only be used for integer values. As a consequence any time this program is used for data that are not all integers (that is, values like 17.3), it will warn the user (after the fact) that he is in trouble. The program "works" for some sets of data but it is not a correct program for the given problem.

Many people seem to regard testing in a negative sense -- as an extra phase of the computing process that must be performed only if there appear to be errors. In fact, it is an essential part of programming. One must take positive action to try and force latent errors into revealing themselves -- so that one can reasonably infer correctness if no errors are exposed by determined and persistent testing. This must be done not just for a few simple test cases, but for maliciously contrived test cases that exercise a program more strenuously than is likely to occur in actual use. Contriving sufficiently difficult test cases is something of an art in itself. While testing is listed as a separate phase of the programming process it actually pervades the entire process, and if all consideration of determining correctness is postponed to the final phase it will almost surely be unsuccessful. It is essential that the necessity of demonstrating correctness be considered at the time that the overall structure of the program is chosen and that provision for testing be incorporated in the program as it is written, rather than as an afterthought.

1.5 Loading, Translation and Execution of a Program

When the program is complete and data have been prepared, both must be transmitted to the computer. The usual means of communication is the "punched card" or "IBM card". A machine called a "keypunch" is used to encode information in a card by punching holes in it. Each different character has a different pattern of holes; each character in the program and data is represented by the pattern in one vertical column of the card.

An alternative method of introducing information into a computing system is by means of a "terminal" directly connected to the computer. The keyboard of such a terminal is like that of the keypunch -- but instead of punching holes in a card which will later be detected by the computer, the terminal transmits its information directly to the computer, essentially as the key is struck. This has the virtue of immediate response -- the user is notified of errors after each line of the program, and sees results as the program is being executed. Although the use of such terminals is increasing rapidly it is still more expensive than using punched cards, and the majority of introductory instruction still uses cards. For our purposes it makes little difference which type of access is used and we will speak of program lines, input lines, and cards almost interchangeably.

The key point in understanding the loading and execution of a program is the timing of the reading of the cards. The card deck consists of two parts -- the program (lines 1 to 25 of (1.1e)) and the data (line 27). The cards for the entire program are read initially -- before any execution of the program begins; the cards for the data are not read until specifically called for during execution of the program. The computer does not read a card and execute the statement on it, read the next card and execute, etc. Instead it reads the entire program, creates a copy of the program in "memory", and then begins execution with the first statement of the program. In the course of execution the "card read" statements (such as lines 14 and 20 of (1.1e)) will cause the data cards to be read.

The initial loading of the cards of the user's program is controlled by execution of another program called a "compiler" (or sometimes a "translator" or "interpreter"). As the user-program cards are read a translation is performed by the compiler with the result that the "copy" of the program in memory, while functionally equivalent to the initial program, is very different in appearance. During this translation the compiler checks the program statements for "syntactical" (grammatical) errors and reports these to the user. If any errors are discovered during this loading-translation process most compilers will halt after loading and refuse to initiate execution of the user-program; a few compilers will effect some repair of minor errors and permit execution to begin. Most users will become aware of the existence of a compiler only through this error checking and will never have occasion to see the strange form their program has assumed in memory.

The printed output for a program can also be divided into two parts, corresponding to the loading and execution phases described above. During loading, a copy of the user-program is printed, including announcement of any errors discovered. This much of the printing is automatic -- a service performed by the compiler. Further printing will be done only as called for by the "output" statements (such as lines 23 and 24 of (1.1e)) of the program. If the user fails to include any such statements there will be no output during execution and the results of the computation will never be known.

Section 1 Exercises

The following all refer to the program example given in (1.1e). You cannot be expected to answer all of these questions at this point, but attempting to do so should be interesting and educational.

1. What would have to be done to cause this program to obtain the maximum of the following eight numbers:
    2 4 6 15 3 9 7 9

2. What would happen if the program were used to find the maximum of the following nine numbers:
    6 45 -3 14 0 2 -1 52 143

3. What would happen if line 27 looked like the following:
    5 5 5 -1 -1 -1

4. What would happen if the order of lines 18 and 19 were reversed? Lines 13 and 14? Lines 19 and 20?

5. Suppose the problem definition were broadened to require the program to work for negative as well as positive numbers. What changes would have to be made?

6. How could the program be changed to obtain the minimum rather than the maximum of the numbers?

7. How could the program be changed to produce both the maximum and the minimum of the numbers?

8. What would happen if line 18 were accidentally left out (say the card was dropped) before the program was submitted to the computer? Line 20? Line 24?

9. What would happen if line 23 were replaced by the following line?

```
(* WRITELN('NUMBER OF VALUES =', COUNT); *)
```

10. How could the program be changed to produce the sum of the numbers in addition to the maximum?

11. What would happen if line 1 were replaced by the following line:

```
(* COMPUTE THE PRETTIEST OF THE GREEN NUMBERS *)
```

and no other change were made in the program?

12. Construct a set of test data (a replacement for line 27) that would cause the program to produce incorrect results.

Section 2 Variables

A program describes how a set of values is to be manipulated. However, the description deals not directly with these values, but with entities called "variables". For example, instead of writing

```
        2 + 3          one could write         X + Y
```

and make arrangements so that "X had the value 2" and "Y had the value 3". The difference is essentially the same as that between arithmetic and algebra, and yields roughly the same advantage. One gains the ability to specify a procedure which may be applied, without change in the written form, to many different sets of values.

A variable is a place or location in the memory of a computer which can hold a value, and to which a name may be attached. The following line pictorially represents three variables:

A ——> 20   TOTAL ——> 456.003   ACCOUNT ——> -20.7

The first variable is named A and has the value 20 in its location (on its line). The second variable is named TOTAL and has the value 456.003. Variable ACCOUNT has the value -20.7.

We often omit the arrow in the pictorial representation, if the name and location are close enough so that no misunderstanding can take place:

A 20   TOTAL 456.003   ACCOUNT -20.7

A variable is relatively permanent -- it is created when execution of a program begins and lasts until execution is completed. The value is generally more transient, and may change often during execution. At any given instant, a variable contains a single, specific value, which is referred to as the current value of the variable. The current value of the variable named A above is 20. The phrase "current value of the variable named A" is long, and is often shortened to "value of A". A's value changes whenever a different value is placed in the location named A.

It is important to clearly distinguish between creating a variable and assigning a value to a variable. A variable is created only once -- when a physical location in the memory of the computer is set aside to hold its value. The creation process is also referred to as "declaring" or "defining" a variable. Once a variable has been created it may have a value assigned to it, and that value may be frequently changed. This "assignment process" is the topic of Section 3.

In PASCAL, "declarations" give the name to be attached to each variable and describe the kinds of values each variable can contain. The actual assignment of memory locations is performed automatically by the computing system and the programmer need not be concerned with it. He must only give a declaration for each variable. For example,

```
VAR MINVALUE, CUMSUM: INTEGER
```

defines two different variables named MINVALUE and CUMSUM, each of which can contain a decimal integer. The declaration does not automatically assign an initial value to the newly created variables; hence they exist, they have a location ready to receive a value, but have not as yet received one.

Variables play an important role in programs. Each variable contains a value with a specific meaning -- for example, the minimum value of a list of numbers, or the cumulative sum of a list of numbers. Knowledge of the variables and their meaning is essential for any person trying to understand a program. In order to help the reader, declarations for all variables are placed at the <u>beginning</u> of the program, before any statement which uses the variables.

It is a good practice to describe the use of each variable with a "comment". In PASCAL, "(*" marks the beginning of a comment and "*)" marks the end. The comment may contain any characters on the keypunch -- except the sequence "*)" which would be interpreted as the end of the comment. For example:

```
VAR MINVALUE,      (* MIN VALUE OF X'S SO FAR; >= 0 *)
    CUMSUM:        (* SUM OF X'S PROCESSED SO FAR *)
          INTEGER
```

Clarity and precision in defining the role of each variable in a program is of vital importance in producing a correct and understandable program. Many programming difficulties can be traced to fuzziness in the meaning of key variables. We find it useful, when asked to help "debug" (find the mistakes in) a program, to start by asking such questions as:

"What does this variable represent?"
"Does it have the same meaning everywhere in the program?"
"What are the extreme limits on the values it may contain?"

This approach is aided by following a consistent practice of supplementing the declaration of each variable with comments.

2.1 Identifiers

The sequence of characters that forms the name of a variable is called an "identifier". Each programming language has a set of rules that control the choice or construction of identifiers. These rules sometimes seem arbitrary, and at this stage it is best just to accept and learn them. Among the most widely used programming languages -- FORTRAN, COBOL, PL/I and ALGOL -- the rules are quite similar, but just enough different to be a nuisance to the unwary programmer. In almost any language, however, an identifier can consist of a letter, followed by a sequence of other letters and digits, and this is the kind of identifier you will use most often. For example, the following are all valid PASCAL identifiers:

```
I              SUM            MAXIMUM
X              VALUE          TEMPVALUE
X2             FEB3DATUM      TEMPERATURE
LOCATION       XPTR           JUNE5
```

You should choose variable names that suggest the role the variables play in the program. While it may seem clever to name variables after girls or flowers, it doesn't help to make a program understandable. For example, although SUSAN is a legal identifier, using SUSAN as the name of a variable which holds the average of 10 numbers is not helpful. AVERAGE or AVG would be better since it would help to indicate the role of the variable.

The keywords of PASCAL have been "reserved" and are not allowed to be used as identifiers. These words are:

```
AND        END        NIL         SET
ARRAY      FILE       NOT         THEN
BEGIN      FOR        OF          TO
CASE       FUNCTION   OR          TYPE
CONST      GOTO       PACKED      UNTIL
DIV        IF         PROCEDURE   VAR
DO         IN         PROGRAM     WHILE
DOWNTO     LABEL      RECORD      WITH
ELSE       MOD        REPEAT
```

It is easy to remember the keywords that are used frequently -- BEGIN, IF, FOR, etc. -- however, a problem will arise when you happen to choose an identifier that coincides with some PASCAL statement you have never been told about. For example, there is a WITH statement in PASCAL, but we do not use it in the Primer. Nevertheless, the word WITH is reserved and cannot be used as an identifier. We do not expect you to memorize this list -- just remember that such a list exists. Then when PASCAL objects to one of your identifiers with an error message about "identifier expected", check back here to see if you happen to have stumbled onto part of the PASCAL language you were never told about. There is no shortage of potential identifiers, so the loss of these few words should not seriously inhibit your creativity.

2.2 Values

Programming languages allow a variety of different types of values to be stored in variables. The most important types for ordinary numeric computation are signed integers (..., -2, -1, 0, 1, 2, ...) and real numbers -- such as 20.3, -463.2, 0.000043, and 4.3×10^{-5}. (Note that the last two real numbers look different but represent the same quantity.) Since each value is placed in a physical location in the computer's memory, there must obviously be a limit on the number of digits allowed. Eventually one must become aware of such limits, but they are not necessary for our present purposes. We assume here that all numerical values will be represented in the computer in conventional decimal notation, and that a reasonably adequate number of digits is permitted in each value.

Constant values are often written in a program. In general, they can be written in their usual form:

```
-20      10365     0.4      0.15     -0.0043      49.65
```

One restriction is that there must always be some digit to the left of the decimal point, whenever a decimal point is given. Hence .4 must be written 0.4. Alternatively, constants can be written in "scientific" or "exponential" form:

```
-20E0      1.0365E+4      4E-1      0.15E0      -4.3E-4
```

The exponent "E0" following the number specifies that the fractional number is to be multiplied by 10^{0}, which is 1. In general, one can put any integer after the "E" to represent a power of 10. Thus 125 could be alternatively written as 12.5E1, 1.25E2 or 0.125E3. As another example, the following are all equivalent values:

```
4.3E-5      0.43E-4      0.000043E0      0.00000043E+2
```

This is often called "floating point format", since the position of the decimal point "floats" depending on the exponent following "E".

A value may also be a character, such as 'A'. Variables with such "character" values are discussed in Section 9. The values "true" and "false" are important in certain contexts and we will discuss them in Section 4. But for the moment we will consider only values that are integers and real numbers.

2.3 Type Attributes

In PASCAL each variable is restricted to one particular type of value. The value may change, but the type of value (like the name) is permanent for the life of the variable. For example, if variable COUNT is defined to hold only integer values it might at different times have values such as 2, 1501, -3 and 0, but it could never have values such as 20.3 or 'J'.

The properties that determine the type of value that can be stored in a variable are called "attributes" of the variable. We represent attributes by putting them in brackets [and] after the variable. The following examples illustrate how the names, values and attributes of variables will be indicated in the text:

MAX	20 [integer]	MAX may only contain integers (e.g. -3, 0, 1, +5)
TB42	-.002 [real]	TB42 may contain real numbers (e.g. 20.3, 20, -.82)
Z4	-20.0 [real]	Z4 may contain real numbers

You may have assumed that these numbers would be represented in the computer's memory as shown here -- that is, in the decimal number system. However, this is not the case. The "binary number system" is extensively used in computing, and PASCAL's numbers are represented in memory using this system. Fortunately, they will be automatically converted from decimal to binary on input and binary to decimal on output, so at least for our purposes you can ignore the fact that the internal representation of numbers is in the binary system.

A variable always has some particular set of type attributes. When we neglect to mention them it is only because the type of value is not relevant to the point under discussion -- not because attributes do not exist for that variable.

In PASCAL type attributes are specified by listing them in the declaration of the variable. For example:

```
VAR MAX: INTEGER

VAR TB42: REAL; Z4: REAL
```

When several variables have the same set of attributes, the names may be separated by commas and the attributes given only once. For example, the following declarations are equivalent:

```
VAR TB42, Z4: REAL

VAR TB42: REAL; Z4: REAL
```

Simple programs such as we are considering at this point can only have one declaration of variables. That is, the keyword VAR can only appear once, followed by a list of all the variables that will be used. (In Part IV we will introduce programs with several procedures, each of which can have one declaration.) This means that the following is a correct declaration:

```
VAR MAX, MIN, COUNT: INTEGER;
    AMT, RATE: REAL
```

but the following similar form is not correct since VAR appears twice:

```
VAR MAX, MIN, COUNT: INTEGER;
VAR AMT, RATE: REAL
```

This is a curious and unfortunate restriction, but that is just the way the language was defined.

Section 2 Summary

1. A variable is a named location in computer memory into which a value may be placed.

2. All variables to be used in a procedure must be defined (created) by specifying their names and type attributes in a declaration placed at the beginning of the program. The name should be chosen to reflect the role the variable plays in the program, and the declaration should be supplemented by a comment that describes the role exactly and clearly. The keywords of the language -- BEGIN, VAR, IF, etc. -- cannot be used as names of variables.

3. The standard type attributes for integer values and real values are INTEGER and REAL, respectively.

4. Numeric constants may be written in a program in either conventional form: 32, -61, 4.3, 0.198, or in exponential form: 3.2E1, -61E0, 4.3E0, 198E-3. If a decimal point is given, there must be at least one digit to its left -- that is, .198 must be written 0.198.

Section 2 Exercises

Exercises 1 to 4 concern the following variables:

LASTONE	-20 [integer]
ANSWER	-30.2 [real]
BAD20	0 [integer]
COSINE	-30.2 [real]
TEXT	30.0 [real]
MINIMUM	+30.2 [real]

1. a) What is the current value of variable ANSWER?
   b) What is the current value of variable COSINE?
   c) What is the current value of variable TEXT?
   d) Which variables have the value -30.2?
   e) Which variables have the value 20?

2. Which of the following values:

   -30, -30.1, 0, 0.0050, 43981, 43981.5, 4.3891E4

   can be stored in variable:

   a) LASTONE ?
   b) BAD20 ?
   c) MINIMUM ?

3. Define the term "variable".

4. Write a PASCAL declaration for the variables given above.

5. Consider the following declaration:

```
VAR SUM: INTEGER;
    POSTOT: REAL;
    COUNT: INTEGER
```

   a) Write an equivalent declaration that does not require the repetition of a type attribute.

   b) Write an equivalent declaration that also includes comments describing the role of each variable. For example

   TOTAL OF X'S > 0 for POSTOT
   SUM OF Y'S for SUM
   NO. OF PTS for COUNT

Section 3 Assignment of Value

The computing process involves the assignment of values to variables. The basic assignment process, in any programming language, has two distinct stages:

1. The production of a new value.

2. The assignment of that new value to a variable.

The construction for specifying a new value is called an "expression". Examples are:

```
26          X          Y+1          (X3+ABC)/ZZZ
```

where X, Y, X3, ABC, and ZZZ are variable names. In the evaluation of an expression the current value of each variable referenced is used, but this does not change the values of those variables. Regardless of the length and complexity of an expression the result of its evaluation is a single value.

The second stage of the assignment process is the assignment of the new value. A logical form for describing this would be:

```
X + Y —> Z
```

A precise description of the execution of this process is:

> Evaluate the expression X + Y, by adding a copy of the current value of the variable named X to a copy of the current value of the variable named Y. Store this sum as the new value of variable Z (replacing and destroying whatever previous value Z may have had).

Note that the values of X and Y are only copied and are not changed in the process. Typical values of X, Y and Z before and after such an assignment are:

before:	X 1	Y 3	Z 2
after:	X 1	Y 3	Z 4

3.1 The PASCAL Assignment Statement

The syntax for an "assignment statement" in PASCAL is:

```
variable name := expression
```

The expression on the right gives the formula to obtain a new value; the variable on the left receives this new value. The ":=" denotes the assignment process (instead of the arrow used on the previous page). The following are examples of PASCAL assignment statements:

```
A := 4.3
Z := X + 1
I := I + 1
LOW := CTR - 1.43E-1
SUM := 0
SUM := A1 + A2 + A3
SUM := SUM + NUMBER
TEMP := (A3 + B4)/BASE
RATIO := (A+B) / (C+D)
SUP := Z3 + P / (A + B/4E0)
```

These examples are shown as individual statements; any consecutive statements in PASCAL must be separated by a semi-colon. Hence if the first two of these statements were given consecutively in a program they would be written

```
A := 4.3;
Z := X + 1
```

Unfortunately, the form of the assignment statement tempts you to read it in the usual left-to-right manner, and the similarity to an algebraic equation is also deceptive. For example, consider the assignment of a value to the variable X:

```
X := Y
```

This should be read "get a copy of the value of Y, and store it in X". It might seem that this is equivalent to saying "let X take on the value of Y", but consider the following statement:

```
X := X + Y
```

It is clearer to read this as "add together the current values of X and Y, and store the result in X", than it would be to say "let X take on the value of X plus the value of Y".

Many programming languages use "=" in their assignment statement; PASCAL uses ":=" to minimize the similarity to an algebraic equation. The assignment statement is a command to perform a sequence of actions, whereas an equation is a statement of fact. If equality between the left and right sides already existed, there would be no point in writing the statement at all, since no action would be required. One might try to salvage this "equation interpretation" by suggesting that it is a command to "make the equation become true". However, this interpretation just cannot explain examples such as:

```
X := X + Y     and     W := W + 2
```

The assignment statement <u>must</u> be considered a command to perform <u>two distinct actions</u>: first, <u>produce</u> a value from the expression on the right; second, <u>assign</u> this value to the variable on the left.

Note that the two sides of an assignment statement are not symmetric in role. The following two statements have different meanings, although as equations they would be equivalent:

```
X := Y     and     Y := X
```

Assignment statements are executed in the order in which they appear (reading from left to right, and top to bottom). Consider the two statements

```
X := Y + Z     and     Z := X + Y
```

Assuming a set of initial values, the effect of executing these statements in one order would be:

```
before                  X  3     Y  5     Z  2
after  X := Y + Z       X  7     Y  5     Z  2
after  Z := X + Y       X  7     Y  5     Z 12
```

With the same initial values the effect of executing these same statements in the opposite order would be:

```
before                  X  3     Y  5     Z  2
after Z := X + Y        X  3     Y  5     Z  8
after X := Y + Z        X 13     Y  5     Z  8
```

As a further example, consider the task of interchanging, or "swapping", the values of two variables. Suppose we want to

```
change      A 3     B 5

to          A 5     B 3
```

Since there is no single statement in PASCAL to perform this, it must be done with a sequence of assignment statements. Let T be a variable not used in the program so far. The following uses T as a "temporary" variable to accomplish the swap:

```
(* SWAP VALUES OF A AND B *)
   T := A;
   A := B;
   B := T
```

Given the initial values of the variables as shown below, we show the contents of the variables after execution of each statement. Question marks ??? are used as the value of a variable that has not yet been assigned a value.

before	A 3	B 5	T ???
after T := A	A 3	B 5	T 3
after A := B	A 5	B 5	T 3
after B := T	A 5	B 3	T 3

The comment (* SWAP VALUES OF A AND B *) summarizes the actions of the group of statements that follow it (and are indented with respect to it). When reading a program that includes this segment, to find out _what_ is being performed we read the comment _instead_ of the statements indented underneath it. The detailed statements under the comment need be read only to find out _how_ the swap is being performed. Comments are entirely for the benefit of human readers; they have no effect on the execution of the program by the computer. When used properly, comments make it significantly easier for us to read and understand a program, but when badly used they obscure rather than clarify.

3.2 Arithmetic Expressions

Expressions are used in many different contexts in programs. Wherever they occur they always have the same basic purpose -- to provide a _formula by which a value can be obtained_. The simplest expressions are constants, like 3 or 20.6E0, or variables, like I or TOTAL. In general, an expression can include a number of terms or "operands", and "operations" by which the operand values are to be combined to yield a single value. Examples of expressions are shown in the right side of the assignment statements of Section 3.1.

3.2.1 Symbols for Operations

The PASCAL symbols for arithmetic operations are:

+	for addition of both real numbers and integers
-	for subtraction of both real numbers and integers, and to indicate negation (that is, -4 and -X)
*	for multiplication of both real numbers and integers
/	for division giving a real number result; the operands may be either real or integer
DIV	for division giving an integer result; the operands must both be integers
MOD	for the remainder of an integer division; the result is an integer, both operands must be integers.

The symbol for an operation is often called an "operator". The * operator is used for multiplication in most programming languages, because all the familiar means of indicating multiplication lead to confusion and ambiguity. (For example, a period could get confused with a decimal point -- would 2.34.5 mean 2.34 times 5 or 2 times 34.5?)

Unlike many programming languages, PASCAL has no special operator for exponentiation.

3.2.2 Precedence of Operations

Some concern must be given to the order in which arithmetic operations are performed. For example, should the expression

```
A + B * C
```

be evaluated as A+(B*C) or (A+B)*C? The difference is obviously important. For example, if A, B and C have values 2, 3 and 4, respectively A+(B*C) evaluates to 14 while (A+B)*C evalutes to 20.

In any expression, however complicated, a lavish enough use of parentheses will remove any possible ambiguity. However, to avoid too many parentheses, PASCAL has conventions corresponding to normal algebra to determine the order in which operations are to be performed. For example, in algebra:

	$a + bc$,	$a - b + c$,	$-a^2$
mean	$a + (bc)$,	$(a - b) + c$,	$-(a^2)$
and not	$(a + b)c$,	$a - (b + c)$,	$(-a)^2$.

The PASCAL rules for evaluation of an expression are:

1. Expressions in parentheses are evaluated independently of preceding or succeeding operators.

2. Subject to rule 1, the order of operations is:
   first: negation (-)
   next: multiplication (*) and division (/,DIV,MOD)
   last: addition (+) and subtraction (-)

3. Sequences of operations in the same category under rule 2 are evaluated from left to right.

   For example:

   X/Y*Z is equivalent to (X/Y)*Z

   X-Y+Z is equivalent to (X-Y)+Z

PASCAL will always follow these rules, whether you want it to or not! If you give an expression

```
X + Y * Z
```

PASCAL will multiply the values of Y and Z first, and then add the value of X to the product. If you want the addition to be performed first you must override this inherent precedence with parentheses by writing

```
(X + Y) * Z.
```

If you prefer not to learn these rules you can get along by always using enough parentheses to make the required order explicit -- but this sometimes takes a lot of parentheses.

3.2.3 Conversion of Values

Some concern must also be given to the manner in which operands of different types can be intermixed and interchanged. In ordinary arithmetic the integers are just a subset of the real numbers and we use them together quite casually. In computing, INTEGERs and REALs are distinctly different types and the programmer must understand and be careful about the difference.

There are three rules that you must remember:

1. When PASCAL expects a REAL value it will generally accept an INTEGER value.

2. When PASCAL expects an INTEGER value it will generally *not* accept a REAL value.

3. When REAL values and INTEGER values are combined in an expression the result is generally of type REAL.

For example, suppose there are four variables used in a program:

```
VAR RL1, RL2: REAL;
    IN1, IN2: INTEGER
```

The three expressions

```
RL1 + RL2,    RL1 + IN1   and   IN1 + RL1
```

all produce a result of type REAL. Only an expression with *all* operands of type INTEGER, such as

```
IN1 + IN2
```

will produce a result of type INTEGER. This means, for example, that you can write constants as integers in expressions where the variables are REAL. That is

```
(RL1 + RL2)/2
```

can be given instead of having to write

```
(RL1 + RL2)/2.0    or    (RL1 + RL2)/2E0
```

The following assignment statements are all legal, since they assign REAL values to REAL variables and INTEGER values to INTEGER variables:

```
RL1 := RL2
RL1 := RL1 + RL2
RL1 := RL1 + IN1
RL1 := 45.6

IN1 := IN2
IN1 := IN1 + IN2
IN1 := 45
```

The following assignments are also legal since, although a REAL value is expected, an INTEGER value will be accepted:

```
RL1 := IN1
RL1 := IN1 + IN2
RL1 := 45
```

However, the following assignments are not legal since an INTEGER value is expected and a REAL value will not be accepted:

```
IN1 := RL1
IN1 := IN2 + RL1
IN1 := 45.6
```

PASCAL does have a means of converting a value of type REAL to type INTEGER, which could be used to make these assignments legal. This uses the TRUNC and ROUND built-in functions, which are described in the next section.

This is an area in which different programming languages do very different things. PASCAL seems to us to be quite reasonable in this regard. You wouldn't believe what FORTRAN and PL/I do under similar circumstances.

3.3 Built-in Functions

Some common "functions" are used so often in programming that they have been included in the language. (This is only a convenience since the task of each of these functions could be accomplished by explicitly writing all the statements needed to evaluate the function.) For example, to obtain the square root of the value of variable X or of an expression X+Y/Z, write

```
SQRT(X)     or     SQRT(X+Y/Z)
```

The expression whose square root is sought is called the "argument" of the function.

This functional form can be used as an operand in an expression, just as one would use a variable:

```
X + SQRT(Y)
SQRT(TEMP - SQRT(T4K/PRESSURE))
B4 * (SQRT(SQRT(J3) + R2PEAK) + SIDE4)
```

The built-in functions included in a language depend heavily on the problem area for which the language is designed. FORTRAN, designed primarily for mathematical and engineering computation, has a different set of built-in functions from COBOL, which was designed for business data processing problems. A partial list of PASCAL built-in functions is given below. This includes most of the functions commonly needed in introductory programming examples. For a complete list, consult a PASCAL reference manual.

ABS(x) -- The result is the absolute value of x.

ARCTAN(x) -- The result (REAL) is the arctangent, in radians, of x.

CHR(x) -- See Section 9.2.4.

COS(x) -- The result (REAL) is the cosine of x, where x is expressed in radians.

EOF(x) -- See Section 4.3.1.3.

EOLN(x) -- See Section 4.3.1.3.

EXP(x) -- The result (REAL) is e raised to the power x, where e is the base of the natural logarithm system.

LN(x) -- The result (REAL) is the natural logarithm of x. x must be greater than 0.

ODD(x) -- See Section 4.3.1.3.

ORD(x) -- See Sections 8.3 and 9.2.4.

PRED(x) -- See Sections 8.3 and 9.2.4.

ROUND(x) -- The result (INTEGER) is the value of x rounded. x must be REAL. Used to convert a REAL value to an INTEGER value.

SIN(x) -- The result (REAL) is the sine of x, where x is expressed in radians.

SQR(x) -- The result is the square of x; that is, x * x. The type of the result is the same as that of x, which must be either REAL or INTEGER.

SQRT(x) -- The result (REAL) is the square root of x. x must be greater than or equal to 0.

SUÇC(x) -- See Sections 8.3 and 9.2.4.

TRUNC(x) -- The result (INTEGER) is the value obtained by truncating the fractional part of x. x must be REAL. Used to convert a REAL value to an INTEGER value.

3.4 Assignment from External Data

Evaluation of an expression generates a new value in terms of values that are already in the computer memory. One also needs a mechanism to enter values from outside the computer. Execution of an "input" statement causes an auxiliary device -- such as a punched card reader, a magnetic tape reader, or a typewriter terminal -- to deliver one or more values to the memory of the computer. The form of the simplest input statement is

```
READ(variable-names, separated by commas)
```

An example is:

```
READ(AMOUNT)
```

Its execution causes the next value to be read from the data list which is given on cards after the program, and assigned to variable AMOUNT. The value is assigned using the same rules as in an assignment statement. That is, if the target variable is REAL the value assigned can be either REAL or INTEGER. If the target variable is INTEGER the value <u>must</u> be INTEGER.

Execution of the statement

```
READ(X, Y)
```

would cause the next two values to be read (from the data list) and assigned to X and Y, respectively.

Recall (from Section 1.5) that the cards bearing data at the end of the program are not read automatically into memory as the program is being loaded. Loading ends with the last card of the program body, and the cards bearing data wait to be read if and when the program calls for them by executing READ statements. The cards supply a list of values; the reading process moves through this list from left-to-right, one card to the next, as demanded by the execution of READ statements. Each value is read only once from this list. Suppose there are three READ statements in a program, where all variables are REAL:

```
...
READ(BASE, HEIGHT);
...
READ(WIDTH, TEMP, TIME);
...
READ(LIMIT);
...
```

and the data list for this program is:

```
          17.5
          83.72
(3.4a)    23.05
          76
          0.2314
          964.122
```

When the first READ statement is executed the first two values are read from the data list (two values because there are two variables listed in the statement) and 17.5 becomes the value of BASE and 83.72 becomes the value of HEIGHT. When the next READ statement is executed the next three values are read; 23.05 is assigned to WIDTH, 76 to TEMP and 0.2314 to TIME. When the third READ is executed 964.122 is read and assigned to LIMIT.

A total of six values are read in by the three READ statements and exactly six values are provided in the data list. If more than six had been provided, the extra values would simply have been ignored since the program never calls for them to be read. This could be intentional -- the amount of data processed might depend upon some test the program performs upon the early values. This could also happen by accident if the programmer did not properly coordinate his input statements and data list.

The opposite condition is more common; a READ statement is executed and an inadequate number of data values remain on the list to satisfy all of the variables in the READ. Different languages react to this situation in different ways. It is essentially an error, but is often considered a legitimate way to stop execution. (The PASCAL "EOF" condition is a neat way of handling this situation. See Section 4.3.1.3.) In order to detect the end of the data from within the program, we often add some marker value at the end of the actual data. This should be a value that is clearly recognizable -- it cannot be a possible data value -- so that the program can test for it after each READ statement. This technique was used in the example of (1.1e).

An alternative way of recognizing the end of a data list is to provide an initial control value that specifies the length of the list. This technique was illustrated in (1.1d).

The variables listed in the READ statement and the values on the data list must be synchronized with respect to order as well as quantity. The variable to which each value is assigned is entirely determined by the order in which the variable names appear in the READ statements. (For this purpose the order of the READ statements is the order in which they are executed, and not the order in which they are written. This distinction is the topic of Section 4.) Hence the programmer must know exactly what the order of the variables in the "READ lists" will be and arrange the data values accordingly. This is not always easy and is a common source of errors. For example, in the data list above there is nothing in the list that suggests that 17.5 is intended to be assigned to BASE and 83.72 to HEIGHT. If the position of these two values had been reversed the computer would have uncomplainingly assigned 83.72 to BASE and 17.5 to HEIGHT.

3.4.1 Data Format

The data associated with the READ statements is a list of values. The values are separated by blanks -- one or more blanks are given between values. The order of values in the list, and on the card, is critical, as noted in the last section, but position on the card is not at all critical. You can have one value per card, or many values on a card. Values can be spaced so they begin in certain card columns, or packed tightly together (with at least one blank between values). The entire card can be used -- a value can begin in column 1 and a value can end in column 80. However, a value cannot be split over two cards. That is, 437 could not be given with 43 in columns 79 and 80 of one card and 7 in column 1 of the next card. REAL values can be given in either conventional decimal form or in exponential form. Recall from Section 3.2.3, however, that INTEGER values must not contain either a decimal point or an exponent. (If they contain either they will be considered REAL.)

In example (3.4a) the values were given on six different cards. Each of the following forms is equivalent to (3.4a), although (3.4.1d) is best for humans since the arrangement suggests which values will be read by each READ statement. (3.4.1a) is the least attractive because of the inconsistent (although legal) means of separating values.

```
(3.4.1a)      17.5
              83.72 23.05       76 0.2314    964.122

(3.4.1b)          17.5 83.72 23.05 76 0.2314 964.122

(3.4.1c)      1.75E1 8.372E1 2.305E1 7.6E1 2.314E3 9.64122E2

(3.4.1d)      17.5 83.72
              23.05 76 0.2314
              964.122
```

There is an alternative form of input statement, READLN, for which the arrangment of values on the cards is significant. We postpone discussion of this form to Section I.9.2.2.

Note that no commas can appear in the data. The common convention of including commas within a number cannot be used. That is, 23109 cannot be given as 23,109. Also, unlike other places where a list appears in PASCAL, commas cannot be used to separate the elements of a data list.

Only values can be given as data. It would not make sense to give a variable as a datum -- each datum will be assigned as the value of a variable, and variables of the kind we are using cannot have another variable as value. Arithmetic operations are not allowed in the data -- for example, .5 cannot be given as 1/2.

Section 3 Summary

1. The form of an assignment statement is:

   variable := expression

To execute an assignment statement, evaluate the expression and assign the result to the variable on the left of the :=.

2. + and - denote addition and subtraction. * denotes multiplication. / denotes REAL division. DIV gives the quotient and MOD gives the remainder of INTEGER division.

3. Expressions in parentheses are evaluated independently of operators outside the parentheses.

4. When not overruled by parentheses, the order of operations is:
   a. Negation
   b. Multiplication and division
   c. Addition and subtraction

Within these categories a sequence of operations proceeds from left to right.

5. Either REAL or INTEGER values can be assigned to a REAL variable. Only INTEGER values can be assigned to an INTEGER variable.

6. A library of built-in functions such as SQRT(...) is provided.

7. The form of the simplest input statement is:

   READ(variable-names, separated by commas)

8. The order of data values on cards is crucial, but the format is quite flexible. The entire card may be used; adjacent values should be separated by one or more blanks. (Commas cannot be used to separate values.)

Section 3 Exercises

1. In each of the following assignment statements delete all "redundant" parentheses -- that is, parentheses whose deletion does not change the result of the statement:

```
a) ALT := ALT + (BASE + COL4) + DIV

b) PRESSURE := (TEMP + ENTROPY) * SPEC22

c) GRADIENT := (GRADIENT - (HGT-SLOPE))

d) EFF := (EFF + (FULL * (EXP(H3 * LN(LOSS)))))

e) X := -B + SQRT((B*B -(4*(A*C))))
```

2. Suppose the following were the values of four variables at a certain point in a program:

BASE	4	[real]
HGT	3	[real]
SIDE	0	[real]
TOP	14.2	[real]

Starting at that point, the following four assignment statements are executed in the order shown below:

```
SIDE := SIDE + BASE/HGT;
SIDE := SIDE + BASE/HGT;
TOP := BASE + HGT + SIDE + TOP;
TOP := TOP/HGT
```

What are the resulting values of the four variables?

3. The following are all intended to be assignment statements. Which ones contain at least one syntax error?

```
a) A := B + C

b) A := B, C;

c) A = (B + C)

d) A + B := C

e) (A := B + C);

f) A := (B) + C

g) A := B (+) C

h) A := (B + C;)
```

4. Write a READ statement and a data list that will assign the same values as the following pair of assignment statements:

```
XPLUS := 93.17;
XMINUS := -45.93
```

5. Suppose the data given with a program are the following:

```
2 4 6 8 10 12 14
```

What would be the values of the variables T4, LOW and VAL after execution of the following statement (assuming it is the first READ statement to be executed in the program):

```
READ(VAL, LOW, LOW, T4, LOW, VAL)
```

Give a different data list and READ statement that will produce exactly the same result (but are shorter and more reasonable than the example shown).

Section 4 Flow of Control

4.1 General Program Structure; Executing Programs

A complete "job" to be processed by a computer consists of a program and data, in that order. In PASCAL the form of a job is:

```
(* Comment summarizing program function *)  ┐
PROGRAM name(INPUT, OUTPUT);                 | main
   Definitions and declarations              | proc-
BEGIN (* name *)                             |  edure
   Body of program                           |
END. (* name *)                              ┘
   eor
   Data cards
```

The program consists of a "main procedure". The "name" that appears after PROGRAM and as a comment after the first BEGIN and the last END is also called an "entry-name" of the procedure, and can be used to refer to the program as a whole. Program or entry-names are chosen subject to the same rules as variable identifiers (see Section 2.1) and should be chosen to suggest the action the procedure performs. A period is given after the END of the main procedure.

A procedure consists of a "heading" and a "body". The heading consists of definitions and declarations. The first line of the heading defines the program name and declares the names of the "files" through which the program will communicate with its environment. We will use a file called INPUT to refer to the card reader, and another file called OUTPUT to refer to the printer. These names vary at different computer installations and you may have to use other file names where we use INPUT and OUTPUT.

Other definitions and declarations include the declaration of all of the variables that will be used in the program, as described in Section 2.3. Other types of definitions will be described in Section 8 and Part IV.

The body of the procedure consists of imperative statements that direct the computer to perform certain actions -- such as assign a new value to a variable, read new data values from cards, and print results. Normal execution order of the statements is like the normal order of reading English text -- from left to right, top to bottom, from the beginning to the end of a procedure.

4.1.1 Writing Simple Programs

At this point you have seen almost enough of PASCAL to be able to write simple programs; we need only explain how to get "output" -- how to cause the computer to write numbers out in a readable form.

The simplest form of output statement is the "write line" statement:

```
WRITELN(variable-names, separated by commas)
```

For example, execution of the statement

```
WRITELN(X, Y, Z)
```

causes the values of variables X, Y and Z to be printed in a readable form, on one line. The output resulting from execution of such WRITELN statements will accompany the "listing" of the program you receive after your program has been executed on the computer. A more detailed discussion of the control and interpretation of output is given in Sections 6 and 7.

We now show two examples of complete programs -- the kind you should be able to write, keypunch and submit for execution.

```
          (* READ TWO VALUES, PRINT THEM AND THEIR SUM *)
          PROGRAM ADDER(INPUT, OUTPUT);
          VAR X, Y,       (* INPUT NUMBERS *)
              Z:   REAL;  (* SUM OF X AND Y *)
(4.1.1a)  BEGIN (* ADDER *)
              READ(X, Y);
              Z := X + Y;
              WRITELN(' INPUTS AND ANSWER:');
              WRITELN(X, Y, Z)
          END.  (* ADDER *)
              eor
          15.5 10.2
```

The second example is:

```
(* READ A NUMBER, PRINT IT AND ITS SQUARE ROOT *)
PROGRAM SROOT(INPUT, OUTPUT);
VAR ARG,            (* INPUT NUMBER *)
    SRARG: REAL;    (* SQUARE ROOT OF ARG *)
BEGIN (* SROOT *)
    READ(ARG);
    SRARG := SQRT(ARG);
    WRITELN(' INPUT AND ANSWER:');
    WRITELN(ARG, SRARG)
END.  (* SROOT *)
    eor
25.01
```

The complete output resulting from computer processing of (4.1.1a) is shown below. It will be explained in detail in Section 7, but you should be able to recognize the listing of the source program and the answer printed as a result of executing the two WRITELN statements.

```
000006 (* READ TWO VALUES, PRINT THEM AND THEIR SUM *)
000006
000006 PROGRAM ADDER(INPUT,OUTPUT);
000464
000464 VAR  X,Y,           (* INPUT NUMBERS *)
000464      Z:  REAL;      (* SUM OF X AND Y *)
000467
000467 BEGIN (* ADDER *)
000467   READ(X,Y);
000030   Z := X + Y;
000032   WRITELN(' INPUTS AND ANSWER:');
000040   WRITELN(X,Y,Z)
000054 END.  (* ADDER *)

INPUTS AND ANSWER:
 1.5500000000000E+001  1.0200000000000E+001  2.5700000000000E+001
```

4.1.2 Tracing Execution

You should understand both the meaning of each PASCAL statement and the manner in which they are executed, well enough to be able to follow the execution of a program on a statement-by-statement basis. In fact, you should be able to simulate the action of the computer and "trace" the execution of a program on paper. Your action should differ from the computer's only in speed (by a factor of 10^6 or more).

For example, a detailed trace of the loading and execution of (4.1.1a) is given below:

1. The cards, from the initial comment through eor are read; a copy of the program (in translated form) is created in memory.

2. Execution begins by entering the main procedure ADDER.

3. As ADDER is entered three variables are created (recall that ??? is used to indicate that no value yet exists):

```
X ??? [real]
Y ??? [real]
Z ??? [real]
```

4. The first statement in the body of ADDER is READ(X, Y). Execution of this statement reads the two numbers on the first (and only) data card and assigns them to variables X and Y. At this point, the variables are:

```
X 15.5 [real]
Y 10.2 [real]
Z ???  [real]
```

5. Execution of the next statement, Z := X + Y, changes the value of Z. The variables now are:

```
X 15.5 [real]
Y 10.2 [real]
Z 25.7 [real]
```

6. Execution of the next statement:

```
WRITELN(' INPUTS AND ANSWER:')
```

causes an output line to be printed:

```
INPUTS AND ANSWER:
```

7. Execution of the next statement, WRITELN(X, Y, Z), causes another output line to be printed:

```
1.55000000000000E+001 1.02000000000000E+001 2.57000000000000E+001
```

8. The end of ADDER is reached; execution of the program is finished.

Having completed ADDER, the computer begins execution of some other program. The next program "overwrites" and destroys the ADDER program, and its variables X, Y and Z.

This example has the property that the statements are executed just as they are written. There are four executable statements in the body of ADDER, and those statements are executed, once, in the order written. This is true only of the most trivial programs. Our purpose in the rest of Section 4 is to describe the means by which we can cause the statements executed to be <u>very</u> different in quantity and order from the statements written in the program.

4.2 Compound Statements

We will often have to refer to groups, or sequences, of statements. We need to be able to refer to some arbitrary sequence of statements as if it were a <u>single entity</u>. We call such a sequence a "compound statement" and denote its beginning and end with the keywords BEGIN and END:

```
BEGIN
  statement 1;
  statement 2;
  ...
  statement n
END
```

We have already used this construction in each of our previous program examples, since the body of a PASCAL program is in fact a compound statement. Other examples are:

```
BEGIN
  READ(VALUE);
  WRITELN(VALUE);
  SUM := SUM + VALUE;
  QTY := QTY - 1
END

BEGIN
  ERRCNT := ERRCNT + 1;
  WRITELN(' IMPROPER VALUE', VALUE);
  VALUE := 1
END
```

A compound statement can be given a name by giving a comment after the end markers:

```
BEGIN (* ADD NEGATIVES *)
  NEGCOUNT := NEGCOUNT + 1;
  NEGSUM := NEGSUM + NEWVAL
END (* ADD NEGATIVES *)
```

This naming is not required by PASCAL but it does help identify the END with the corresponding BEGIN. (We will soon have many BEGIN,END pairs in our programs.) We will follow the practice of giving name comments to BEGIN,END pairs whenever the compound statement they enclose includes another BEGIN,END pair.

Notice the manner in which the semi-colon is used to separate statements in the examples. It is given after each of the component statements in the compound statement except the last. The BEGIN and END markers are not statements, hence do not need separation from the statements in the body of the compound statement. Although the semi-colon is usually placed immediately after a statement (in the same manner as it is used in ordinary English text) it is not considered to be part of the statement it follows.

4.3 Repetitive Execution

Most programs require statements, or usually sequences of statements, to be executed repeatedly, so it is essential to have convenient mechanisms to control repetition. In PASCAL a sequence of consecutive statements whose execution is to be repeated, or "iterated", is written as a compound statement and this is given as the body of a "loop". There are various different types of loops, described in the following sections.

The complete loop is a single unit -- a single complex statement. It can appear wherever any other statement can appear.

4.3.1 Conditional Repetition

PASCAL provides two different types of loops that permit the execution of the body to depend upon a specified condition. They are called the "while loop" and the "repeat loop", and are quite similar in concept and purpose.

4.3.1.1 The WHILE Loop

The most frequently used conditional repetitive statement has the general form:

```
WHILE condition DO
    statement
```

When the statement to be repeated is compound the WHILE loop has the following form:

```
WHILE condition DO
  BEGIN (* loop-name *)
    statement 1;
    statement 2;
    ...
    statement n
  END (* loop-name *)
```

The loop-name comments are given if any of the statements in the body of the loop is itself a compound statement.

The WHILE loop is executed as follows:

1. Evaluate the condition. If the result of evaluation is "false", execution of the loop is completed; if "true", proceed to step 2.

2. Execute the body of the loop. Upon completion, return to step 1.

The action is suggested by the English meaning of the keywords -- the body is iterated while the condition remains true. The action can be shown graphically by a "flow-diagram":

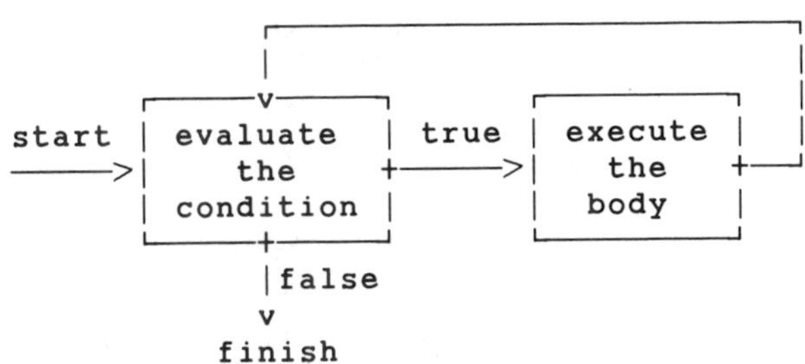

Figure 1. Execution of the WHILE loop

An example of a trivial WHILE loop is the following:

```
I := 0;
WHILE I < 3 DO
    I := I + 1
```

In execution this loop would have the same effect as execution of the following sequence of statements:

```
I := 0;
I := I + 1;
I := I + 1;
I := I + 1
```

While in this case it might be easier to write out the sequence, this quickly becomes impractical as the number of repetitions becomes large or when a compound statement is to be repeated. Go back and reread examples (1.1c) and (1.1d) which illustrate this same point on a slightly less trivial task. This concept of a loop -- of repeating a sequence of statements -- is a very important idea in programming and you must understand it thoroughly.

As another example of a WHILE loop, suppose you wanted to sum the integers from 14 through 728. (There is a simple formula to sum consecutive integers so this program would not actually be used, but it provides a simple and clear example of the control of repetition.) The following program segment could be used:

```
            (* SUM INTEGERS FROM 14 THRU 728 *)
               I := 14;
               SUM := 14;
               WHILE I < 728 DO
(4.3.1.1a)       BEGIN
                    I := I + 1;
                    SUM := SUM + I
                 END
```

The first two assignment statements establish initial values for the variables I and SUM. Then the WHILE loop is executed. Since the condition I < 728 is true (I=14) the loop body is executed. This changes I to 15 and SUM to 14+15=29. Then the condition is re-evaluated. It is still true (since the value of I is now 15) so the body is again executed. This repetition continues until finally the value of I becomes 728. At this point the condition is found to be false, and the execution of the WHILE loop is finished. The required task has been accomplished -- the variable SUM contains the sum of the integers from 14 to 728.

We can "prove" that (4.3.1.1a) performs the desired task by showing that, just before and after each execution of the loop body,

(4.3.1.1b) SUM contains the sum of the numbers from 14 to I.

Before executing the loop I=14 and SUM=14, so that (4.3.1.1b) holds initially. The body of the loop always increases I by 1 and then adds the new I to SUM, so that the relation (4.3.1.1b) does indeed hold after every execution of the body. Hence after the last execution we have I=728 and SUM contains the sum of the integers from 14 to 728.

As another example, in which the body is a single statement rather than a compound statement, a WHILE loop could be used to scan the data list to find the first negative number:

```
            (* DISCARD DATA UP TO FIRST NEGATIVE VALUE *)
               READ(DATUM);
(4.3.1.1c)     WHILE DATUM >= 0 DO
                    READ(DATUM)
```

Execution of the body of a WHILE loop must provide some action that affects the condition, so that it eventually becomes false. For example, in (4.3.1.1a) an assignment statement increases the value of I to serve this role. If the body never affects the condition, then if it is initially true it will remain true and the body of the WHILE loop will be iterated indefinitely. This is a classic program error called an "infinite iterative loop" and every programmer produces one once in a while. In practice, of course, each program is subject to a time limit so that repetition does not continue forever.

The condition may be false when the WHILE loop is first encountered. In this case the body is not executed -- not even once -- so the statements of the body have no effect upon the condition or upon anything else.

It is important to understanding the action of a WHILE loop to know when the condition is evaluated. This is done before the body itself is executed. If the condition is true then the entire body is executed. Even if statements within the body change the values of variables to make the condition false, the condition is not under continuous review during execution of the body. The condition is not re-evaluated until after execution of the body is completed. For this reason the following program is not correct since it will print the value of the negative number as well as those of the discards.

```
            (* DISCARD AND LIST DATA UP TO FIRST NEG VALUE *)
               READ(DATUM);
               WRITELN(DATUM);
               WHILE DATUM >= 0 DO
(4.3.1.1d)       BEGIN
                    READ(DATUM);
                    WRITELN(DATUM)
                 END
```

We leave it as an exercise for you to figure out how to change this program segment to make it correct.

4.3.1.2 The REPEAT Loop

The second conditional repetitive statement in PASCAL has the general form:

```
REPEAT
    statement
  UNTIL condition
```

If the statement to be repeated is compound the form is:

```
REPEAT
    statement 1;
    statement 2;
    ...
    statement n
  UNTIL condition
```

In this case the keywords REPEAT and UNTIL serve as end markers for the compound statement so it is not necessary to use the BEGIN and END markers. The REPEAT loop is executed as follows:

1. Execute the body of the loop.

2. Evaluate the condition. If the result of evaluation is false, return to step 1; if the result is true, execution of the loop is completed.

The action is suggested by the English meaning of the keywords -- repeat the body of the loop until the condition becomes true. The action can be shown by a flow-diagram:

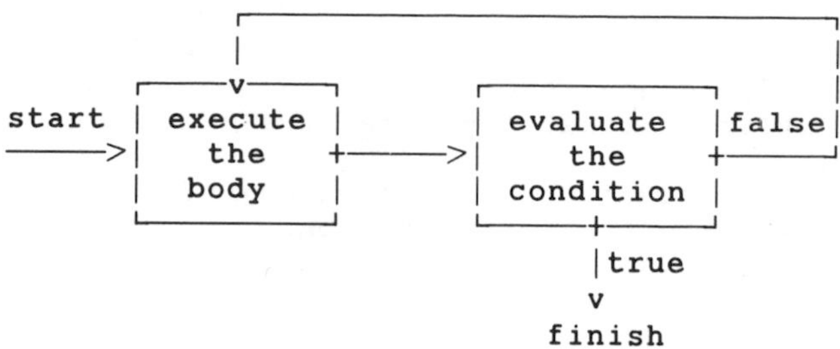

Figure 2. Execution of the REPEAT loop

The summing task, which was written with a WHILE loop in (4.3.1.1a), can also be written with a REPEAT loop:

```
(* SUM INTEGERS FROM 14 THRU 728 *)
    I := 14;
    SUM := 14;
    REPEAT
         I := I + 1;
         SUM := SUM + I
      UNTIL I = 728
```

Similarly, the examples of (4.3.1.1c) and (4.3.1.1d) can also be written with REPEAT loops:

```
(* DISCARD DATA UP TO FIRST NEGATIVE VALUE *)
    REPEAT
         READ(DATUM)
      UNTIL DATUM < 0

(* DISCARD AND LIST DATA UP TO FIRST NEG VALUE *)
    REPEAT
         READ(DATUM);
         WRITELN(DATUM)
      UNTIL DATUM < 0
```

Both of these examples are shorter and clearer when written with a REPEAT loop than they were when written with a WHILE loop, but note that the error in (4.3.1.1d) is still present in the REPEAT version.

In general, any repetitive task can be put in either the WHILE or the REPEAT forms. In fact, most programming languages offer only one of these forms. PASCAL has the advantage of providing both -- but to take advantage of this you have to learn when to use the WHILE loop and when to use the REPEAT loop. There are two significant differences:

1. In the WHILE loop the condition is evaluated <u>before</u> the execution of the body; in the REPEAT loop the condition is evaluated <u>after</u> the execution of the body.

2. As a consequence of this the body of a REPEAT loop is always <u>executed at least once</u>, whereas the body of a WHILE loop may not be executed at all.

With practice you will learn to choose whichever of these forms is the most natural for a given task. For example, if the task must be performed before the condition has any meaning, then the REPEAT loop is a clearer way to describe it. (4.3.1.1c) and (4.3.1.1d) were examples of this type of task. A similar example is the task of making a list of data up to, and including, the first zero value. The clearest way to program this is:

```
(* LIST DATA THRU FIRST 0 *)
    REPEAT
         READ(DATUM);
         WRITELN(DATUM)
      UNTIL DATUM = 0
```

The equivalent WHILE loop is shown below. (The symbol "<>" in the fourth line means "not equal".)

```
(* LIST DATA THRU FIRST 0 *)
    READ(DATUM);
    WRITELN(DATUM);
    WHILE DATUM <> 0 DO
      BEGIN
         READ(DATUM);
         WRITELN(DATUM)
      END
```

The WHILE loop in this case requires the body to be written twice -- once as a preparatory step, and once inside the loop -- so the REPEAT form is preferable. However, there are other cases where the WHILE loop is more natural, but we need an additional statement type to give plausible examples.

4.3.1.3 Simple Conditions

A simple "condition" or "relational expression" is a special type of expression that involves a "relation". The symbols for the PASCAL relations are the following:

symbol	meaning
=	is equal to
<>	is not equal to
>	is greater than
>=	is greater than or equal to
<	is less than
<=	is less than or equal to

(The double-character symbols cannot have a blank between characters.) A condition consists of two arithmetic expressions (as described in Section 3.2) separated by a relation:

```
arith-expr    relation    arith-expr
```

A condition describes a relationship that is either true or false. For example, 2<3 is a condition that is always true; 2=3, a condition that is always false; J=K, a condition that may be either true or false depending upon the values of the variables J and K at the instant the condition is evaluated.

Other examples are:

```
TEST = 0
J+2 < K
TEMP*(PRESSURE-4*PI) <= BASEPRESSURE
```

Three of the built-in functions listed in Section 3.3 have results that are either true or false. These functions may also be used as a simple condition:

ODD(x) -- The value of the result is true if x is an odd number; otherwise the result is false. x must be an INTEGER.

EOLN(INPUT) -- The value of the result is true if, while reading a card, the end of the card is reached; otherwise the result is false. "INPUT" is the default file, so the function can be given without an argument, simply as EOLN, and EOLN(INPUT) is assumed. We use this form in our examples.

EOF(INPUT) -- The result is true if, while reading the data cards, the "end-of-file" or end of the data cards is reached; otherwise the result is false. (An example of the use of EOF is given in the next section.) "INPUT" is the default file, and is assumed if EOF is given without an argument.

4.3.1.4 Compound Conditions

Conditions can be made more complex by the use of "Boolean operators". These are "and", "or" and "not". "And" and "or" are used to combine two conditions to form a "compound condition". "Not" is used to reverse the truth of a condition. Letting A and B represent conditions which are true or false, we describe the symbols and meanings of the three operations:

English	symbol	meaning	
"and"	AND	A AND B	is true if both A and B are true
"or"	OR	A OR B	is true if either A or B is true (or if both are true)
"not"	NOT	NOT A	is true only if A is not true

The following table gives the values of these compound conditions for different values of the conditions A, B, C and D.

A	B	A AND B	A OR B	NOT A
true	true	true	true	false
true	false	false	true	false
false	true	false	true	true
false	false	false	false	true

WHILE and REPEAT loop conditions can be simple or compound:

```
WHILE (I > 56) AND (I < 729) DO
    ...

REPEAT
    ...
  UNTIL (PRESSURE > PRESSMIN) AND (TEMP < TEMPMAX)

WHILE (REGGAP <= 15.2 * GAP) OR (FLAG = 2) DO
    ...
```

The parentheses in these compound conditions are required by PASCAL, since the Boolean operators have higher precedence than relations.

Precedence rules for these operators are analogous to those for arithmetic operations given in Section 3.2.2. AND is considered before OR, so that

```
(A=B) AND (C=D) OR (E=F)
```

is equivalent to

```
((A=B) AND (C=D)) OR (E=F)
```

However, it is a good idea to use parentheses in compound conditions to be certain that the order of consideration is what you intended.

NOT should be used sparingly, since it tends to make programs harder to understand. When NOT must be used parentheses should generally be given to enclose the condition to which it applies. An exception is when NOT is applied to a built-in function, as for example

```
NOT EOF    or    NOT EOLN
```

where an extra set of parentheses does not help make the meaning clearer. The same thing is true when NOT is applied to Boolean variables, which are introduced in the next section.

In many cases, NOT can be avoided by choosing the opposite relation:

```
NOT(A = B) is equivalent to A <> B
NOT(A <= B) is equivalent to A > B
```

The following example will illustrate a reasonable use of the NOT operator, as well as the use of the EOF function and a contrast between a WHILE loop and a REPEAT loop. Suppose that at some point in a program we have to read and compute the sum of the remaining data on the data list, but there is no special datum at the end of the list by whose value the program can recognize that the end of the list has been reached. The EOF built-in function provides a means of recognizing the end of the list, but it is not entirely obvious how to use it. What we would like to do is repeat a pair of statements such as

```
READ(ITEM);
SUM := SUM + ITEM
```

Obviously these statements could be made the body of a loop, but there will be a problem when the end of the data list is reached. When that happens READ(ITEM) will not assign a new value to ITEM, so the subsequent execution of SUM := SUM + ITEM would be incorrect. Hence the problem is to terminate repetition immediately after READ(ITEM) encounters the end of the data list. This can be done in the following way:

```
(* READ AND SUM REMAINING DATA *)
    SUM := 0;
    ITEM := 0;
    REPEAT
         SUM := SUM + ITEM;
         READ(ITEM)
      UNTIL EOF
```

This will work, but it is the kind of "tricky" program we would like to avoid whenever possible. In this case, since the body of the loop sums before reading, we have to provide a "dummy read" so the loop will work properly on the first repetition. This is done by the statement ITEM := 0, which assigns a value carefully chosen so the summing statement in the body is harmless on the first repetition. A much better way to accomplish this task is the following:

```
(* READ AND SUM REMAINING DATA *)
    SUM := 0;
    READ(ITEM);
    WHILE NOT EOF DO
      BEGIN
         SUM := SUM + ITEM;
         READ(ITEM)
      END
```

4.3.1.5 BOOLEAN Values

As noted in Section 4.3.1.3, conditions are special kinds of expressions. They are expressions whose result is a new type of value called "Boolean" (named for the English logician George Boole). BOOLEAN is a value type in PASCAL, comparable to the types INTEGER and REAL introduced in Section 2.3. It is a curious type of value in that there are only two values allowed: TRUE and FALSE. TRUE and FALSE are BOOLEAN constants in the same sense that 5 and 8 are INTEGER constants. However, TRUE and FALSE happen to be the only BOOLEAN constants.

Variables can be declared to be of type BOOLEAN:

```
VAR ERRORFLAG, TEST: BOOLEAN
```

Such variables can be the target of assignments, but the right-side expressions that produce the value to be assigned must yield a BOOLEAN value. For example

```
ERRORFLAG := TRUE
TEST := FALSE
ERRORFLAG := TEST
ERRORFLAG := X < 0
ERRORFLAG := (X < 0) OR (X > 100)
```

However, BOOLEAN variables cannct be assigned values from external data. That is, the values TRUE or FALSE cannot be placed on data cards and assigned to a BOOLEAN variable by means of a normal READ statement.

In effect, BOOLEAN variables allow you to save the result of a condition. You can perform the test at one point in a program, and use the result at some other point. For example, instead of writing

```
IF (X < 0) OR (X > 100) THEN ...
```

if XTEST is a BOOLEAN variable you could write

```
...
XTEST := (X < 0) OR (X > 100)
...
IF XTEST THEN ...
```

4.3.2 Repetition with Different Values

An alternative type of loop is used to specify that execution of the body is to be repeated with consecutive values of a key variable, called the "index" variable. Example (4.3.1.1a) could be rewritten in this form as

```
          (* SUM INTEGERS FROM 14 THRU 728 *)
              SUM := 0;
(4.3.2a)      FOR I := 14 TO 728 DO
                   SUM := SUM + I
```

The *index variable* I is set equal to 14 and the body is executed; then I is set equal to 15 and the body is executed; etc. The final execution of the body has I equal to 728.

The general form of the FOR loop is:

```
FOR index-variable := initial-value TO final-value DO
    statement
```

If the statement to be repeated is compound the form is:

```
FOR index-variable := initial-value TO final-value DO
  BEGIN (* loop-name *)
    statement 1;
    statement 2;
    ...
    statement n
  END (* loop-name *)
```

The loop-name comments are given on the BEGIN,END lines if any of the statements in the loop body are compound. The index variable and the expressions giving initial value and final value *must all be of type INTEGER*. (This restriction will be relaxed in Section 8, but the key point here is that they *cannot be REAL.*) The expressions giving initial and final values will be evaluated just *once* -- before any execution of the body of the loop. If, in this evaluation, the initial value is greater than the final value the body is not executed at all.

Execution of such a FOR loop can be most easily and precisely explained by exhibiting an equivalent WHILE loop. Suppose that INDEX, INITIAL and FINAL are INTEGER variables representing the index variable, initial value and final value of the FOR loop, respectively. Assume that none of these variables is assigned a value in the body of the FOR loop. Then the equivalent WHILE loop is

```
INDEX := INITIAL;
WHILE INDEX <= FINAL DO
  BEGIN (* loop-name *)
    Statements in the body of the FOR loop;
    INDEX := INDEX + 1
  END (* loop-name *)
```

The only difference between these two loops is that after completion of the WHILE loop the value of INDEX is FINAL + 1. After execution of the FOR loop the value of the index variable is "undefined". Since the language does not define what it should be, different compilers for for PASCAL could very well result in different values. You should treat the index variable after a FOR loop just as you would a newly created variable -- assign it a value before you use it.

Studied carefully, the equivalent WHILE loop reveals some interesting properties of the FOR loop:

1. An assignment is performed in the control of the FOR loop; the index variable is changed just as if it were the left-side variable of an ordinary assignment statement.

2. It is not necessary to use the index variable in the body. Frequently it serves only as a "counter" to determine the number of iterations of the body.

Two other properties of the FOR loop are:

3. Assignment within the body to a variable that appears in the expressions for the initial value or the final value has no effect on the control of iteration; these expressions are only evaluated before the first iteration of the body.

4. The index variable cannot be the target of assignment within the body. That is, the index variable is assigned a new value automatically for each iteration of the body, but that value cannot be changed within the body.

The FOR loop we have shown provides repetition for a sequence of increasing values. There is an alternative form that provides repetition for a sequence of decreasing values:

```
FOR index-variable := initial-value DOWNTO final-value DO
    statement
```

The comparable WHILE loop is:

```
INDEX := INITIAL;
WHILE INDEX >= FINAL DO
  BEGIN (* loop-name *)
    Statements in the body of the FOR loop;
    INDEX := INDEX - 1
  END (* loop-name *)
```

In this case, if the initial value is less than the final value the body of the loop is not executed. (4.3.2a) could be rewritten as a decreasing loop:

```
(* SUM INTEGERS FROM 728 THRU 17 *)
    SUM := 0;
    FOR I := 728 DOWNTO 14 DO
         SUM := SUM + I
```

The FOR loop can be quite useful. It's most common use is to index over the elements of an array -- the topic of Section 5. However, you should recognize that it is just a special case of the more general WHILE loop. When iteration is of this special form it is certainly easier to write "I := 14 TO 728" than to write the statements necessary to initialize and increment the index variable in a WHILE loop. Another desirable characteristic of the FOR loop is that there is no question of termination. The maximum number of repetitions for a FOR loop is always exactly specified in the TO or DOWNTO phrase, whereas it is possible for a WHILE loop never to terminate (if the controlling condition never becomes false).

However, not all iteration has the form appropriate for a FOR loop, and you should not try to force it to do work for which it was not intended. The WHILE or REPEAT loop is the general form, and one of those should be used except in special cases.

4.3.3 Nesting of Loops

Since the body of a loop is a sequence of statements, and since an entire loop is itself effectively a statement, one loop can be included in the body of another. For example, suppose the input data consists of a list of pairs of numbers, and for each pair (LOW, HIGH) we want to print the sum of the integers from LOW to HIGH. We always have LOW <= HIGH, and the last pair is followed by the pair (1,0). For the input "1 2 2 3 1 0" we should print "3 5". The program segment given in (4.3.3a) is designed to perform this task, but the segment has not been completed. Part of the action is given as a comment -- which describes what has to be done, but not how.

```
              (* READ INPUT PAIRS (LOW,HIGH) UNTIL LOW > HIGH *)
              (* FOR EACH PAIR PRINT LOW + (LOW+1) + ... + HIGH *)
                  READ(LOW, HIGH);
                  WHILE LOW <= HIGH DO
(4.3.3a)            BEGIN
                       (* SET SUM = LOW + (LOW+1) + ... + HIGH *)
                       WRITELN(SUM);
                       READ(LOW, HIGH)
                    END
```

We already have a program segment (4.3.2a) to perform the required summing task, so we simply insert (4.3.2a) in (4.3.3a) as a "refinement" or implementation of the comment describing the summing task. (4.3.2a), which is itself a loop, just becomes one statement in the body of the loop of (4.3.3a):

```
(* READ INPUT PAIRS (LOW,HIGH) UNTIL LOW > HIGH *)
(* FOR EACH PAIR PRINT LOW + (LOW+1) + ... + HIGH *)
    READ(LOW, HIGH);
    WHILE LOW <= HIGH DO
      BEGIN
         (* SET SUM = LOW + (LOW+1) + ... + HIGH *)
              SUM := 0;
              FOR I := LOW TO HIGH DO
                   SUM := SUM + I;
         WRITELN(SUM);
         READ(LOW, HIGH)
      END
```

One loop is said to be "nested" within another. We have indented the statements to show the nesting structure. As the nesting level increases and the length of the compound statements increases indentation is very helpful in making the structure of a program quickly and clearly obvious to the human reader. It is immaterial to PASCAL -- which doesn't care where a statement is placed on the line.

We also use a consistent comment convention to help make the nature of nested loops clearer to the reader. The BEGIN,END delimiters of any loop are followed by matching comments if the body of that loop contains another BEGIN,END pair. That is

```
BEGIN (* loop name *)
    ...
    BEGIN
         ...
    END;
    ...
END (* loop name *)
```

Only the BEGIN,END delimiters of the innermost loop are not identified by matching comments. We always give matching comment-names to the BEGIN,END delimiters of a procedure, whether or not it contains another BEGIN,END pair.

Note that when (4.3.2a) becomes a "statement" in another compound statement it is followed by a semi-colon to separate it from the following statement.

As another example of nested loops, consider the program segment

```
OUTSUM := 0;
INNERSUM := 0;
FOR OUTINDEX := 1 TO 5 DO
  BEGIN
    OUTSUM := OUTSUM + 1;
    FOR ININDEX := 1 TO 4 DO
         INNERSUM := INNERSUM +1
  END
```

Both index variables OUTINDEX and ININDEX are counters that control the number of iterations but are not used within the body. The segment does nothing useful, but study it until you understand very clearly why after its execution the values of the variables are:

OUTSUM <u>5</u>   INNERSUM <u>20</u>

Also make sure you understand why semi-colons are placed where they are.

Note that each segment in these examples could be presented and discussed out of context -- it was not necessary to specify whether it was part of some larger, unseen loop. Each segment could in fact be buried in the interior of a nest of loops several layers deep, so that its execution would be repeated many times.

4.4 Conditional Execution

It is often necessary to execute a statement conditionally -- that is, to decide whether or not to execute it, depending upon some condition. For example, this was done in the sample program in (1.1e) to find the maximum of a set of values:

```
IF NUMBER > MAXNBR
    THEN MAXNBR := NUMBER
```

The candidate number in NUMBER was compared to the largest that had been encountered up to that point. If the new candidate was larger, then execution of the assignment statement recorded it as the largest encountered. If the new number was not larger, then that assignment statement had to be skipped.

In PASCAL the conditional statement has two forms. The simpler one, used in the example above, is

```
IF condition
    THEN statement¹
```

The interpretation is suggested by the English meaning of the keywords "IF" and "THEN":

> *If* the condition is true *then* execute statement^1. If the condition is false, do not execute statement^1.

This flow-of-control is as follows:

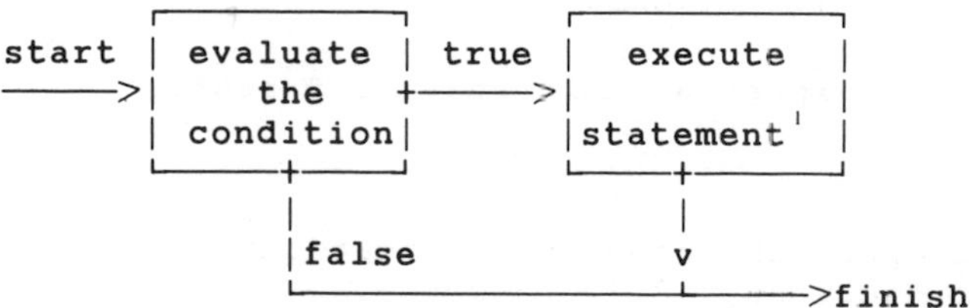

Figure 3. Conditional Execution

The second form of the IF statement is very similar:

```
IF condition
    THEN statement¹
    ELSE statement²
```

The interpretation is:

> If the condition is true then execute statement^1. If the condition is false execute statement^2.

That is, one or the other of statement^1 and statement^2, but not both, will be executed, depending upon the truth or falsity of the condition. The flow-of-control is:

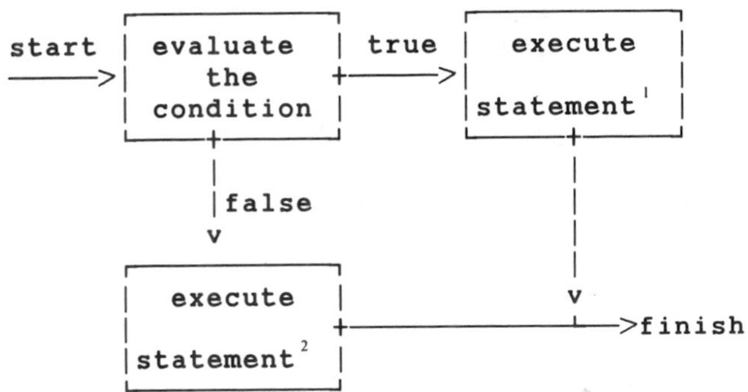

Figure 4. Alternative Execution

Either simple or compound conditions can be used, as described in Sections 4.3.1.3 and 4.3.1.4.

Examples of conditional statements are given below. The parentheses are actually required only in the last example. The others have been added only to make the meaning clearer to a human reader.

```
IF (NEWVALUE > MAXVALUE)
    THEN MAXVALUE := NEWVALUE

IF QTY < 0
    THEN NEGCOUNT := NEGCOUNT + 1
    ELSE POSCOUNT := POSCOUNT + 1

IF (B*B - 4*A*C) < 0
    THEN WRITELN(' IMAGINARY ROOT')

IF (CONTROL = J+1) OR (VALUE = 0)
    THEN READ(VALUE)
```

The "THEN statement" following the condition is mandatory; the "ELSE statement" is optional, since it is only present in the second form. Situations arise where it seems useful to have only an "ELSE statement" -- that is, a statement to be executed only if a condition is false. This could be done by giving a "dummy THEN statement":

```
IF condition
    THEN
    ELSE statement¹
```

However, this seems artificial and confusing to the reader and it is generally preferable to avoid this by <u>reversing the sense</u> of the condition. For example, instead of writing

```
IF A > B
    THEN
    ELSE statement
```

you should write

```
IF A <= B
    THEN statement
```

Instead of writing

```
IF (A = B) OR (C < D)
    THEN
    ELSE statement
```

you should write

```
IF NOT((A = B) OR (C < D))
    THEN statement
```

or

```
IF (A <> B) AND (C >= D)
    THEN statement
```

In all of the examples above what is shown as a single statement can also be a compound statement. The general form is

```
IF condition
    THEN BEGIN
             statement 1;
             statement 2;
             ...
             statement m
         END
    ELSE BEGIN
             statement 1;
             statement 2;
             ...
             statement n
         END
```

Note that there is never a semi-colon immediately before an ELSE. The ELSE phrase is part of the overall conditional statement. Since semi-colons separate statements, inserting one in the middle of a conditional statement is obviously improper. It would effectively sever the ELSE phrase from the conditional statement. The separated ELSE is then considered an error, since there is no statement in PASCAL that begins with ELSE.

4.4.1 Exit from a Program Segment

Greater flexibility in choosing program structures is possible if one can "exit" from a program segment "prematurely"; that is, if one can terminate execution of a program segment before its normal completion. In the case of a loop this means terminating execution of the body, or terminating execution of the entire loop. In PASCAL this type of exit must be accomplished by a "conditional branch". In addition to the conditional statement, this involves the "goto statement" and the concept of a "statement label".

A statement label is just an integer, of not more than four digits. Any statement may be identified so it can be referred to, by giving it a prefix consisting of a statement label followed by a colon. For example

```
24: SUM := 0
32: BEGIN ...  END
7000: FOR I := 1 TO N DO ...
555: WRITELN('INVALID DATA')
```

Since the purpose of a label is to identify a statement, obviously two statements must not be given identical labels.

Integers which are used as statement labels must be declared as such in the procedure heading. For example

```
LABEL 24, 32, 555, 7000
```

This declaration must precede the declaration of variables in the heading.

The GOTO statement refers to such a label:

```
GOTO label
...
label: statement
```

Execution of the GOTO statement causes control to "branch" or "jump" to the statement whose label is specified. That is, the next statement to be executed is the one whose label is referenced in the GOTO, rather than the statement immediately following the GOTO.

As an example, the program below uses a GOTO to terminate execution of the loop body (not the whole loop). Here, label 43 is a prefix on an "empty" or "null" statement. This null statement has no effect on execution, since its execution does nothing; its sole purpose is to provide a statement on which to hang the label. (This example uses integer division -- the MOD operator defined in Section 3.2.1.)

```
          (* SUM AND COUNT THE INTEGERS FROM BASE TO TOP
              WHICH ARE DIVISIBLE BY 3 OR 5 *)
          PROGRAM COUNTSUM(INPUT, OUTPUT);
          LABEL 43;
          VAR BASE, TOP, (* INPUT VALUES *)
              KSUM,      (* SUM OF NBR DIVISIBLE BY 3 OR 5 *)
              KCOUNT,    (* COUNT OF NBR DIVISIBLE BY 3 OR 5 *)
              K:         (* LOOP INDEX *)
                   INTEGER;
(4.4.1a)  BEGIN (* COUNTSUM *)
              READ(BASE, TOP);
              KSUM := 0;
              KCOUNT := 0;
              FOR K := BASE TO TOP DO
                BEGIN
                   IF (K MOD 3 <> 0) AND (K MOD 5 <> 0)
                        THEN GOTO 43;
                   KSUM := KSUM + K;
                   KCOUNT := KCOUNT + 1;
                   43:
                END;
              WRITELN(' BASE =', BASE, 'TOP =', TOP);
              WRITELN(' SUM =', KSUM, 'COUNT =', KCOUNT)
          END.  (* COUNTSUM *)
```

The GOTO exit is not really necessary in this example, since the same result could be achieved much more clearly with a compound statement:

```
              ...
              KSUM := 0;
              KCOUNT := 0;
              FOR K := BASE TO TOP DO
(4.4.1b)        BEGIN (* SUM LOOP *)
                   IF (K MOD 3 = 0) OR (K MOD 5 = 0)
                        THEN BEGIN KSUM := KSUM + K;
                                   KCOUNT := KCOUNT + 1
                             END
                END (* SUM LOOP *)
```

The style of (4.4.1b) is certainly preferable in this case, and should be employed whenever practical. However, as loops become larger and more complex, situations arise in which the structure is made clearer if one can branch directly to the END and thus terminate (or skip) a particular iteration of the body.

In general, branches make it harder to understand execution of a program, and make it harder to show that it is correct. Consequently, the GOTO should be used sparingly and only when necessary.

It is also useful to be able to escape from a loop earlier than provided by the control phrase, by branching to a null statement following the loop. For example:

```
          (* SUM INTEGERS FROM BASE TO TOP, SUBJECT TO KLIMIT *)
              KSUM := 0;
              FOR K := BASE TO TOP DO
(4.4.1c)        BEGIN
                   IF KSUM + K > KLIMIT THEN GOTO 9001;
                   KSUM := KSUM + K
                END;
              9001:
```

The same result would be achieved by assigning the label to the first statement of the next section of the program, but the logical role of the exit would be less clear. The GOTO is being used to exit from this program segment, and not to enter the next segment. Hence the target label should be positioned, and the label should be chosen, as the last statement of this segment, rather than as the first statement of the next.

We have adopted the convention of having all exit labels used in this way be integers above 9000 so that the role of the GOTO in terminating the loop is unmistakable. This is just an arbitrary convention -- not a rule of the programming language -- but this type of consistency makes a program more predictable and easier for a human reader to understand.

We generally try to use two-digit labels for those that serve to terminate one execution of the loop-body, as for example, the label 43 in (4.4.1a). However, this distinction cannot always be maintained. Note that in (4.4.1g) the label 9002 is an exit from the inner FOR loop, and a termination of one execution of the loop-body for the outer WHILE loop.

Notice the different indentation of the labels 43 and 9001 in examples (4.4.1a) and (4.4.1c). In (4.4.1a) the label 43 is indented to show that it is part of the body of the loop. In (4.4.1c) the label 9001 is aligned with the END to show that it follows the loop.

As in the case of (4.4.1a), the GOTO exit is not necessary in (4.4.1c). It would be better to use a WHILE loop and include the exit condition in the main control phrase. (4.4.1d) is equivalent to (4.4.1c) in function and preferable in style:

```
          (* SUM INTEGERS FROM BASE TO TOP, SUBJECT TO KLIMIT *)
              KSUM := 0;
              K := BASE;
              WHILE (K <= TOP) AND (KSUM + K <= KLIMIT) DO
(4.4.1d)        BEGIN
                   KSUM := KSUM + K;
                   K := K + 1
                END
```

As another example, suppose we are given integer variables A, B, C, and Y, and we desire a program segment which will print Y if the following is true:

(4.4.1e) There is <u>no</u> integer n such that

$$1 \le n \le Y \quad \text{and} \quad Y = A + B \cdot n + C \cdot n^2$$

This can be detected by examining values of $A+B \cdot n+C \cdot n^2$ for n = 1,2,...,Y. The following segment uses a GOTO to end execution of the segment when it has attained its goal:

```
          FOR I := 1 TO Y DO
(4.4.1f)      IF A + B*I + C*I*I = Y
                   THEN GOTO 9002;
          WRITELN(Y);
          9002:
```

We now write a segment which prints up to 5 values of Y, for Y = 1, 2, ..., 50, which satisfy property (4.4.1e). The following segment illustrates the use of a GOTO to end execution of a program segment, in performing this function.

```
          (*  PRINT UP TO 5 VALUES OF Y (FOR I=1,2,...,50) WHICH
              SATISFY PROPERTY (4.4.1E) *)
              Y := 0;
              COUNT := 0;
              WHILE (Y < 50) AND (COUNT < 5) DO
(4.4.1g)        BEGIN
                   Y := Y + 1;
                   (* PRINT Y IF IT SATISFIES (4.4.1E) *)
                        FOR I := 1 TO Y DO
                             IF A + B*I + C*I*I = Y
                                  THEN GOTO 9002;
                        WRITELN(Y);
                   COUNT := COUNT + 1;
                   9002:;
                END
```

The GOTO should be used sparingly. It <u>can</u> be used much more widely, and many programming texts consider it to be the principal control mechanism. With ingenious use of labels, IFs and GOTOs one can "handcraft" control structures equivalent to all the others described in Section 4, but it does not follow that this is desirable. Such programs are not necessarily more efficient and seldom exhibit their logical structure as clearly as programs using the more complex control statements. One philosophy of programming -- called "structured programming" -- considers the GOTO to be both inelegant and dangerous. We agree wholeheartedly, and use the GOTO only when PASCAL does not offer a more natural alternative. The principal example of such use is as an exit, as has been described in the preceding paragraphs. (Further discussion of this "exit problem" is given in Section 4.6.)

As a general rule, never resort to the use of a GOTO until you have tried to design the program in another way that would avoid it. <u>Use a GOTO only when the alternative is even more awkward</u>.

4.4.2 Indefinite Repetition

In some cases, a program is clearer and more logical if the control of iteration is performed entirely within the body of the loop. The exit technique described in 4.4.1 can be used, but some mechanism must be provided to continue the iteration until the exit takes effect. This can be done just by using the constants TRUE and FALSE in the conditions in the loop control. The loop

```
WHILE TRUE DO
    ...
```

will continue to be executed until some internal exit takes effect. Similarly, the loop

```
REPEAT
    ...
  UNTIL FALSE
```

will also repeat indefinitely.

For example, consider the following problem:

> The input consists of integers which are to be read and printed <u>until</u> one is read which satisfies one of the following three conditions:
> a) the number is negative
> b) the number ends in "3"
> c) the number is a power of two (1,2,4,8,16,...)

The requirement is not complicated or difficult, but the termination test cannot be conveniently written as the condition of a WHILE loop. The following is a reasonable solution:

```
(* PRINT NON-NEGATIVE INTEGERS WHICH DO NOT END IN 3
    AND WHICH ARE NOT POWERS OF TWO *)
    WHILE TRUE DO
      BEGIN
         READ(A);
         IF (A MOD 10 = 3) OR (A < 0) THEN GO TO 9010;
         (* TEST A FOR POWER OF 2 *)
              POWEROF2 := 1;
              WHILE POWEROF2 < A DO
                   POWEROF2 := POWEROF2 * 2;
              IF POWEROF2 = A THEN GOTO 9010;
         WRITELN(A)
      END;
    9010:
```

4.4.3 Nesting of Conditional Statements

The statement following THEN or ELSE in a conditional statement can be another conditional statement. When this occurs they are said to be "nested". For example, the form of a complete, symmetric nest of three conditional statements, each with both THEN and ELSE statements, is:

```
           IF condition^1
              THEN IF condition^2
                      THEN statement^1
(4.4.3a)              ELSE statement^2
              ELSE IF condition^3
                      THEN statement^3
                      ELSE statement^4
```

The flow-of-control in this nest is:

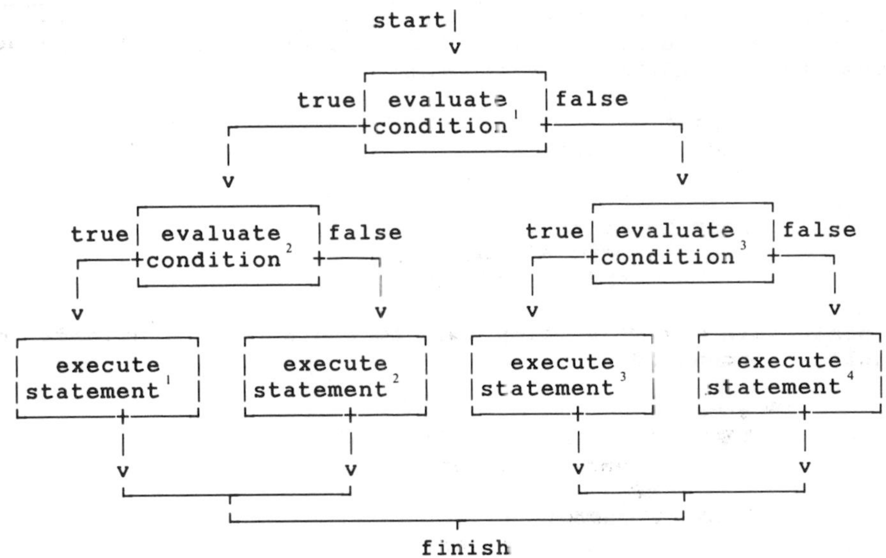

Figure 5. Nested Conditional Statements

Great care is required in using nested conditional statements since it is very easy to write nests that are syntactically correct (hence do not receive any warning messages) but do not do exactly what was intended. For example, suppose in (4.4.3a) the second conditional statement did not have an ELSE statement. If the fourth line were simply removed from (4.4.3a) the program would look like:

```
           IF condition^1
              THEN IF condition^2
(4.4.3b)               THEN statement^1
              ELSE IF condition^3
                       THEN statement^3
                       ELSE statement^4
```

The indenting in (4.4.3b) is deceptive and does not accurately show the program structure. (Remember that the PASCAL compiler ignores indentation.) The lines should be indented as:

```
IF condition^1
   THEN IF condition^2
           THEN statement^1
           ELSE IF condition^3
                   THEN statement^3
                   ELSE statement^4
```

This is because an ELSE belongs with the last preceding conditional statement that lacks an ELSE. To achieve the intended flow-of-control a null ELSE statement could be provided for the second conditional statement:

```
IF condition^1
   THEN IF condition^2
           THEN statement^1
           ELSE
   ELSE IF condition^3
           THEN statement^3
           ELSE statement^4
```

A preferable way of writing this to avoid the clumsiness of the null statement is:

```
IF condition^1
   THEN BEGIN IF condition^2
                 THEN statement^1
        END
   ELSE IF condition^3
           THEN statement^3
           ELSE statement^4
```

If you find these schematic nests hard to follow you may well believe that when written with actual conditions and statements (including compound statements), and even deeper nesting, this construction becomes very difficult to understand.

Fortunately the most obvious and common type of nested conditional statements can usually be replaced by a single conditional statement with a compound condition. The following examples are effectively equivalent:

```
IF  condition^1
   THEN IF condition^2
     THEN statement^1
```

```
IF condition^1 AND condition^2
   THEN statement^1
```

4.4.4 The CASE Statement

The IF ... THEN ... ELSE statement is used to choose one of two alternatives. When there are more than two alternatives there is a generalization of the IF statement that should be used. The general form is:

CASE expression OF
    case-label^{1}: statement^{1};
    case-label^{2}: statement^{2};
        ...
    case-label n: statement n
  END

For example:

```
(* WRITE MESSAGE, BASED ON ERROR NUMBER *)
    CASE ERRNBR OF
         1: WRITELN(' DATA VALUE TOO LARGE');
         2: WRITELN(' DATA VALUE TOO SMALL');
         3: WRITELN(' INSUFFICIENT DATA');
         4: WRITELN(' EXCESSIVE DATA');
         5: WRITELN(' IMPROPER VALUE')
      END
```

In executing the CASE statement the expression is evaluated and its value must be the value of one of the case-labels listed in the body of the statement. In the example above, ERRNBR must have value 1, 2, 3, 4 or 5 and depending upon that value one of the five alternative statements will be selected and executed. That completes execution of the CASE statement.

An alternative statement can have more than one case-label:

```
(* WRITE MESSAGE, BASED ON ERROR NUMBER *)
    CASE ERRNBR OF
         1: WRITELN(' DATA VALUE TOO LARGE');
         2: WRITELN(' DATA VALUE TOO SMALL');
         3,4,5: WRITELN(' IMPROPER DATA')
      END
```

The value of the CASE expression must be one of the case-labels listed in the body of the statement. If it is not, the result of executing the CASE statement is "undefined" -- that is, there is just no telling what PASCAL will do. (It may be more-or-less reasonable, but you are not supposed to count on it.) To avoid this embarassment it is a good idea to make sure the value of the expression is proper before executing the CASE statement. For example:

```
(* WRITE MESSAGE, BASED ON ERROR NUMBER *)
    IF (ERRNBR > 0) AND (ERRNBR < 6)
         THEN CASE ERRNBR OF
                1: WRITELN(' DATA VALUE TOO LARGE');
                2: WRITELN(' DATA VALUE TOO SMALL');
                3,4,5: WRITELN(' IMPROPER DATA')
            END
         ELSE WRITELN(' IMPROPER ERROR NUMBER')
```

These are presumably two different types of messages. "IMPROPER ERROR NUMBER" is a message to the programmer telling him the program has done something unexpected, and probably wrong. The other messages are directed to the user of the program telling him that he is not following the rules for submitting data.

At this point we must restrict the CASE expression to be of type INTEGER. We will be able to relax this restriction when we introduce other data types in Section 8.

As another example, suppose there is an "ill-behaved" mathematical function called the "Wooster function", that must be defined differently on different intervals:

if $0 \leq x < 1$, $y = 5x^2 + 3x + 2$;
if $1 \leq x < 4$, $y = 8.3x^3 - 2x^2 + 0.67x - 5$;
if $4 \leq x < 5$, $y = 2x + 3$; and
if $5 \leq x < 10$, $y = 8$;
otherwise $y = 0$.

Assuming X and Y are REAL, this might be programmed as follows:

```
(* EVALUATE WOOSTER FUNCTION OF X *)
    IF (X < 0) OR (X >= 10)
         THEN Y := 0
         ELSE CASE TRUNC(X) OF
                0: Y := 5 * SQR(X) + 3*X + 2;
                1,2,3: Y := 8.3*X*X*X - 2*X*X +
                                0.67*X - 5;
                4: Y := 2*X + 3;
                5,6,7,8,9: Y := 8
            END
```

Although we have not shown an example of such, <u>any of the alternative statements can itself be a compound statement</u>.

"Case-labels" are not equivalent to the statement labels of Section 4.4.1, although they happen to have the same form. In particular

1. Case-labels <u>cannot</u> be referenced by a GOTO statement.

2. Case-labels are <u>not</u> listed in a LABEL declaration.

Case-labels are "local" to the particular CASE statement in

which they appear. They must be unique within that statement -- the same label cannot appear more than once in the same CASE statement. However, the same case-label may appear in different CASE statements, and a case-label may be identical to a statement label (although this is likely to confuse the reader, and is not a good idea).

4.5 Tracing Execution

Tracing was introduced in Section 4.1.2, before our examples had loops. Now we would like to consider tracing of programs with loops. To trace execution of a loop, construct a table with a row for each variable, and a column for the execution of each statement that changes the value of at least one variable. For example, consider the following program, which is a variation of (1.1d):

```
(* SUMMING PROGRAM *)
PROGRAM WILLSUM(INPUT, OUTPUT);
VAR N: INTEGER;   (* NUMBER OF DATA *)
    I: INTEGER;   (* LOOP COUNTER *)
    X: REAL;      (* NEW DATUM *)
    SUM: REAL;    (* SUM OF DATA *)
BEGIN (* WILLSUM *)
    READ(N);
    SUM := 0;
    FOR I := 1 TO N DO
      BEGIN
         READ(X);
         SUM := SUM + X
      END;
    WRITELN(' SUM IS:', SUM)
END.  (* WILLSUM *)
    eor
3 5.6 42.1 31.7
```

The first part of the trace table for this program is:

Vari-able	Values as execution proceeds ->									
N	???	3	3	3	3	3	3	3	3	3	3
I	???	???	???	1	1	1	2	2	2	3	3
X	???	???	???	???	5.6	5.6	5.6	42.1	42.1	42.1	31.7
SUM	???	???	0	0	0	5.6	5.6	5.6	47.7	47.7	47.7

Tracing execution is for the programmer's benefit -- to help him understand a program or to help him detect an error in it. Thus, tracing occurs mainly when he is in difficulty of one sort or another. It must be done with care, one step at a time. While tracing, the programmer must execute the program the way the machine does, without thinking about the task being performed. Too often, a programmer executes what he *thinks* is there, and not what really *is* there, which of course doesn't help at all.

It is not necessary to write down each value in each column, but only that value that is being changed. The trace table shown above would then be

Vari-able	Values as execution proceeds ->										
N	???	3									
I	???			1			2			3	
X	???				5.6			42.1			31.7
SUM	???		0			5.6			47.7		

Often, the trace table becomes complicated and messy, and it is difficult to go back and analyze it. To aid in studying it, one often uses an extra row to indicate which statement is being executed, or to indicate the result of evaluating a condition. Labels can be given to statements so they can be unambiguously identified in the trace table. For example, consider the program segment

```
1: SUM := 0;
READ(X);
WHILE X <> 0 DO
  BEGIN
     2: IF X < 0
            THEN SUM := SUM - X
            ELSE SUM := SUM + X;
     READ(X)
  END;
SUM := SUM + 1;
...
eor
8 -5 0
```

In the trace table below, the top row indicates either the statement executed (by giving its label) or the result of evaluating a condition of a loop or conditional statement.

Vari-able		1:		loop true	2: X>0				loop true	2: X<0	
SUM	???	0	0	0	0	8	8	8	8	13	13
X	???	???	8	8	8	8	-5	-5	-5	-5	0

The amount of information needed in the trace table varies from program to program, depending on how difficult it is and how much trouble the programmer is having. But get in the habit of putting in as much information as possible.

4.6 Initialization and Exit Problems

Most problems with iteration involve starting and stopping the iteration, or equivalently, entering and exiting the program segment that performs the iteration. If one can get the first and last iterations to work properly, the iterations in between generally pose much less of a problem. Developing correct loops is one of the hardest parts of programming. We give some direction in this matter here; the subject is discussed again in Section II.1.5.

4.6.1 Exit Problems in Loops

Exit problems seem to have two principal sources:

1. Design of the stopping condition -- in particular, treatment of the "=" case.

2. Position of the "increment step" relative to the rest of the body.

These problems are more often associated with the WHILE and REPEAT forms since these tasks are handled more or less automatically in the FOR loop. However, since the WHILE loop is the more general and important form these questions can neither be ignored nor avoided.

For example, consider an integer summing task, similar to (4.3.1.1a):

```
          (* SET SUM TO SUM OF INTEGERS 14-728 *)
              I := 14;
              SUM := 0;
              WHILE I < 729 DO
(4.6.1a)        BEGIN
                   SUM := SUM + I;
                   I := I + 1
                END
```

The condition in this segment could just as well have been written (I <= 728). That is, it could be written to include the case of equality, and with a test value that is to be used in the body. Either form is equally correct -- they result in exactly the same execution -- and there are no general grounds for preferring one form to the other. However, there are two other possibilities that are likely to occur:

condition	result in (4.5.1a)
(I< 728)	one iteration too few
(I<=728)	correct number
(I< 729)	correct number
(I<=729)	one iteration too many

As indicated, the improper matching of the stopping value and the condition will cause improper timing of the exit. This is an exceedingly common type of error, even among experienced programmers.

Similarly, the position of the increment step can be critical. Changing its position, (4.6.1a) could be written as below. The comment notwithstanding, (4.6.1b) sums the integers from 15 through 729.

```
            (* SET SUM TO SUM OF INTEGERS 14-728 *)
                I := 14;
                SUM := 0;
                WHILE I < 729 DO
(4.6.1b)          BEGIN
                     I := I + 1;
                     SUM := SUM + I
                  END
```

If it is important to have the increment step in the position used in (4.6.1b) other parts of the segment could be changed. For example, (4.6.1c) is a corrected version of (4.6.1b):

```
            (* SET SUM TO SUM OF INTEGERS 14-728 *)
                I := 13;
                SUM := 0;
                WHILE I < 729 DO
(4.6.1c)          BEGIN
                     I := I + 1;
                     SUM := SUM + I
                  END
```

4.6.2 Initialization and Entry Problems

Typically, one or more variables must be "initialized" prior to entry of a loop, as for example, SUM in (4.6.1a). This is obvious, and logically straightforward, but nevertheless it is overlooked surprisingly often.

The benign form of error, in this regard, is to accidentally place the initialization within the body of the loop, as in (4.6.2a). This form of error is annoying but is usually revealed during testing, since it makes the loop ineffective.

(4.6.2a)

```
(* SET SUM TO SUM OF INTEGERS 14-728 *)
    I := 14;
    WHILE I < 729 DO
      BEGIN
         SUM := 0;
         SUM := SUM + I;
         I := I + 1
      END
```

The malignant form of error is to omit initialization altogether. For example, if the SUM := 0 statement were omitted from (4.6.1a), the result of execution would depend upon what value SUM happened to have when this segment was encountered. If this happened to be zero throughout testing the error would not be detected and this faulty program would be proclaimed "correct". Later, in production use, different initial values for SUM might arise, and this latent error would affect the results of the program. If the user is fortunate, the effect will be so dramatic that it is obvious that something is wrong. If he is less fortunate the error will remain hidden, and it will intermittently injure the results by varying amounts.

Initialization problems can be much more subtle than the previous example might suggest. For example, consider the following task:

> Read data from cards and sum the values, until a value of -1 is encountered. Do not include the -1 in the sum.

Execution of a program for this task will involve the following sequence of actions:

```
Read a value
Add the value just read to a running sum
Read a value
Add the value just read to a running sum
...
Read a value and discover it is -1
```

Obviously this will involve a loop whose body includes a READ and an assignment statement, but the entry and exit from the loop are not as obvious. Note that the sequence must both begin and end with a read. That is, at least one value must be read, and when the last value (the -1) is read, it must not be followed by an addition.

If you think of this program in terms of iteration of a pair of actions

```
Read a value
Add the value just read to a running sum
```

then the simple WHILE loop cannot be used, since it is unable to prevent the addition from following the last read. You could use the techniques described in Sections 4.4.1 and 4.4.2:

```
            (* READ AND SUM DATA UNTIL FIRST -1 *)
                SUM := 0;
                WHILE TRUE DO
(4.6.2b)          BEGIN
                     READ(VAL);
                     IF VAL = -1 THEN GOTO 9020;
                     SUM := SUM + VAL
                  END;
                9020:
```

Alternatively, you can think of the program in terms of iteration of the pair

    Add the value just read to a running sum
    Read another value

This simplifies the exit problem considerably, and a normal WHILE loop can be used:

```
                WHILE VAL <> -1 DO
                  BEGIN
                     SUM := SUM + VAL;
                     READ(VAL)
                  END
```

However, now the problem is to get the loop started properly. One method would be to read the first value as an initialization action, WHILE loop:

```
            (* READ AND SUM DATA UNTIL FIRST -1 *)
                SUM := 0;
                READ(VAL);
                WHILE VAL <> -1 DO
(4.6.2c)          BEGIN
                     SUM := SUM + VAL;
                     READ(VAL)
                  END
```

It is not very clean to have to rewrite a portion of the body of the loop as initialization, but all things considered, for most simple tasks the style of (4.6.2c) is preferable to that of (4.6.2b). Since <u>at least</u> one number must be read, having the first number read outside of the loop makes sense.

The style of (4.6.2c) begins to become burdensome as the size and complexity of the initialization action grows. If an appreciable number of statements in the body must be rewritten outside, the risk increases that they will not be exactly the same. They might start out identical, but subsequent changes in one location might not be faithfully repeated in the other. In such cases, one sometimes contrives a way to get the iteration started, with minimal initialization. For example:

```
          (* READ AND SUM DATA UNTIL FIRST -1 *)
              SUM := 0;
              VAL := 0;
              WHILE VAL <> -1 DO
(4.6.2d)        BEGIN
                   SUM := SUM + VAL;
                   READ(VAL)
                END
```

(4.6.2d) differs from (4.6.2c) only in the replacement of READ(VAL) with VAL := 0, but the difference in philosophy is quite significant. A dummy value has been contrived to force execution of the loop body; and the first statement in the body is executed pointlessly but harmlessly. This was done just to avoid having to write a duplicate of a portion of the body outside the loop. It should be obvious that this is a tricky and dangerous practice.

The previous examples illustrate three unattractive ways of performing a very common kind of task: (4.6.2b) requires a GOTO exit; (4.6.2c) requires rewriting a portion of the body outside the loop; and (4.6.2d) requires a devious contrivance to get the loop started. The least unattractive of these will vary, depending upon context and other circumstances. Basically, the problem is that PASCAL does not offer a natural and convenient way to perform this task. In this regard PASCAL is better than the other languages in general use today, but there is still room for improvement.

Section 4 Summary

1. A PASCAL job consists of a "main procedure", optionally followed by data. The execution of a program consists of a single execution of the main procedure.

2. The normal order of statement execution is the order in which the statements are written.

3. A loop is a control mechanism to provide iteration of a group of consecutive statements. The four forms of loop control in PASCAL are:

```
WHILE condition DO
    statement

REPEAT
    statement
  UNTIL condition

FOR index-variable := initial-value TO final-value DO
    statement

FOR index-variable := initial-value DOWNTO final-value DO
    statement
```

In each case the statement to be iterated may be compound.

4. A condition is an expression involving a relational operator, and possibly Boolean operators. Its evaluation results in a value of either TRUE or FALSE.

5. There are two forms of conditional execution of a statement:

```
IF condition
    THEN statement¹

IF condition
    THEN statement¹
    ELSE statement²
```

Statement[1] and statement[2] can be either simple or compound statements.

6. A conditional branch may be used to terminate execution of a program segment. This is the primary use of the GOTO:

```
IF condition THEN GOTO statement label
...
label:
```

The label can be inside the body of the loop, in which case it causes execution to skip the rest of this particular iteration of the body of the loop. Alternatively, the label can be placed after the end of the body, in which case the entire loop is terminated.

7. One of several alternatives may be selected for execution by means of the CASE statement:

```
CASE expression OF
    case-label 1: statement 1;
    case-label 2: statement 2;
          ...
    case-label n: statement n
  END
```

Section 4 Exercises

1. Write a separate, complete program (similar to the examples in Section 4.1.1) to perform each of the following tasks:

a) Read five data values, compute their sum and print the sum.

b) Read three data values, compute the first times the sum of the second and third, and print the result.

c) Without reading any data (no READ statements) compute the sum of the integers from 1 to 8 and print the result.

d) Read four data values, print the maximum of the four values.

2. Write a single program that will perform all four of the tasks listed in Exercise 1, one after another.

3. Trace the execution of the programs in Exercise 1.

4. Keypunch and run the programs in Exercise 1.

5. Trace the execution of the following program segments:

a)
```
TOTAL := 0;
WHILE TOTAL < 5 DO
    TOTAL := TOTAL + 1
```

b)
```
R1 := 0;
R2 := 0;
R3 := 0;
FOR I := 1 TO 3 DO
  BEGIN (* R1 LOOP *)
    FOR J := 3 DOWNTO -1 DO
      BEGIN
         FOR K := 3 TO 4 DO
              R3 := R3 + 1
      END
  END (* R1 LOOP *)
```

c)
```
A := 2;
B := 5;
(* COMPUTE Z = A TO THE B POWER,
    ASSUMING A>0 AND B>0 ARE INTEGERS *)
    Z := 1;
    X := A;
    Y := B;
    WHILE Y <> 0 DO
      BEGIN (* NONZERO LOOP *)
         WHILE TRUNC(Y/2E0)*2 = Y DO
           BEGIN
              Y := Y/2E0;
              X := SQR(X)
           END;
         Y := Y - 1;
         Z := Z * X
      END (* NONZERO LOOP *)
```

d) Same as c), but with "A:=2; B:=5" replaced by "A:=1; B:=1".

e)
```
(* PRINT THE FIRST 7 FIBONACCI NUMBERS *)
    N := 7;
    FIRST := 0;
    WRITELN(FIRST);
    SECOND := 1;
    WRITELN(SECOND);
    FOR I := 3 TO N DO
      BEGIN
         NEXT := FIRST + SECOND;
         WRITELN(NEXT);
         FIRST := SECOND;
         SECOND := NEXT
      END
```

f)
```
READ(N);
FOR I := 1 TO N DO
  BEGIN (* PRINT LOOP *)
    READ(X);
    IF X < 0 THEN
      BEGIN
         Y := X + 1;
         WRITELN(Y)
      END;
         ...
  END (* PRINT LOOP *)
         ...
    eor
0 8 8 9 8 3
```

g) Same as f), but with the data

```
    5 -30 40 50 -60 -70 -80
```

6. The following exercises are to be written using only conditional statements, assignment statements, and READ and WRITELN.

a) Write a single conditional statement with only an assignment statement as a substatement, for the following:

```
IF X < 0 THEN
   IF Y < 0 THEN
     IF Z = 5 THEN A := X + Y + Z
```

b) Rewrite the following using a single conditional statement:

```
IF X < 0
  THEN BEGIN IF Y < 0
               THEN A := X + Y + Z
       END
  ELSE IF X = 5
         THEN A := X + Y + Z
```

c) Given three variables A, B and C, write a program segment to interchange the values of A, B and C so that the largest is in A and the smallest is in C.

d) Given three variables X, Y, and Z, write a program segment to determine if they are the sides of a triangle (X, Y, and Z are the lengths of the sides of a triangle if all are greater than 0 and if X+Y>Z, X+Z>Y, and Y+Z>X.)

e) Write a program segment to print '1' if X, Y, and Z are the lengths of the sides of an equilateral triangle, and '2' if they are the sides of a non-equilateral triangle. A triangle is equilateral if all its sides are the same.

f) A, B and C are three variables with different values. One of these variables has the "middle value" -- one other is greater, one smaller. Write a program segment that will set variable D to this middle value. Compare this to the program for c).

7. Exercises with loops.

a) Write a WHILE loop with initialization that is equivalent to:

```
FACT := 1;
FOR I := 2 TO N DO
     FACT := FACT * I
```

b) Write a program segment to read in a sequence of 50 numbers and print out those numbers that are > 0.

c) Given a variable N with a value greater than 0, write a program segment to print N, N^2, ..., N to the Nth.

d) Given variables N and M, both with values > 0, write a segment to print all powers of N that are less than M. That is, print the value N to the power i, for all i such that N to the i is less than M.

e) The <u>Fibonacci numbers</u> are the numbers 0, 1, 1, 2, 3, 5, 8, 13, 21, ... The first one is 0, the second is 1, and each succesive one is the sum of the two preceding ones. The segment of Exercise 1 e) calculates the first 7 Fibonacci numbers and prints them out. Given a variable N≥2, write a program segment to print out all Fibonacci numbers which are less than N (<u>not</u> the first N Fibonacci numbers).

<u>8</u>. Write complete programs for the following problems. Most of these use the program segments written in earlier exercises.

a) The input consists of groups of three numbers. The last group is an end-of-list signal consisting of three zero values. Write a program to read each group in, print it out, and print an indication of whether the three numbers represent the sides of a triangle. (See Exercise 6d.)

b) The input consists of an integer N ≥ 0, followed by N groups of three numbers. Write a program to read the groups of numbers in, print them out, and then print the middle value of the three. Each group and its middle value should appear on a separate line.

c) The input consists of a single integer N. Write a program to read in N and print the first N Fibonacci numbers. (If N < 1, don't print any out.)

d) The input consists of two positive integers M and N, with M ≥ N. Write a program to print all Fibonacci numbers which lie between M and N.

e) The input consists of a positive integer N. Write a program to read N and to print out the first, second, third and fourth powers of the integers 2, 3, ..., N. The beginning of your output should look like

```
2    4    8    16
3    9    27   81
```

9. Rewrite the program segment of problem 5c using REPEAT loops instead of WHILE loops.

10. The following exercises are to be written using CASE statements:

a) Write a program segment which will read a one digit positive integer and print the integer. If it is 2, 3 or 7 also print the square of the number which follows it in the number sequence. (That is, if it is 3 then print 16.) If it is 5 or 8 print the square root of the number which precedes it. Otherwise print the number which is 5 greater than the given number.

b) Write a program segment which will read the pair of numbers I (which is INTEGER) and X (which is REAL). Print X. If I = 0 then print Y = X^2; if I = 1 then print Y = e to the power X; if I = 2 then print Y = sine X; if I = 3 then print Y = cosine X; if I = 4 then print Y = natural logarithm of X; and if I = 5 then print Y = absolute value of X-3.

Section 5 Multiple-Valued Variables

5.1 Arrays of Subscripted Variables

Suppose it is necessary to store and process a large amount of data at the same time. For example, we might want to calculate a set of numbers, then sort them into increasing order, and finally print them in sorted order. If there were 50 different numbers, using 50 different variables with different names would be cumbersome. In order to handle such situations, most programming languages use a "data structure" called an "array".

An array is a set of variables, each having a separate value just like an ordinary simple variable, but with <u>all the variables of the set sharing a common identifier</u>. A "subscript" is added to this common identifier to produce a unique name for each individual element of the set. For this reason these are often called "subscripted variables". For example, an identifier X could refer to a set of five variables:

```
          X[1]    20
          X[2]    -2
(5.1a)    X[3]     6
          X[4]   217
          X[5]     8
```

Programming languages are unable to use conventional subscripts because the keypunch (and most other input devices) lack the capability of depressing a character below the normal printing line. As a consequence subscripts are generally identified by being enclosed in parentheses. PASCAL uses square brackets, as in (5.1a), to make them distinct from ordinary parentheses.

In (5.1a), X is called an "array of subscripted variables". Each of the variables named X[1], X[2], X[3], X[4] and X[5] is itself called a "subscripted variable". (Unsubscripted variables -- those discussed before this section, whose names are just simple identifiers -- will now be called "simple" or "scalar" variables.) The "name" of a subscripted variable has the form:

```
identifier[index]
```

where "index" is any "scalar" value, except REAL. For the time being, consider index to be of type INTEGER, but other types can be used, as will be noted in Section 8, and illustrated in Section 9.3. Thus X[1], X[0], X[+1], and X[-1] are all valid subscripted variable names. X[1] and X[+1] refer to the same variable. Note that the brackets are necessary: X[2] is a subscripted variable, while X2 is just a simple variable with no relation whatever to the array X of subscripted variables.

Subscripted variables often have positive integer subscripts, but zero and negative subscripts can also be used when convenient.

For example, suppose we need a table whose values represent the number of minutes in a day that the temperature is between i and i+1 degrees Fahrenheit. For each integer i, we can store the number of minutes that the temperature is between i and i+1 in the appropriate element of an array named MINUTES. Thus, the value of MINUTES[2] represents the number of minutes the temperature is between 2 and 3 degrees; MINUTES[47] represents the number of minutes between 47 and 48 degrees, MINUTES[-3] the number of minutes between -3 and -2, etc.

The name of a subscripted variable can be used exactly as the name of a simple variable is used. For example, execution of

```
A := X[3] * X[1]
```

causes the current value of X[3] (which is given as 6 in (5.1a)) to be multiplied by X[1] (which is 20), and the result 120 to be stored in simple variable A. Similarly, a subscripted variable can be given as the target of an assignment process:

```
X[2] := X[4] * 5
```

The value of X[4] (which is 217) is multiplied by 5 and the result (1085) is stored in X[2]. At this point, then, there seems to be little difference between a simple and subscripted variable, except that the name of the latter has a somewhat more complicated form. The real power of subscripted variables is shown in the next section.

5.1.1 Referencing Subscripted Variables

Suppose we wish to write a program to obtain the sum of the values of 50 different variables. We could use 50 simple variables named V1, V2, V3, ..., V50, and obtain their sum using a single, long assignment statement:

```
(* SET SUM TO SUM OF V1 THROUGH V50 *)
    SUM := V1 + V2 + V3 + V4 + V5 + V6 + V7 + V8 +
         V9 + V10 + V11 + V12 + V13 + V14 + V15 +
         V16 + V17 + V18 + V19 + V20 + V21 + V22 +
         V23 + V24 + V25 + V26 + V27 + V28 + V29 +
         V30 + V31 + V32 + V33 + V34 + V35 + V36 +
         V37 + V38 + V39 + V40 + V41 + V42 + V43 +
         V44 + V45 + V46 + V47 + V48 + V49 + V50
```

Alternatively the sum could be obtained using a sequence of 51 assignment statements:

```
(* SET SUM TO SUM OF V1 THROUGH V50 *)
    SUM := 0;
    SUM := SUM + V1;
    SUM := SUM + V2;
    SUM := SUM + V3;
       ...
    SUM := SUM + V50
```

A slight modification of this second method would be to use an array U of subscripted variables:

```
           (* SET SUM TO SUM OF U[1..50] *)
               SUM := 0;
               SUM := SUM + U[1];
(5.1.1a)       SUM := SUM + U[2];
               SUM := SUM + U[3];
                  ...
               SUM := SUM + U[50]
```

The term U[1..50] in the heading comment is a convenient way of saying "all of the variables U[1] through U[50]", but only as a comment -- you cannot use this form in an assignment statement.

Now suppose there is a simple variable I with value 2:

I <u>2</u>

and suppose we execute the following assignment statement:

```
SUM := SUM + U[I]
```

This is interpreted as follows:

> Add a copy of the current value of variable SUM to a copy of the current value of one of the subscripted variables of the array U. The subscripted variable to be used is

determined by the value of the variable I. Since I's value is currently 2, the term U[I] refers to U[2]. Hence a copy of the value of U[2] is added to the value of SUM. The result is stored as a new value for SUM.

Note that the assignment process remains the same except that a preliminary evaluation of variable I is required to determine which of the subscripted variables of U is to be used. This may not seem significant on first encounter, but it is, in fact, exceedingly powerful. Using this method of referencing subscripted variables and the means of controlling repetition introduced in Section 4.2, (5.1.1a) can be written as

```
            (* SET SUM TO SUM OF U[1..50] *)
                SUM := 0;
                I := 0;
                WHILE I < 50 DO
(5.1.1b)          BEGIN
                     I := I + 1;
                     SUM := SUM + U[I]
                  END
```

Assuming a set of values for the array U, after execution of the first two assignment statements of this program the values might be the following:

U[1]	5	I	0
U[2]	7	SUM	0
U[3]	1		

Execution of the WHILE loop starts with the evaluation of the condition. The condition is true, since the current value of I, 0, is less than 50, and the body of the loop is executed. First I is increased to 1. The second assignment statement in the body involves a subscripted variable. The current value of I, which appears as the subscript, is 1 so the current value of U[1], which is 5, is added to the value of SUM. Thus 5 is stored as the new value of SUM. At this point the values of the variables are:

U[1]	5	I	1
U[2]	7	SUM	5
U[3]	1		

The condition is then evaluated. I is still less than 50 so the body is again executed. The first assignment statement increases I to 2. Since I is now 2, the value of the subscripted variable U[2] is added to SUM to give 12. This is stored as the new value of SUM.

You should continue this exercise until convinced that the result is the same as that obtained by (5.1.1a). Of particular interest is the last execution of the loop body, when I is 49. At this time I is increased to 50, and the value of U[50] is added to SUM (which by then contains the sum of the first 49 elements of the array U). Evaluation of the condition now yields FALSE and execution of the loop is finished.

(5.1.1b) could also be written as a FOR loop:

```
(* SET SUM TO SUM OF U[1..50] *)
    SUM := 0;
    FOR I := 1 TO 50 DO
         SUM := SUM + U[I]
```

As a further example, suppose the problem required the sum of the variables U[1], U[2], ..., up to the first variable with zero value. This is given below in two different forms, one with a WHILE loop and one with a FOR loop.

```
(* SET SUM TO SUM OF U[1..50] THRU FIRST 0 *)
    I := 1;
    SUM := U[I];
    WHILE (U[I] <> 0) AND (I < 50) DO
      BEGIN
         I := I + 1;
         SUM := SUM + U[I]
      END

(* SET SUM TO SUM OF U[1..50] THRU FIRST 0 *)
    SUM := 0;
    FOR I := 1 TO 50 DO
      BEGIN
         IF U[I] = 0 THEN GOTO 9005;
         SUM := SUM + U[I]
      END;
    9005:
```

An expression may be given for a subscript -- the constants and variables in the examples so far are just special cases of expressions. The only restriction is that when evaluated the <u>expression must yield an appropriate scalar (not REAL) value</u>. Expression subscripts can be very useful. For example, suppose there were two arrays, LEFT and RIGHT, each consisting of 15 variables. The following segment of program would copy the values of LEFT into RIGHT in inverted order:

```
(* SET RIGHT[1..15] TO REVERSE-ORDER OF LEFT[1..15] *)
    FOR I := 1 TO 15 DO
         RIGHT[I] := LEFT[16-I]
```

5.2 Variables with Multiple Subscripts

It is sometimes convenient to use more than one subscript to designate a particular variable from an array. This is done when there is more than one natural pattern for referencing variables from the array. For example, suppose one had grades for up to fifty students in as many as nine courses apiece. Assume variables NUMCRS and NUMSTUD give the number of courses and number of students, respectively. We store these grades in an array GRADE of doubly-subscripted variables so that GRADE[I,J] represents the grade of the jth student in the ith course. That is, GRADE[3,17] is the grade of the 17th student in the 3rd course. Then to obtain the average grade in a certain course you could write:

```
(* SET AVGGRADE TO AVERAGE GRADE IN ITH COURSE *)
    TOTGRADE := 0;
    FOR J := 1 TO NUMSTUD DO
         TOTGRADE := TOTGRADE + GRADE[I,J];
    AVGGRADE := TOTGRADE/NUMSTUD
```

To obtain the average for a particular student for all of his courses you could write:

```
(* SET STUDAVG TO AVERAGE GRADE FOR JTH STUDENT *)
    SUMGRADE := 0;
    FOR I := 1 TO NUMCRS DO
         SUMGRADE := SUMGRADE + GRADE[I,J];
    STUDAVG := SUMGRADE/NUMCRS
```

Note that this assumes that each student has exactly the same number of grades -- the number given by NUMCRS. If a student had fewer grades than NUMCRS and the omitted grades were represented by zeros in GRADE this program segment will produce incorrect averages. To remedy this we would need another array NBRCOURSES[1..50] to give the number of courses for each student. The program to produce an average for an individual student would be:

```
(* SET STUDAVG TO AVERAGE GRADE FOR JTH STUDENT *)
    SUMGRADE := 0;
    FOR I := 1 TO NBRCOURSES[J] DO
         SUMGRADE := SUMGRADE + GRADE[I,J];
    STUDAVG := SUMGRADE/NBRCOURSES[J]
```

The overall average (all students in all courses) could be obtained by executing

```
(* SET OVAVG TO OVERALL AVERAGE GRADE *)
    GSUM := 0;
    FOR J := 1 TO NUMSTUD DO
      BEGIN
         (* SET STUDAVG TO AVG GRADE FOR JTH STUD *)
            SUMGRADE := 0;
            FOR I := 1 TO NBRCOURSES[J] DO
                 SUMGRADE := SUMGRADE +
                             GRADE[I,J];
            STUDAVG := SUMGRADE/NBRCOURSES[J];
            GSUM := GSUM + STUDAVG
      END;
    OVAVG := GSUM/NUMSTUD
```

However, note that the following might be an equally plausible interpretation of the same problem:

```
(* SET OVAVG TO OVERALL AVERAGE GRADE *)
    GSUM := 0;
    STUDSUM := 0;
    FOR J := 1 TO NUMSTUD DO
      BEGIN
         STUDSUM := STUDSUM + NBRCOURSES[J];
         FOR I := 1 TO NBRCOURSES[J] DO
              GSUM := GSUM + GRADE[I,J]
      END;
    OVAVG := GSUM/STUDSUM
```

Only under certain circumstances would these two interpretations give the same answer -- can you see why? In general, one or the other of these program segments is not interpreting "overall average" in the way intended by the person asking the question. This may begin to suggest why it is so easy to come up with programs that are not quite right.

An array of singly-subscripted variables is a "list" of variables -- with the subscript specifying the position on the list. The analogous interpretation of an array of doubly-subscripted variables is a "table" or "matrix". The first subscript specifies the row position and the second specifies the column:

```
GRADE[1,1]  GRADE[1,2]  GRADE[1,3]  GRADE[1,4]  ...

GRADE[2,1]  GRADE[2,2]  GRADE[2,3]  GRADE[2,4]

GRADE[3,1]  GRADE[3,2]  GRADE[3,3]  GRADE[3,4]

...
```

It is also common to visualize the variables of an array as being distributed in a geometric space. An array of singly-subscripted variables is said to be a "one-dimensional array" or "vector". The values are considered to be positioned along a line, with the subscript giving the position on the line. An array of doubly-subscripted variables is called a "two-dimensional array" or "matrix" and the pair of subscripts specifies a position in the plane of values. Although singly- and doubly-subscripted variables are the most common, three or more subscripts can be used if required.

5.3 Declaration of Arrays

An array declaration specifies the number of subscripted variables to be created and the number of subscripts to be used for referencing each variable, as well as the type of value each variable can contain. The most common form for a one-dimensional array is

```
VAR identifier: ARRAY[lower-bound..upper-bound] OF type
```

An example is:

```
VAR TEMP: ARRAY[1..50] OF REAL
```

This defines an array of 50 variables named TEMP[1], TEMP[2], ..., TEMP[50], each capable of holding one REAL number. As another example, to declare an array of 22 INTEGER variables named POP[-1], POP[0], ..., POP[20] use

```
VAR POP: ARRAY[-1..20] OF INTEGER
```

Multiple subscripts are indicated by two or more sets of bounds, separated by commas. For example, to define an array of 450 doubly-subscripted variables with the values of the first subscript ranging from 1 to 9, and the second from 1 to 50, use

```
VAR GRADE: ARRAY[1..9,1..50] OF REAL
```

Don't confuse the role of the comma and the two periods in the bounds declaration. The comma separates bounds, indicating how many dimensions the array has and how many subscripts each reference to an element in the array must have. The two periods separate lower and upper bounds of a <u>single</u> dimension. The two periods are always present to separate the lower and upper bounds; the comma is present only if there is more than one dimension. For example

```
VAR TABLE1: ARRAY[3..4] OF REAL;
    TABLE2: ARRAY[1..3,1..4] OF REAL
```

creates two arrays: TABLE1 with one dimension and only two elements, and TABLE2 with two dimensions and twelve elements.

As a final example, the following declaration defines a three-dimensional array of 60 integer variables, each with three subscripts. The values of the first subscript range from -5 to -2; the second from 1 to 3; and the third from 0 to 4.

```
VAR POINT: ARRAY[-5..-2,1..3,0..4] OF INTEGER
```

In referring to arrays in the text we will generally use the same form as the declaration. That is, MAT[1..5,1..9] refers to the array defined by the declaration

```
VAR MAT: ARRAY[1..5,1..9] OF type
```

We also use the notation to refer to an array segment -- a part of the array. For example, if A[1..100] is an array, we might discuss the segment A[1..50], or A[1..N] where N contains the subscript value. A[1..1] refers to the single element A[1], while A[1..0] would refer to the array segment containing _no_ elements, the _empty_ segment.

5.4 Program for the Example of 1.2.1

In Section 1.2.1 the analysis of a problem description was carried through several levels, but the programming was postponed until subscripted variables could be employed. The analysis in Section 1.2.1 had reached the following stage:

> 3.1 Read a sequence of 100 or fewer positive integers from cards until a zero value is encountered; store these integers in memory, preserving order.
>
> 3.2 Find the position of the integer with maximum value in this sequence.
>
> 3.3 Print the early values of the sequence, from the first to the maximum value, one per line.

Each of these subtasks is well defined and detailed program design can begin. The next step is to specify the data structures that will be used.

The principal data structure will have to be an array since there are many values to be stored at once. Call it INT to remind us that only integer values are allowed. It needs at least 100 elements since there may be that many data values, and should be INTEGER. There should be a variable TOP (say) to indicate the number of values currently in the array, and a variable MAXP (say) to mark the position of the maximum value. Later, as we design the different subtasks, we may find that other variables will be needed.

Now the problem statement can be rewritten in terms of the variables that will be used:

> 4.1 Read data into INT[1..TOP] until a zero value is encountered (keeping the value of TOP as defined above).
>
> 4.2 Set MAXP to mark the position of the maximum value in INT[1..TOP].
>
> 4.3 Print the values in INT[1..MAXP], one per line.

This description is now very close to programming language terms. Although it may not seem so to one who is just learning the language, the hardest part of the programming process is bringing the problem description to this level. The analysis and design have been completed -- from here on it is just a matter of translating into the proper form.

We will program the sub-tasks one at a time, taking them in reverse order just to demonstrate their relative independence. The program for 4.3 is obviously a loop:

```
FOR I := 1 TO MAXP DO
    WRITELN(INT[I])
```

Problems concerning extreme values of MAXP might arise in this subtask. If MAXP<1 no values will be printed. This makes sense since MAXP<1 means that <u>no</u> values appeared in the input -- only the end signal 0. If MAXP>100 an invalid subscript will be used, so prior statements must ensure that MAXP<=100.

The program for 4.2 must take into account that no values may be supplied in the data -- only the end-of-list signal may appear. We set MAXP to zero initially, to indicate that no maximum has been found yet. We also find it advantageous to introduce a variable MAXVAL to contain the maximum value encountered so far; we initialize it to -1, which is less than any possible value. If there is actually no list then the body of the loop labeled FINDMAX will never be executed and MAX will remain at zero.

```
MAXVAL := -1;
MAXP := 0;
FOR I := 1 TO TOP DO
  BEGIN (* FINDMAX LOOP *)
    IF INT[I] > MAXVAL THEN
      BEGIN
         MAXVAL := INT[I];
         MAXP := I
      END
  END (* FINDMAX LOOP *)
```

This routine has potential problems if TOP>100. However, note that if $0 \le TOP \le 100$, this segment automatically guarantees a value for MAXP that will be acceptable to the routine for 4.3.

The program for 4.1 is less obvious and could be done in several different ways. It must make provision for a number of extreme conditions with respect to the input data:

1. It must work properly for every valid quantity of data -- as little as none, to as much as 100 values.

2. It must provide adequate warning when it encounters improper data -- no data at all, too much data, data without the proper end signal, or improper values as described in 3 below.

3. The problem statement specifies that the data will be positive integers. A fundamental decision must be made as to whether the program will <u>trust</u> that it will only be presented with such proper data, or whether it will <u>test</u> to make sure that this is the case. As a general philosophy, programs should <u>be suspicious and trust no one</u>.

Reading each value directly into an INTEGER variable would cause execution errors if a REAL value is encountered. So that we can test for non-integers, each value will instead be read into a temporary variable TREAL which is of type REAL. The following segment (which still includes English statements) contains a loop which reads and processes the data until the endmarker 0 is read or until 100 values have been processed. The last statement prints an error if the endmarker has not been read. The segment also relies on PASCAL to provide a warning if it runs out of data unexpectedly; this would occur if the endmarker was missing and there were 100 or fewer proper values. By "process TREAL" we mean to check for errors in TREAL and store it in the array. Remember, TOP always indicates the number of values in the array.

```
TOP := 0;
READ(TREAL);
WHILE (TOP < 100) AND (TREAL <> 0) DO
  BEGIN
    Process TREAL;
    READ(TREAL)
  END;
IF TREAL <> 0 THEN Print error.
```

The complete program, after further refinement, is

```
(* LIST POSITIVE INTEGERS FROM FIRST TO MAXIMUM *)
PROGRAM LISTTOMAX(INPUT, OUTPUT);
VAR INT: ARRAY[1..100] OF INTEGER;
            (* THE POSITIVE VALUES READ *)
    TOP,    (* ARE IN INT[1..TOP].  *)
    MAXVAL, (* IF NO VALUES, MAXP=0, ELSE *)
    MAXP,   (* MAXP MARKS MAXVAL POSITION.  *)
    I:      (* MAXVAL = MAX(INT[1..TOP]).  *)
            INTEGER;
    TREAL: REAL; (* LAST VALUE READ IN *)
BEGIN (* LISTTOMAX *)
    (* READ DATA, CHECK, AND STORE IN INT[1..100]
         UNTIL 0 IS FOUND *)
         TOP := 0;
         READ(TREAL);
         WHILE (TOP < 100) AND (TREAL <> 0) DO
           BEGIN (* LOAD LOOP *)
              IF (TREAL > 0) AND (TRUNC(TREAL) = TREAL)
                   THEN BEGIN
                       TOP := TOP + 1;
                       INT[TOP] := TRUNC(TREAL)
                     END
                   ELSE WRITELN(' IMPROPER DATA:', TREAL);
              READ(TREAL)
           END; (* LOAD LOOP *)
         IF TREAL <> 0
              THEN WRITELN(' MORE THAN 100 VALUES');
    (* SET MAXP TO MARK POSITION OF MAX IN INT[1..TOP] *)
         MAXVAL := -1;
         MAXP := 0;
         FOR I := 1 TO TOP DO
           BEGIN (* FINDMAX LOOP *)
              IF INT[I] > MAXVAL THEN
                BEGIN
                   MAXVAL := INT[I];
                   MAXP := I
                END
           END; (* FINDMAX LOOP *)
    (* PRINT NUMBERS IN INT[1..MAXP] *)
         FOR I := 1 TO MAXP DO
              WRITELN(INT[I])
END.  (* LISTTOMAX *)
    eor
```

Section 5 Summary

1. An array is a set of subscripted variables. These are distinct variables but all have the same identifier and contain the same type of value.

2. A subscripted variable reference consists of an identifier with a subscript -- an expression enclosed in square brackets. Upon evaluation the subscript expression must yield an appropriate scalar value. (Of the types presented up to this point, it must be INTEGER.) Multiple subscripts are expressions separated by commas.

3. An identifier is declared to be an array name by:

```
VAR identifier: ARRAY[lower-bound..upper-bound] OF type
```

For multiple subscripts the sets of bounds are separated by commas.

4. References to an array in the text will generally be in the same form as a declaration; for example, MATRIX[1..5,1..10], SET[0..4].

Section 5 Exercises

1. The following are values of certain arrays and simple variables: (??? means no value has been assigned yet.)

```
B[-3]   20        AGE[1]   1         I  1
B[-2]   25        AGE[2]  13         J  2
B[-1]   42        AGE[3]  21         K  3
B[0]     9        AGE[4]   6         M  4
B[1]     8        AGE[5]   7       SUM  ???
B[2]    13        AGE[6]  12         C  ???
B[3]   -20        AGE[7]   8       MAX  ???
B[4]   -40        AGE[8]   0       MIN  ???
B[5]    50
```

a) Give the values of B[-2], AGE[5], B[I], AGE[I+J].

b) Give the name of the variable containing the largest value in array B[-3..5]; in array AGE[1..8].

c) Evaluate the following expressions:

```
B[1] + AGE[4]
B[3] * AGE[1]
5 + B[5]
AGE[6]/6
AGE[6] DIV 6
```

d) Give the value of B[1], B[I+1], B[I+J].

e) Which of the following refer to existing variables?

```
AGE[I-M]     B[I-M]     AGE[I+M]     B[I+M]
```

f) Give the values of:

```
B[AGE[1]]   B[AGE[M]-1]   AGE[AGE[4]]   AGE[AGE[M+I]-2]
```

g) Evaluate the following expressions:

```
M + AGE[M]
M + AGE[K]
B[3]*3 - AGE[3]
AGE[J+J]/AGE[J]
B[M-I]
```

h) Give declarations for all of the arrays and variables shown. (Assume INTEGER values for I, J, K and M; REAL for the others.)

i) Write assignment statements to assign the values to the variables as shown.

j) Write READ statements and a data list to assign the values to the variables as shown.

2. Assuming variables with initial values as in Exercise 1, trace the execution of the following program segments and show the values that result from their execution.

a)
```
(* SET SUM TO SUM OF AGE[J..M] *)
      C := J;
      SUM := 0;
      WHILE C <= M DO
        BEGIN
           SUM := SUM + AGE[C];
           C := C + 1
        END
```

b)
```
(* SET MAX TO MAX OF AGE[I..M] *)
      MAX := AGE[I];
      C := I + 1;
      WHILE C <= M DO
        BEGIN
           IF MAX < AGE[C] THEN MAX := AGE[C];
           C := C + 1
        END
```

c)
```
(* ADD THE SUBSCRIPT VALUE I TO EACH VARIABLE B[I] *)
      C := -3;
      WHILE C <= 5 DO
        BEGIN
           B[C] := B[C] + C;
           C := C + 1
        END
```

d)
```
(* SET AGE[1..8] TO "FIBONACCI SEQUENCE" VALUE *)
           (* THAT IS, AGE[1] = 0; AGE[2] = 1; *)
           (* AGE[I] = AGE[I-2] + AGE[I-1] FOR I > 2 *)
      AGE[1] := 0;
      AGE[2] := 1;
      C := 3;
      WHILE C <= 8 DO
        BEGIN
           AGE[C] := AGE[C-1] + AGE[C-2];
           C := C + 1
        END
```

e)
```
(* SET B[-3..5] TO ABS(B[-3..5]) WITHOUT ABS FUNCTION *)
      C := 5;
      WHILE C >= -3 DO
        BEGIN
           IF B[C] < 0 THEN B[C] := -B[C];
           C := C - 1
        END
```

f)
```
(* MOVE EACH VALUE IN B[-3..5] UP 1 POSITION *)
      (* STORE 0 IN B[-3], DISCARD B[5] *)
      C := 5;
      WHILE C > -3 DO
        BEGIN
           B[C] := B[C-1];
           C := C - 1
        END
      B[-3] := 0
```

3. Draw lines (locations) like those shown in Exercise 1 for variables declared as follows:

a) VAR A, B: INTEGER

b) VAR AGE: ARRAY[1..3,1..4] OF INTEGER

c) VAR COST: ARRAY[-3..0] OF REAL

d) VAR PAY, AMOUNT: ARRAY[0..10] OF REAL; I: REAL

4. Write program segments to accomplish each of the following tasks, using the variables declared in Exercise 3:

a) Set all of the variables in the array AGE[1..3,1..4] to zero.

b) Set each variable in the array AGE[1..3,1..4] equal to the sum of its own subscripts -- that is, AGE[I,J] equal to I + J.

c) Set each variable in the array COST[-3..0] equal to whatever is the minimum of the initial values of the variables in COST.

d) Subtract the value of each variable in the array AMOUNT[0..10] from the variable in the corresponding position in the array PAY[0..10].

e) Compute the sum of the values of all of the variables in the array PAY[0..10].

f) Swap the values of PAY[1..10] to put the largest in PAY[10]. Thus if initially PAY is

PAY 10 9 8 7 6 5 4 3 2 1

then after execution, the array might be

PAY 9 8 7 6 5 4 3 2 1 10
or PAY 1 9 8 7 6 5 4 3 2 10

5. Suppose array B[1..N] contains a sequence of values, some of which appear more than once. Write a program segment to "delete" duplicates, moving the unique values towards the beginning of the array. Assign to variable M the number of unique values. The order of the values should be preserved. For example, if we have

N 7   B 1 6 1 8 3 7 6

after execution the variables should be as follows (where "-" indicates that the value is immaterial):

N 7   M 5   B 1 6 8 3 7 - -

6. The following segment searches array segment B[1..N] for a value equal to X. When it finds it, it sets J to the index of X in B so that B[J] = X. (This is called a "linear" search algorithm since execution time is proportional to the length of the segment.)

```
J := 1;
WHILE B[J] <> X DO
     J := J + 1
```

a) What value is in J after execution if X is not in the array?

b) Change the program to set 0 in J if X is not in the array.

c) What happens if N = 0? Change the program segment to store 0 in J if this is the case. (Such a case actually arises in programming, and is not always a mistake.)

7. The following questions refer to the program in Section 5.4.

a) Suppose there is a tie for maximum -- several input numbers are the same and are greater than all others. What should the program do in this case; what does the program do?

b) What does the program do if several improper data values are included?

c) Precisely what happens if 110 data values followed by the end-of-input signal appear in the input?

d) What would the output look like if the following data were presented?

14 13 -3 15 2 7 15 12 0 23

Section 6 Display of Results

Printed output from a program is produced by execution of "output" statements. The detailed discussion of these statements is prefaced by two general comments on output.

First, output during execution of a program is entirely the programmer's responsibility. A copy of the program, called a "source listing", is produced automatically, but once execution begins, the only further printing is the result of executing output statements of the program. All values produced during execution are lost unless specifically printed. Unless you specifically ask to have results displayed you will not know what happened during execution of the program.

Second, the statements that control output are typically the most complex statements in a programming language. If not the most difficult in concept they are at least the richest in detail and the most tedious to learn to use. This seems to be required in order to give the programmer flexible control over what information is to be displayed and the format in which it is to appear. PASCAL is certainly not an exception in this regard, and the following paragraphs offer a brief introduction to only the simplest type of PASCAL output statements.

6.1 Display of Values of Variables

The simplest output statement in PASCAL has the form

```
WRITELN(variable-names, separated by commas)
```

The variables may be simple or subscripted. For example:

```
(6.1a)     WRITELN(TOTAL, I, PLACE[I])
```

There is a standard output format for each different type of variable. For REAL variables the standard format is a "field" of exactly 22 horizontal "print positions". Each column is one print position and contains one character. (Some of these characters may be blank, but blank is a perfectly respectable character.) Regardless of the particular value of a REAL variable the output format is always exactly 22 columns. Similarly, for INTEGER variables the standard format is a field of 10 positions. (The number of positions in these fields is a "local installation option", and may be something other than 22 and 10 at your installation. In any event it should be a constant.)

Each variable listed in the WRITELN statement results in one field being placed in the output line; a field of either 22 or 10 positions depending upon whether the type of the variable is REAL or INTEGER. In (6.1a), assuming I is INTEGER and TOTAL and PLACE are both REAL, the value of TOTAL will be printed in the first (leftmost) 22 positions of the line. The value of I will appear in the next 10 positions and the value of PLACE[I] in the next 22 positions. (The particular variable from the array PLACE to appear in the third field will, of course, depend upon the value of the subscript I at the time the statement is executed.) This is all that will appear on this line -- the rest of the positions to the right of these three fields will be filled with blanks. Subsequent WRITELN statements will cause printing on a following line.

INTEGER variables are printed in decimal integer form, right-justified in the 10 position field. That is, a value 273 will result in a 10 character field consisting of seven blanks (which we sometimes denote by "b̸") followed by the digits 2, 7 and 3:

b̸b̸b̸b̸b̸b̸b̸273

REAL variables are printed in exponential form. The decimal point is always given after the first digit, and the power of ten required to properly position the decimal point is given after the digits of the number. One blank always precedes a REAL value. (This may not be the case with an INTEGER value if it occupies all ten positions with digits.)

For example, if the values of the variables are as shown below:

TOTAL	-0.0036	[real]
I	2	[integer]
PLACE[1]	-124.3	[real]
PLACE[2]	63.7	[real]

the values displayed by the WRITELN statement of (6.1a) would be:

```
 -3.600000000000E-003          2  6.370000000000E+001
```

BOOLEAN variables are right-justified in a 10 character field, similar to that of INTEGER variables.

6.1.1 Construction of Print Lines

Sometimes it is not necessary or desirable to produce a separate line of output for each output statement. In such cases the WRITE statement can be used:

```
WRITE(variable-names, separated by commas)
```

Both the WRITE and WRITELN statements operate by copying the values of the variables listed into a "print buffer" -- a space set aside just for the construction of lines to be printed. (The number of positions in this buffer is a local installation option -- lengths anywhere from 80 to 136 positions are used.) The values are placed in this buffer, from left to right, in the order that the variable-names are listed in the statement. The format and length of each value depends upon its type, as noted above. Whenever the print buffer is filled, its contents are printed. It is then cleared (to blanks) to begin receiving the values for the next line. The order in which variables are listed determines their position on the line, but the partition of the variable list into separate statements is not significant. That is,

```
WRITE(X, Y, Z)
```

is exactly equivalent to

```
WRITE(X);
WRITE(Y, Z)
```

In each case, the value of X, then the value of Y, and finally the value of Z is placed in the print buffer. Whether or not a line is printed by either of these versions depends upon what happened before -- what was in the print buffer beforehand. If the buffer happened to be empty, the values of X, Y and Z will be placed in the buffer but they will not be printed at that time. They will wait there until some further WRITE statement supplies additional values to complete filling of the buffer.

The difference between the WRITE and WRITELN statements is just that when the last variable of the WRITELN list has been placed in the print buffer, the printing of the buffer is forced, whether or not it is full. In contrast, the last variable of the WRITE list is not particularly significant. It will not force printing of the line -- unless it happens to have filled the print buffer, but that is true of each variable on the WRITE list.

For example, compare the output of (6.1.1a) and (6.1.1b). (6.1.1a) produces fifty lines of output, each containing a single value of I.

```
          FOR I:= 1 TO 50 DO
(6.1.1a)      WRITELN(I)
```

(6.1.1b) prints the same fifty values of I, but on fewer than fifty lines, since values are accumulated in the print buffer until it is filled, and only then is a line printed. The number of values per line will depend upon the length of the print buffer of the computer on which (6.1.1b) is executed.

```
           FOR I := 1 TO 50 DO
(6.1.1b)       WRITE(I);
           WRITELN
```

Note that (6.1.1b) ends with a WRITELN statement without any variables listed. This simply forces the printing of whatever exists in the print buffer at that time.

The option of having both WRITE and WRITELN output statements gives you more flexibility in formatting your output, and more freedom in placing your output statements at a logical position in your program. In "real" programs the WRITE statement is used more often than WRITELN since the programmer generally wants to control the construction of each line. We have used the WRITELN statement in our examples up to this point because it is simpler to explain -- you don't have to understand the print buffer mechanism. It is also simpler since if every output statement in a program is a WRITELN statement, then each output statement is independent of the others. Each prints a line with the variables listed, regardless of what output statements preceded and follow it. On the other hand, the action of a WRITE statement is independent of other output statements only in the sense that it always places values in the print buffer. Exactly where the values will appear on the line, and whether or not a line is printed by that particular WRITE statement depends upon the output statements that preceded it.

6.2 Titling and Labeling Results

The appearance of printed results can be improved by adding appropriate titles and labels. This can be done by placing a "literal" instead of a variable in the list of a WRITELN or WRITE statement. A literal is a string of characters enclosed in single quotes. For example:

```
'TOTAL'
'TEMPERATURE ='
'RESULTS FOR 9/23/72 ARE:'
'*-*-*-*-*-*-*'
' '      (blank is a valid character)
```

The character string is printed exactly as given -- without the quotes. The printing begins in the next available column. For example, if TOTAL and SUM have values

```
TOTAL   642.17  [real]
SUM    -1043.7  [real]
```

then execution of the statements

```
WRITELN(' TOTAL =', TOTAL);
WRITELN(' SUM =', SUM)
```

would produce the output

```
TOTAL =  6.4217000000000E+002
SUM = -1.0437000000000E+003
```

Literals are often used to identify different values, using their variable names. For example, assuming the last preceding output statement was a WRITELN (so the print buffer is empty):

```
WRITELN(' X', X)
```

will print a line with the name X in the first column, and the value of X starting in the second column. Whatever is included in the literal is printed; the content of the literal has no significance to PASCAL. For example, execution of the following would cause the deceptive label to be printed, without complaint:

```
WRITELN(' THE VALUE OF Y IS:', X)
```

Blank literals can be used to control the spacing of other values on the printed line. For example, the following WRITE statement would cause the values of X and Y to be separated by three blanks more than provided by the standard format.

```
WRITE(X, '   ', Y)
```

WRITELN statements whose list consists of a single literal are frequently used for "messages". For example,

```
WRITELN(' IMPROPER DATA ENCOUNTERED')
WRITELN(' UNEXPECTED NEGATIVE VALUE')
```

Since the output statement preceding such a message statement may have been a WRITE statement, which left a partially filled print buffer, it is good practice to force the printing of the contents of the buffer before printing such a message:

```
WRITELN;
WRITELN(' IMPROPER DATA ENCOUNTERED')
```

In this form the message is assured of having a line to itself, regardless of what output statements preceded it.

Another example of the use of messages is shown in the sample program of Section 5.4. Such statements announce to the programmer that the flow-of-control has reached a certain point in the program or that an exceptional condition has occurred. One often includes such statements to help test a new program; they are removed after the correctness of the program has been established. This technique is discussed in Section V.4.

Literals may be of any length, although if they are longer than a single "print line" they will spill over onto the next line.

A literal is the only "element" of PASCAL that can be split between two lines in the program. Other elements, such as keywords, variable names, and arithmetic constants must be on a single line, but a literal can begin on one line and continue onto the next line. For example, the following is a valid statement:

```
WRITELN(TOTAL, SUM, AVERAGE, MEDIAN, 'THESE STATISTICS
ARE OBTAINED FROM 9/7/75 DATA')
```

However, it is easier for the human reader if you avoid splitting literals over lines whenever possible. For example, the statement above would be better if it were divided between elements:

```
WRITELN(TOTAL, SUM, AVERAGE, MEDIAN,
    'THESE STATISTICS ARE OBTAINED FROM 9/7/75 DATA')
```

Since a quote _ends_ a literal it is not obvious how you can get a quote to appear _in_ a literal. The solution to this dilemma is to require _two consecutive quotes_ when you want _one quote to appear_ in the literal. That is, a quote does not end a literal if it is immediately followed by another quote. For example, the execution of

```
WRITELN(' SOLUTION BY CRAMER''S RULE')
```

would cause the printing of

```
SOLUTION BY CRAMER'S RULE
```

As another example, the execution of

```
WRITELN(' '',''')
```

would cause the printing of

```
','
```

6.2.1 Line and Page Control

You have probably noticed that in each of our examples, if a WRITE or WRITELN list begins with a literal, the first character of that literal is always a blank. This is because the first character of each print line has special significance. It is a "control character", specifying line and page control instructions to the printer. This control character is not printed.

There are five characters that can be given in the first position to control the line feed of the printer:

blank	advance carriage one line before printing
0 (zero)	advance carriage two lines before printing
-	advance carriage three lines before printing
+	print without advancing carriage
1	advance carriage to first line of next page

Our examples, always having a blank in first position, would all provide normal, single-spaced printing. If we had consistly given a zero in place of the blank, the output would have been double-spaced.

For example, the sequence

```
WRITELN('1', 'DATA TABLE');
WRITELN('+', 'DATA TABLE');
WRITELN(' ', '----------');
WRITELN('0', 'FEB.  1975')
```

would place a two-line, double-spaced title on the top of a new page of output. The first line of the title would appear darker (since it is printed twice) and would be underlined.

You can use sequences of these basic operations to achieve any kind of page and line control. For example, the following statement will insert an arbitrary number of blank lines -- the number given by the value of N:

```
FOR I := 1 TO N DO
    WRITELN(' ')
```

Section 6 Summary

1. The forms of the simplest PASCAL output statements are:

```
WRITE(variables and literals, separated by commas)

WRITELN(variables and literals, separated by commas)
```

Both forms place the values listed in the print buffer, which is printed whenever it becomes full. WRITELN forces the printing of the buffer after placement of the last value on the list.

2. The format of each value is determined by its type:

- -REAL values are printed in exponential form in a field of 22 positions
- -INTEGER values are right-justified in a field of 10 positions
- -BOOLEAN values are right-justified in a field of 10 positions.

3. A "literal" is a quoted string of characters that will be printed exactly as given. The output field is determined by the number of characters in the literal. Literals can be used to title and label results, and to print messages.

4. Line and page control is specified by the first character of each print line. This character, which is not printed, should be one of the following:

```
blank - advance carriage one line before printing
0     - advance carriage two lines before printing
-     - advance carriage three lines before printing
+     - print without advancing carriage
1     - advance carriage to first line of new page
              before printing
```

Section 6 Exercises

1. Write a single WRITELN statement to produce the same printed output as the following sequence:

```
WRITE(TOTAL);
WRITE(MAX);
WRITELN(MINIMUM, AVG)
```

2. What would the output from the following segment look like?

```
FOR I := 1 TO 5 DO
   WRITELN(I, I, I, I, I)
```

3. What is the result of executing the following statement?

```
WRITE(' ',' ')
```

4. What is printed by execution of the following statement?

```
WRITELN(' WRITELN(X)')
```

5. What is printed by execution of the following statement?

```
WRITELN(' ' (* CHECKPOINT 19 *))
```

6. What is printed by execution of the following statement?

```
WRITELN('1',',',(*4*)'3','(*2*)')
```

7. What is printed by execution of the following statement?

```
WRITELN(' ',',',',',',',',',')
```

8. Write statements that would print a reasonable approximation of the Greek letters theta (θ) and phi (ø).

Section 7 The Execution of Programs

After a program has been written, and painstakingly checked for errors in logic and syntax, it must be transmitted to a computer for execution. This is usually done by "punching" both the program statements and suitable test data onto cards. Each card generally contains one line of the program as it was written on paper, and columns should be skipped at the left of the card to reflect the indentation of the program lines.

"Keypunching" is a <u>major source of errors</u>. Many programs, correct on paper, reach the computer in garbled form simply because the lines are not exactly represented by the information actually punched in the cards. Much time and effort is saved if the cards are checked against the written form, with great care, before the deck is submitted for processing. If at all possible, you should get a "listing" of the cards and check this listing, rather than attempt to read the cards directly.

When cards containing keypunch errors have been replaced, the deck is arranged as follows for presentation to the computer:

```
Control cards
    eor
(* Comment summarizing program function *)
PROGRAM name(INPUT, OUTPUT);
Cards containing definitions and declarations
BEGIN (* name *)
    Cards containing program statements
END.  (* name *)
    eor
Cards containing data
    eof
```

The control cards indicate the beginning of a new job, identify the author (or user) of the program, and indicate that the program is written in the PASCAL language. The exact form of these cards is peculiar to the particular computer installation that you use to run your program. Some information is given in Appendix B.1, but you will also need local instructions as to exactly what is required. The form of the "end-of-record" (eor) and "end-of-file" (eof) cards is also a local option and you will need local instructions. Control cards, eor, and eof cards are generally very <u>sensitive to format</u>. In particular, they must have certain punches in the first columns that allow the computer to recognize the special nature of these cards.

On the other hand, the other cards in the deck are rather insensitive to format. As far as PASCAL is concerned, you can start in any column of the card, split statements over several cards (as long as you do not split an individual word or number), or place several statements on the same card. We have tried to be very careful about format, but entirely for the benefit of the human reader of the program. It is very helpful to the reader if the form of the program reflects its logical structure and we have used a system of careful indentation to achieve this. Appendix B.1 has further information on card formats.

The following page shows the output resulting from processing the program given in Section 5.4. The following data were supplied to the program:

15 23 46.9 -5 29 17 5.5 6 0 52

```
000006 (* LIST POSITIVE INTEGERS FROM FIRST TO MAXIMUM *)
000006
000006 PROGRAM LISTTOMAX(INPUT,OUTPUT);
000464
000464 VAR INT:  ARRAY[1..100] OF INTEGER;
000630                 (* THE POSITIVE VALUES READ *)
000630     TOP,        (* ARE IN INT[1..TOP].  *)
000630     MAXVAL,     (* IF NO VALUES, MAXP = 0; ELSE  *)
000630     MAXP,       (* MAXP MARKS MAXVAL POSITION.  *)
000630     I:          (* MAXVAL = MAX(INT[1..TOP]  *)
000630          INTEGER;
000634     TFLOAT: REAL; (* LAST VALUE READ IN *)
000635
000635 BEGIN (* LISTTOMAX *)
000635     (*READ DATA, CHECK, AND STORE IN*)
000635     (*INT[1..100] UNTIL 0 IS FOUND*)
000635         TOP := 0;
000023         READ(TFLOAT);
000026         WHILE (TOP < 100) AND (TFLOAT <> 0) DO
000034             BEGIN (*LOAD LOOP*)
000034                IF (TFLOAT > 0) AND (TRUNC(TFLOAT) = TFLOAT)
000042                     THEN BEGIN
000043                             TOP := TOP + 1;
000044                             INT[TOP] := TRUNC(TFLOAT)
000047                          END
000050                     ELSE WRITELN(' IMPROPER DATA:', TFLOAT);
000062                 READ(TFLOAT)
000065             END; (*LOAD LOOP*)
000066         IF TFLOAT <> 0 THEN WRITELN(' MORE THAN 100 VALUES');
000077
000077     (*SET MAXP TO MARK POSITION OF MAX IN INT[1..TOP]*)
000077         MAXVAL := -1;
000101         MAXP := 0;
000101         FOR I := 1 TO TOP DO
000103             BEGIN (*FINDMAX LOOP*)
000105                 IF INT[I] > MAXVAL THEN
000112                     BEGIN
000112                         MAXVAL := INT[I];
000115                         MAXP := I
000115                     END
000116             END; (*FINDMAX LOOP*)
000120
000120     (*PRINT NUMBERS IN INT[1..MAXP]*)
000120         FOR I := 1 TO MAXP DO
000122             WRITELN(INT[I])
000132 END. (* LISTTOMAX *)
```

```
IMPROPER DATA:  4.6900000000000E+001
IMPROPER DATA: -5.0000000000000E+000
IMPROPER DATA:  5.5000000000000E+000
       15
       23
       29
```

7.1 Loading, Translation and Execution

Processing a program takes place in two distinct stages. First, the program is "loaded" into the memory of the computer; second, it is executed. In order to load a program, the deck of cards is placed in a device called a "card reader". The card reader examines the cards one at a time, in the order presented, detects the position of holes in the cards, and transmits this information to the computer. The card-reading operation appears to proceed very rapidly (300 to 1000 cards per minute) but it is in fact very slow compared to the speed with which statements are executed once the program is loaded.

The loading of a program for processing is actually performed by another program, called a "PASCAL compiler", which is already in the computer. During loading, the compiler scans the program for errors and translates the PASCAL statements into an internal form that the computer can understand and execute. (Strictly speaking, there is another program after the compiler called a "loader" which manipulates this internal form of the program and prepares it for execution. This phase is irrelevant for our purposes and we will ignore it. We will speak of the "loading of a program" as the process by which the source program statements are initially read into the computer.)

A crucial point is that the program is <u>not executed as it is loaded and translated</u>. Only after the entire program has been loaded and translated, does the second, or execution, stage begin. Execution begins with the first statement of the main procedure, and proceeds from statement to statement until the procedure is completed. Since generally many statements will be repeatedly executed (in accordance with the control statements described in Section 4) the total <u>number of statements executed</u> will <u>far exceed</u> the <u>number of statements loaded</u>.

At the moment that execution begins only the cards containing the program statements have been read. Cards containing data remain in the card reader -- ready to be read when called for by the execution of READ statements in the program.

7.2 Analysis of Printed Output

The amount and type of printed output produced during the processing of a program can vary considerably. Certain portions are always provided, some portions depend upon the choice of "options" for the particular program, and some depend upon the execution of output statements in the program.

Each computing facility has predetermined a set of standard or "default" choices for the various options. These are presumably chosen to be the most appropriate for the greatest number of users of the computer. The default options are automatically assigned to each program -- but you can <u>override</u>

<u>the defaults</u> by specifying your own choice of options. In PASCAL, options are specified by special comment cards. Many of the important options are described in the following sections; a complete list is given in Appendix B.1.

The complete printed output produced during loading, translation and execution of a PASCAL program can be divided into the following sections, to be described in more detail subsequently:

> <u>Header Pages</u>: Several pages produced by a general supervisory program (called the "operating system") to identify the beginning of a new program, report its cost, the language used -- and scores of other statistics that are of little importance to the neophyte programmer. (These pages are not included in the previous sample output.)
>
> <u>Source Listing</u>: A copy of the program, with additional information such as statement numbers and error messages.
>
> <u>Execution Output</u>: The result of executing WRITE and WRITELN statements in the program. This output may also contain error messages for error conditions detected by PASCAL during execution of the program.
>
> <u>Post-Mortem Dump</u>: A listing of the final values of variables (values after the end of execution), and various summary statistics.
>
> <u>Trailer Pages</u>: Additional more-or-less incomprehensible pages supplied by the operating system. (These pages are not included in the previous sample output.)

7.2.1 <u>Source Listing</u>

The source listing is a copy of the program, to which certain other information has been added.

1) At the left of the program statements in the source listing is a column of six-digit numbers. These numbers actually indicate the location in computer memory where the internal form of each of the program statements has been placed. The internal-form-statements are placed in consecutive locations, corresponding to the order in which the PASCAL statements were given in the program. You might note that different PASCAL statements require different amounts of memory for their internal form. But for our purposes this column of numbers serves simply as <u>statement numbers</u>. They provide a means by which PASCAL can refer to particular statements in the program.

2) When errors are detected during the translation of a program an "error line" is printed. This is marked with asterisks in

the statement number column, and has an arrow under the character where the error was detected. (The "arrow" character depends upon the particular character set used at your installation.) For example:

```
000467      X := Y*(X+Z;
******                 ^4
```

The number following the arrow is the "PASCAL error number". It refers to a list of PASCAL error messages -- a copy of which is given in Appendix B.4. In this case, error message 4 -- "')' expected" -- is quite reasonable. Sometimes the messages appear much less reasonable, and occasionally downright confusing. One source of confusion is that the point when the error is detected may be long after the point at which it actually occurred, and the message may describe a result rather than the cause. In the example above, the problem might just as well be the presence of an extra left parenthesis, but PASCAL cannot know that, so it cannot point to the left parenthesis and say that it is extra.

Errors in declarations and definitions are particularly serious in this regard. Their effect tends to propagate throughout the program. For example, suppose that in the declaration of variables the keyword "VAR" is accidentally misspelled as "VAL". This error would be detected, but the declaration would fail. That is, the variables would not be created. Hence every time one of the variables appeared in the program the error of using an undeclared variable would be announced. There might be dozens or even hundreds of such "errors". They would, of course, all be cleared up just by repairing the declaration. As another example, suppose that a variable that is supposed to be an array, is not properly declared as an array. Then each time that variable name appears followed by a subscript, PASCAL will consider it incorrect. When there are errors in declarations you can't take the error messages in the rest of the program too seriously. It may be worth looking at them quickly to see if errors independent of the declarations are reported -- punctuation errors, for example -- but in general, you will have to repair your declarations and rerun the program to find out anything helpful about the rest of it.

PASCAL detects many errors, but it does not correct any. You must punch a new card with a corrected statement, and resubmit the entire program.

7.2.2 Execution Output

The output generated by the actual execution of a program is completely dependent upon execution of WRITE and WRITELN statements in the program. If no such statements are executed, there is no execution output. PASCAL intrudes in this output only if it detects an error during execution. For example, suppose a program is required to take the square root of the value of an expression. The built-in function that obtains the square root checks to make sure that the argument it receives is non-negative. If it is not, then an error is reported. This is shown in the following example. The source listing of the program is the following:

```
000006 (* SQUARE ROOT DEMONSTRATION *)
000006
000006 PROGRAM DEMO(INPUT,OUTPUT);
000464
000464 VAR I:     INTEGER;   (* LOOP COUNTER *)
000465     LEFTPT,           (* INPUT NUMBER *)
000465     BASEVALUE:        (* SQRT OF LEFTPT *)
000465          REAL;
000467
000467 BEGIN (* DEMO *)
000467   FOR I := 1 TO 10 DO
000023   BEGIN (* I/O LOOP *)
000025     READ(LEFTPT);
000030     WRITE(' ', I, '     LEFTPT =', LEFTPT);
000047     BASEVALUE := SQRT(LEFTPT);
000053     WRITELN('    BASEVALUE =', BASEVALUE)
000064   END (* I/O LOOP *)
000065 END. (* DEMO *)
```

Suppose this program were run with the following data:

17.3 4.82 16 22.91 -44 8.999 5.0 12.5 49 -54.6

The execution output would begin as shown below:

```
1    LEFTPT =  1.7300000000000E+001    BASEVALUE =  4.1593268686171E+000
2    LEFTPT =  4.8200000000000E+000    BASEVALUE =  2.1954498400100E+000
3    LEFTPT =  1.6000000000000E+001    BASEVALUE =  4.0000000000000E+000
4    LEFTPT =  2.2910000000000E+001    BASEVALUE =  4.7864391775097E+000
5    LEFTPT = -4.4000000000000E+001
```

At this point, when SQRT is confronted with a negative value of LEFTPT, PASCAL objects:

```
* NEGATIVE ARGUMENT OF SQRT
* AT ADDR 000051 IN PROCEDURE DEMO
```

The first line tells you what is wrong -- a negative argument given to the square root function -- and the second line tells you where this occurred in your program. This is given in terms that allow you to find the proper statement in the source listing. "ADDR 000051" refers to the memory addresses listed on the left margin of the source listing. Since 000051 falls between 000047 and 000053 it indicates the problem occurred in the statement

```
BASEVALUE := SQRT(LEFTPT)
```

In this case there is nothing wrong with the statement, the problem lies in the data supplied to the program.

When an execution error is detected, PASCAL terminates execution of the program. In this example, the execution output would be terminated with the following information:

```
  PROGRAM TERMINATED AT% 000051 IN DEMO


DEMO

  BASEVALUE   =    4.7864391775097E+000
  LEFTPT      =   -4.4000000000000E+001
  I           =              5
```

This final information is called a "post mortem dump", because it is given after the program has "died". In general, the dump includes the following information:

1. The cause of the termination and where it occurred.

2. A description of each procedure that is "active" at the point execution was terminated. (In the example above, there is only one procedure, DEMO, but we will later have programs with more than one procedure.)

3. The final values of all scalar variables in each active procedure

At the time of writing, the principal PASCAL compiler is one written for Control Data Corporation computers, and we have used this version for the specific examples in the Primer. This is not a particularly distinguished compiler in terms of the amount of help it provides during the testing of a program. (However, we admit to being especially critical in this regard, because we have been involved in the development of PL/C, which emphasizes diagnostic assistance to the user. A highly-diagnostic compiler is not yet available for the PASCAL language.)

Section 8 Declarations and Definitions

In previous sections we have already introduced the concept of declarations to create objects used by the program. Briefly, we have already said the following:

1. Every variable must be listed in a VAR declaration, placed at the beginning of the program. (Section 2.)

2. Each individual variable can store only one <u>type</u> of value. The type is permanently established by the VAR declaration. The standard types presented so far are REAL and INTEGER (Section 2.2) and BOOLEAN (Section 4.3.1.5).

3. Statement labels (prefixes to a statement to serve as a target for a GOTO) must be listed in a LABEL declaration. This must be placed at the beginning of the program (ahead of the VAR declaration). (Section 4.4.1.)

4. ARRAYs are variables with multiple values (all of the same type). (Section 5.3.)

The purpose of Section 8 is to review (and repeat) what has already been said about declarations, and then give more detail and introduce other types of declaration. We will discuss four different declarations:

```
LABEL
CONST
TYPE
VAR
```

They are listed here in the <u>order in which they must appear</u> in the program. Not all of these declarations appear in every program, but those present must be given in this order.

8.1 Declaration of Labels

There is not much to the declaration of labels -- simply list all of the labels that are used in the procedure:

```
LABEL label1, label2, ... ;
```

If there is more than one label in the declaration, the labels are separated by commas. The declaration is followed by a semi-colon, to separate it from the next declaration. The LABEL declaration must be the first declaration in the procedure.

The labels themselves are integers:

```
LABEL 45, 9001, 9005;
```

Any integers can be used, as far as PASCAL is concerned, but it is helpful to the human reader of a program if consistent conventions are followed in the choice of labels. For example, we always use 9000 labels to indicate a "loop exit label". It is also helpful if labels are chosen so that they are always in increasing order as you read down the lines of a program. It is good practice to list the labels in increasing order in the declaration so you can find a particular label easily, and check the list against the body of the procedure.

Note that the labels in the body of a CASE statement are not considered statement labels and hence are not included in the LABEL declaration.

Although the LABEL declaration is given at the very beginning of a procedure it is almost always written last and then inserted at the beginning. You don't know what labels you are going to need until you are writing the actual statements of the procedure. So in practice, you just invent labels as you need them -- but then must remember to go back over your procedure and copy all the labels into a LABEL declaration. It is easy to forget to do this, or to miss one label in the process. PASCAL will detect such an error and remind you of the omission. (This is just a nuisance. Most programming languages don't require the declaration of labels -- but PASCAL does, and you will just have to go along with it.)

Note that only one LABEL declaration is permitted in a procedure. If you discover you have omitted a label, you cannot simply add a second declaration:

```
LABEL 45, 9002;
LABEL 9005;
```

The additional label would have to be inserted in the existing list:

```
LABEL 45, 9002, 9005;
```

8.2 Definition of Constants

Constants in PASCAL can be given directly wherever they are needed, as we have done in many earlier examples. Constants can be of different forms, corresponding to the various different types of values:

```
AREA := 5E-1 * HEIGHT * WIDTH
X[I] := X[I+1]
WRITE(' HEIGHT =', HEIGHT)
WHILE TRUE DO ...
```

However, in some circumstances it is useful to define a particular constant value in the heading of a procedure, and give the constant a name. For example, suppose a program frequently uses a high-precision value of pi, say 3.1415926536. You should object to having to write all those digits each time the value of pi is required, and in fact, the high probability of making an error would make it unwise to do so. Alternatively, you could define a constant:

```
CONST PI = 3.1415926536;
```

With this definition you can write the name PI instead of the numeric value wherever the value is required.

Why is this needed? After all, you could declare a variable PI and assign it the same value:

```
VAR PI: REAL;
    ...
PI := 3.1415926536
```

In fact, in most programming languages this is precisely what you would do, but PASCAL offers the additional feature of being able to define constants. The difference is simply that a constant name cannot be made the target of an assignment. Neither an assignment statement nor a READ statement can accidentally (because of some latent program error) change the value of the constant. Constants defined in this way are also useful in TYPE definitions and VAR declarations, as will be described in Sections 8.3 and 8.4.

As another example, suppose a program involved considerable printed output that had to be elaborately titled and formatted. The following constants might be convenient:

```
CONST AUTH = 'JEFFREY ZIMMERMAN';
      PDATE = 'SEPTEMBER 29, 1975';
      DASHLINE = '--------------------';
      STARLINE = '********************';
```

It will be easier to use these names in WRITE and WRITELN statements than to repeat writing the equivalent literal each time it is needed.

The general form of the definition of a constant is:

```
CONST name¹ = value¹;
      name² = value²;
      ...
```

The constant-names are identifiers, chosen subject to the same rules as variable-names. That is, they must begin with a letter, and the same list of reserved keywords (Section 2.1) must be avoided. The name is followed by "=" (not the ":=" of the assignment statement) and the value to be permanently associated with this name. The individual name-value phrases are separated by semi-colons. The last name-value phrase is followed by a semi-colon to separate it from the next declaration. There can be any number of name-value phrases, but there can be only one CONST definition in a procedure -- that is, the keyword CONST can appear only once. If present, the CONST definition must follow the LABEL declaration (if any) and precede the TYPE definition (if any) and the VAR declaration.

8.3 Definition of Types

Up to this point we have considered only "standard" types of values -- REAL, INTEGER or BOOLEAN. A fourth standard type, CHAR, will be introduced in Section 9. These four types are adequate for any programming task -- in fact, many programming languages do not even provide all four of these. However, PASCAL goes beyond this and permits you to define additional types. Any user-defined types are available only to the procedure in which they are defined. They are used in the declaration of variables in a manner quite analogous to the standard types. The definition of additional types is never absolutely necessary -- you can always find a way to write the program with standard types, but the addition of a new type allows you to write a program in a clearer and more reliable manner.

A user-defined type is somewhat similar to the standard type BOOLEAN, in the sense that there are a small number of values, and the values themselves are identifiers. A type is defined by enumerating, in order, all of the values that it represents. The form is:

```
TYPE type-name = (value¹, value², ... )
```

The values are identifiers -- that is, words such as those used for the names of variables. For example:

```
TYPE DAY = (SUN, MON, TUES, WED, THURS, FRI, SAT)
```

In this example DAY is a type that permits seven different values, in the same sense that BOOLEAN is a type that permits only two values. SUN, MON, ..., SAT are the specific values that may be assigned to a variable of type DAY, just as TRUE and FALSE are the values that can be assigned to a BOOLEAN variable. If a TYPE definition were required for the standard type BOOLEAN (which is not the case) it would look like the following:

```
TYPE BOOLEAN = (FALSE, TRUE)
```

Since BOOLEAN is a standard type its definition is built-in and you do not have to give it; this is shown to explain what the TYPE definition accomplishes.

Note that in the example above, SUN is a _value_ of type DAY, and not a _variable_ of type DAY. DAY will be used to define a variable (or many variables) of this new type:

```
VAR DAYOFWEEK: DAY
```

which means that SUN is one of the seven values that can be assigned to the variable DAYOFWEEK. A particular identifier used as a value cannot be also used for some other purpose. Since SUN is a value in this example, you could not also have a variable named SUN.

A user-defined type can be used in many of the same ways as the standard type INTEGER. In particular, it can be used as an index-variable:

```
FOR DAYOFWEEK := MON TO FRI DO ...
```

For a suitably declared array (see Section 8.4.2) it may be used as a subscript:

```
CUMSALES[MON] := CUMSALES[MON] + DAILYSALES[MON]
```

It may be used as the basis of a CASE statement:

```
CASE DAYOFWEEK OF
    SAT, SUN: statement;
    MON: statement;
    ...
  END
```

Any of these examples could be programmed by "coding" using the integers:

    Let 1 stand for "Monday",
        2 stand for "Tuesday", etc.

but it is clearer to use the intended values directly, rather than have to establish an artificial code. Moreover, by using a user-defined type, PASCAL will _automatically monitor_ variables of this type to ensure that they can only be assigned one of the legitimate values. There is no risk of having the program somehow erroneously produce a value "8", which is not defined in the code, and hence produce some unpredictable and unwanted result.

The order in which the values are listed in a type definition is significant; it establishes an inherent ordering of the values. In the example above, TUES is the predecessor of WED because it comes immediately before WED in the list of values. (This has nothing to do with "alphabetical ordering" of the identifiers used as values -- SUN comes before MON.) One consequence of this ordering is that when you use such a variable as an index variable:

```
FOR DAYOFWEEK := MON TO FRI DO ...
```

the index variable is assigned values in the order in which they are listed in the definition. In this case, that would be MON, TUES, WED, THURS and FRI. This means that it would be improper to write

```
FOR DAYOFWEEK := THURS TO MON DO ...
```

since THURS follows MON in the definition list, and the keyword "TO" requires "increasing" order. However, you could write

```
FOR DAYOFWEEK := THURS DOWNTO MON DO ...
```

User-defined types are for internal use only. Values can be assigned, used and tested within the program, but these values cannot be displayed by means of the WRITE or WRITELN statements. They also cannot be assigned from external data by means of the READ or READLN statements. That is, with DAYOFWEEK as declared above, you could not give the value THURS on a data card and assign this value to DAYOFWEEK by executing READ(DAYOFWEEK).

Three of the built-in functions of PASCAL (see Section 3.3) pertain to user-defined types:

ORD(x) -- The result (INTEGER) is the ordinal number of the argument x in the set of values of which x is a member. That is, the result is the position of the argument on the list in which it was defined as a value. Referring to the definition of type DAY above, ORD(MON) = 1.

SUCC(x) -- The result is the successor value, relative to the argument value. That is, the result is the value that follows the argument value on the definition list. Referring again to DAY, SUCC(THURS) = FRI. It is an error if the argument is the "last" value, and hence has no successor.

PRED(x) -- The result is the predecessor value, relative to the argument value. That is, the result is the value that precedes the argument value on the definition list. Referring again to DAY, PRED(WED) = TUES. It is an error if the argument is the "first" value, and hence has no predecessor. PRED is the inverse of SUCC:

```
PRED(SUCC(TUES)) = TUES
SUCC(PRED(FRI)) = FRI
```

A particular value can appear in only one TYPE definition. For example, the following would be <u>improper</u>:

```
TYPE WEEKDAY = (MON, TUES, WED, THURS, FRI, SAT);
     WEEKEND = (SAT, SUN)
```

The difficulty here is that the value SAT is included in both types WEEKDAY and WEEKEND. Although this is not allowed, one type can consist of a subset of another type, as described in the next section.

As with each of the other kinds of declaration and definition there can be any number of phrases (definitions) in the TYPE definition, with the phrases separated by semi-colons, but the keyword TYPE can appear <u>only once</u> in a procedure. TYPE definitions must come after LABEL declarations and CONST definitions, if any, and before VAR declarations.

8.3.1 <u>Subrange Types</u>

Another version of a user-defined type specifies the values as a subset of some standard, or previously defined, type. The form is:

```
TYPE type-name = lowest-value .. highest-value
```

The new type is called a "subrange" of the previous type. For example:

```
TYPE CODENUMBER = 20 .. 30;
     ERRORFLAG = -1 .. 1;
     WEEKDAY = MON .. FRI
```

In each case the first value given <u>must be less than</u> the second value. It would be <u>improper</u> to write:

```
TYPE WEEKDAY = FRI .. MON
```

or

```
TYPE CODENUMBER = 30 .. 20
```

Note that one type must be a proper subset of another type -- they cannot just overlap partially, as in the case of WEEKDAY and WEEKEND in the improper example of the last section. The following would be a proper definition:

```
TYPE DAY = (MON, TUES, WED, THURS, FRI, SAT, SUN);
     WEEKDAY = MON .. FRI;
     WEEKEND = SAT .. SUN
```

A subrange type can be defined relative to INTEGER or relative to a user-defined type, as shown in the examples above. It could also be defined relative to the standard types BOOLEAN or CHAR. However, a subrange of type REAL is not allowed.

The usefulness of subrange definitions will become clear in Section 8.4.1.

8.4 Declaration of Variables

Every variable to be used in a procedure must be declared. The general form of the declaration is:

VAR $name_1$: $type\text{-}specification_1$;
    $name_2$: $type\text{-}specification_2$;
    ...

The variable names are identifiers, as described in Section 2.1. They must begin with a letter and cannot be identical to any of the reserved keywords listed in Section 2.1. The type-specification can be one of the standard PASCAL types -- REAL, INTEGER, BOOLEAN or CHAR (the topic of Section 9) -- or a non-standard type you have defined in a TYPE definition. There can be any number of name:type phrases, separated by semi-colons. The last name:type phrase is followed by a semi-colon to separate it from the first statement of the procedure. All of the phrases are part of a single declaration. The keyword VAR can appear only once in a procedure.

If there is more than one variable to be declared with the same type-specification, these variables may be listed in the same phrase:

$name_{11}$, $name_{12}$, $name_{13}$, ... : $type\text{-}specification_1$;

It is usual practice to collect variables of similar type in this way, but it is not required by PASCAL -- there can be two or more phrases with REAL, for example, as the type-specification. The punctuation of the VAR declaration is critical. Note that:

Semi-colons separate phrases.

Commas separate names in a single phrase.

A colon separates the last name in a phrase from the type-specification.

The declaration of a variable does not assign any initial value to that variable. The declaration simply creates the variable, preparatory to the execution of some statement assigning it a value. In the interval between creation and the first assignment of value, the value of a variable is said to be "undefined". If displayed during this interval, an undefined value will appear as the character "U" on printed output. A variable must be assigned a value before it can be expected to provide a value. That is, in the assignment statement

```
X := Y
```

the variable Y is being asked to provide a value, and the variable X is being assigned a value. Prior to execution of this statement the variable Y must have been assigned a value by the execution of some other statement, but this can be the first statement is which X is used, since it is receiving rather than providing a value.

Each variable has three fundamental characteristics: a name, a type, and a value. The name and type of a variable are permanent characteristics, and are established as the variable is created by the VAR declaration. The particular value of a variable will change from time to time as it is the target of various assignment or READ statements. However, no matter how many different values a variable may have had during its lifetime, they will all have been of the same type. Each variable is restricted to a single type of value.

Examples of the declaration of variables are the following:

```
VAR X: REAL;
    I: INTEGER

VAR X: REAL;
    Y: REAL;
    I: INTEGER

VAR X, Y: REAL;
    COL, ROW: INTEGER

VAR ITEM, LIMIT, SUM: REAL;
    I, J, POSNMAX: INTEGER;
    ERRORFLAG, ZEROFOUND: BOOLEAN
```

It is crucial that the declarations of a procedure be very carefully done. As noted in Section 7.2.1, errors in the declaration of variables are felt throughout the program -- wherever the variables are used. (An example of the result of a declaration error is shown in Section V.3.3.1.) You cannot begin to test the correctness of the rest of the program until the declarations are correct. It is obviously good practice to check the spelling and punctuation in declarations very carefully before ever trying to run the program.

The declaration is a fine place to establish the role of each variable. This is not a formal characteristic as far as PASCAL is concerned -- it is an announcement for the benefit of the human reader, usually the programmer himself. You should state, in a comment, what the meaning of the value of each variable will be. For example:

```
VAR ITEM,        (* LAST DATUM READ *)
    MAXITEM,     (* MAXIMUM ITEM SO FAR *)
    SUMITEM:     (* SUM OF ITEMS SO FAR *)
          REAL;
```

The variable name should be chosen to help suggest the role of the variable, but it is usually not adequate in itself. Since the variable-name will, in general, be written many times in the statements of a procedure it is convenient to keep it relatively short -- too short to be completely descriptive. On the other hand, an explanatory comment is written only once and you can afford to make it reasonably precise.

8.4.1 Limitation of Values

It is useful to be able to restrict the values that can be assigned to a variable. For example, suppose a variable named CODE is of type INTEGER and is used as the "selector" of a CASE statement:

```
CASE CODE OF
    1: statement1;
    2: statement2;
    3: statement3;
    4: statement4
  END
```

If the value of CODE at this point in execution is one of the integers 1, 2, 3 or 4, one of the four component statements of the CASE statement is selected for execution. However, if the value is anything else, the execution of the CASE statement is undefined -- you simply don't know what PASCAL will do. Since this would be intolerable, you must ensure that the value of CODE will be in the proper range. The crude way to do this (which is the way used in most programming languages) would be to write your own test:

```
IF (CODE < 1) OR (CODE > 4) THEN
    BEGIN WRITELN(' CODE VALUE OUT OF RANGE', CODE);
         GOTO 9900
    END;
CASE CODE OF
    1: statement¹;
    ...
```

In PASCAL you can achieve this more clearly and conveniently by declaring CODE in such a way that it can never be assigned any value except 1, 2, 3 or 4. There are two ways to do this; either:

```
TYPE CODELIMIT = 1 .. 4;
VAR CODE: CODELIMIT
```

or

```
VAR CODE: 1 .. 4
```

The second is essentially a shorthand form of the first. It would probably be generally preferable, except when the same limits are to be applied to more than one variable. Then it would be convenient to have a subrange type, rather than write the limits for each variable separately.

If these limits are constant for a particular version of the program but are likely to change in future versions, it might be worth going one step farther and defining the limits as constants:

```
CONST LOWERCODE = 1; UPPERCODE = 4;
TYPE CODELIMIT = LOWERCODE .. UPPERCODE;
VAR CODE: CODELIMIT
```

Now when the program has to be changed, perhaps to introduce a new code value and a new statement alternative in the CASE statement, you only have to change the CONST definition and everything else is adjusted automatically. You don't have to scan the entire program to make sure you have changed the limit 4, given as a constant each time it is needed.

The power of this automatic limitation of value is that it is applied unfailingly throughout the program. It does not depend upon your remembering that a test is required, and recognizing each of the possibly many places where is must be performed.

Unfortunately, this limitation only applies to INTEGER, CHAR, BOOLEAN and user-defined types. You cannot use it to automatically limit the values of a REAL variable.

8.4.2 Declaration of Arrays

Arrays were introduced in Section 5, and the form of the declaration of an array was given in 5.3 as:

```
VAR array-name: ARRAY[lower-bound..upperbound] OF type
```

Now, having CONST and TYPE definitions at our disposal, we can show a more general form:

```
VAR array-name: ARRAY[index-type] OF element-type
```

"Index-type" is any type with finitely-many values. Since one element of the array will be created for each distinct value of the index-type, the limit in practice is the amount of memory available in the computer. Neither REAL nor INTEGER can be given as index-type since neither has only finitely-many values (as least not for practical purposes). Index-type can be a subrange of INTEGER, which is the most commonly used form, and the form we gave in Section 5.3. But it can also be given as any user-defined type. "Element-type" can be any of the type-specifications that can be applied to a simple, single-valued variable; that is, any of the standard types REAL, INTEGER, BOOLEAN or a subrange type as described in Sections 8.3.1 and 8.4.1.

For example, suppose there were a number of arrays in a procedure, all of which had to have the same number of elements. The way to write this would be:

```
CONST LBOUND = 1;
      UBOUND = 50;
TYPE ARSIZE = LBOUND .. UBOUND;
VAR X: ARRAY[ARSIZE] OF REAL;
    Y: ARRAY[ARSIZE] OF REAL;
    COUNT: ARRAY[ARSIZE] OF INTEGER;
    CONTROL: ARRAY[ARSIZE] OF INTEGER
```

This form makes it clear to the reader that these arrays are related -- that the size of one cannot be changed without also changing the size of the others. Moreover, if the size does have to be changed it can be done easily and surely with a minimum possibility of error, since only the CONST definition needs to be changed.

Suppose the following TYPE definitions are given:

```
TYPE DAY = (MON, TUES, WED, THURS, FRI, SAT, SUN);
     DECADE = 1 .. 10
```

Then the following array declarations could be given.

```
VAR WEEK: ARRAY[1..5] OF DAY
```

This creates an array of five elements, each of which is of type

DAY, and can be assigned any of the values SUN, MON, ... etc.

```
VAR DAYCOUNT: ARRAY[DAY] OF DECADE
```

This creates an array of seven elements (one for each value of type DAY) each of which is a subrange INTEGER type and can be assigned as values any of the integers 1, 2, ..., 10. The values MON, TUES, ... etc. would be the subscripts used with this array. For example, DAYCOUNT[TUES] is the second element of the array. As in the case of integer subscripts, these subscripts can be given by a variable rather than a constant. For example, if DATE is a variable of type DAY:

```
VAR DATE: DAY
```

then an element of DAYCOUNT can be referenced by writing

```
DAYCOUNT[DATE]
```

The value of DATE is one of MON, TUES, ..., etc., so this subscripted name references one of the seven elements of the array DAYCOUNT.

As indicated in Section 5.3, there can be multi-dimensional arrays. The form of declaration is:

```
VAR  array-name: ARRAY[index-type¹, index-type², ... ]
                 OF element-type
```

The most common form is to have INTEGER subranges for each index-type. For example:

```
VAR SCORES: ARRAY[1..10, 1..20] OF REAL
```

However, the index-types do not have to be similar. For example:

```
VAR DAYTOTAL: ARRAY[DAY, 1..5] OF REAL
```

This will create an array of thirty-five elements, each of type REAL:

```
DAYTOTAL[MON,1]   DAYTOTAL[MON,2] ...   DAYTOTAL[MON,5]
DAYTOTAL[TUES,1]  DAYTOTAL[TUES,2] ...
...
DAYTOTAL[SUN,1]   DAYTOTAL[SUN,2] ...   DAYTOTAL[SUN,5]
```

Note that all elements of all dimensions of an array have the same type of value.

Section 8 Summary

1. Declarations and definitions are placed at the beginning of a procedure to describe some of the objects that will be used in the procedure, and to give names to these objects. There are four kinds of declarations and definitions:

```
LABEL
CONST
TYPE
VAR
```

All are optional, and are used only as needed by the particular procedure. However, the VAR declaration is almost always required, since all variables in PASCAL must be explicitly declared. Those declarations and definitions present must be in the order shown above.

2. Each of the declarations and definitions can appear only once in a procedure. That is, the keyword that starts the declaration or definition -- LABEL, CONST, TYPE or VAR -- can be given only once. The keyword can be followed by any number of defining phrases. Phrases are separated from each other and from other declarations and statements by a semi-colon.

3. The LABEL declaration lists all the integers that are used as statement labels in the procedure, but does not include labels used within a CASE statement. The form of the declaration is:

LABEL $label^1$, $label^2$, ... ;

4. The CONST definition is used to give names to particular constant values. Such a name is then used whenever the constant is required in the procedure. The form of the CONST definition is:

CONST $name^1$ = $value^1$;
      $name^2$ = $value^2$;
      ...

5. The TYPE definition is used to add new value types to the language for this particular procedure; that is, value types in addition to the standard types REAL, INTEGER, BOOLEAN and CHAR. The form of the TYPE definition for a new user-defined value type is:

TYPE type-name = ($value^1$, $value^2$, ...)

in which all of the values included in the type are listed in "increasing" order. The values themselves are identifiers. These user-defined types are for internal use only. Such values can neither be displayed by means of WRITE, nor read from data by means of READ.

A second form of TYPE definition establishes a new type as a "subrange" of another type. The form of a subrange definition is:

TYPE type-name = lowest-value .. highest value

6. The VAR declaration is used to create all variables and arrays used in the procedure, and to specify the type of value for each. The form of the VAR declaration for a simple variable is:

VAR name^{11}, name^{12}, ... : type-spec^{1};
    name^{21}, name^{22}, ... : type-spec^{2};
    ...

where the names separated by commas are variables of identical type. The type-specification is either a standard type -- REAL, INTEGER, BOOLEAN or CHAR -- or a type previously given in a TYPE definition. Alternatively, a subrange definition can be given directly as a type-specification:

VAR name^{1}, name^{2}, ... : lowest-value .. highest-value

The form of an array declaration is:

VAR array-name: ARRAY[index-type] OF element-type

Index-type is either a user-defined or subrange type specifying the number of elements in the array. Several index-types can be given (separated by commas) for multi-dimensional arrays. Element-type is a standard type, a user-defined type, or a subrange type specifying the type of value of each element of the array.

7. Neither simple variables nor arrays are automatically assigned any initial value by PASCAL as they are created. They must be assigned a value by a program statement before they can be asked to provide a value to use in an expression or to be displayed.

8. Declarations and definitions are critical parts of a program. They should be written and keypunched with special care. The testing of program statements cannot really begin until the declarations and definitions are correct.

Section 8 Exercises

1. Write a declaration to create a variable named TOTAL that will hold values such as -123.79 and 0.00062.

2. Write a declaration equivalent to the following, but one that does not group the variables of similar type:

```
VAR X, I, J: INTEGER;
    Y, Z: REAL
```

3. Write a declaration that will create variables with the following names and types:

```
TOP[1] [real]
TOP[2] [real]
BOT[1] [real]
BOT[2] [real]
SIDE   [real]
WIDE   [integer]
```

4. What is the value of the variables created in exercise 3 at the start of execution of the procedure? How can you arrange to have the variables have the following values:

```
TOP[1] 5
TOP[2] 6.5
BOT[1] 5
BOT[2] 6.5
SIDE   5
WIDE   5
```

5. Define a new type COLOR made up of the values RED, BLUE, GREEN, YELLOW, and ORANGE.

6. Declare an array X of twelve elements, each of type COLOR.

7. Write a program segment that would assign the value GREEN to each of the elements of the array X of exercise 6.

8. Define a new type so that TOP and BOT in exercise 3 may be declared as follows:

```
VAR TOP, BOT: NEWTYPE
```

9. Write constant definitions for

   a. The mathematical constant e, the base of the natural logarithms.

   b. The string 'PAGE'.

   c. The integer 66.

Section 9 Character-Valued Variables

Up to this point we have considered numeric-valued variables. We have used non-numeric "strings" of characters as literals in a WRITE statement (Section 6.2), but not as values to assign to variables. Some languages (current FORTRAN, for example) are only capable of processing numeric values, and are considered useful primarily for mathematical and engineering applications. However, in many types of applications it is useful to be able to store, manipulate, and display values that include other characters besides digits. Values that include letters and special symbols as well as digits are called "character data", or "strings".

For example, programs called "text editors" take a sequence of words, punctuation marks, and format commands, and format the words and punctuation marks into lines, paragraphs, and pages. This book was produced by such a program.

Many important applications involve both numeric and character data. Consider a program to maintain a customer charge account system for a retail store. Each account includes numeric information on charges, payments, balance due, arrears, finance charges, etc. It also contains character information giving the name of the customer, his address, credit references, etc. A majority of the world's computers are used primarily for file processing, and on the whole computers process more character data than numeric data.

Since PASCAL was designed to serve both mathematical and file processing applications it includes facilities for processing strings of characters. However, its string processing features are not PASCAL's greatest strength. Even much-maligned PL/I offers string facilities that are more convenient for the programmer. There are also specialized languages, such as SNOBOL, designed especially for string processing.

There is surprisingly little agreement as to exactly what characters should be allowed in such a facility. There is general agreement that the letters A to Z and the digits 0 to 9 should be included, but there is little agreement as to what punctuation and special characters should be allowed. The decision is partly dependent upon the language being used -- PASCAL generally uses a different character set than PL/I -- and partly dependent upon equipment. The humble keypunch is an important consideration, since the characters represented on its keyboard can be easily entered. Other characters must be "encoded" by combinations of keys. Even more important is the printer used by the computer, since this determines what characters can be displayed. It would seem reasonable that there would be some accepted standard in this regard -- but there isn't. You will just have to find out from your own computer installation what character set can be used (and displayed) by PASCAL on your computer. (See Appendix B.2.1.)

A typical character set for PASCAL on Control Data Corporation computers is shown below. (The blank character follows the "=".)

```
:ABCDEFGHIJKLMNOPQRSTUVWXYZ0123456789+-*/()$= ,.'[]%"↰!&#?<>@\↑;
```

String processing is in a sense more fun than numeric processing. After learning a few details, you will find it easy to format output nicely, to write programs to print out graphs and pictures, and to perform other interesting tasks.

9.1 Declaration of Character Variables

There is a fourth standard type, CHAR, in PASCAL (in addition to REAL, INTEGER and BOOLEAN) to handle character values. Variables of this type are declared:

```
VAR name¹, name², ... : CHAR
```

A CHAR variable represents a <u>single character</u>. That is, the value of a CHAR variable is <u>one</u> of the characters in the allowed character set. The particular value may, of course, change from time to time during execution of a program, but a CHAR variable will always have as value some single character. Like any other type of variable in PASCAL, CHAR variables do not automatically receive a value when they are created. Their value is "undefined" until a value is assigned. Note that "undefined" is not the same as "blank", which is a normal (and often used) value.

Subranges are often used with CHAR variables. Two common examples are:

```
TYPE LETTER = 'A' .. 'Z';
     DIGIT = '0' .. '9'
```

These subrange types can be used in the declaration of character-valued variables to limit their values to a particular section of the overall character set (see Section 8.4.1).

A constant of type CHAR is written as the particular character value, enclosed in quotes. Examples are:

```
'A'
'8'
' '
'+'
```

Since the quote itself is a valid character, a special rule is needed to represent it as a constant. If the quote is itself a value it must be repeated -- that is, two consecutive quotes represent the quote value. This value is then enclosed in quotes in the usual way, so the constant consisting of a single quote character is written as four consecutive quotes: ''''.

The quoting convention is necessary to distinguish character constants from other elements of the language. No special convention was necessary with numeric constants since the form of numeric constants is recognizably different from that of other elements. For example, 15, 2E4 and -0.7 cannot be anything but constants. But when arbitrary characters are allowed as values, then things become more complicated. For example, since X could be a <u>variable</u> or a <u>value</u>, some means is needed by which the programmer can unambiguously indicate whether he means the variable X, or the constant character value X. Similarly, "+" is a valid character value, but it is also an arithmetic operator, and the two must be written so there is no possible confusion. PASCAL and most other programming languages require character constants to be quoted.

9.1.1 Declaration of Character Arrays

Most programs that deal with character values deal with sequences of values -- representing "words" or "lines" -- rather than individual characters. In general, a <u>sequence of characters</u> is called a "string". In PASCAL, a string is represented as an <u>array of CHAR variables</u>. For example,

```
VAR WORD: ARRAY[1..10] OF CHAR
```

is a string, named WORD, consisting of ten characters. WORD[1] is the first character in the string, WORD [2] the second, etc.

PASCAL actually has two different ways to represent strings: as ARRAYs and as PACKED ARRAYs. This difference has primarily to do with the efficiency with which values are stored in and retrieved from computer memory, and the amount of memory space required per character. Neither of these considerations is appropriate for a primer, so we will only use PACKED ARRAYs, since these make life a little easier for the programmer.

Although strings are not a "standard" type in PASCAL, they are used so frequently that it is useful to adopt a standard practice in their declaration. We will (almost) always give a TYPE definition for strings, of the following form:

```
TYPE STRINGn = PACKED ARRAY[1..n] OF char-type
```

"Char-type" is either the standard type CHAR, or a user defined subrange of CHAR. "n" is the "length" -- the number of characters -- of the string. Examples of string declarations are the following:

```
TYPE STRING132 = PACKED ARRAY[1..132] OF CHAR;
VAR LINE: STRING132

TYPE STRING80 = PACKED ARRAY[1..80] OF CHAR;
VAR CARD1, CARD2: STRING80

TYPE LETTER = 'A' .. 'Z';
     LETTERSTRING20 = PACKED ARRAY[1..20] OF LETTER;
VAR WORDIN, WORDOUT, WORDTEMP: LETTERSTRING20
```

In our examples, when we do not show a complete program we will not always show the TYPE declaration for a string, but you must remember that STRINGn is not a standard PASCAL type and hence a TYPE declaration is required in an actual program.

In some contexts in PASCAL you can use a string-name directly -- as if it were actually a standard type. For example, this can be done in assignment statements (Section 9.2.1) and WRITE statements (Section 9.2.5). In other contexts, such as a READ statement (Section 9.2.2), the string cannot be regarded as a single object. You must then remember that a string is really an array of characters, and act upon each character separately. If STR is a string, then STR[I] refers to the Ith character in the string.

You will often need <u>arrays of strings</u> -- which are really just doubly-subscripted arrays of CHAR variables. An example of declaration of a string array is:

```
CONST LINES = 55;
TYPE STRING132 = PACKED ARRAY[1..132] OF CHAR;
VAR PAGE: ARRAY[1..LINES] OF STRING132
```

With this declaration PAGE is a 55 by 132 array of characters -- 55 lines of 132 characters each. PAGE[2] refers to the second line of this array, and PAGE[3,5] refers to the 5th character in the 3rd line.

9.2 Use of Character Variables

9.2.1 Assignment of Value

The assignment statement for a character-valued variable has the same form as that for a numeric variable:

```
variable-name := expression
```

The expression on the right side is evaluated to provide a character value, which is then assigned to the variable specified on the left side. However, in this case the expression on the right is of a very restricted form. In PASCAL there are no operators for character values corresponding to the arithmetic operators for numeric values. Hence the expression must consist of a single term -- a constant, a variable or a built-in function. For example, suppose two variables C1 and C2 have been declared:

```
VAR C1, C2: CHAR
```

Then a value could be assigned by giving that value as a constant:

```
C1 := 'D'
```

A value could also be assigned by copying the value of another character variable:

```
C2 := C1
```

Certain built-in functions also yield a character value, as noted in Section 9.2.4, and hence could be given as the right side of an assignment statement.

The variables in an assignment can be subscripted. For example, suppose the following character variables and arrays have been declared:

```
TYPE STRING4 = PACKED ARRAY[1..4] OF CHAR;
VAR C1, C2: CHAR;
    STR: STRING4
```

Then the following are valid assignment statements:

```
C1 := 'F'
STR[1] := 'G'
STR[3] := C1
C2 := STR[1]
STR[4] := STR[3]
```

A value can be assigned to the individual elements of a string, as in the example above, but it is also possible to assign a value to all elements of a string simultaneously. For example, if a string named WORD is declared:

```
VAR WORD: STRING4
```

then a value could be assigned to each element of WORD by a statement such as the following:

```
WORD := 'ABCD'
```

The value on the right is a "literal" -- a string constant -- which was first introduced in Section 6.2. The action of this assignment statement is equivalent to the action of four statements, assigning value element by element:

```
WORD[1] := 'A';
WORD[2] := 'B';
WORD[3] := 'C';
WORD[4] := 'D'
```

Suppose each element of WORD was to be assigned the same value, say a blank. The assignment statement

```
WORD := '    '
```

would be equivalent to the loop:

```
FOR I := 1 TO 4 DO
    WORD[I] := ' '
```

The same shortcut can be used to copy a value from one string to another, but only if both strings have the <u>same length</u>. For example, suppose declarations are given as:

```
VAR WORD1, WORD2: STRING10;
    LINE: STRING50
```

You could write:

```
WORD1 := 'XXXXXXXXXX';
WORD2 := WORD1
```

which would be equivalent to writing:

```
FOR I := 1 TO 10 DO
    WORD1[I] := 'X';
FOR I := 1 TO 10 DO
    WORD2[I] := WORD1[I]
```

However, you could <u>not</u> write:

```
LINE := WORD1
```

since LINE and WORD1 do not have the same length. You could copy WORD1 into a portion of LINE, but you would have to do it element by element:

```
FOR I := 1 TO 10 DO
    LINE[I] := WORDI[I]
```

Character values cannot be involved in arithmetic operations. For example, suppose S and R are character-valued variables:

```
VAR S, R: CHAR
```

You cannot write an expression such as:

```
S + R
```

This seems reasonable, since you probably wouldn't think of writing such an expression in terms to character constants, such as letters:

```
'A' + 'B'
```

However, it may surprise you that character variables cannot ever be involved in an arithmetic operation, not even when their values happen to be digits. For example, the following is not valid:

```
S := '3';
R := '4';
S := S + R
```

This will not assign the value '7' to the variable S, because the sum of two characters values is not defined, no matter what those values are.

We should also point out the distinction between string values and the values assigned to variables whose type is user-defined (Section 8.3). String values are literals, or constants, and are quoted whenever they appear in a program. The values of a user-defined type are identifers and are never quoted. For example, SUN is a value that can be assigned to a variable of type DAY (defined in Section 8.3), and 'SUN' is a value that can be assigned to a variable of type STRING3. Note also that string variables can be used on either input or output, but user-defined types are for internal use only.

9.2.2 Assignment from External Data

The assignment of value to character-valued variables from external data is a little surprising, and more than a little confusing, since it is not quite analogous to the assignment to numeric variables. Recall that with numeric variables the forms for external and internal assignment were similar. That is, if X is of type INTEGER, one could assign the value 9 to X either by writing

```
X := 9
```

or by putting the value 9 on a data card and executing the statement:

```
READ(X)
```

in the program. In both cases the form of the constant is the same.

However, with character variables this is not the case. For example, suppose S is a CHAR variable. A value could be assigned to S by an assignment statement:

```
S := 'M'
```

but if the same value were to be assigned by execution of the statement READ(S) the value would have to be given on a data card without quotes. Stated in another way, a quote on a data card is just a character, and not a punctuation mark. In fact, there is no punctuation on a data card supplying values for character variables. Even the blank, which is used to punctuate (separate) numeric values on a data card, is just another character on a card supplying values to character variables. Every column of the card supplies a character, reading from left to right.

For example, suppose A, B and C are CHAR variables and the statement

```
READ(A, B, C)
```

is executed. The next three card columns will be read, and whatever they contain will be assigned as values to A, B and C, respectively. If they happen to be blank, then blank will be assigned as value to each of these variables. In reading values for CHAR variables, PASCAL will not scan along the card looking for a non-blank value, as it would for numeric variables. Suppose the card contained

```
'M' 'N' 'P'
```

probably because the programmer forgot that you do not quote values on a data card. The value "M" would be assigned to variable B, and the value "'" would be assigned to both A and C.

To control this assignment you obviously need a means of controlling the position on the card from which the reading starts. There are two aspects to this. You can move to the right just by reading into a variable set aside for this purpose. For example, suppose SKIP is a CHAR variable not used for anything else in the procedure. Then, to skip over N columns of a card, write:

```
FOR I := 1 TO N DO
    READ(SKIP)
```

To advance the reading position to the first column of the next card, regardless of where it was before, there is a READLN statement. It is comparable to READ except that after it is executed the rest of the card being read is discarded. The next READ or READLN statement begins reading with column 1 of the next card. This provides all sorts of opportunities to make errors. For example, suppose you have one character in the first column of each of a set of data cards and you want to read these values into the elements of a CHAR array named ALPHA. The following program segment might be used:

```
FOR I := 1 TO N DO
    READLN(ALPHA[I])
```

This might, or might not, work properly, depending upon what came before it in execution of the program. If this is the first READ or READLN action in the program it will work all right, but if some previous READ statement has read part of a card, then this segment will give improper results. To make this segment independent of what goes before you might precede it by a READLN statement without any list of variables. It reads nothing, but causes the next following READ to begin on a new card.

```
READLN;
FOR I := 1 TO N DO
    READLN(ALPHA[I])
```

But now what happens if the last input statement executed was a READLN? The modified segment will discard one card without reading it. This too could produce improper results. It is possible to write programs that will read character values properly, but it is not easy.

9.2.2.1 Mixed Character and Numeric Data

The situation really gets complicated when you try to intermix character and numeric data. We will give some indication how this can be done, but strongly recommend that you avoid doing this until you are sure you thoroughly understand the reading process. If you have any control over the format of the data cards that your program will read, keep numeric and character values on separate cards. However, if you must read cards with mixed character and numeric values, the following should help you understand the difficulty.

Suppose that X and Y are INTEGER variables and SA and SB are CHAR variables. Consider execution of the statement:

```
READ(X, SA, Y, SB)
```

Assume that the "next" data is the following:

5P79Q

The result of executing the READ is:

X = 5, SA = P, Y = 79, SB = Q

However, suppose the next data had been:

5 79Q5

The result would be:

X = 5, SA = blank, Y = 79, SB = Q

If the data had been:

543P 79 Q

the result would be:

X = 543, SA = P, Y = 79, SB = blank

The rules are the following:

1. For a numeric variable, the scan ignores blanks to find the start of a numeric value. It continues as long as the next character is a valid continuation of a numeric value. That is, it terminates with the first character that cannot be included in the numeric value -- say a blank or a letter. (Note that the decimal point, the plus and minus signs and the letter E can be in a numeric value, in addition to the digits.)

2. For a character variable, the next character is read, regardless of what it is. In particular, blank has no special significance -- it is simply one possible character.

In light of this, suppose you wanted the results to be:

X = 5, SA = 6, Y = 79, SB = Q

There is simply <u>no way</u> that execution of

READ(X, SA, Y, SB)

can produce this result. For example, suppose the data were:

5679Q

The result would be:

X = 5679, SA = Q, Y = ?

since there is nothing to terminate the reading of X with the single digit 5. On the other hand, if you terminate the value of X with a blank:

```
5 679Q
```

the result would be:

```
X = 5, SA = blank, Y = 679, SB = Q
```

One way to achieve the desired results would be to modify the READ statement so that it reads and discards the blank required to terminate the numeric value for X:

```
READ(X, SA, SA, Y, SB)
```

Then the correct form of the data would be:

```
5 679Q
```

Good luck.

9.2.2.2 String Assignment from External Data

The final surprise (and disappointment) is that you cannot read a string from a data card without a loop. Suppose STR has been declared to be a string of length 4:

```
VAR STR: STRING4
```

Although you can assign a value to each element of STR with a 4-character literal in an assignment statement:

```
STR := 'ABCD'
```

you cannot write

```
READ(STR)
```

and give the literal

```
ABCD
```

on a data card. You must use a loop, and read the four characters from the data card, one at a time:

```
FOR I := 1 TO 4 DO
    READ(STR[I])
```

9.2.3 Conditions

Character and string expressions can be used in conditions. The form is:

expression^1 relation expression^2

The expressions are like those that appear on the right side of an assignment statement. That is, they can consist of a variable, a literal, or certain built-in functions that produce a character value (see Section 9.2.4). The relations are the same as those used for arithmetic-expression conditions (listed in Section 4.3.1.3). Conditions may be simple or compound, as described in Section 4.3.1.4.

The values being compared in a condition <u>must be of the same length</u>. The relationship between the two values depends upon an ordering that has been defined over all of the valid characters that might be included in such a value. This ordering is called the "collating sequence" of the characters. Like the choice of characters that are used, the ordering of the characters differs between languages and between computers. The particular ordering that is used for PASCAL characters on Control Data Corporation computers is:

```
:ABCDEFGHIJKLMNOPQRSTUVWXYZ0123456789+-*/()$= ,.'[]%"↰!&#?<>@\^;
```

Any character is this sequence is said to be "less than" a character to its right in the sequence. This is, in effect, an extension of "alphabetical order", with the digits higher than Z, and the special characters higher than 9. Note that the blank character lies between "=" and ",". (The particular order shown here is quite different from that used on IBM computers -- be careful.)

The consequences of this ordering are illustrated by the following examples of conditions. All of these examples are <u>true</u>:

```
'A' = 'A'
'A' <> any other character
'AB' = 'AB'
'A5' <> 'AB', 'A5' > 'AB'
'A ' <> ' A', 'A ' < ' A'
'MOORE, C. G.' > 'MOORE  C. G.'
'MOORE, CHAS.' < 'MOORE, C.    '
```

The position of the blank and the special characters <u>above</u> the letters and digits results in some orderings that don't agree with common usage. For example:

```
'4.5' > '450'
'  1' > '1.5'
'WILLIAM ' > 'WILLIAMS'
```

Normal usage would be better preserved if the special characters were below the letters and digits, but CDC PASCAL doesn't do it that way.

9.2.4 Built-in Functions

Several of the PASCAL built-in functions, listed in Section 3.3, are concerned with character values. Some require a character-valued argument, some produce a character-valued results, and some do both.

ORD(x) -- The result (INTEGER) is the ordinal number of the argument x in the set of values of which x is a member. When x is a character value, the result is the position of that value in the collating sequence. (The collating sequence depends upon the particular computer being used, and even the particular installation.) Position numbers begin with 0. For example, ORD('A') is 1, ORD(':') is 0, ORD('2') is 29.

CHR(x) -- The result (CHAR) is the character in the position in the collating sequence given by the argument. Only integers 0 to 63 are allowed as arguments. (Any other argument causes an error.) For example, CHR(0) is ':', CHR(26) is 'Z'.

Note that ORD and CHR are inverse functions, relative to the character set. That is:

```
CHR(ORD('A')) = 'A'
ORD(CHR(5)) = 5
```

SUCC(x) -- The result is the successor value, relative to the argument value. If the argument is a character value, the result is the 'next" value in the collating sequence. (The collating sequence depends upon the particular computer being used, and even the particular installation.) For example, SUCC('G') is 'H', SUCC('5') is '6'. It is an error if the argument is the "last" value, and hence has no successor.

PRED(x) -- The result is the predecessor value, relative to the argument value. If the argument is a character value, the result is the preceding value in the collating sequence. For example, PRED('0') is 'Z', PRED('A') is ':'. It is an error if the argument is the "first" value, and hence has no predecessor.

Note that SUCC and PRED are inverse functions, relative to the character set. That is:

```
SUCC(PRED('A')) = 'A'
PRED(SUCC('A')) = 'A'
```

9.2.5 Display

The display of character and string values is relatively straightforward. Such variables may be included in the list of WRITE and WRITELN statements. There is no fixed field width for these variables, as in the case of numeric and BOOLEAN variables. Instead, the field width is just equal to the number of characters to be printed. That is, a simple CHAR variable prints a single column, and a string prints in a field whose width is equal to the length of the string.

Note that, unlike the READ statement, strings *may* be given on a WRITE list and have their value displayed without having to write a loop to print the value character by character.

9.3 Examples of Character Processing

Consider the following problem:

> Given a deck of data cards, each containing a person's name consisting of first-name followed by last-name, print a list of the last-names that begin with the letter "T".
>
> The deck will have exactly 50 cards, and each name will be at most 20 characters long.

Three different programs to perform this task are given below. The first program (9.3a) reads all the names into an array, then selects and prints. In this case, the array is not necessary, since the names could be examined as they are read. Note that the selection criterion is a search for the sequence "ƀT", which presumably indicates the beginning of a last name starting with "T". This program illustrates the topics of Section 9, but is highly vulnerable to errors in the data. For example, each of the following names would be considered to have a last-name beginning with "T":

```
ROBER T JONES
ROBERT T. JONES
 TOM BROWN
```

The second program (9.3b) does not read all the names in advance, and hence does not need an array to store them. It simply reads one character at a time, and prints characters beginning with a "T" following a blank. BOOLEAN variables are used to remember what characters have been seen.

The third alternative (9.3c) is similar to (9.3b), but uses the EOF and EOLN built-in functions to limit the reading. In this case this ignores the given information about the number and length of names -- but in real problems such information is usually not given. In this respect (9.3c) is probably the most realistic of the three alternatives, and the most suggestive of what would actually be done in practice. Note also that (9.3c) uses only one BOOLEAN variable to remember the state of the reading process.

We must also note that there is a peculiarity of the CDC operating system that affects programs of this type. This is discussed in Appendix B.2.4.

(9.3a)

```
(* PRINT LAST NAMES BEGINNING WITH 'T' *)
PROGRAM PRINTNAMES(INPUT, OUTPUT);
LABEL 9001;
TYPE STRING20 = PACKED ARRAY[1..20] OF CHAR;
VAR NAME: ARRAY[1..50] OF STRING20; (* LIST OF NAMES *)
    NM: STRING20; (* CURRENT NAME *)
    I, J, K: INTEGER;
BEGIN (* PRINTNAMES *)
  (* LOAD NAME[1..50] *)
    FOR I := 1 TO 50 DO
      BEGIN (* LOAD LOOP *)
         J := 1;
         WHILE NOT EOLN AND (J <= 20) DO
           BEGIN
              READ(NM[J]);
              J := J + 1
           END;
         READLN;
         FOR K := J TO 20 DO
              NM[K] := ' ';
         NAME[I] := NM
      END; (* LOAD LOOP *)
  (* PRINT NAMES IN NAME[1..50] WITH ' T' *)
    FOR I := 1 TO 50 DO
      BEGIN (* NAME LOOP *)
         NM := NAME[I];
         FOR J := 1 TO 19 DO
           BEGIN (* SCAN LOOP *)
              IF (NM[J] = ' ') AND (NM[J+1] = 'T') THEN
                BEGIN
                   WRITE(' ');
                   FOR K := J+1 TO 20 DO
                        WRITE(NM[K]);
                   WRITELN;
                   GOTO 9001
                END
           END; (* SCAN LOOP *)
         9001:;
      END (* NAME LOOP *)
END.  (* PRINTNAMES *)
```

(9.3b)

```
(* PRINT LAST NAMES BEGINNING WITH 'T' *)
PROGRAM PRINTNAMES(INPUT, OUTPUT);
VAR CH: CHAR; (* CURRENT CHARACTER *)
    BSEEN: BOOLEAN; (* BLANK HAS BEEN SEEN *)
    PRINT: BOOLEAN; (* NAME IS BEING PRINTED *)
    CHL: INTEGER; (* LENGTH OF NAME *)
    CARD: INTEGER;
BEGIN (* PRINTNAMES *)
    WRITE(' ');
    READ(CH);
    FOR CARD := 1 TO 50 DO
      BEGIN (* NAME LOOP *)
         BSEEN := FALSE;
         PRINT := FALSE;
         CHL := 1;
         WHILE NOT EOLN AND (CHL <= 20) DO
           BEGIN (* CHAR LOOP *)
              IF NOT PRINT AND BSEEN AND (CH = 'T')
                THEN PRINT := TRUE
                ELSE BSEEN := FALSE;
              IF NOT PRINT AND (CH = ' ')
                THEN BSEEN := TRUE;
              IF PRINT
                THEN WRITE(CH);
              READ(CH);
              CHL := CHL + 1
           END (* CHAR LOOP *)
         IF PRINT THEN
           BEGIN
              WRITELN;
              WRITE(' ')
           END
      END (* NAME LOOP *)
END.  (* PRINTNAMES *)
```

(9.3c)

```
(* PRINT LAST NAMES BEGINNING WITH 'T' *)
PROGRAM PRINTNAMES(INPUT, OUTPUT);
VAR CH: CHAR; (* CURRENT CHARACTER *)
    TSEEN: BOOLEAN; (* 'T' HAS BEEN SEEN *)
BEGIN (* PRINTNAMES *)
    WRITE(' ');
    READ(CH);
    WHILE NOT EOF DO
      BEGIN (* CHAR LOOP *)
         TSEEN := FALSE;
         WHILE NOT EOLN DO
           BEGIN (* T LOOP *)
              IF NOT TSEEN AND (CH = ' ') THEN
                BEGIN
                   READ(CH);
                   TSEEN := (CH = 'T')
                END;
              IF TSEEN
                THEN WRITE(CH);
              READ(CH)
           END; (* T LOOP *)
         IF TSEEN THEN
           BEGIN
              WRITELN;
              WRITE(' ')
           END
      END (* CHAR LOOP *)
END.  (* PRINTNAMES *)
```

A second example is a program to convert commas to colons. The input is a deck of punched cards containing textual information which may include commas. Each line of text is contained on one card. For example, each line of text in this book would be given as a separate card. The program should read each card, and print a line with the card contents -- except that each occurrence of a comma on the card should appear as a colon in the printed line.

The basic strategy is to build an array of characters, one element of the array for each member of the character set. The program then replaces the comma in that array by a colon. Then it reads each character of the text, one at a time, and writes the corresponding element of the array. The specific task of replacing commas with colons could be performed by a much simpler program. We have chosen this strategy to illustrate a much more powerful and general technique. This strategy could make any number of character substitutions as easily as the single substitution required for this problem.

Two different programs are given below, both implementing this same strategy. They differ only in the programming technique used to implement this strategy. (9.3d) is the more obvious version, since it uses integer subscripts for the character array CS, as we have done with arrays in all previous examples. However, (9.3e) takes advantage of the fact that PASCAL allows any scalar type (and not just integers) to be used as a subscript of an array. It this case it is appropriate to use type CHAR for the subscripts.

(9.3d)
```
(* CONVERT COMMAS TO COLONS *)
PROGRAM CONVCC(INPUT, OUTPUT);
VAR CS: ARRAY[0..63] OF CHAR; (* CHAR SET *)
    CH: CHAR; (* INPUT CHARACTER *)
    I: INTEGER;
BEGIN (* CONVCC *)
    (* SET UP CHARACTER SET ARRAY *)
        FOR I := 0 TO 63 DO
            CS[I] := CHR(I);
        CS[ORD(',')] := ':';
    (* PROCESS TEXT *)
        WHILE NOT EOF DO
          BEGIN (* TEXT LOOP *)
            WHILE NOT EOLN DO
              BEGIN
                READ(CH);
                WRITE(CS[ORD(CH)])
              END;
            WRITELN;
            READLN
          END (* TEXT LOOP *)
END.  (* CONVCC *)
```

(9.3e)
```
(* CONVERT COMMAS TO COLONS *)
PROGRAM CONVCC(INPUT, OUTPUT);
VAR CS: ARRAY[CHAR] OF CHAR; (* CHAR SET *)
    CH: CHAR; (* INPUT CHARACTER *)
    IC: CHAR; (* INDEX CHAR *)
BEGIN (* CONVCC *)
    (* SET UP CHARACTER SET ARRAY *)
        FOR IC := ':' TO ';' DC
            CS[IC] := IC;
        CS[','] := ':';
    (* PROCESS TEXT *)
        WHILE NOT EOF DO
          BEGIN (* TEXT LOOP *)
            WHILE NOT EOLN DO
              BEGIN
                READ(CH);
                WRITE(CS[CH])
              END;
            WRITELN;
            READLN
          END (* TEXT LOOP *)
END.  (* CONVCC *)
```

By using CHAR values as subscripts (9.3e) avoids the use of the CHR and ORD functions required in (9.3d). Probably (9.3e) would be considered the better PASCAL style, but it is not obvious whether this is because it is clearer to read, or only because it exploits a special feature of PASCAL not available in most other programming languages.

Section 9 *Summary*

1. CHAR is a standard type in PASCAL -- in addition to types REAL, INTEGER and BOOLEAN. The value of a CHAR variable is a single character. The set of valid character values is dependent on the language and the computer, but includes the letters, the digits and various special characters and punctuation marks. The declaration of a character-valued variable has the form:

VAR name^1, name^2, ... : CHAR

2. A "string" is an array of CHAR variables. The form of declaration is:

TYPE STRINGn = PACKED ARRAY[1..n] OF CHAR;
VAR name^1, name^2, ... : STRINGn

An array of strings is declared:

```
VAR name: ARRAY[index-type] OF STRINGn
```

3. The assignment statement for a CHAR variable has the form:

```
variable-name := character-valued-expression
```

The expression can be a variable, a character-constant, or a character-valued built-in function.

The assignment statement for a string is:

```
string-name := string-valued-expression
```

The expression can be a string variable or a literal. In either case its length must be identical to that of the target variable.

4. Character-valued variables may appear in the list of a READ or READLN statement. However, a string *cannot* appear in the list and be read directly -- a string must be read character-by-character by means of a loop. READ for a character-valued variable reads the *next* card column, whatever character it may contain. Character values on a data card are *not* quoted.

5. Both character-valued-variables and strings can be given in the list of a WRITE or WRITELN statement. The width of the printing field corresponds to the number of characters in the variable.

6. Character-valued or string-valued expressions of the same length can be compared in a condition. The comparison is based on an ordering (the collating sequence) of all valid characters.

7. The built-in functions ORD, CHR, SUCC and PRED can be used in character processing. EOF and EOLN are also useful.

Section 9 Exercises

Write programs for the following problems.

1. Read a string of variable length up to 40 characters, reverse the order of the characters in the string and print it out. For example, 'EVIL' becomes 'LIVE'. You may determine the input form.

2. Read a string of variable length up to 40 characters, using READ. Delete all blanks up to the first non-blank; print the result.

3. Read a string of variable length up to 40 characters, delete all characters 'A', and print the result. You may determine the input form.

4. Read in three strings, call them A, PATTERN, and REPLACEBY. Replace every occurrence of PATTERN in A by the string REPLACEBY. Print the result. For example, if we have

A BIG, BIGGER, BIGGEST   PATTERN BIG   REPLACEBY SMALL

the program should print the string

'SMALL, SMALLGER, SMALLGEST'.

Be careful. If we have

A LAST   PATTERN A   REPLACEBY EA

A should not be changed to 'LEAST', then to 'LEEAST', and then to 'LEEEAST', etc. Stop with 'LEAST'.

5. Read a string of variable length up to 40 characters and determine whether or not it is a "palindrome". (A palindrome is a string whose characters are the same whether read from left-to-right or right-to-left. For example: AHA, NOON, I, LEVEL, LON NOL.)

6. Read a three-digit integer and print it in English. For example, print 182 as ONE HUNDRED EIGHTY TWO.

7. The input consists of three two-digit numbers representing a date. The first is the day, the second the month, and the third the last two digits of the year. For example 25 12 75. Read the date in this numeric form and print it in the usual text form. For example, DECEMBER 25, 1975. Use an array for the names of the months.

8. Read in a list of words and print out (1) the number of words made up of 1 to 6 characters, (2) the number with 6 to 12 characters, and (3) the number of times the word 'THE' appears. The words appear on one card each, left-justified in columns 1 through 12.

9. Rewrite the second example in Section 9.3 so that LINE LOOP may be written:

```
READ(CH);
WRITE (CS[CH])
```

10. Write appropriate declarations for the following variables and arrays:

a. A single string of 100 letters.

b. An array of 12 strings of digits.

c. An array to count occurrences of each letter. There should be 26 elements, each to store an integer count.

Part II
Program Structure

Part II introduces no new PASCAL features. It is entirely concerned with ways in which the statements presented in Part I should be used to enhance the clarity, readability and understandability of programs. We assume not only that you can now write PASCAL statements to perform simple tasks, but also that you realize that there are various different ways of performing the same task. Once you pass the first threshold of being happy to find any way at all of programming a given task, you should become concerned with which of several possible ways is better.

A program to solve a particular problem is not unique -- many different programs could solve the same problem. But although different programs may produce the same final answers, there may still be significant differences between them and hence strong reasons to prefer one form of program over another. Some of the possible reasons for prefering one program over another are:

1. One is easier to write than the other.

2. One is easier to test and show correctness than the other.

3. One is easier to change, if problem requirements are later altered.

4. One takes less computer time to execute than the other.

5. One is shorter and requires fewer variables -- hence requires less computer memory space during execution.

In Part II we are concerned with the first three of these reasons, which are generally involved with a form of programming that is <u>easy to read and understand</u>. This form does not necessarily produce programs that are efficient as far as the computer is concerned (reasons 4 and 5), but neither are they obviously inefficient. At this point <u>human efficiency</u> is more important to us than computer efficiency and we will concentrate on a type of programming that is oriented to human understanding.

Programs are <u>not only</u> meant to convey information to a computer; programs are written by people <u>to be read</u> by people, and for many reasons:

1. Except for trivial problems, programs are rarely completed at a single sitting. Programs take several days to over a year to complete, and you must often review what you have done before.

2. Programs are rarely entirely correct on the first try, and the testing process requires that the program be read.

3. A programming task is often divided among several people who must read and understand portions of each other's work, so that their sections communicate properly.

4. Program segments are often reused in contexts other than the one for which originally written. To do so it is necessary to understand exactly what the segment does.

5. Programs often need to be modified to meet changes in problem requirements.

Most people read programs not for enjoyment, but in order to <u>understand what the program does when executed by a computer</u>. This does not just mean what it will do in one particular execution with one particular set of input data, but what it will do in general, for any possible set of data, any choice of execution options, and any other conditions of context or environment. This is a difficult task at best, and the reader needs all the help he can get.

We must of course understand the precise meaning of each statement type in the programming language so that we can, if necessary, trace or simulate the action of the computer. In theory, we can simulate the entire execution and thereby understand the meaning of any program. In practice this just isn't reasonable. Even for programs of modest size we lack the time or patience to read them as if we were a computer. So we are forced to try to read programs in a way that is quite different from a computer. For example, consider the simple program segment:

```
TOTAL := 0;
FOR I := 1 TO N DO
    TOTAL := TOTAL + ARR[I]
```

Depending upon the value of N, the computer may execute hundreds or even thousands of statements from this segment. Regardless of the value of N, the human reader should regard this as a single task: <u>compute the sum of the values of ARR[1..N]</u>. Instead of making the reader figure this out for himself, the writer can help by describing the task just this way in a heading comment:

```
(* SET TOTAL TO SUM OF VALUES OF ARR[1..N] *)
    TOTAL := 0;
    FOR I := 1 TO N DO
         TOTAL := TOTAL + ARR[I]
```

As far as the computer is concerned the program is unchanged -- the presence or absence of comments, and the contents of comments are immaterial. But the human reader now has a choice as to what to read: either the heading comment or the program indented under the comment. He can read the comment to find out what the segment does, or the program statements to find out how the task is performed.

Being able to understand substantial programs depends on our being able to understand them at a level higher than that of the individual PASCAL statement. To facilitate reading a program in this way the programmer must structure the program in terms of higher-level units, and organize and present the program so that its structure is clear and obvious. If this is carefully done it is much easier to view the program in terms of larger units and to understand its action without a statement-by-statement trace of execution.

For example, consider the two program segments given below. These segments give identical results; they include exactly the same PASCAL statements. They differ only in that in (IIb) the statements have been slightly reordered into a more logical grouping, indentation has been used to show the relationship between various statements, and comments have been added to summarize the purpose of various subsections. These two segments are equivalent as far as the computer is concerned, but the second is much clearer and easier for us to understand. This particular task is simple enough that either form of the program can be figured out, but it is easier to understand (IIb). If the program required several hundred statements the form illustrated by (IIa) would be very difficult to understand -- and yet several hundred statements is not really a large program. The larger the program, the more important it is to use an understandable style.

```
(IIa)   TOTAL := 0; NREAD := 0;
        FOR I := 1 TO T DO M[I] := 0;
        I := 0; WHILE NREAD < N DO BEGIN
        READ(A); IF A = 0 THEN GOTO 9020;
        IF A > 0 THEN BEGIN TOTAL := TOTAL + A;
        I := I + 1; M[I] := A; NREAD := NREAD + 1
        END END; 9020:
```

```
(IIb)
     (* SET M[1..T] TO ZEROES *)
         FOR I := 1 TO T DO
              M[I] := 0
     (* READ VALUES UNTIL N HAVE BEEN READ OR UNTIL 0 IS READ *)
     (* STORE POSITIVE VALUES IN M[1..I] AND TOTAL IN SUM *)
         I := 0;
         TOTAL := 0;
         NREAD := 0;
         WHILE NREAD < N DO
           BEGIN (* READ LOOP *)
              READ(A);
              IF A = 0 THEN GOTO 9020;
              IF A > 0 THEN
                BEGIN
                   TOTAL := TOTAL + A;
                   I := I + 1;
                   M[I] := A;
                   NREAD := NREAD + 1
                END
           END; (* READ LOOP *)
         9020:
```

Consider the ways in which the <u>writer</u> of (IIb) has undertaken to help the <u>reader</u>. Most importantly, he shows with comments and indentation that the program consists of two subtasks that are relatively independent. The first clears M to zeroes; the second reads and sums. The same two subtasks are present in (IIa), but the reader must discover this for himself. Not only does he not have comments and indentation to aid him; the statement order does not suggest this logical division. (IIa) starts with two statements that are part of the initialization of the second subtask. As far as the computer is concerned these can just as well be first, but it diverts the human reader to find these statements that are not related to or needed by their immediate successors. The point is that <u>(IIa) must be studied as a single entity</u>, while <u>(IIb) can be studied as a sequence of smaller, simpler subtasks</u>. Even the task of understanding the individual statements is easier in (IIb). To understand the extent of a loop in (IIa) the reader must scan the entire program and count ENDs very carefully. In (IIb) the extent of each loop is indicated by indentation, and for longer loops confirmed by the matching comments following the BEGIN and END of the loop.

The style of (IIb) is recommended, not as a matter of consideration for some hypothetical reader of your program, but simply as a matter of self-interest. You will repeatedly have to <u>read and understand your own programs</u>. The process of completing later parts requires re-reading earlier parts; the process of testing requires frequent re-reading. The time spent in carefully organizing and presenting a program is handsomely repaid before you have finished with the program.

Section 1 Basic Program Units

The previous section stated our objective of making programs more readily understandable to a human reader. Now we propose a systematic method by which this can be done.

The easiest program construction to understand is a sequence of actions that has no loops or branches. That is, given a sequence

```
S1
S2
S3
```

we know that S1 will be executed first, then S2, and finally S3. However, it must be obvious from the examples of Part I, and even from the statement types of PASCAL, that programs must have loops and branches. In a sense, what we are going to do is try to hide that fact. We will try to write programs that actually contain loops and branches in such a way that they can be read and understood as if they were a simple sequence of actions. In effect, we will say that it is useful to be able to regard the execution of a program as "first S1, then S2, and finally S3", even though we know that internally S2 involves a loop.

We are interested in identifying patterns of statements that can be usefully regarded as a single unit for purposes of reading and understanding the action of a program. The three patterns that dominate are called "the compound statement", "the repetition unit" and "the alternate selection unit". Each of these basic units behaves as if it were a single "statement" in some language that is at a higher level than PASCAL. The key point is that, as a statement, each of these units has a single entry point and a single exit point. The only control of flow between such units is the normal sequential order -- the order in which they are written.

1.1 The Compound Statement

Any simple sequence of statements that follow one after another can be considered a "compound statement". For example, a sequence of three assignment statements could be considered a compound statement, or unit, to interchange the values of two variables:

```
(* INTERCHANGE VALUES OF A AND B *)
   T := A;
   A := B;
   B := T
```

We require only that the statements perform some logically related task and that the statements follow one another in normal sequential order. Other examples are:

```
(* PRINT TITLE AND HEADING FOR TABLE *)
   WRITELN('0',
     'TEMPERATURE-PRESSURE EQUIVALENTS');
   WRITELN('0',
     'STANDARD CONCENTRATION WITHOUT CATALYST');
   WRITELN('0',
     'TEMPERATURE    PRESSURE    REACTION TIME')

(* INITIALIZE TABLE LINE GENERATION *)
   LINECOUNT := 0;
   COLUMNSUM := 0;
   TIMEBASE := TEMPBASE/EQUILCONST
```

We want to be able to regard an entire sequence of PASCAL statements as if they were a single statement in some even-higher-level language than PASCAL. A single statement has a single entry point and a single exit point:

```
          ┌────┐
enter───>│ Si │───>exit
          └────┘
```

So if a sequence is to behave as a single statement we require that the entire sequence has a single entry point and a single exit point:

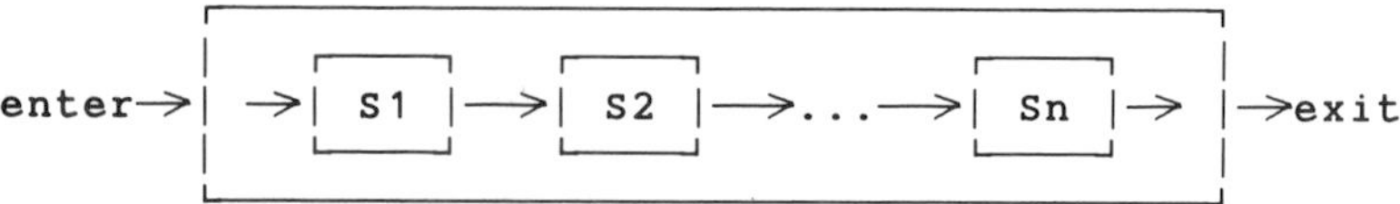

Figure 1. A Compound Statement

The heading comment of a compound statement summarizes the action of the entire statement; the individual PASCAL statements indented beneath the heading comment specify <u>how</u> this action is performed.

We used the concept of a compound statement in Sections I.4.2 and I.4.4 to specify that a sequence of statements were to act as a single statement for purposes of repetition or conditional execution. For example, the form for conditional execution is:

```
IF condition THEN
  BEGIN
    S1;
    S2;
    ...
    Sn
  END
```

In that context the compound statement is significant to PASCAL and we must indicate that the entire sequence S1;...Sn is to be treated as a single unit by marking the beginning and end of the sequence with BEGIN and END. A heading comment and indentation would not suffice since neither of these is recognized by PASCAL. Now we are talking about structuring a program for the benefit of a human reader -- to whom comments and indentation are significant, but for whom the BEGIN-END delimiters are unnecessary. The general rules for format of a compound statement are:

> Write a comment to summarize the purpose (or action) of the compound statement and indent the comment so it is left-aligned with the heading of the preceding unit. The individual components of the unit are left-aligned with respect to each other and indented with respect to the heading comment.

1.2 <u>The Repetition Unit</u>

Repetition is a common task in programs, and it is relatively difficult for a human reader to comprehend. With the other types of units the execution sequence is at least similar to the sequence that appears on the program listing; with repetition it is very different. Hence it is crucial that sections involving repetition be carefully organized and clearly presented.

<u>Repetition is always accomplished with some type of loop</u>. The loop may be preceded by initialization statements and it may be followed by termination statements. The idea of the "repetition unit" is to regard this entire sequence as a single entity:

```
(1.2a)    (* Description of what the unit does *)
               Sequence of statements to initialize for loop;
               Loop control
                 BEGIN (* loop-name *)
                    Body of loop
                 END; (* loop-name *)
               Sequence of statements to terminate the unit
```

The general form of a WHILE loop is shown in Figure 2. The "cond" represents the condition of a WHILE loop and indicates by becoming false when the loop should terminate. The statements S1 through Sn form the body of the loop. This form of loop was discussed in Section I.4.3.1.1. The repetition unit can also be built around the other forms of loop -- the REPEAT loop (Section I.4.3.1.2) and the FOR loop (Section I.4.3.2).

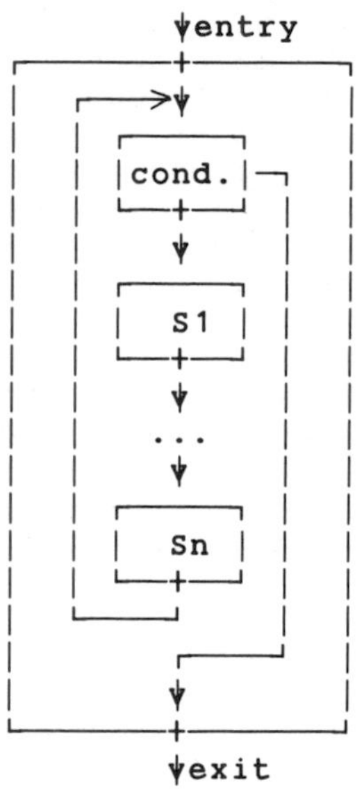

Figure 2. WHILE Loop

Although the individual statements in a loop may be repeated, and the condition causes a branch, taken as a whole, the loop has a single entry point and a single exit point. It can be regarded as a single statement, so that with the initializing and terminating statements (1.2a) is a single-entry, single-exit compound statement. But because of the presence of the loop we recognize it as a special type of compound statement and call it a "repetition unit". Examples are given below.

```
(* SET SUM TO SUM OF INTEGERS FROM 14 THRU 728 *)
    INT := 14;
    SUM := 14;
    WHILE INT < 728 DO
      BEGIN
         INT := INT + 1;
         SUM := SUM + INT
      END

(* MOVE A[J..K] TO B[J..K] *)
    FOR I := J TO K DO
         B[I] := A[I]

(* READ INTO X[1..N] UNTIL EOF OR X FULL *)
    I := 0;
    REPEAT
         I := I + 1;
         READ(X[I])
      UNTIL (I = N) OR EOF

(* TITLE AND PRINT A[1..M] *)
    WRITELN('0VALUES OF A[1..M]');
    WRITELN;
    FOR J := 1 TO M DO
         WRITELN(' ', A[J]);
    WRITELN('0END OF A[1..M]')
```

The general rules for the format of a repetition unit are:

1. Write a heading comment that summarizes <u>what</u> the <u>entire</u> unit does. Indent this comment so it is left-aligned with the heading of the preceding unit.

2. The individual components of the unit -- initialization, loop and termination -- are left-aligned with respect to each other, and indented with respect to the heading comment.

3. The statements that constitute the body of the loop should be indented with respect to the WHILE, REPEAT, or FOR statement that controls the loop (which means two levels of indentation with respect to the heading comment of the unit). The BEGIN and END have an intermediate indentation -- indented to the right with respect to the control statement, to show that they delimit the compound statement being repeated; but with the statements of the body further indented so that the BEGIN and END are easily identifiable. In the case of a REPEAT loop the BEGIN and END are usually omitted, in which case the UNTIL phrase is given the same indentation that an END would have.

4. If the loop body is long or complex it should be treated as a compound statement (or as several compound statements), with a heading comment that describes what the body does <u>on each repetition</u>.

5. If the body of a loop is more than a few statements, or if there is more than one level of nesting, the BEGIN should be followed with a comment that assigns a name to the loop. The identical comment should also be given on the END so that the matching of BEGINs and ENDs is clear to the reader. We have adopted the convention that these loop-names always end in the characters "LOOP" to make the nature of these comments immediately obvious.

1.3 The Alternate Selection Unit

1.3.1 The Single-Alternative Unit

The third basic type of unit occurs when one of several alternative tasks is to be selected for execution. The simplest and most common case is when there are two alternatives, but one of the two is null. That is, there is one statement that may or may not be executed. This is of course the "conditional execution" described in Section I.4.4 and programmed with the IF construction. However, now we want to make the IF construction (Figure 2 of I.4.4) conform to our single-entry, single-exit requirement. We do this simply by regarding the entire construction as a single unit, as shown in Figure 3.

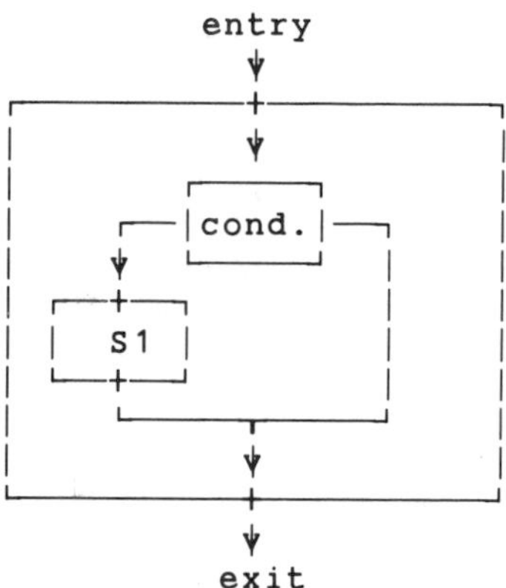

Figure 3. The Single-Alternative Unit

There is a single entry-point and a common exit-point whether or not the conditional statement is executed. The following are examples of single-alternative or conditional units:

```
(1.3.1a) (* REPLACE NEGATIVE X BY 0 *)
             IF X[I] < 0
                  THEN X[I] := 0
```

```
(1.3.1b) (* REPLACE NEGATIVE DATUM *)
              IF DATUM < 0
                   THEN READ(DATUM)

(1.3.1c) (* DISCARD AND REPORT NEGATIVE DATUM *)
              IF DATUM < 0 THEN
                BEGIN
                   ERRORCOUNT := ERRORCOUNT + 1;
                   WRITELN('0ERROR NUMBER', ERRORCOUNT);
                   WRITELN(' NEGATIVE DATUM', DATUM);
                   READ(DATUM)
                END

(1.3.1d) (* SAVE NEW MAXIMUM VAL *)
              IF VAL > MAXVAL
                   THEN MAXVAL := VAL

(1.3.1e) (* SAVE MAXVAL AND POINTER MAXLOC IF NEW MAXIMUM*)
              IF VAL[I] > MAXVAL THEN
                BEGIN
                   MAXVAL := VAL[I];
                   MAXLOC := I
                END
```

Since single-alternative units are often short and obvious, as in these examples, we often shortcut the full-blown unit format shown above. The criteria, as always, are readability and clarity. If the actual PASCAL statements are clear and obvious then a summary comment is not needed. In fact, being redundant, the comment then tends to clutter and obscure the program rather than clarify it. Some judgement is required. In the examples above (1.3.1a), (1.3.1b) and (1.3.1d) need no heading comment and perhaps are clearer without it. The indentation is also not necessary in these cases. They would be better written as:

```
IF X[I] < 0 THEN X[I] := 0

IF DATUM < 0 THEN READ(DATUM)

IF VAL > MAXVAL THEN MAXVAL := VAL
```

On the other hand, (1.3.1c) is probably large enough that the heading comment is useful, and (1.3.1e) could be written either way.

Note that if the conditional statement is itself a compound statement the BEGIN and END delimiters must be used. The extent of the conditional statement must be conveyed to PASCAL as well as the human reader, and PASCAL does not consider comments and indentation.

The general rules for the format of a single-alternative unit are:

1. If the unit is long or complex it should be treated

formally as a distinct unit, with a heading comment left-aligned with the heading of the preceding unit. The IF should be indented with respect to the heading, and the alternative should be indented with respect to the IF. (It doesn't matter whether the THEN is on the line with the IF or is considered part of the body. The structure is quite clear either way.)

2. If the unit is short and obvious it should just be written as a simple statement. That is, there should be no heading comment and the IF should be left-aligned with the preceding statement. If the alternative does not entirely fit on the line beginning with IF, its continuation should be indented with respect to the IF (just like any other continuation line).

1.3.2 The Two-Alternative Unit

The case with two non-null alternatives, programmed with the IF-THEN-ELSE construction (see Section I.4.4), can still be viewed as a unit with a single exit point, as shown in Figure 4.

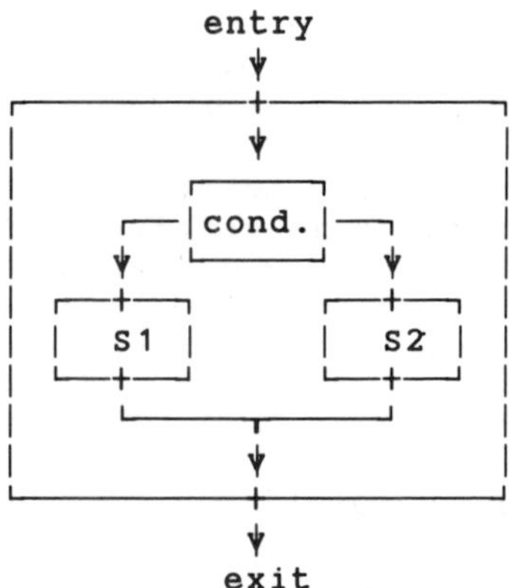

Figure 4. The Two-Alternative Unit

Examples of two-alternative units are the following:

```
IF A < B
    THEN X := B
    ELSE X := A

(* SET VAL FROM A OR DATA LIST *)
    IF A[I] <> 0
         THEN VAL := A[I]
         ELSE READ(VAL)
```

```
IF NEWVAL >= 0
    THEN POSCOUNT := POSCOUNT + 1
    ELSE NEGCOUNT := NEGCOUNT + 1

(* READ NEXT VALUE INTO NUMBER OR LETTER *)
    IF TYPEFLAG = 1
      THEN BEGIN
          READ(NUMBER[I]);
          I := I + 1
        END
      ELSE BEGIN
          READ(LETTER[J]);
          J := J + 1
        END
```

The two-alternative unit should <u>not be used to combine two unrelated tasks</u>. The following is an example of <u>poor usage</u>:

```
(* PRINT TITLE OR ERROR MESSAGE *)
    IF N > 50
      THEN BEGIN
          WRITELN('0EXCESSIVE DATA');
          GOTO 85
        END
      ELSE BEGIN
          WRITELN('0LIST OF INPUT DATA');
          WRITELN
        END
```

The title in this example should not be viewed as an alternative to the error message. It would be clearer when presented in the following way:

```
(* TEST FOR EXCESSIVE DATA *)
    IF N > 50
      THEN BEGIN
          WRITELN('0EXCESSIVE DATA');
          GOTO 85
        END;
WRITELN('0LIST OF INPUT DATA');
WRITELN
```

The general rules for the format of a two-alternative unit are:

1. If the unit is long or complex it should be treated formally as a distinct unit, with a heading comment left-aligned with the heading of the preceding unit. The IF should be indented with respect to the heading, and the two alternatives should be indented with respect to the IF.

2. The THEN and ELSE lines should be indented with respect to the IF and left-aligned with respect to each other. If the body of the alternative cannot be completed on the same line as the THEN or ELSE its continuation lines should be

indented with respect to the THEN or ELSE. The critical aspect is that the parallel relationship between the THEN and ELSE alternatives be made clear.

1.3.3 The Multiple-Alternative Unit

The general case, with more than two alternatives, is shown in Figure 5. S1 to Sn are the alternatives, one of which is to be executed; "cond" is the condition by which selection of one alternative is made.

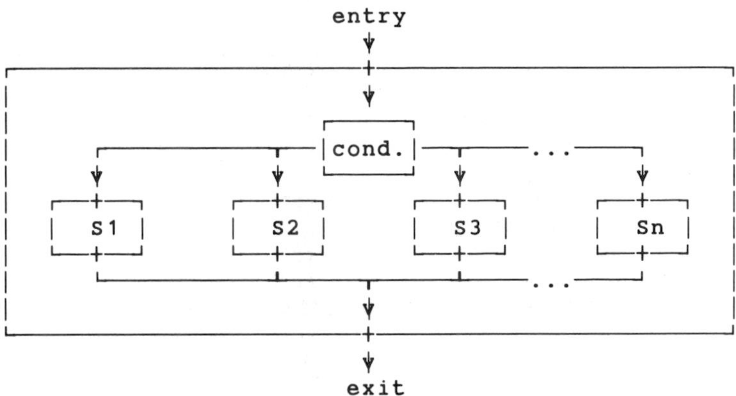

Figure 5. An Alternate Selection Unit

The entire construction has a single entry-point and a single exit and can be treated as a single unit. It is preferably programmed using the CASE statement. Examples are:

```
(1.3.3a)   (* COMPUTE TOLL, DEPENDING ON CLASS *)
               CASE CLASS OF
                    1: TOLL := 0.25;
                    2: TOLL := 0.25 + WEIGHTFACTOR;
                    3: TOLL := 0.10 + NBRPASSENGERS;
                    4: TOLL := 0.0125 * MILESDRIVEN
                 END (* CASE CLASS *)
```

```
(1.3.3b)  (* COMPUTE SCORE, DEPENDING ON RESPONSE *)
              CASE RESPONSE OF
                   'A', 'C', 'D', 'E':
                     WRITELN(' WRONG ANSWER.  THE CORRECT',
                         'ANSWER IS B) GEORGE WASHINGTON');
                   'B': BEGIN
                         WRITE('0GOOD.');
                         SCORE := SCORE + 1;
                         IF SCORE > 30 THEN
                           WRITE('  YOU KNOW THIS',
                               ' MATERIAL WELL.',
                               '  KEEP UP THE GOOD WORK.');
                         WRITELN
                       END
                END (* CASE RESPONSE *)

(1.3.3c)  TYPE QUALVAL = (POOR, FAIR, MEDIUM, GOOD, BEST);
          VAR QUALITY: QUALVAL
          ...
          (* COMPUTE PRICE, DEPENDING ON QUALITY *)
              CASE QUALITY OF
                   POOR: PRICE := QUANTITY * 0.10;
                   FAIR: PRICE := QUANTITY * 0.15;
                   MEDIUM: PRICE := QUANTITY * 0.25;
                   GOOD: PRICE := QUANTITY * 0.35;
                   BEST: PRICE := QUANTITY * 0.50 + 1.00
                END (* CASE QUALITY *)
```

There are situations in which the selection condition cannot be easily based on the values of a particular variable. Then you must construct a multiple-alternative unit using the IF statement. To illustrate the technique, we will use a variation of the toll computation example of (1.3.3a). The contrast of (1.3.3a) with (1.3.3d) and (1.3.3e) should make it obvious why the CASE statement is a clearer construction, which should be used whenever possible. Unfortunately, most programming languages lack the equivalent of PASCAL's CASE statement, hence programmers using those languages must always use the techniques illustrated in (1.3.3d) and (1.3.3e).

Two possible constructions using only the IF statement are shown in (1.3.3b) and (1.3.3e). Both are functionally equivalent and have the desirable single entry and single exit. We prefer (1.3.3d) since it is simpler and seems to exhibit more clearly the parallel relationship between the alternatives. Deeply nested IF constructions, such as (1.3.3e), are difficult to write correctly, difficult to test and to change, and very difficult to read and understand. (1.3.3d) does require the use of GOTOs, but only in a restricted way that is entirely internal to the unit. They do not add any exit points to the unit. This is an example of a situation in which the GOTO is less unattractive than the available alternatives. The GOTO is just being used to simulate the natural higher level control structure (the CASE statement), which cannot accomodate the particular selection condition required.

```
(1.3.3d)  (* COMPUTE TOLL, DEPENDING ON CLASS AND CODE *)
              IF (CLASS = 1) AND (CODE = 'P') THEN
                BEGIN
                    TOLL := 0.25;
                    GOTO 700
                END;
              IF (CLASS = 2) AND (CODE = 'P') THEN
                BEGIN
                    TOLL := 0.25 + WEIGHTFACTOR;
                    GOTO 700
                END;
              IF (CLASS = 3) AND (CODE = 'G') THEN
                BEGIN
                    TOLL := 0.10 * NBRPASSENGERS;
                    GOTO 700
                END;
              (* FOR ALL OTHER CLASSES AND CODES: *)
                    TOLL := 0.0125 * MILESDRIVEN;
              700:
```

```
(1.3.3e)  (* COMPUTE TOLL, DEPENDING ON CLASS AND CODE *)
              IF (CLASS = 1) AND (CODE = 'P')
                   THEN TOLL := 0.25
                ELSE IF (CLASS = 2) AND (CODE = 'P')
                   THEN TOLL := 0.25 + WEIGHTFACTOR
                ELSE IF (CLASS = 3) AND (CODE = 'G')
                   THEN TOLL := 0.10 * NBRPASSENGERS
                ELSE (* ALL OTHER CLASSES AND CODES *)
                   TOLL := 0.0125 * MILESDRIVEN
```

The general rules for the format of an alternate selection unit with more than two alternatives are:

1. Write a heading comment that summarizes what the entire unit does, emphasizing that one of many alternatives is to be executed. Indent this comment so it is left-aligned with the heading of the preceding unit.

2. The individual alternatives are indented with respect to the heading comment and left-aligned with respect to each other. Their alignment should show their parallel role.

3. The CASE statement should be used whenever possible to select from the alternatives. The clearest indentation convention is the following:

```
(* unit comment *)
  CASE ...
      alternative1;
      alternative2;
      ...
    END (* CASE ...  *)
```

4. When the CASE statement cannot be used and the unit must be constructed of IF statements, the indentation must be especially carefully done in order to emphasize the parallel nature of the alternatives. If the strategy shown in (1.3.3d) is used, the IF statements should be left-aligned. If the strategy of (1.3.3e) is used the ELSEs should be left-aligned. In either event the body of the alternatives should be indented with respect to the IF or ELSE so that the beginning of each alternative is emphasized.

5. If an individual alternative is long or complex it should be treated as a compound statement with its own heading comment, etc.

1.4 Units and Levels

In the preceding sections the basic units were generally described as if their components were simple PASCAL statements. Actually the components can just as well be units, since units have a single entry and exit point and in that regard behave as if they were single statements. An entire compound statement (Figure 1), a repetition unit (Figure 2) or an alternate unit (Figures 3, 4 and 5) could be inserted in the position of any one of the Si blocks in any of these figures. The properties of the units, and the rules for their presentation, remain the same whether their components are simple statements, or program units -- which in turn can have units as their components.

This means that in general there is a hierarchy of these units. At the highest level there will be a compound statement -- a simple sequence of units. Each of these can be a unit of any type, whose components are in turn also units, etc. At some lowest level the components will be single PASCAL statements. Since there is no limit either to the size of an individual unit or to the number of levels in the structure, there is no limit to the size or complexity of program that can be organized and presented in this manner.

For example, consider a program to read 100 numbers, sort them into ascending order, and print the sorted list:

```
(* READ, SORT AND PRINT A LIST OF 100 NUMBERS *)
PROGRAM RSP(INPUT, OUTPUT);

VAR A: ARRAY[1..100] OF REAL;
    T: REAL; (* TEMP FOR INTERCHANGE OF A'S *)
    I,J: INTEGER;

BEGIN (* RSP *)
  (* LOAD A[1..100] FROM DATA *)
    FOR I := 1 TO 100 DO
         READ([I]);

  (* SORT A[1..100] *)
    FOR J := 1 TO 100 DO
      BEGIN (* SORT LOOP *)
        (* PUT MIN OF A[J..100] IN A[J] *)
          FOR I := 100 DOWNTO J+1 DO
            BEGIN (* MIN LOOP *)
              IF A[I] < A[J] THEN
                BEGIN
                  T := A[I];
                  A[I] := A[J];
                  A[J] := T
                END
            END (* MIN LOOP *)
      END; (* SORT LOOP *)

  (* PRINT A[1..100] *)
    FOR I := 1 TO 100 DO
        WRITELN(' ', A[I])
END. (* RSP *)
```

The overall program RSP is a compound statement. This "statement" has three components, each of which is itself a unit. The unit actions are described by their heading comments:

```
(* LOAD A[1..100] FROM DATA *)
(* SORT A[1..100] *)
(* PRINT A[1..100] *)
```

Note that alignment clearly indicates these three statements constitute the components of RSP. That is, they are aligned with respect to each other, and they are the only lines in RSP with that alignment. The lines indented with respect to each of these lines are <u>lower levels</u> of the program. They elaborate <u>how</u> each of these tasks is to be performed. Reading the program RSP at the highest level, you see that it consists of a sequence of three actions: LOAD, then SORT, and finally PRINT. You do not need to read all of the lines to discover this. To find the action that follows LOAD, you simply scan down until you come to the <u>next line that has the same indentation</u> as LOAD. In this case, this is SORT.

Now go one level deeper, and read LOAD, SORT, or PRINT just as you read RSP. That is, look at the lines indented under SORT (those between SORT and PRINT) to see how SORT is performed. These lines constitute the components of SORT, just as LOAD, SORT, and PRINT are the components of RSP. The lines under SORT have the same indentation convention -- with respect to each other -- that was used for LOAD, SORT and PRINT at the higher level.

LOAD, SORT, and PRINT are each repetition units. The load and print units are simple repetition units, such as the examples given in Section 1.2. The sort unit is more complex. It is a repetition unit, with the body of the loop performing the task:

```
(* PUT MIN OF A[J..100] IN A[J] *)
```

This body is itself a repetition unit containing a loop named MIN LOOP. The body of MIN LOOP is a single-alternative unit (although it is not formally presented as such).

In summary, <u>every level of a program is just a compound statement</u> -- a simple sequence of tasks to be performed in order. At the higher levels the components of this compound statement are themselves units. At the lowest level the components are individual PASCAL statements.

1.5 <u>Termination of a Unit</u>

A unit normally terminates by reaching its exit. It is then followed in execution by the unit appearing next on the listing (if any). However, it is often convenient (and sometimes necessary) to permit a unit the option of terminating not only itself, but also <u>some unit at a higher level</u>.

For example, suppose that in some compound statement such as shown in Figure 1, you would like the unit represented by S2 to have the option of terminating the entire compound statement as shown in Figure 6.

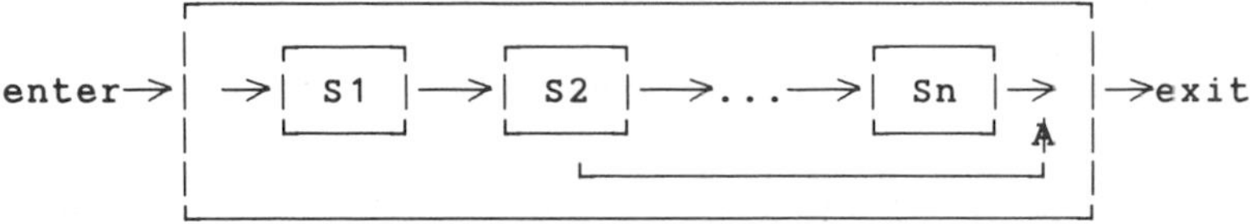

Figure 6. Compound Statement with Termination Exit

This could be implemented with a conditional GOTO and a target label at the end of the compound statement:

```
          (* Purpose of compound statement *)
               (* S1 *)
                    ...
               (* S2 *)
                    ...
(1.5a)              IF condition THEN GOTO label
                    ...
               ...
               (* Sn *)
                    ...
               Label:
```

In Figure 6 and example (1.5a) unit S2 has been given a conditional second exit, whose purpose is to terminate the entire compound statement -- the unit at the next higher level. The compound statement itself still has a single exit point.

It is generally possible to avoid a termination exit such as the one shown in Figure 6 and example (1.5a). For example, (1.5b) uses a termination exit and (1.5c) is a revision of (1.5b) that avoids the need for the exit.

```
(1.5b)    (* LOAD AND OPTIONALLY PRINT A[1..N] *)
               (* LOAD A[1..N] *)
                    FOR I := 1 TO N DO
                         READ(A[I];
               IF PRINTFLAG = 0 THEN GOTO 55;
               (* PRINT A[1..N] *)
                    FOR I := 1 TO N DO
                         WRITELN(' ', A[I]);
               55:

(1.5c)    (* LOAD AND OPTIONALLY PRINT A[1..N] *)
               (* LOAD A[1..N] *)
                    FOR I := 1 TO N DO
                         READ(A[I]);
               (* PRINT A[1..N] IF PRINTFLAG IS ON *)
                    IF PRINTFLAG <> 0 THEN
                         FOR I := 1 TO N DO
                              WRITELN(' ', A[I])
```

Compare (1.5b) to the model shown in Figure 6. There are three components to this compound statement unit -- LOAD, IF and PRINT. The IF component contains a termination exit such as the one shown for S2 in Figure 6. The label 55 is placed so that this exit terminates the entire unit.

Even though the strategy used in (1.5c) is always possible, it is not always preferable to the one shown in (1.5b). If the portion of the unit to be skipped is large and complex it may be clearer to use a termination exit as in (1.5b) rather than have to make a large section of program conditional, as in (1.5c). Particularly when the "normal", or "most frequently followed" path of the execution is to continue through the remainder of the compound statement, it can be less clear to make this portion conditional and indent it further than the initial portion. This is another situation in which the use of a GOTO is sometimes less unattractive than the alternative. However, this use of the GOTO and provision of a second exit point to a unit should always be subject to these restrictions:

1. It should be used only to terminate a unit at a higher level.

2. The target label must be positioned below the GOTO. That is, always go forward; never go back.

3. The target label must always be positioned at the end of a unit; never at the beginning of the "next" unit. The name should be chosen to suggest the end of something rather than the beginning of whatever comes next.

The body of a loop (S1 to Sn in Figure 2) can be considered a compound statement. Then the termination shown in Figure 6 is the means of terminating one particular execution of the body. The target label would be attached to a null statement preceding the END that denotes the end of the body. This technique was introduced in Section I.4.4.1, and is illustrated in example (I.4.4.1a).

Termination arises sometimes when one of the repeated components (say S2 in Figure 2) of a repetition unit needs to terminate the <u>entire loop</u>, or <u>some outer unit</u>, rather than just one particular repetition of the loop. This can be accomplished by a GOTO with a target label at the end of that unit. (1.5d) illustrates both kinds of termination exits.

```
(1.5d)     (* SET SUM TO SUM OF POSITIVE ELEMENTS OF A[1..N], *)
           (* STOP ON 0 *)
               SUM := 0;
               FOR I := 1 TO N DO
                 BEGIN
                    IF A[I] = 0 THEN GOTO 9999;
                    IF A[I] < 0 THEN GOTO 33;
                    SUM := SUM + A[I];
                    33:
                 END
               9999:
```

(1.5d) could easily be written without requiring the 33 exit, in the manner of (1.5c), but it is presented this way to contrast the two types of exit. Note the indentation of the 9999 label, showing that it is not part of the body of the loop.

In effect, a unit can have three different kinds of exits, as shown in Figure 7. Allowing more than one exit from a unit obviously makes a program more difficult to understand, but it is sometimes just unavoidable. The contortions required to preserve the strict single-exit property sometimes do more harm than good. Good judgement is required to decide what is the best and clearest structure in each situation.

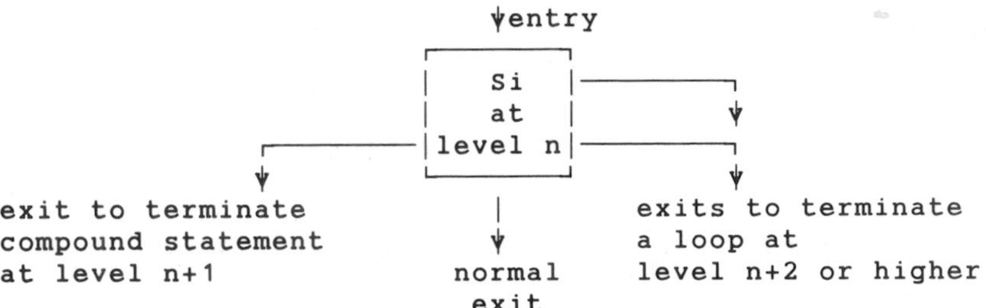

Figure 7. Termination Exits of a Unit

1.6 The Well-Structured Program

A program is said to be "well-structured" if it is organized so that the entire program is itself a unit of one of the types described above. The components of this unit are themselves units, etc., to however many levels are required. This means that the program consists of segments that are readily understandable at a level higher than individual PASCAL statements, and that the control paths between segments are few in number and simple in form.

Structure and format are actually two different issues, although the preceding sections have treated both together. A program is well-presented if its structure is clearly and quickly apparent to the reader. This means grouping statements in a logical way, and providing heading comments so the purpose of each group is apparent without having to figure it out from the individual PASCAL statements. It also means using indentation in a clear and consistent way to emphasize the grouping, and to indicate the flow-of-control during execution.

A program that is both well-structured and well-presented has a high degree of predictability, and this is useful to the reader. For example, suppose you encounter the following line in reading a program:

```
(* SET MINPN TO MIN OF PN FUNCTION *)
```

If, at the moment, you are looking for something else in the program and don't need to know how the program actually finds that minimum, you can confidently skip over the lines indented with respect to that heading comment. The next line below that is left-aligned with this comment will be the next line to consider. Note that it is the commenting and indenting convention that helps you find this next line quickly, but it is the unit structure convention that allows you to go directly to that line without worrying that the program might have executed a random GOTO somewhere in the SET MINPN unit. Knowing that the

SET MINPN unit has a single exit point you know that it will reach that next line, without having to trace through the detail of SET MINPN to make sure.

In a well-structured program the different PASCAL statements will always be used in a consistent manner. For example, repetition is always controlled by a WHILE, REPEAT, or FOR loop, and never with some construction handcrafted from IF, GOTO, and a label. This means that when you encounter an IF or a GOTO you never have to wonder whether it might be part of a homemade loop control.

You can read and understand a well-structured program more quickly, simply because you actually have less to learn about the program. You know in advance how the program will be organized, how it will be presented, and how each PASCAL statement type will be used. If a program doesn't use these conventions, then you must approach it with much less of a headstart. All you have is your knowledge of the meaning of each individual PASCAL statement. For example, when you encounter a GOTO in a well-structured program, you know that some unit is being terminated early. You know that that label is assigned to some statement further down the page, and when you locate it, its indentation will confirm the level of the unit being terminated. You do not have to figure out what the role of the GOTO is -- you know that in advance. All that has to be determined is which unit is being terminated.

Variation in program style is not desirable. A given programmer, when confronted with similar tasks at different points in a program, should solve those tasks in a similar way. From the point of view of the reader, when he encounters apparently similar tasks that are handled in different ways, he should take this as a warning that he does not fully understand the tasks -- and not just that the programmer got bored with one approach and decided to try another. For example, suppose that in the process of reading a program you encounter the following three segments at three different points:

```
(* MOVE A[1..N] TO B[1..N] *)
   FOR I := 1 TO N DO
        B[I] := A[I]

(* REPLACE X[1..N] WITH Y[1..N] *)
   FOR I := N DOWNTO 1 DO
        X[I] := Y[I]

(* COPY R[1..N] INTO S[1..N] *)
   I := 0;
   WHILE I < N DO
     BEGIN
        I := I + 1;
        S[I] := R[I]
     END
```

First you might wonder whether "move", "replace", and "copy" mean exactly the same thing to the writer, or whether there are subtle differences in objective. You should certainly wonder if there is something peculiar about X and Y that makes it necessary to index backward (that is, from N to 1) over their elements. Finally, you should be concerned with why the writer chose to use a WHILE loop for R and S when he has used a FOR loop in other cases. If it turns out that these are in fact exactly comparable tasks, and the writer simply amused himself by seeing how many different ways he could find to write the same task, you will have wasted time looking for differences that don't exist and are entitled to be annoyed -- especially if you were the writer at some earlier time.

Effectively, you are asked to yield some of your freedom of choice in writing a program. But this compromise is for your own benefit. It is in _your_ best interest to do this, since you the programmer are the most frequent reader of the program. _You_ must find the errors in it; _you_ must be sure of its correctness.

Another major virtue of the structure recommended above is the _limitation of context_. This structure makes it possible to understand a particular unit with relatively little knowledge about surrounding units. Without this type of discipline it may be necessary to examine and understand an entire program before one can understand much about a particular small segment. This same characteristic allows units of a program to be written, and later modified or replaced, while only considering a carefully circumscribed local environment of that unit. This makes it possible to produce relatively large programs and achieve the same confidence in their correctness as is possible for small programs.

The harmful effect of the unrestricted use of the GOTO statement should be obvious from this discussion. If a unit is allowed to branch arbitrarily to other sections of the program its successor is no longer unique or apparent. The sequence of statements executed is very different from the sequence as written. Similarly, if other units have the privilege of unrestricted branching then the entry point and entry conditions of the unit under consideration are not easily determined.

This structure is not always the most obvious or natural for a problem. But it is the most desirable structure for a program, and it is worth trying to organize a problem so that it takes this form. It is not always easy to do so and it takes a good deal of practice. For non-trivial programs the effort is clearly worthwhile. The additional time spent in initial planning is more than recovered by a reduction in testing time, and the overall result is a significant improvement in clarity and reliability.

For very small programs a less structured organization may suffice, and a well-structured program does require some extra work in the initial writing. While an experienced programmer who knows how to produce a good program might be permitted to "shortcut" under special circumstances, a beginner trying to learn the art of programming should practice using the proper style at every opportunity. Even for the professional a casual approach is risky since very often little programs reappear later as pieces of big programs.

If there is a "break-even point" with regard to these practices it occurs at a surprisingly small size of program. The extra effort pays off for programs as small as 20 statements just in a reduction in the time required to adequately test the program. This means it will be valuable even for exercises that are encountered in a first programming course.

1.6.1 The Art of Writing Comments

It is comparatively difficult to learn to write good, useful comments in a program, and many programmers never deign to learn. The difficulty lies in the complete freedom that is allowed. A programming language specifies precisely the form of the statements that are allowed, and the translator enforces those rules, but for comments the language and translator require only that they be properly identified. Thus the programmer must develop his own rules, and there is no mechanism to remind him when he departs from his rules. We have tried to use comments in a consistent manner throughout the book, but there are undoubtedly lapses where we should have done better. Ours is admittedly an extreme position among programmers with regard to comments and you will encounter much skepticism among knowledgeable programmers. Ultimately, you will have to decide for yourself whether our comments help you to understand our examples, and more importantly, whether your comments help you to write and test your own programs.

The rules that we are trying to observe, and that we recommend to you, are the following:

1. In many contexts and for many purposes comments should be read as an alternative to a group of program statements. To be able to read comments in this way the reader must have complete confidence that a comment is a valid alternative -- that it says the same thing as the program statements, but in a different form. To maintain this confidence, comments must be precise and accurate. For example, compare the following possible heading comments for a segment to read data:

```
(* LOAD AR[1..50] FROM DATA, STOP ON FIRST -1 *)

(* READ DATA *)

(* LOAD AR *)
```

The first example specifies fairly precisely what is going to be done, and for many purposes it would be unnecessary to read the corresponding program statements. The second and third possibilities just generally describe the purpose of the statements, but with these comments you would be more likely to have to read the statements to understand the action of that part of the program.

Use specific variable names in comments. For example, compare the following alternatives:

```
(* SET MINA TO MIN OF A[J..K] *)

(* FIND MINIMUM *)
```

Keep your comments up-to-date. When you change program statements, adjust the comments accordingly. No matter how well-written the comments were initially, unless they are kept current the reader can have no confidence in them. This confidence is a fragile thing -- once the reader has discovered one inaccurate or obsolete comment in a program he must be suspicious of all other comments.

There must be some convention (usually indentation) to indicate the precise scope of each comment -- that is, the program statements to which it is an alternative. Our convention is that program statements are indented with respect to the corresponding comment. The next line that is left-aligned with a comment (whether that next line is itself a comment or a statement) is the beginning of the next unit of the program. For example

```
(* LOAD X[1..N] FROM DATA *)
    READLN(N);
    FOR I := 1 TO N DO
         READ(X[I]);
SUM := 0;
COUNT := 0;
(* WRITE TITLE AND COLUMN HEADINGS *)
    WRITELN('1');
    WRITE('0               ');
    WRITELN('DEMOGRAPHIC PROFILE');
    WRITELN(' WAYNE COUNTY, 1970 CENSUS');
    WRITELN('0SIZE          NUMBER',
         '        SOURCE         INCOME');
    WRITELN('0')
```

2. The reason for having comments as an alternative description for a human reader is to provide a form that is more efficient for him -- that is, a form that is both more concise and more comprehensible. The comments should be written in a semi-formal higher-level language. They should never simply duplicate the program statements. For example, the following are examples of poor comments -- in each case the program would be at least as clear without them so there is no reward for the effort of writing them.

```
SUM := 0 (* INITIALIZE SUM TO 0 *)

(* GET NEW VALUE OF N *)
    READLN(N)

(* EXIT IF ITEM IS NEGATIVE *)
    IF ITEM < 0 THEN GOTO 747

(* MOVE WORD[1] TO WORD[2] *)
    WORD[2] := WORD[1]
```

The purpose of a comment is _not_ to explain the action of a program statement to a reader who does not understand the programming language. Start with the assumption that the reader _could_ read and understand the program statements, if necessary, but your job is to make it unnecessary for him to do so in many cases. Remember that you are going to be the most frequent reader, hence the principal beneficiary of this kindness.

In summary, comments can be useful, but only _if you take them seriously_. Time spent in writing comments that are precise, concise alternatives to program segments is generously repaid later in the programming and testing process. Comments that are casually written -- and inserted more because of compulsion than conviction -- are probably not worth the bother. Evaluate our examples critically in this regard and decide what your own "comment conventions" should be.

Other types of comments are also used. For example, we have often shown comments with declarations to precisely define the role of a variable. A group of comments at the beginning of a program can give instructions to the user. They may also identify the author, date, title, etc. Occasionally a comment can be used to explain the strategy of a program (or a segment) by giving a reference to the computing literature.

1.6.2 _A Comparative Example_

With this discussion as background we now give another example, presenting the same program in both "well-structured" and "conventional" form, as we did in (IIa) and (IIb). Consider a program which is to read in a 2-dimensional array of integers A[1..N,1..N], and then determine and report the following three values:

1. The largest element on the principal diagonal -- the maximum of A[I,I] for I=1,2,...,N. Call this maximum DMAX.

2. The largest element in row I, the row in which DMAX occurs. Calls this RMAX.

3. The largest element in column I, the column in which DMAX occurs. Call this CMAX.

The input consists of a number N, less than 25, followed by the N^2 numbers of the array in row-major order -- that is, the numbers of the top row, left to right, followed by the numbers of the second row, left to right, etc. The required output is a display of the array and the values of DMAX, RMAX and CMAX.

(1.6.2a) and (1.6.2b) are alternative programs which are correct and solve the problem. (1.6.2a) is typical of conventional programming style and format. (Although we are obviously trying to persuade you that (1.6.2b) is preferable we have tried not to make (1.6.2a) deliberately obscure.) (1.6.2b) is written following the recommendations of the preceding sections. As you consider these two programs, realize that they are identical, as far as the computer is concerned. They differ only in the manner in which they are organized and presented for a human reader.

(1.6.2a)

```
PROGRAM MAXELMT(INPUT,OUTPUT);
LABEL 9005;
VAR A: ARRAY[1..24,1..24] OF INTEGER;
N,LD,LR,LC,I,J: INTEGER;
BEGIN READLN(N); LD := 1; LR := 1; LC := 1;
IF (N<1) OR (N>24) THEN BEGIN WRITELN(' WRONG SIZE',N);
GOTO 9005 END;
FOR I := 1 TO N DO BEGIN WRITELN;
FOR J := 1 TO N DO BEGIN READ(A[I,J]); WRITE(A[I,J])
END END; WRITELN; FOR I := 2 TO N DO
IF A[I,I] > A[LD,LD] THEN LD := I;
WRITELN('0DMAX IS: ',A[LD,LD],' IN ROW, COL',LD);
FOR I := 2 TO N DO BEGIN
IF A[LD,I] > A[LD,LR] THEN LR := I;
IF A[I,LD] > A[LC,LD] THEN LC := I END;
WRITELN('0RMAX IS:',A[LD,LR],' IN COL',LR);
WRITELN('0CMAX IS:',A[LC,LD],' IN ROW',LC);
9005:; END.
```

(1.6.2b)

```
(* FIND DMAX, RMAX AND CMAX IN A[1..N,1..N] *)
PROGRAM MAXELMT(INPUT, OUTPUT);

LABEL 9005;
VAR A: ARRAY[1..24,1..24] OF INTEGER;
    N,              (* SIZE OF ARRAY, <= 24 *)
    LD,             (* ROW, COL OF DMAX *)
    LR,             (* COL OF RMAX *)
    LC,             (* ROW OF CMAX *)
    I,J: INTEGER;
```

```
BEGIN (* MAXELMT *)
  (* READ IN ARRAY A, STOP IF IMPROPER SIZE *)
    READLN(N);
    IF (N<1) OR (N>24) THEN
      BEGIN (* WRONG SIZE *)
         WRITELN(' SIZE OF ARRAY WRONG:', N);
         GOTO 9005
      END; (* WRONG SIZE *)
    FOR I:= 1 TO N DO
      BEGIN
         FOR J := 1 TO N DO
              READ(A[I,J])
      END;

  (* PRINT ARRAY A *)
    FOR I := 1 TO N DO
      BEGIN
         WRITELN;
         FOR J := 1 TO N DO
              WRITE(A[I,J])
      END;
    WRITELN;

  (* FIND INDEX OF DMAX *)
    LD := 1;
    FOR I := 2 TO N DO
         IF A[I,I] > A[LD,LD]
              THEN LD := I;

  (* FIND INDEX LR OF RMAX AND LC OF CMAX *)
    LR := 1;
    LC := 1;
    FOR I := 2 TO N DO
      BEGIN
         IF A[LD,I] > A[LD,LR]
              THEN LR := I;
         IF A[I,LC] > A[LC,LD]
              THEN LC := I
      END;

  (* PRINT RESULTS *)
    WRITELN('0DMAX IS:  ', A[LD,LD],
              ' IN ROW, COL ', LD);
    WRITELN(' RMAX IS: ', A[LD,LR], ' IN COL ', LR);
    WRITELN(' CMAX IS: ', A[LC,LD], ' IN ROW ', LC);

  9005:; (* FROM WRONG SIZE *)
END.  (* MAXELMT *)
```

(1.6.2b) is more readily understandable than (1.6.2a) even though it has more lines to read. (1.6.2b) makes it obvious that the program is a compound statement -- a simple sequence of five subtasks:

```
Read in array A;
Print array A;
Find index LD of DMAX;
Find index LR of RMAX and LC of CMAX;
Print results.
```

Each of these subtasks is itself a compound statement, and four of them involve looping, but that does not obscure the fact that there are essentially five steps in executing the program. Within each of the subtasks the extent and purpose of each loop are made clear by labelling and indentation.

It is probably not obvious at this stage of your programming development, but real programs are often modified. That is, after a program is completed and tested, and has been used for awhile, it is not unusual for problem requirements to be slightly changed. Then someone -- not always the original author -- must go back and re-read the program and find the appropriate points at which to make changes. Consider (1.6.2b) from the point of view of making changes. It is easier to find the place to make the change, easier to write the new statements, and we have greater confidence that the change is correct and does not disturb other sections of the program. In effect, we really have to study (1.6.2a) in order to find out information that is readily apparent in (1.6.2b). For example, consider the relative ease and confidence with which (1.6.2a) and (1.6.2b) could be modified to make one or more of the following changes:

1. The program is to be run only on "sparse" arrays -- arrays where most of the elements are 0. To make it easier to keypunch the input data, change the program to accept input of the following form, where the user need only specify the non-zero elements:
    a) card 1 contains the integer N
    b) each successive card describes one non-zero array element by giving its row number, its column number and its value
    c) the last card contains three zero values.

2. The output is difficult to read if N>5 because a row of the array will be printed on several successive lines. Change the output format so that each row begins a new print line, and continuations of the row are given on lines that are indented with respect to the first line of the row.

3. Change the output format so the array is printed with 2 stars "**" on either side of the values DMAX, RMAX and CMAX.

4. Change the program so that DMAX is the largest value on the lower-left-to-upper-right diagonal.

Section 1 Summary

1. A well-structured program is a hierarchy of program units. The highest level is a unit, whose components are also units, etc. The lowest level consists of simple PASCAL statements.

2. A program unit is a group of statements that are logically related to each other in that they perform some well-defined task. There are three principal kinds of units: "compound statement", "repetition" and "alternate selection".

3. A unit should begin with a comment that is left-aligned with the heading of the preceding unit. The components of the unit should be left-aligned with each other and indented with respect to the heading comment.

4. A unit has a single entry point and a single normal exit point. It may also have a termination exit that terminates execution of either the body or the entire containing unit at a higher level.

5. Comments are principally used as a "higher-level" description of the action of a program segment. If well-written, they can often be read instead of the corresponding program statements.

Section 1 Examples

```
000006 (* COUNT LETTERS IN TEXT *)
000006 PROGRAM LTRCOUNT(INPUT,OUTPUT);
000464
000464 VAR COUNTS: ARRAY['A'..'Z'] OF INTEGER; (* COUNTERS *)
000516     INTEXT,          (* INPUT CHARACTERS *)
000516     J:   CHAR;       (* LOOP CONTROL VARIABLE *)
000520
000520 BEGIN (* LTRCOUNT *)
000520     (*SET COUNTS TO ZERO*)
000520         FOR J := 'A' TO 'Z' DO
000023             COUNTS[J] := 0;
000034
000034     (*READ TEXT AND COUNT LETTERS*)
000034         READ(INTEXT);
000041         WHILE NOT EOF DO
000042             BEGIN
000042                 IF (INTEXT >= 'A') AND (INTEXT <= 'Z') THEN
000045                     COUNTS[INTEXT] := COUNTS[INTEXT] + 1;
000053                 READ(INTEXT)
000060             END;
000061
000061     (*PRINT RESULTS*)
000061         WRITELN('0  LETTER FREQUENCY COUNTS');
000067         WRITELN;
000070         FOR J := 'A' TO 'Z' DO
000071             WRITELN('      ', J, COUNTS[J])
000115 END.  (* LTRCOUNT *)
```

```
 LETTER FREQUENCY COUNTS

    A        36
    B         7
    C        16
    D        22
    E        79
    F         9
    G         9
    H        23
    I        30
    J         1
    K         1
    L        18
    M        12
    N        22
    O        42
    P        17
    Q         2
    R        48
    S        40
    T        62
    U        28
    V         5
    W         7
    X         2
    Y        11
    Z         0
```

```
000006 (*WORD TABLE LOOK-UP*)
000006 PROGRAM LOOKUP(INPUT,OUTPUT);
000464
000464 LABEL 9800;
000464 CONST SIZE = 100;  (* MAX TABLE SIZE *)
000464 TYPE  WORD = PACKED ARRAY[1..10] OF CHAR;
000464       DEFINITION = PACKED ARRAY[1..50] OF CHAR;
000464 VAR WDS:  ARRAY[1..SIZE] OF WORD;          (*TABLE WORDS*)
000630     DEFS: ARRAY[1..SIZE] OF DEFINITION;   (*TABLE DEFINITIONS*)
001760     INWORD: WORD;                         (*WORD FOR SEARCH*)
001761     N,             (*NO. OF TABLE ENTRIES, <= SIZE*)
001761     I, J, K:  INTEGER;
001765
001765 BEGIN  (*LOOKUP*)
001765     (*FILL THE TABLE*)
001765         READLN(N);
000026         FOR I := 1 TO N DO
000030             BEGIN (*TABLE READ LOOP*)
000032                 FOR J := 1 TO 10 DO
000033                     READ(WDS[I,J]);
000055                 J := 1;
000056                 WHILE NOT EOLN DO
000057                     BEGIN
000057                         READ(DEFS[I,J]);
000101                         J := J + 1
000101                     END;
000103                 FOR K := J TO 60 DO
000105                     DEFS[I,K] := ' ';
000127                 READLN
000127             END; (*TABLE READ LOOP*)
000133
000133     (*PRINT COLUMN HEADINGS*)
000133         WRITELN('1  WORD       DEFINITION---------');
000141         WRITELN;
000142
000142     (*READ WORDS AND LOOK UP DEFINITIONS*)
000142         WHILE NOT EOF DO
000143             BEGIN (*LOOK-UP LOOP*)
000143                 J := 1;
000144                 WHILE NOT EOLN DO
000145                     BEGIN
000145                         READ(INWORD[J]);
000160                         J := J + 1
000160                     END;
000162                 FOR K := J TO 10 DO
000164                     INWORD[K] := ' ';
000176                 READLN;
000177
000177                 (*COMPARE INPUT WORD TO TABLE ENTRIES*)
000177                     FOR I := 1 TO N DO
000201                         BEGIN (*SEARCH LOOP*)
000203                             IF INWORD = WDS[I] THEN
000207                                 BEGIN
000207                                     WRITE(' ', INWORD);
000216                                     WRITELN(' ', DEFS[I]);
000232                                     GOTO 9800
000233                                 END
000233                         END; (*SEARCH LOOP*)
000236                     WRITELN('0', INWORD, ' NOT IN TABLE');
000253                     9800:;
000253             END (*LOOK-UP LOOP*)
000253 END.  (*LOOKUP*)
```

```
  WORD       DEFINITION---------

SMITTEN     GRIEVOUSLY AFFLICTED.
PRAIRIE     A TRACT OF GRASSLAND.

BORE        NOT IN TABLE
KARMA       LOOSELY, DESTINY,FATE.
DOGTROT     A GENTLE TROT LIKE THAT OF A DOG
BOER        A SOUTH AFRICAN OF DUTCH OR HUGUENOT DESCENT.
```

Section 2 Program Schemata

When we introduced the IF construction in Section I.4.4 we gave the model of the construction as

IF condition THEN statement.

This gave the form or "schema" of that conditional statement in PASCAL. The symbol "statement" in the schema stands for any simple or compound PASCAL statement. The symbol "condition" stands for any simple or compound condition. Written in this form, before some particular statement and particular condition is specified, the schema is said to be "uninterpreted" when some of its elements are given in general terms, rather than as some specific example -- that is, given as "condition" rather than "A = B". We defined the action of the IF construction in terms of an uninterpreted schema; that is, we described its action independent of what particular statement and particular condition might be given in a specific example.

This seems like a complicated way of explaining something that was fairly obvious on first encounter, but we would like to extend this argument to larger program constructions. For example, (2a) is a schema for a particular kind of repetition unit, one in which the body is to be repeated a definite number of times:

```
           (* Comment describing action of the unit *)
               i := 0;
               WHILE i < n DO
                 BEGIN (* loop name *)
                    i := i + 1;
(2a)                Body
                 END (* loop name *)
```

This is a schema uninterpreted with respect to the body, the index variable i, the stopping value n, the loop name and the heading comment -- the elements given in lower-case letters. A particular example or interpretation of this schema would have these lower-case elements replaced by specific PASCAL elements. For example, the following are specific interpretations of (2a):

```
(* MOVE A[1..K] TO B[1..K] *)
    J := 0;
    WHILE J < K DO
      BEGIN
         J := J + 1;
         B[J] := A[J]
      END

(* PRINT 12 LINES OF 10 *'S EACH *)
    I := 0;
    WHILE I < 12 DO
      BEGIN
         I := I + 1;
         WRITELN(' **********')
      END


(* CLEAR X[1..K] TO ZERO *)
    M := 0;
    WHILE M < K DO
      BEGIN
         M := M + 1;
         X[M] := 0
      END


(* CLEAR A[1..K,2..M] IF < A[1..K,1] *)
    I := 0;
    WHILE I < K DO
      BEGIN
         I := I + 1;
         (* CLEAR ITH ROW *)
              FOR J := 2 TO M DO
                   IF A[I,J] < A[I,1]
                       THEN A[I,J] := 0
      END
```

Although these examples perform very different tasks, in each case the basic structure is the same -- some task is repeated a definite number of times. That subtask may be a single statement or a substantial program segment, but the statements that control its repetition are the same (except for the particular names used). Each of these examples follows the pattern shown in (2a) with the lower-case elements of (2a) replaced by particular PASCAL elements. These different interpretations of (2a) *differ* from each other *only in the choices of specific elements to replace the lower-case elements of (2a)*.

Definite repetition is a common task, and (2a) can be regarded as a schema for a "statement" to accomplish this task. You can learn this schema and use it more-or-less automatically each time that you need to repeat some action a definite number of times. It means that you will not have to "re-invent" a mechanism for definite repetition each time it is required.

There are many other common tasks and corresponding schemata. For example, suppose some action is to be performed on each item of a data list, where the end of the list is recognized by the presence of some distinctive value. (2b) gives an appropriate schema.

```
          (* Comment describing task and stopping flag *)
              Initialize;
              READ(item);
              WHILE item <> stopping flag DO
                BEGIN (* loop name *)
(2b)                Perform action on item;
                    READ(item)
                END (* loop name *)
```

Each of the following is an example (or interpretation) of (2b):

```
          (* FIND MAX X, STOPPING AT FIRST 0 *)
              XMAX := 0;
              READ(X);
              WHILE X <> 0 DO
                BEGIN
                    IF X > XMAX
                         THEN XMAX := X;
                    READ(X)
                END

          (* PRINT, SUM AND COUNT DATA UNTIL -999 *)
              WRITELN('0LIST OF INPUT DATA:');
              WRITELN;
              SUM := 0;
              COUNT := 0;
              READ(ITEM);
              WHILE ITEM <> -999 DO
                BEGIN
                    WRITELN(' ', ITEM);
                    SUM := SUM + ITEM;
                    COUNT := COUNT + 1;
                    READ(ITEM)
                END
```

An especially common task in programs is to perform some action on each element of an array, or on some portion of an array. (2c) gives a schema for this task.

```
          (* Perform action on each element of a[j..k] *)
              Initialize;
              FOR i := j TO k DO
                BEGIN (* loop name *)
(2c)                Perform action on a[i]
                END (* loop name *)
```

The following are examples of interpretations of (2c):

```
(* DISPLAY VALUES OF AR[A..B] *)
    WRITELN('0VALUES OF AR[A..B]');
    WRITELN(' A = ', A, ' B = ', B);
    WRITELN;
    FOR I := A TO B DO
         WRITELN(' ', AR[I])
```

```
(* LOAD X[1..N] FROM DATA *)
    FOR I := 1 TO N DO
         READ(X[I])
```

```
(* MOVE X[1..N] TO Y[1..N] *)
    FOR J := 1 TO N DO
         Y[J] := X[J]
```

Sometimes a task can be viewed in several different ways. For example, suppose you are required to read data values into an array X[1..N], but not past the first -1 in the data list. That is, the reading process will read N values, or up to the first -1, whichever occurs first. This could be written as an interpretation of (2c):

```
(* LOAD X[1..N], UP TO FIRST -1 *)
    FOR I := 1 TO N DO
      BEGIN
         READ(X[I]);
         IF X[I] = -1 THEN GOTO 9009
      END;
    9009:
```

Alternatively, the same task could be written as an interpretation of (2b):

```
(* LOAD X[1..N], UP TO FIRST -1 *)
    I := 1;
    READ(X[I]);
    WHILE X[I] <> -1 DO
      BEGIN
         I := I + 1;
         IF I > N THEN GOTO 9009;
         READ(X[I])
      END
    9009:
```

These segments are quite comparable and there is no strong reason to prefer one over the other. However, you might note that it is <u>possible that neither is correct</u>, depending upon the precise requirements of the problem. Both will include the stopping flag value (-1) as an element of X, if it occurs within the first N items on the data list. This may well not be a valid element for X and probably should not be included. Also note that for either example the only way of knowing how many items were actually loaded is the value of I after finishing the loop, and this value is 1 too large. That is, the final value is I is either N+1 or the subscript of the element containing -1. Either version could be written to avoid this flaw. For example:

```
(* LOAD X[1..N], UP TO FIRST -1 *)
    I := 0;
    READ(Y);
    WHILE (Y <> -1) AND (I < N) DO
      BEGIN
         I := I + 1;
         X[I] := Y;
         READ(Y)
      END
```

As a final example of a schema, another common task is to perform some action on each element of a data list, when the list is preceded by an integer specifying the number of items on the list. An appropriate schema is given in (2d).

```
          (*  Read n, and perform action on n following items *)
                Initialize;
                READLN(n);
                WHILE n > 0 DO
                  BEGIN (* loop name *)
                     READ(item);
(2d)                 Perform action on item;
                     n := n - 1
                  END (* loop name *)
```

An interpretation of (2d) is the following:

```
(* READ M, LOAD M ELEMENTS INTO A[1..N] *)
    I := 0;
    READLN(M);
    WHILE M > 0 DO
      BEGIN (* LOAD LOOP *)
         IF I = N THEN
           BEGIN
              WRITELN('0 EXCESS DATA');
              GOTO 9050
           END;
         I := I + 1;
         READ(A[I]);
         M := M - 1
      END; (* LOAD LOOP *)
    9050:
```

We cannot catalog all common program tasks for you and give schemata for them. We are just trying to make you aware that there are certain patterns that recur frequently, and that you should learn to recognize them. You should develop your own repertoire of schemata, and apply them whenever a familiar task appears. This will save you the time and effort of re-inventing solutions to these problems, and make your programs more consistent and predictable.

Notice that it is the control structure of the segment that recurs more often than the specific action. The action will vary from problem to problem, but the manner in which it is repeated is often familiar. There are infinitely many different problems to be solved -- you will rarely meet one that is identical to one you have solved before. But any problem can be broken down into sections, and many of the sections may be recognizable as some action to be repeated in some familiar way. Viewed in this way, even large problems are not quite so formidable.

2.1 A Classification of Very Simple Programs

For many of the very simple problems used as examples and exercises in introductory programming courses one can give schemata for the entire program, rather than just for segments of it. Many of these simple problems consist of some repetition of three actions:

1. Read an item of data;
2. Perform some action upon the item;
3. Print some result.

The problem requirements will detail the action to be performed, and the result to be printed. This will dictate which of two basic strategies must be used.

The simplest strategy consists of dealing with the data items one at a time. There is never any need to have more than one item available at any point in execution of the program. The entire program is just an interpretation of schema (2b) or (2d). For example, (2.1a) gives a schema for the entire program based upon (2b).

```
           (* Read, process and print, one item at a time *)
           PROGRAM name(INPUT, OUTPUT);

           Definitions and declarations;

           BEGIN (* program name *)
               Initialize;
               READ(item);
               WHILE NOT EOF DO
                 BEGIN (* loop name *)
(2.1a)              Perform action on item;
                    WRITELN(' ', item result);
                    READ(item)
                 END; (* loop name *)
               WRITELN(' ', final result)
           END.  (* program name *)
               eor
           data list
```

A simple interpretation of (2.1a) is a program to print a copy of the data list:

```
(* PRINT LIST OF DATA *)
PROGRAM PRINTDATA(INPUT, OUTPUT);

VAR VALUE: REAL;

BEGIN (* PRINTDATA *)
    WRITELN('0 MCLAUGHLIN DATA LIST:');
    WRITELN;
    READ(VALUE);
    WHILE NOT EOF DO
      BEGIN (* PRINT LOOP *)
         WRITELN(' ', VALUE);
         READ(VALUE)
      END; (* PRINT LOOP *)
    WRITELN('0 END OF LIST')
END.  (* PRINTDATA *)
```

Another example of an interpretation of (2.1a) would be to print running sums of the values on a data list:

```
(* PRINT RUNNING SUMS OF DATA LIST *)
PROGRAM RUNSUM(INPUT, OUTPUT);

VAR ITEM,  SUM: REAL; (* VALUE READ, AND SUM SO FAR *)
    COUNT: INTEGER; (* NUMBER OF ITEMS SO FAR *)

BEGIN (* RUNSUM *)
    COUNT := 0;
    SUM := 0;
    READ(ITEM);
    WHILE NOT EOF DO
      BEGIN
         SUM := SUM + ITEM;
         COUNT := COUNT + 1;
         WRITELN(' ', SUM);
         READ(ITEM)
      END;
    IF COUNT = 0
         THEN WRITELN('0 NO DATA GIVEN')
         ELSE WRITELN('0 SUM OF', COUNT,
                    ' ITEMS IS ', SUM)
END.  (* RUNSUM *)
```

Now suppose the problem requirements were changed just enough to make it necessary to retain many data values at the same time. (2.1a) can no longer be used since it is limited to a single data value at a time. The program will now require an array to hold the data list, and will likely involve two principal steps, each one being a loop over the elements of the array. A schema such as (2.1b) would be required. The "load-loop" in (2.1b) could be of the form of either schema (2b) or (2d). The "process-loop" is likely to be of the form of schema (2c).

```
          (* Summary of program action *)
          PROGRAM name(INPUT, OUTPUT);

          Declaration of array to hold data;
          Declaration of other variables;

          BEGIN (* program name *)
              (* Load array from data list *)
(2.1b)              Load-loop
              (* Process elements of array *)
                    Process loop
          END.  (* program name *)
              eor
          data list
```

A simple example of an interpretation of (2.1b) would be a problem requiring printing some summary result <u>before</u> printing a copy of the data list. For example:

```
(* COUNT, TITLE, AND PRINT DATA *)
PROGRAM CTPDATA(INPUT, OUTPUT);

LABEL 9001;
VAR DLIST: ARRAY[1..50] OF REAL;
    DTEMP: REAL;
    DCOUNT, (* NBR OF DATA ITEMS SO FAR *)
    J: INTEGER;

BEGIN (* CTPDATA *)
    WRITELN('1 BARBU DATA LIST');
    (* LOAD DLIST[1..50] FROM DATA AND SET DCOUNT TO
              INDEX OF LAST ELEMENT *)
         DCOUNT := 0;
         READ(DTEMP);
         WHILE NOT EOF DO
           BEGIN (* LOAD LOOP *)
              IF DCOUNT = 50 THEN
                BEGIN
                   WRITELN('0 EXCESS DATA');
                   GOTO 9001
                END;
              DCOUNT := DCOUNT + 1;
              DLIST[DCOUNT] := DTEMP;
              READ(DTEMP)
           END; (* LOAD LOOP *)
         9001:;

    (* COMPLETE THE TITLE *)
         WRITELN('0', DCOUNT, ' ITEMS READ AS DATA');
         WRITELN('0');

    (* PRINT DLIST[1..DCOUNT] *)
         FOR J := 1 TO DCOUNT DO
              WRITELN(DLIST[J])
END.  (* CTPDATA *)
```

A good way to get started on your first programming exercise is to study the problem requirements to see whether it is a "one at a time" problem or an "all at once" problem. Then view your program, not as an entirely original creation, but just as an interpretation of either (2.1a) or (2.1b). This prescription won't handle all of your assigned problems, but it should help with many of them.

Section 2 Examples

```
000006 (* COPY INPUT TO OUTPUT *)
000006 PROGRAM COPY(INPUT,OUTPUT);
000464
000464 VAR CH:  CHAR;
000465
000465 BEGIN (* COPY *)
000465     WHILE NOT EOF DO
000023         BEGIN (*LINE COPY LOOP*)
000023             WRITE(' ');  (*FOR VERTICAL SPACING*)
000025             WHILE NOT EOLN DO
000026                 BEGIN
000026                     READ(CH);
000033                     WRITE(CH)
000037                 END;
000040             READLN;
000041             WRITELN
000041         END (*LINE COPY LOOP*)
000042 END. (* COPY *)
```

```
0...I....1....I....2....I....3....I....4....I....5

THIS IS A TEST OF THE COPY PROGRAM.

A
 B
  C
   D            . . .                 X
                                       Y
                                        Z
         *    *    *    *    *    *    *
```

```
000006 (* CALCULATE MEAN AND STANDARD DEVIATION *)
000006 PROGRAM EASYSTAT(INPUT,OUTPUT);
000464
000464 LABEL 9200;
000464 VAR X:  ARRAY[1..200] OF REAL;           (* DATA VALUES *)
000774     XTEMP,                               (* TEMPORARY DATA HOLDER *)
000774     SUMX,                                (* SUM OF X S *)
000774     MEAN,                                (* ARITHMETIC MEAN *)
000774     SUMDSQ,                              (* SUM OF SQUARED DIFFERENCES *)
000774     STDEV:  REAL;                        (* STANDARD DEVIATION *)
001001     N,                                   (* NUMBER OF DATA VALUES *)
001001     I:  INTEGER;                         (* LOOP COUNTER *)
001003
001003 BEGIN  (* EASYSTAT *)
001003     (*LOAD X[1..200] FROM DATA AND SET N TO THE NO. OF DATA VALUES*)
001003         N := 0;
000023         READ(XTEMP);
000026         WHILE NOT EOF DO
000027             BEGIN (*LOAD LOOP*)
000027                 IF N = 200 THEN
000031                     BEGIN
000031                         WRITELN('0  TOO MUCH DATA ');
000037                         GOTO 9200
000040                     END;
000040                 N := N + 1;
000042                 X[N] := XTEMP;
000045                 READ(XTEMP)
000050             END; (*LOAD LOOP*)
000051         9200:;
000051
000051     (*TITLE AND PRINT X[1..M]*)
000051         WRITELN('1    MEAN AND STANDARD DEVIATION RESULTS');
000057         WRITELN('0', N, ' DATA VALUES ARE:');
000073         WRITELN;
000074         FOR I := 1 TO N DO
000076             WRITELN(X[I]);
000112
000112     (*CALCULATE AND PRINT MEAN*)
000112         SUMX := 0;
000115         FOR I := 1 TO N DO
000117             SUMX := SUMX + X[I];
000126         MEAN := SUMX / N;
000132         WRITE('0 MEAN =', MEAN);
000143
000143     (*CALCULATE AND PRINT STANDARD DEVIATION*)
000143         SUMDSQ := 0;
000146         FOR I := 1 TO N DO
000150             SUMDSQ := SUMDSQ + SQR(X[I] - MEAN);
000161         STDEV := SQRT(SUMDSQ / N);
000167         WRITELN('  STANDARD DEVIATION =', STDEV)
000200 END.  (* EASYSTAT *)
```

```
   MEAN AND STANDARD DEVIATION RESULTS

        12 DATA VALUES ARE:

1.5000000000000E+001
1.5500000000000E+001
1.6000000000000E+001
1.7000000000000E+001
1.8000000000000E+001
1.9000000000000E+001
1.1000000000000E+001
1.0000000000000E+001
2.0000000000000E+001
2.1200000000000E+001
5.3000000000000E+001
2.2000000000000E+001

MEAN =  1.9808333333333E+001  STANDARD DEVIATION =  1.0607580491747E+001
```

Part III
Program Development

Section 1 The Phases of Development

Our task is to write a program to solve some problem. Given the problem description in English, we have to figure out a way in which a computer can be used to solve the problem, and then describe this plan very precisely in some programming language. This process has four distinct phases:

1. Clarify the problem requirements.

2. Design a program strategy.

3. Specify critical data structures.

4. Write the program statements.

Although the phases should occur roughly in the order listed, there is a good deal of overlap and backtracking, and particularly for small problems they are difficult to separate. Nevertheless they each represent a distinct function that must be performed in every programming process. At least initially, while struggling to learn the details of a programming language, phase four may look the most formidable. With practice and experience you will discover that if the other three phases are properly done then writing the program statements is quite straightforward. It may still be time-consuming and error-prone, but it will not be the critical phase.

In this section we give a brief introduction to each of these phases. In Section 2 we illustrate the complete process for several simple programs. In Section 3 we elaborate upon general problems and considerations that arise in various phases of the process.

1.1 Clarification of the Problem

Surprisingly, clarification of the problem is a major phase of the process. It would seem reasonable that a clear and precise statement of the problem would be given, but in fact this is rarely the case and more programming disasters can be blamed on failure in this regard than any other. It is very easy to misunderstand the precise requirements of a problem and proceed to write a program that solves the wrong problem. This phase is hard enough even in a programming course where the problem is stated by someone who (presumably) understands what can be programmed, and chooses problems to be only interestingly difficult. Real problems are usually posed by someone who isn't sure exactly what he wants done, much less how the computer is going to contribute to a solution, and the problem definition often becomes precise only in response to persistent and pointed questions on the part of the programmer.

A substantial fraction of the clarification dialog is concentrated on three key issues:

1. Input. What is its format and order? What are the limits of volume that may occur and how will the end of the input be recognized? What are the limits on values that will be encountered?

2. Output. What is the content, format and order of output? What titling is appropriate? What limits on volume may be expected?

3. Errors. What types of errors (both in input and in processing) must the program guard against, and what action should be taken when they are encountered? Which problem specifications can be taken as guaranteed, and which only as good intentions -- to be checked by the program?

For example, suppose you are given the following problem:

(1.1a) Write a program to compute the sum of a list of numbers.

This statement gives only a general idea of the objective of the program; much more detailed information is required before you could begin to design the program. For example:

1a. Can the data be presented on punched cards in a format acceptable to the READ statement?

b. How many values can there be? How can the end of the list of values be recognized?

c. What types and sizes of values might be expected?

2a. In what form should the sum be displayed?

b. What identifying title should be provided?

3a. What action should be taken for values on the list that violate the specifications of 1c?

b. What action should be taken if the quantity of values violates instructions given in 1b?

After obtaining specific answers to these questions you might have the following refinement of (1.1a):

(1.1b) Write a program to compute the sum of a list of positive integers, given in READ format. The end of the data list will be denoted by two consecutive values of -999. Improper values on the list should be rejected (excluded from the sum) and printed on a list titled "REJECTED VALUES:". Any irregularity in termination should result in a warning message. The result should be given in three lines, after the list of rejects (if any):

```
SUM OF POSITIVE INTEGERS

    n VALUES INCLUDED

    SUM IS s
```

As a second example, consider a simple text-processing problem:

(1.1c) Write a program to delete duplicates from a word list.

Clarification of (1.1c) might result in something like the following:

(1.1d) Write a program to print a list of words, one per line, in the order given, but excluding any word that has appeared earlier in the list. The data will be given as an integer n (not more than 100), followed by n words, each a character string of length 20 or less. Each word should consist of a sequence of letters A-Z; no digits, blanks or special characters are allowed. The output should be given as follows:

```
WORD LIST WITHOUT DUPLICATES:
    m ENTRIES

    first word
    second word
    ...
```

The value m given in the title indicates the length of the final list, after duplicates and improper words have been rejected. Report any difficulties with the length of the list, but produce some list if at all possible.

(1.1b) and (1.1d) have obviously been written by someone who understands programming, and who is anticipating many of the difficulties the program must face. Given a description in this form and this much detail, the program is well-specified and not very difficult to write. But, in general, (1.1a) and (1.1c) are samples of what you can expect to be given as an initial problem statement. (1.1b) and (1.1d) are the corresponding samples of what you must produce by asking the right questions. In a programming course your assignments may look more like (1.1b) and (1.1d), but someday you will face problems like (1.1a) and (1.1c).

Whenever possible, obtain samples of input and corresponding output. English is a disappointingly ambiguous descriptive tool, and a concrete example often clarifies a voluminous description.

When beginning on a problem don't even think about the program you are to write; concentrate on the problem until it becomes absolutely clear. Make up several sets of input data, and figure out the corresponding output results. This sample data should be designed to test and increase your understanding of the details of the problem, and not just its general nature. It might seem a waste of time to make up input data and perform hand calculations, but in doing so you are actually executing an algorithm to solve the problem. Thus while concentrating on understanding the problem, you are also working toward designing the solution.

While studying the problem you should ask questions like "What is to be done if the input number is incorrect?", "What happens if this particular number is 0? Is it correct or incorrect and what should I do with it?", and "What should I do here -- the problem statement seems to be ambiguous?" It is important that these questions be raised and answered before any programming is done. Proper understanding of the problem before you begin programming is crucial. Without this understanding, the program can never be correct.

The clarification of a significant problem is rarely completed as the first step in development. In general you will discover the omission of some necessary detail in the problem requirements only after you are engaged in the detailed execution of a later phase. For example, you will discover the lack of some detail about the volume of data only when you are attempting to specify the data structures and need a specific value to give as the size of an array. Or you will discover that you don't know how to process a particular error when you are actually writing the conditional unit to check for that error. In either case, you have discovered that the first phase is not quite completed and you must return and work on it further.

1.2 Design of a Solution Strategy

This is certainly the hardest part of the process for which to give general advice as to how to proceed. Whatever creativity exists in programming is concentrated in this phase. We will give some vague suggestions as to where you may get ideas, and will give some helpful procedures for developing ideas once you have them -- but we recognize that we are helping you least just where you need it most. We recommend you read Polya's classic book How to Solve It.

A useful device is to initially ignore the computer and its programming language, and try to figure out how you would solve the problem by hand, if you were presented with the data on cards in such a way that you could see each item only once, and only in the order given. Assume further that the only "scratch paper" available to you is a number of very small cards (one number apiece) on which you can write, erase and rewrite numbers. If you can figure out some way to solve the problem by hand under these restrictions, then you can generally figure out how to describe that method in a program.

The important thing is to separate the process of planning a solution from the task of describing that solution in a programming language. Once you learn to make this separation, the challenging and difficult part of the process will be the planning. For example, if you are unable to write a program to "sort" a list of numbers into increasing order, it is likely because you cannot figure out how to do it by hand in a systematic manner, and not because you don't know PASCAL. Conversely, if your sorting program is particularly efficient it is because you devised a clever plan, and not because a mediocre plan was cleverly described in PASCAL statements.

1.2.1 Algorithms

An algorithm is a sequence of statements to be executed in order, to produce some desired result. It may also contain comments or descriptions to aid us in "executing" or understanding it. A cooking recipe, instructions to put a Heathkit tuner together, or instructions to build a model airplane are all good examples of algorithms.

Algorithms should be written in whatever language and notation will make them most understandable to the reader. Often we assume a certain background and knowledge on the part of the reader and adopt some technical vocabulary that makes the algorithm more precise and compact. Algorithms are written for people to read, rather than for computers and are therefore generally not written in a programming language. We adopt or invent whatever language seems best for the particular problem. Often this is a combination of English, mathematics and whatever technical vocabulary is peculiar to the problem area.

A program is an algorithm that has been translated into a programming language. We regard a program as a specific implementation of an algorithm. The point is that the algorithm comes first, and it is written in an informal (but still precise) English-like language. The program comes later, and its preparation is a process of translation rather than creation.

An algorithm can be translated into different programming languages. However, since we often know in advance what language we will use, we tend to bias the algorithm toward convenient operations of that language. In our case, knowing we are headed for a PASCAL program, we start with a mixture of English and PASCAL, using PASCAL terms where convenient, but inventing terms whenever that seems more convenient. Generally the terms we invent are at a "higher level" than PASCAL statements. For example, we say "Swap A and B". PASCAL has no single statement to "swap" and this will later be translated into three assignment statements:

```
(* SWAP A AND B *)
    T := A;
    A := B;
    B := T
```

We can use terms like "find", "solve", and "search" that are at a much higher level and will eventually be expressed as a substantial segment of program. In our examples, as we illustrate the gradual and systematic conversion of an algorithm into a program, we use upper case (capital) letters for phrases in PASCAL and lower case letters for phrases that have not yet been translated into PASCAL. This is the same convention we used in Section II.2 to present program schemata:

```
(* Comment describing task and stopping flag *)
    Initialize;
    READ(item);
    WHILE item <> stopping flag DO
    BEGIN (* loop name *)
         Perform action on item;
         READ(item)
         END (* loop name *)
```

We will sometimes simply replace the English phrase with its PASCAL equivalent, but usually we will carry the English phrase over into the program as a heading comment, to be followed by the PASCAL implementation of the function described in the comment.

1.2.2 Top-Down Development

The general plan of attack is called "top-down development" or "successive refinement". We try to decompose a problem into a simple sequence of sub-problems. Given a problem P, try to discover a set of smaller problems P1, P2, P3, ... such that solving P1 first, then P2, etc, will be equivalent to solving the original P. Then apply the same approach to each of these sub-problems in turn -- determine a set of sub-sub-problems P11, P12, P13, ... whose solutions in sequence constitute a solution to P1. This leads quite naturally to a well-structured program as described in Section II.1.6.

Each time we find a sequence of sub-problems that correspond to a given problem we are, in effect, refining the statement of that problem into one with more detail and more indication as to how the problem is to be solved. This process continues until we have refined all of the high-level English phrases into PASCAL statements. At this point we have completely specified how the problem is to be solved, and have a program ready for testing.

The top-down analysis of a problem can usefully be guided by constructing a "development tree":

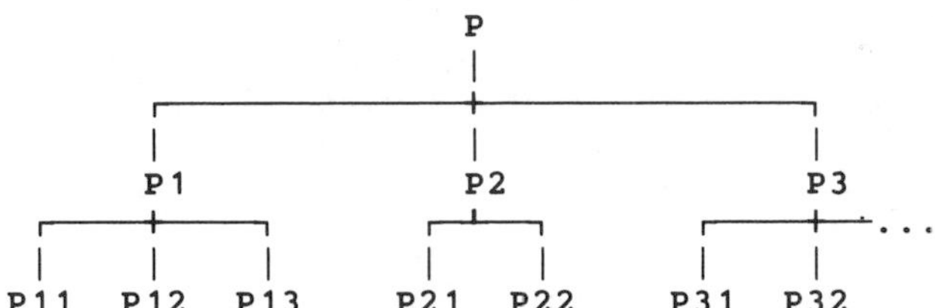

Such a tree is not a "flow-chart". A flow-chart shows alternative paths of flow-of-control; a tree shows the structure of a program. Each horizontal level of the tree is a complete description of the problem; each lower level refines that description to give more detail. All the sub-problems on any horizontal level are to be executed, in left to right order.

1.2.3 A Comment Outline

A convenient way to preserve the information contained in the development tree and at the same time initiate the actual preparation of the program is to transform the tree into a "comment outline". Those phrases in the tree which are not in PASCAL become a separate PASCAL comment, and the vertical position in the tree is reflected by the indentation in the outline. Left-to-right order in the tree becomes normal sequential order (top-to-bottom) in the outline. These comments serve as headings for program units and describe the function performed by the statements indented beneath them. For example, the tree in 1.2.2 would become:

```
(* P ...  *)
PROGRAM P(INPUT, OUTPUT);
    (* P1 ...  *)
         (* P11 ...  *)
         (* P12 ...  *)
         (* P13 ...  *)
    (* P2 ...  *)
         (* P21 ...  *)
         (* P22 ...  *)
    (* P3 ...  *)
         (* P31 ...  *)
         (* P32 ...  *)
         ...
    END.  (* P *)
```

1.3 Choice of Data Structures

Key decisions must be made with regard to what elements of the problem will require storage. Variables have to be specified to accomplish this storage, including names, dimensions, type attributes, and the logical relationship between variables. Much of this information obviously comes from the clarification of the problem with respect to the volume and form of the input data, but the choice of data structures depends equally importantly on the program strategy.

Although we treat them here as separate phases, in general data structure and program strategy are inextricably related. For example, consider the programs classified in Section II.2.1. The strategy represented by (II.2.1a) needs only one datum at a time, while strategy (II.2.1b) requires an array to hold all the data at once.

The choice of data structures takes place after the program strategy has been chosen, and sometimes the final choice can be delayed until after most of the actual program statements are written. In general, postpone the final specification of data structures as long as possible. This will reduce the backtracking that is required. There are often details that don't become clear until much of the program has been written.

Relationships between variables are important, and you should emphasize these relationships to the reader by the order in which you give declarations. For example, consider two sets of declarations (1.3a) and (1.3b) which are equivalent to PASCAL:

```
(1.3a)    VAR PR, TP: ARRAY[1..50] OF REAL;
                    (* PRESSURE AND TEMPERATURE TABLES *)
              MIN, MAX: REAL;
              N, M, POSMAX: INTEGER
                    (* LENGTHS AND POSITION OF MAX *)

(1.3b)    VAR PR: ARRAY[1..50] OF REAL; (* PRESSURE TABLE *)
              PRTOP: INTEGER; (* IS PR[1..PRTOP] *)
              PRMAX,          (* MAX VALUE IN PR[1..PRTOP] *)
              PRMIN: REAL; (* MIN VALUE IN PR[1..PRTOP] *)

              TP: ARRAY[1..50] OF REAL; (* TEMPERATURE TABLE *)
              TPTOP: INTEGER; (* IS TP[1..TPTOP] *)
              TPPOSMAX: INTEGER;
                    (* POSITION OF MAX VALUE IN TP[1..TPTOP] *)
```

It takes a little longer to write declarations like (1.3b) but they are much clearer to the reader. Both the names _and the grouping_ emphasize the relationships between variables. Grouping variables just to avoid repeating attributes is false economy. (1.3b) also uses more suggestive variable names -- TPTOP instead of M; PRMAX instead of MAX.

1.4 Writing the Actual Program Statements

Relatively little needs to be said about the detailed programming phase. If phase two has been adequately done you have a detailed comment outline describing the action of each unit of the program. Phase three has defined the objects upon which those units must act. All that remains is to translate these detailed English-like specifications into statements of PASCAL (or whatever programming language is being employed).

However, as suggested earlier, as you write the detailed program statements you often discover that the data structures are not quite right, so you have to return to phase three. You may also find it necessary to return to phase two to alter the organization of the program. Rarely can you complete the detailed translation without having to return at least once to phase one to clarify some aspect of the problem definition, which in turn may require changes in the program organization or data structures. Backing up and making changes can be a tricky business. The difficulty lies in making sure that you have identified _all_ the implications of the change and have made all the necessary adjustments. The development tree is particularly helpful in indicating what program sections are affected.

Few people compose well at a keypunch. The usual practice is to write the program statements by hand, and then keypunch (or enter on a typewriter terminal) from this handwritten copy. The accuracy of the keypunching depends, to a considerable extent, upon the legibility of the handwritten copy. We often see students punching from copy that is at best only semi-legible.

This inevitably introduces errors into the program. I's get mistaken for 1's; 2's for Z's; O's for zeros; inserts get inserted in the wrong place; and the indentation is generally fouled up. Considering how hard it is to detect and remove errors once they are in a program it is worth spending some time and effort keeping them out in the first place.

The initial writing of a program can be a pretty messy process. Statements have to be added, or deleted, or changed. They sometimes have to be shifted left or right to reflect changes in the nesting level. (An optimist has been defined as someone who programs in ink.) It is usually worthwhile copying a program over to have a clear, readable copy before attempting to keypunch it. This makes keypunching a simple transcription process, rather than a deciphering problem. The time spent in producing the extra initial copy will be more than offset by a reduction in testing time.

Section 2 Examples of Program Development

The following sections present the development of six different examples in varying degrees of completeness. Although we are primarily concerned with the development process rather than the particular problems, three of these examples -- searching, sorting and scanning for symbols -- are in fact important problems with which you should become familiar.

We try to describe the development process in some detail, identifying each phase and presenting some of the alternatives from which one must choose. For short examples this may seem laborious since one obviously can produce a satisfactory program by a much less studied and formal process. However, the process described here is indispensable for larger and more complicated problems. It is not entirely natural or intuitively obvious, so if you are to use this technique when it is needed, you must learn and practice it in simple situations where it may not be absolutely necessary.

2.1 The Example of I.1.2.1

In Section I.1.2.1 the following problem is posed:

> Given a list of numbers, print the first, second, third numbers, etc., but stop printing when the largest number in the list has been printed.

The development begun in I.1.2.1 is later completed in Section I.5.4. You should now reread these sections and try to identify the various phases of the development.

A development tree was not given for this problem. It would be something like the following:

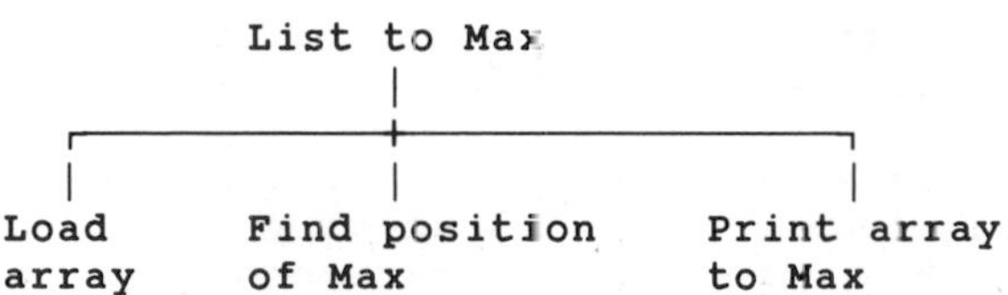

The data structures consist of an array INT of sufficient size to hold all the data, and two variables TOP and MAXP to point to the last position used in INT and to the position of the maximum.

The development tree can be converted to a comment outline:

```
(* PROGRAM TO LIST VALUES FROM FIRST TO MAXIMUM *)
    (* LOAD DATA INTO INT[1..N] UNTIL FIRST ZERO *)
    (* SET MAXP TO POSITION OF MAXIMUM IN INT[1..TOP] *)
    (* PRINT INT[1..MAXP], 1 PER LINE *)
```

Now analyzing the subproblems presented by these headings, the first subproblem is an example of the basic program schema (2b) given in Section II.2. A list of data is to be read, with a specified stopping flag. The task to be performed on each datum is a test, with "good" values to be preserved in an array. The second subproblem is a variation of (I.1.1e), differing only in that the data whose maximum is sought is already in an array, rather than in an external data list. The third subproblem is a straightforward printing task such as the examples given in Section I.6.1. Although this problem may have looked formidable when you first read Section I.5.4, it is apparent now that it actually consists of a simple sequence of three subproblems, <u>each of which is some variation of a task that you have seen previously</u>.

Of course, you are entitled to be suspicious of examples in textbooks, where everything works out neatly and the authors obviously had every opportunity to rig things to make their point. Nevertheless this is not an atypical experience. You will discover that each new problem can be broken down into subproblems, most of which are variations of things you have done before. There are a relatively small number of basic tasks -- perhaps several dozen -- that recur very often in problems that seem entirely different.

2.2 The Problem of Searching a List

Consider the following "list-searching" problem:

> Given is a "list" of numbers, in a particular order, and a set of "inquiries" -- numbers which may or may not be duplicates of those included in the list. For each inquiry determine whether or not it is on the list. If it is on the list, indicate what position it occupies; if it is not on the list report that fact.

For example, if a list consists of the numbers 9, -4.5, 16 and 5, in that order, then the inquiry "16" should result in the report that this number is in third position on the list; the inquiries "12" and "4.5" should result in a report that they are not on the list.

Clarifying the problem will lead to detail about the quantity and the form of the input. This might result in the following specification:

> The input will consist of: a) an integer specifying the length of the list; b) the list values, in order; c) an integer specifying the number of inquiries; d) the inquiries. The list will have not more than 100 values, which can be positive, negative or zero, and in integer, decimal or exponential form.

This means that the example above would be given in the form:

```
4 9 -4.5 16 5
3 16 12 4.5
```

Detailed specifcation of required output might be the following:

> For each inquiry print a line (double-spaced) that gives the value, and either its position on the list or the fact that it does not appear on the list.

With this specification the exact format and wording of the output line is left to the programmer's discretion. Presumably lines such as the following would be acceptable (but it is worth checking in advance to make sure):

```
16 IS IN POSITION 3

12 IS NOT ON THE LIST

4.5 IS NOT ON THE LIST
```

The only data errors that can occur in this problem are in the control values that specify the length of the list and the number of inquiries. Error processing might be specified as follows:

> The list length may be anything from 0 to 100; if not, terminate execution with an appropriate warning. The number of inquiries is arbitrary.

This method of specifying list length with a control value is not a particularly good idea. It is easy to handle in the program, but the program cannot check for certain obvious and ruinous errors. For example, if the list length is specified as 90, but 91 values are actually given, then the 91st will be interpreted as the number of inquiries. If only 89 values are given then the number of inquiries will become the last item on the list, and the first inquiry will be taken to be the number of inquiries. Such miscounting is a common error, and the program can do little against it. On the other hand, the specification that the program should work for a list of length zero, or for no inquiries is not unreasonable. Posed as a separate problem, it would be foolish for anyone to run the program with no list or no inquiries, but such programs are often later incorporated into a larger program. The ability to operate properly for extreme values -- in particular, the ability to do nothing, gracefully -- is very valuable.

Obviously, the entire list must be available for processing each inquiry. This is the reason the list is placed before the inquiries in the input data. On the other hand, each inquiry is processed separately and there is no need to retain an inquiry value after it is processed. Hence the problem does not quite fall in any of the simple categories described in Section II.2.1. But it can be divided into two sub-problems:

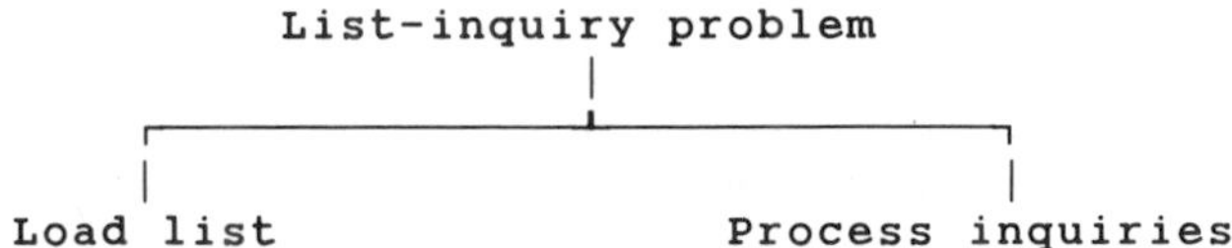

"Load list" is an interpretation of program schema (2d) given in Section II.2. The body of the schema in this case is simply to insert each datum in an array. "Process inquiries" is another interpretation of the same schema. The body in this case is more complex, involving searching the list and reporting results. The second level of development would be:

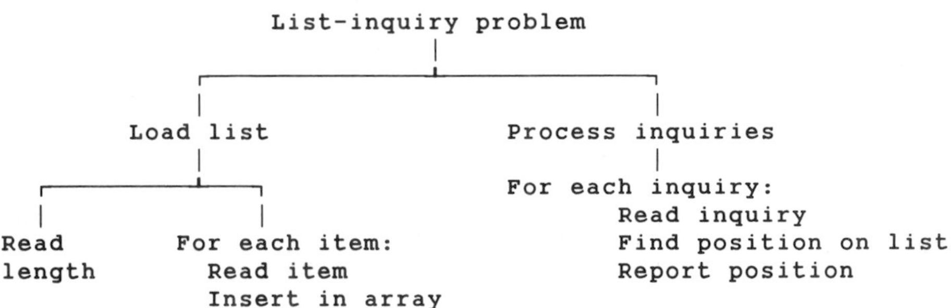

The principal data structure is an array to hold the list, together with a variable to indicate its length. The array must have at least 100 elements since the given list may be that long, and must consist of REAL variables since no restriction assures that the values will be integers. We will call the list "GLIST", for "given list".

No array is necessary to store the inquiries since they can be processed one at a time. A simple REAL variable "INQ" will suffice to hold the current inquiry value. You could not elect to read all the inquiries into a second array and then process them one at a time from that array, because you have no idea how large an array is required. (Some programming languages, such as PL/I, provide a facility that permits the size of arrays to be specified from data, but PASCAL does not allow this. See Section VI.3 of our Introduction to Programming.) We also need variables to store the number of inquiries remaining to be processed, and the position of a particular value in the list. The values of these variables will always be integers.

The development tree can be converted into a comment outline as shown below. The declarations of the required data structures are also included.

```
(* LIST-INQUIRY PROGRAM *)
PROGRAM LISTINQ(INPUT, OUTPUT);
VAR GLIST: ARRAY[1..100] OF REAL; (* GIVEN LIST IS *)
    GLNG,           (* GLIST[1..GLNG] *)
    GPOS: INTEGER; (* A POSITION IN GLIST *)
    INQ: REAL; (* CURRENT INQUIRY VALUE *)
    PRESENT: BOOLEAN; (* TRUE WHEN INQ IS IN GLIST *)
    NINQ: INTEGER; (* NUMBER OF INQUIRIES
                      STILL TO BE PROCESSED *)

    (* LOAD LIST, SKIP IF ERROR *)
         (* READ LENGTH *)
         (* FOR EACH ITEM, READ AND INSERT IN GLIST *)

    (* PROCESS INQUIRIES *)
         (* FIND POSITION ON LIST *)
         (* REPORT POSITION *)

    END (* LISTINQ *)
```

Finally we are ready to write PASCAL statements to perform the actions. "Read length" can be programmed:

```
(* READ LENGTH *)
    READ(GLNG);
    IF (GLNG < 0) OR (GLNG > 100) THEN
      BEGIN
         WRITELN(' IMPROPER LIST LENGTH:', GLNG);
         GOTO 9999
      END
```

Testing, such as that shown here, should take place any time a control value is read. You should think of such testing as an inherent part of "read". In this case the label 9999 must be prefixed to a statement that will terminate execution of the program. This label must also be declared at the head of the program.

The "insert in GLIST" task could be programmed:

```
(* FOR EACH ITEM, READ AND INSERT IN GLIST *)
    FOR GPOS := 1 TO GLNG DO
         READ(GLIST[GPOS])
```

The "process inquiries" task is obviously a repetition unit, modeled after schema (II.2d):

```
(* PROCESS INQUIRIES *)
    READ(NINQ);
    WHILE NINQ > 0 DO
      BEGIN (* INQ LOOP *)
         READ(INQ);
         (* FIND POSITION OF INQ ON LIST *)
         (* REPORT POSITION *)
         NINQ := NINQ - 1
      END (* INQ LOOP *)
```

Two tasks comprise the principal body of this loop. "Find position" is itself a repetition unit:

```
(* FIND POSITION OF INQ ON LIST *)
    PRESENT := FALSE;
    FOR GPOS := 1 TO GLNG DO
      BEGIN (* FIND LOOP *)
         IF INQ = GLIST[GPOS] THEN
           BEGIN
              PRESENT := TRUE;
              GOTO 9000
           END
      END; (* FIND LOOP *)
    9000:
```

FIND LOOP terminates either when a value is found -- in which case it reaches label 9000 with GPOS pointing to that value -- or when the loop has indexed through the last element of GLIST. The program distinguishes between these cases by means of the BOOLEAN variable PRESENT, which is initially set FALSE and remains FALSE if INQ is not found on GLIST. If INQ is found on GLIST, PRESENT is set TRUE.

"Report position" is a "multiple alternative" unit, with selection depending on the outcome of the list search:

```
(* REPORT POSITION *)
    IF PRESENT
         THEN WRITELN('0', INQ, ' IS IN POSITION', GPOS)
         ELSE WRITELN('0', INQ, ' IS NOT ON THE LIST')
```

The complete program can now be assembled from these segments:

```
(* LIST-INQUIRY PROGRAM *)
PROGRAM LISTINQ(INPUT, OUTPUT);

LABEL 9000, 9999;
VAR GLIST: ARRAY[1..100] OF REAL; (* GIVEN LIST IS *)
    GLNG,                    (* GLIST[1..GLNG] *)
    GPOS: INTEGER;           (* A POSITION IN GLIST *)
    INQ: REAL;               (* CURRENT INQUIRY VALUE *)
    PRESENT: BOOLEAN;        (* TRUE WHEN INQ IS IN GLIST *)
    NINQ: INTEGER;           (* NUMBER OF INQUIRIES STILL
                                TO BE PROCESSED *)

BEGIN (* LISTINQ *)
    (* LOAD LIST, SKIP IF ERROR *)
         (* READ LENGTH *)
              READ(GLNG);
              IF (GLNG < 0) OR (GLNG > 100) THEN
                BEGIN
                   WRITELN(' IMPROPER LIST LENGTH:', GLNG);
                   GOTO 9999
                END;
         (* FOR EACH ITEM, READ AND INSERT IN GLIST *)
              FOR GPOS := 1 TO GLNG DO
                   READ(GLIST[GPOS])

    (* PROCESS INQUIRIES *)
         READ(NINQ);
         WHILE NINQ > 0 DO
           BEGIN (* INQ LOOP *)
              READ(INQ);
              (* FIND POSITION OF INQ IN LIST *)
                   PRESENT := FALSE;
                   FOR GPOS := 1 TO GLNG DO
                     BEGIN (* FIND LOOP *)
                        IF INQ = GLIST[GPOS] THEN
                          BEGIN
                             PRESENT := TRUE;
                             GOTO 9000
                          END
                     END; (* FIND LOOP *)
                   9000:;
              (* REPORT POSITION *)
                   IF PRESENT
                     THEN WRITELN('0', INQ,
                          ' IS IN POSITION', GPOS)
                     ELSE WRITELN('0', INQ,
                          ' IS NOT ON THE LIST');
              NINQ := NINQ - 1
           END; (* INQ LOOP *)
         9999:;
END.  (* LISTINQ *)
```

Some final observations with regard to this program:

1. The program should check the value read for NINQ to make sure it is reasonable.

2. The program has many comments relative to the number of statements, but this is because the tasks in this case are simple. As problems grow larger it requires more substantial segments to do what each comment heading specifies.

3. The search algorithm used in "find position" is simple, but not efficient for long lists. Much more efficient algorithms could be used. (Examples are given in Section VII.2.4 of our Introduction to Programming.) Note that the program is structured so the search segment can be easily replaced without requiring a change anywhere else in the program.

2.3 The Problem of Ordering a List

A common task is to reorder the elements of a list so that their values are "in order". For numeric variables this is usually "algebraic order", either increasing or decreasing; for character variables it is usually according to the collating sequence given in Section I.9.2.2, which implies both alphabetical and algebraic order. The process of rearranging values so they satisfy some order relationship is called "sorting". A simple form of sorting problem is:

> Given a list of numbers, sort them so they are in order of increasing value. Display the list before and after sorting.

For example, if the list 5, 0, -7, 6.2, 1 is given, the list -7, 0, 1, 5, 6.2 is to be produced. One possible clarification of the problem is:

> Given data consisting of an integer n (not greater than 50) followed by a list of n numbers, sort these n numbers into increasing order. Display the list in original order in a single column, followed by the sorted list in single column. Provide appropriate titles.

Obviously we need to have all the data available at once, so we cannot use a program like (II.2.1a). But excluding the final printing task the rest of the problem is an interpretation of (II.2.1b). The first level of development might be:

(2.3a)

(2.3a) does not indicate when the display of the initial list will take place. There are two possibilities -- either before or after sorting. The most obvious is to display the initial order before it is changed. This could be done either as part of the "read" task or as a separate task:

(2.3b)

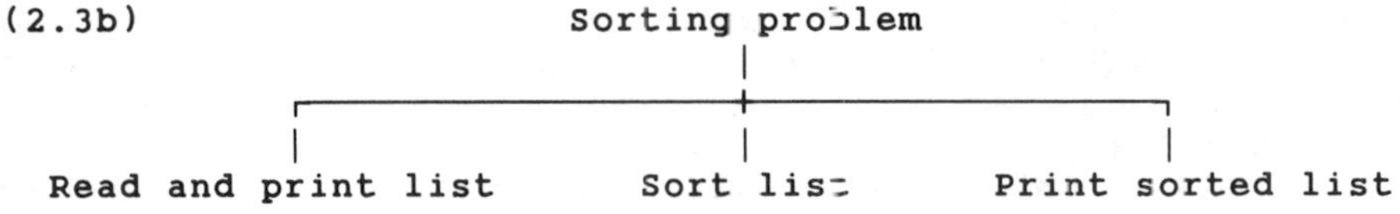

(2.3c)

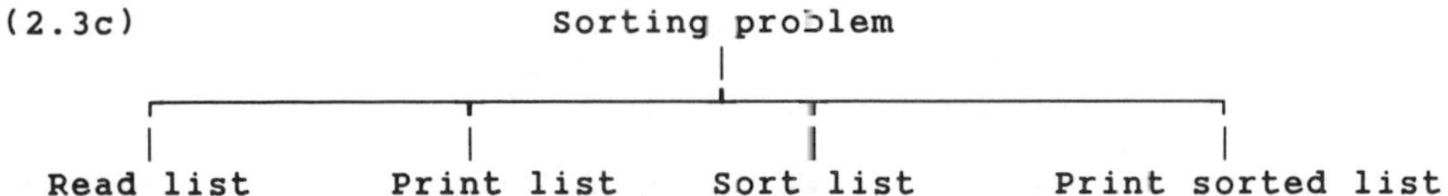

(2.3) results in two separate loops, and (2.3b) in a single loop with two statements (READ and WRITELN) in the body. There seems to be no advantage in separation and we decide, at least tentatively, in favor of (2.3b). If we wanted to have all printing done in one section of the program we would have to make an extra copy of the list, so we could sort one copy and keep the other in initial order. The development then would be:

(2.3d)

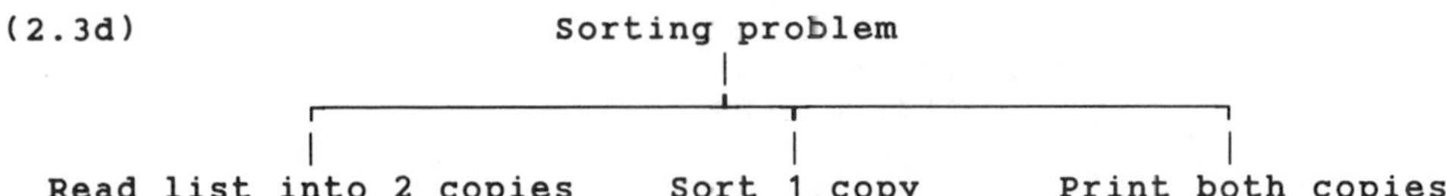

(2.3d) is unnecessary in this case and we will use (2.3b), but note that only a slight variation in the original problem statement -- to require the display in side-by-side columns -- would make strategy (2.3d) necessary.

So now we have separated off two minor tasks "read and print" and "print" -- each an interpretation of schema (II.2b) or schema (II.2.1b). By now the programming of tasks like these should be familiar and almost automatic. It is also clear that the principal data structure will be an array to hold the list and a variable to specify how much of the array is used. The elements of the array will have to be REAL since no restriction on values is implied by the problem statement. What remains is the following task:

Given L[1..N], reorder its elements into increasing order.

To figure out a method for reordering, suppose you had n 3 by 5 cards, each bearing a number, laid out in a row. How would you go about rearranging the cards so the numbers were in increasing order? There is the additional restriction that you can only look at and compare <u>two</u> cards at a time (since PASCAL has this restriction). One way would be to scan over the cards and find the one with the largest value. This card could be interchanged with the one at the end of the row. Now, ignoring that card (which has been properly positioned), you could repeat the process for the remaining n-1 cards. That is, locate the card with the second largest value (the largest of the remaining n-1) and interchange it with the second from last (the last of the n-1). Now with the last two cards in proper position, work on the remaining n-2 cards in the same way. If this is continued until finally the last two cards are put in order, the entire row will have been sorted. Let us transform this idea into an algorithm:

Repeat for lists of diminishing length m=n,n-1,n-2,...,2:
1. Find the maximum value of L[1..m];
2. Interchange the maximum with L[m].

Interchanging values is a familiar task by now, and finding the maximum is similar to a problem you have seen before. This version differs from (I.1.1e) only in that the numbers are already in an array (rather than being an external data list) and in that we need to find the <u>position</u> as well as the value of the maximum. A program segment to do this is:

```
(* SET MAXPOS TO POSITION OF MAX IN L[1..M] *)
    MAXVAL := L[1];
    MAXPOS := 1;
    FOR I := 2 TO M DO
      BEGIN (* MAX LOOP *)
         IF L[I] > MAXVAL THEN
           BEGIN
              MAXVAL := L[I];
              MAXPOS := I
           END
      END (* MAX LOOP *)
```

Given that MAXPOS points to the maximum value in L[1..M] the interchange is simply:

```
(* INTERCHANGE MAX AND LAST IN L[1..M] *)
    TEMP := L[M];
    L[M] := L[MAXPOS];
    L[MAXPOS] := TEMP
```

These two segments must be repeated for lists whose lengths M vary from N down to 2:

(2.3e)

```
(* SORT L[1..N] *)
    FOR M := N DOWNTO 2 DO
      BEGIN (* SUBLIST LOOP *)
         (* SET MAXPOS TO POS'N OF MAX IN L[1..M] *)
              MAXVAL := L[1];
              MAXPOS := 1;
              FOR I := 2 TO M DO
                BEGIN (* MAX LOOP *)
                   IF L[I] > MAXVAL THEN
                     BEGIN
                        MAXVAL := L[I];
                        MAXPOS := I
                     END
                END; (* MAX LOOP *)
         (* INTERCHANGE MAX AND L[M] IN L[1..M] *)
              TEMP := L[M];
              L[M] := L[MAXPOS];
              L[MAXPOS] := TEMP
      END (* SUBLIST LOOP *)
```

The complete program would have (2.3e) inserted in the following:

```
(* SORT AND DISPLAY A LIST OF NUMBERS *)
PROGRAM SORT(INPUT, OUTPUT);

LABEL 9000;
VAR L: ARRAY[1..50] OF REAL;
    N: INTEGER; (* ACTUAL LENGTH OF LIST IN L *)
    M: INTEGER; (* LENGTH OF SUB-LIST *)
    I: INTEGER;
    TEMP: REAL;
    MAXVAL: REAL; (* MAXIMUM VALUE IN SUB-LIST *)
    MAXPOS: INTEGER; (* POSITION OF MAXVAL IN LIST *)

BEGIN (* SORT *)
    (* READ AND DISPLAY INITIAL LIST *)
         READ(N);
         IF (N < 0) OR (N > 50) THEN
           BEGIN
              WRITELN;
              WRITELN('0IMPROPER LENGTH:', N);
              GOTO 9000
           END;
         WRITELN('1LIST IN INITIAL ORDER');
         WRITELN;
         FOR I := 1 TO N DO
           BEGIN
              READ(L[I]);
              WRITELN(' ', L[I])
           END;
    (* SORT L[1..N] *)
         insert (2.3e)

    (* DISPLAY L[1..N] *)
         WRITELN('0SORTED LIST');
         WRITELN;
         FOR I := 1 TO N DO
              WRITELN(' ', L[I])

    9000:;
END.  (* SORT *)
```

Sorting is an important problem in practice, and a very convenient problem to illustrate points in programming. We will refer back to this often in future sections and it will help if you understand this simple version very thoroughly.

2.4 An Accounting Problem

A bank would like to produce records of the transactions during an accounting period in connection with their checking accounts. For each account the bank wants a list showing the balance at the beginning of the period, the number of deposits and withdrawals, and the final balance. (This is a simplified version of a very common and important type of computer application.)

The accounts and transactions for an accounting period will be given on punched cards as follows:

1. First will be a sequence of cards describing the accounts. Each account is described by two numbers: the account number (greater than 0), and the account balance at the beginning of the period, in dollars and cents. There will be one card for each account, containing two numbers. The first gives the account number, and the second gives the account balance. The last account is followed by a "dummy" account consisting of two zero values to indicate the end of the list. There will be at most 200 accounts.

2. Following the accounts are the transactions. Each transaction is given by three numbers: the account number, a 1 or 2 (indicating a deposit or withdrawal, respectively), and the transaction amount, in dollars and cents. The last real transaction is followed by a dummy transaction consisting of three zero values.

The following sample input has been supplied, where the words at the right are not part of the input, but explanatory notes.

Input numbers			meaning
1025	61.50		(account 1025 contains $61.50)
1028	103		(account 1028 contains $103)
1026	100		(account 1026 contains $100)
0	0		(end of accounts)
1025	1	500	(deposit $500 in account 1025)
1028	2	20	(withdraw $20 from account 1028)
1025	2	400	(withdraw $400 from account 1025)
1025	1	50	(deposit $50 in account 1025)
0	0	0	(end of transactions)

For this input, the output should be:

ACCOUNT	PREV BAL	WITHDRAWALS	DEPOSITS	FINAL BAL
1025	61.50	1	2	211.50
1028	103	1	0	83
1026	100	0	0	100

Some of the errors that could occur in the data are:

1. An account is listed two or more times.

2. The end-of-account signal is missing or incorrect.

3. A transaction number is not in the list of accounts.

4. The withdrawal-deposit number is not 1 or -1.

5. The transaction amount is negative.

6. The end-of-transaction signal is wrong or missing.

All these errors could be detected by the program. Detecting other situations such as overdrafts (which are not really input errors) would probably make the program more valuable. Of course, not all errors can be detected by the program. For example, a withdrawal keypunched as a deposit or an error in a transaction amount can not be detected. To keep our program development to manageable size we will ignore the question of data errors. In the real world this is clearly unrealistic, and the program would have to detect and process these errors.

The following steps give a reasonable chronological record of the development of a program for this problem.

Step 1. Discovering the overall structure of the algorithm.

Looking at the problem description, note that the account data precedes the transactions. Thus all accounts must be read and stored internally, before the transactions can be read and "processed". Moreover, while processing the transactions we must be able to access any account at any time, since no ordering of the transactions by account number is mentioned in the description of the problem. The sample data confirm this lack of ordering. Also, since the last transaction may apply to any account, no result may be printed for an account until all transactions have been processed. This analysis indicates that the structure of the program will be:

```
(2.4a)    2a1: Read in and set up the accounts in a "table";
          2a2: Read in and process the transactions;
          2a3: Print the results;
```

In tree form this would be:

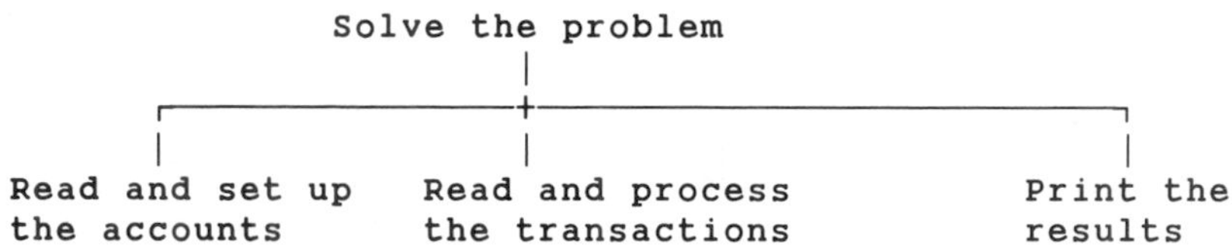

It should already be apparent that the structure of this problem is somewhat similar to the list-searching problem of Section 2.2. Task 2a1 is directly comparable to the first task of 2.2, except that the table of accounts is a more complex data structure than the list of values in 2.2. Task 2a2 searches for a particular entry in the table, but instead of reporting the position of the entry it modifies the entry. Task 2a3 is added; it has no counterpart in 2.2.

(2.4a) is an algorithm using the English commands "read", "set up", "process" and "print". These are not yet precise enough to specify the action to be taken, and our task is to refine them so that they are precise and are expressed in PASCAL terms.

There are now three separate, smaller problems, but they are obviously not entirely independent of each other. All three share the data structures used to contain the accounts and the information connected with them. Whenever we split a problem into several smaller parts, it is important to look at the "interface" or connections between them. Often, several strategies exist for implementing each one, but implementing one in a particular way may reduce the flexibility in designing the others. We must weigh carefully the benefits and disadvantages, including effects on other modules, in choosing a strategy for a given module.

Step 2. <u>The data structures representing the accounts</u>.

We must keep the accounts accessible in a table until all transactions have been processed and the results have been reported. This can be done using an array ACCT (say) to hold the ACCounT numbers and an array IBAL to hold the corresponding Initial BALances. We also need a variable N (say) to hold the number of accounts. Thus, if i is an integer between 1 and N, ACCT(i) contains an account number and IBAL(i) contains the corresponding initial balance. Other alternatives for storing the data exist of course, but this is probably the simplest and easiest.

Now review the problem statement to make sure the accounts have been described completely and accurately. Certainly this is all we need initially, but look at the sample output. After processing the transactions, in addition to the initial balance we must report the number of deposits and withdrawals and also the final balance. This will require three more arrays; we need two arrays to contain the number of withdrawals and deposits, and a third to contain the balances. The arrays holding the number of withdrawals and deposits will be initially set to 0, and will be increased to count the number of withdrawals and deposits that are processed for each account. Similarly, the array holding the final balances will be initialized to the initial balances and will be updated as transactions are processed.

To summarize, we write down the names of the variables which describe the accounts and define <u>as</u> <u>precisely</u> <u>as</u> <u>possible</u> how they will be used:

1. Variable N contains the number of accounts.

2. Five arrays describe the accounts: ACCT, IBAL, WITHDR, DEP and CBAL (meaning Current BALance). If i is an integer between 1 and N, then during execution of the program

   ACCT[i] is an ACCounT number,
   IBAL[i] is the corresponding Initial BALance,
   WITHDR[i] is the number of WITHDRawals processed so far,
   DEP[i] is the number of DEPosits processed so far,
   CBAL[i] is the Current BALance in the account.

CBAL(i) depends of course on the withdrawals and deposits processed so far. In order to fix these definitions more clearly in our minds, consider some examples. Just after reading in all the accounts in the sample input, the arrays are:

	ACCT	IBAL	WITHDR	DEP	CBAL
(1)	1025	61.50	0	0	61.50
(2)	1028	103	0	0	103
(3)	1026	100	0	0	100

Note that each CBAL(i) is the same as IBAL(i), since no transactions have been processed. After processing the first transaction, the arrays are:

	ACCT	IBAL	WITHDR	DEP	CBAL
(1)	1025	61.50	0	1	561.50
(2)	1028	103	0	0	103
(3)	1026	100	0	0	100

At this point we could write PASCAL declarations for these data structures, but it is better to wait. These structures should be considered tentative, and may have to be revised as the detailed design of the program unfolds.

We have looked at the data structures which contain the accounts from the viewpoint of the information that must be available as the program executes. Now consider how this information is accessed and changed -- how the three statements of algorithm (2.4a) use the information. Statement 2a2, "Read in and process the transactions", requires us to locate in the table of accounts the account associated with each transaction. This means a search in the array ACCT of account numbers for each transaction account number. That is, given a transaction like (1028, 1, 100), we have to find an integer i such that ACCT(i) = 1028. Assuming a search algorithm such as the one used in Section 2.2, on the average we must look at half of the accounts in order to find the right one. If there are only a few hundred accounts this may be feasible. But if there are 5000 or more accounts the time to search would be in seconds for each transaction, and we could not afford to structure the table of accounts as we have done.

This search time can be drastically reduced if the accounts are rearranged so that the account numbers are in ascending order: ACCT(1) ≤ ACCT(2) ≤ ... ≤ ACCT(N). If we sort the array of accounts as we read them in, we can process the transactions more efficiently. But sorting takes time too, and we must carefully weigh the sorting time against the efficiency gained in processing, before we decide which approach to take. This depends on the number of accounts relative to the number of transactions, and we now realize that we lack such information. The problem description is not complete, and without such information we cannot design the best program.

An even better solution would be for the bank to keep their accounts in ascending order, so that neither sorting nor a slow search would be required.

This discussion should illustrate the need for thinking about the various ways of implementing each succesive statement of an algorithm, and considering the effects of each. For now, assume that the accounts cannot be kept sorted because of other considerations, and that the simple search algorithm of Section 2.2 is adequate.

Step 3. <u>Refining the statement "Read and set up the accounts."</u>

Statement 2a1 is not yet in PASCAL, so it must be refined further. The required action is

```
Read and set up the first account;
Read and set up the second account;
                  ...
(until the account just read has account number 0)
```

Such a sequence of similar statements can be replaced by a loop which iteratively executes a single statement like "Read and set up the Kth account", where K is of course increased after each execution. There are several ways of writing this loop. One method recognizes that the first statement "Read and set up the first account" must always be executed and can therefore be put outside the loop:

```
K := 1;
Read and set up the Kth account;
WHILE ACCT[K] <> 0 DO
  BEGIN
    K := K + 1;
    Read and set up the Kth account
  END;
N := K - 1
```

The final statement that assigns K-1 instead of K to N is necessary because the last account read is just a dummy account serving as a stopping flag.

An alternative technique uses a dummy account ACCT[0] whose account number is set to 1 so that the loop body is always executed at least once:

```
        K := 0;
        ACCT[0] := 1;
        WHILE ACCT[K] <> 0 DO
          BEGIN
(2.4b)      K := K + 1;
            Read and set up the Kth account
          END;
        N := K - 1
```

Either refinement could be used. If the refinement of the statement "Read and set up the Kth account" turned out to be long and difficult, we would tend to choose (2.4b) because this difficult statement only appears once. (Recall the discussion of this issue in Section I.4.6.2.) At this point we arbitrarily choose (2.4b) and the development tree is:

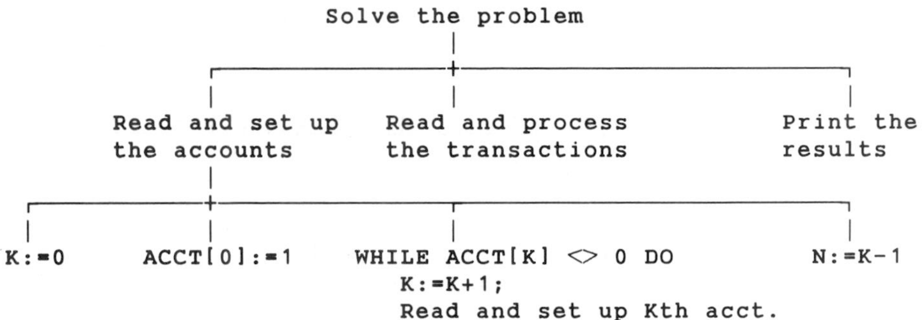

We have introduced a variable K, and should indicate what it means. While executing (2.4b) (and only then), K is the number of accounts read in so far, including the end-of-list signal as an account.

Note that when we declare the array ACCT we must give an upper bound on the number of elements in it. If the input happens to have more than that number of accounts, then (2.4b) will execute incorrectly.

Algorithm (2.4b) still contains an English statement which must be translated into PASCAL. To "read and set up account K", we must obtain values from the input data and store the account number and balance in ACCT[K] and IBAL[K], and initialize the other three variables that comprise account K:

```
(2.4c)  READLN(ACCT[K], IBAL[K]);
        WITHDR[K] := 0;
        DEP[K] := 0;
        CBAL[K] := IBAL[K]
```

As a final step, we insert this refinement into (2.4b) to yield the following program segment. Note that the original statement 2a1 becomes a comment of the program which replaces it:

```
        (* READ AND SET UP THE ACCOUNTS *)
           K := 0;
           ACCT[0] := 1;
(2.4d)     WHILE ACCT[K] <> 0 DO
              BEGIN
                K := K + 1;
                READLN(ACCT[K], IBAL[K]);
                WITHDR[K] := 0;
                DEP[K] := 0;
                CBAL[K] := IBAL[K]
              END;
           N := K - 1
```

Step 4. Refining "Read and process the transactions."

Consider statement 2a2, keeping in mind that the table of accounts is not ordered by account number. Two actions are required -- reading and processing the transactions -- and there may be several ways of performing them. Two possibilities come to mind:

1. First read and store all the transactions, then process all the transactions.

2. Read and process the first transaction, read and process the second transaction, etc.

The first possibility requires arrays in which to store all the transactions. How big should the arrays be? We don't know, since we have no idea how many transactions there may be. To use this method, we would have to determine the maximum number of transactions in any one run. This is essentially the same question we faced with inquiries in Section 2.2 and the distinction between the two simple types of program in II.2.1.

The question with the second method is feasibility. Is it possible to process a single transaction without having access to the others? The answer in this case is yes.

This is not really such a pointless question to ask as it might seem. For example, consider the task "Read in a list of transactions and print them out in order of the account number." We cannot "Read one and print, read one and print, etc.", so we must read all of them before we can begin printing.

With the second method, an array is not needed to hold the transactions, since we need only keep track of one transaction at a time. This second method seems to have no disadvantages compared to the first, and should be used.

Note that without a change in the problem definition, we are forced to use the second method. Since we don't know how many transactions might appear, we cannot assume any maximum and hence cannot use the first method. Quite often, a careful examination of the problem will answer a question for us. We should be continually asking ourselves questions like: "Have I used everything that was given to me?" "Could the problem definition be changed to make the solution easier, clearer, or more efficient?" "Have I assumed something that is not explicitly stated to be true?"

A second point is the question of efficiency. For example, we use the second possibility rather than the first, because it uses less computer storage space but otherwise is essentially the same. We may strive for efficiency with respect to execution time, storage space, or with respect to the time it takes to write the program. There is always a trade-off when trying to gain efficiency; usually what executes faster will take more space, or what is easier to program and understand may be slower. A programmer must know what the value criterion is for each program he is to design.

Our choice, then, for reading and processing transactions is

```
Read a transaction;
Process the transaction just read;
        ...
Read a transaction;
Process the transaction just read;
Read a transaction;
     (until transaction acct. number is 0)
```

This is a sequence of (a pair of) statements which is to be executed several times, and we can use a loop. Since the first statement "Read a transaction" must always be executed and the last transaction is <u>not</u> to be processed, it is easiest to perform the first "read" outside the loop and to let the loop body consist of "Process transaction; Read transaction". That is, we are pairing the statements as indicated by the spacing in the following algorithm:

```
Read a transaction;

Process the transaction just read;
Read a transaction;
        ...

Process the transaction just read;
Read a transaction
     (until transaction acct. number is 0)
```

The algorithm using a WHILE loop is:

```
         Read a transaction;
         WHILE transaction account number <> 0 DO
           BEGIN (* TRAN LOOP *)
(2.4e)       Process the transaction just read;
             Read a transaction
           END (* TRAN LOOP *)
```

Further refinement requires a decision as to how the transactions are to be stored. We should question the format of the input transactions. If we allow a negative amount to specify a withdrawal, then the withdrawal-deposit code is not necessary. Let us assume that the bank says the given form is indeed necessary, and continue with the development.

Since only one transaction need be accessed at any time, only three simple variables are needed:

```
         TACCT   contains the Transaction ACCounT number.
(2.4f)   DEPWITH contains the action code:
                    1 means DEPosit, 2 means WITHdrawal.
         AMT     contains the AMounT of the transaction.
```

This leads to the following refinement of algorithm (2.4e):

```
         READLN(TACCT, DEPWITH, AMT);
         WHILE TACCT <> 0 DO
           BEGIN (* TRAN LOOP *)
(2.4g)       Process the transaction just read;
             READLN(TACCT, DEPWITH, AMT)
           END (* TRAN LOOP *)
```

The final task is to reduce the phrase "Process the transaction just read" to PASCAL terms. Processing a transaction requires us to find the corresponding account in the array ACCT. Suppose that while searching ACCT we store in a new variable J an integer so that TACCT = ACCT[J]. Then account ACCT[J] is to be changed as follows: If DEPWITH[J] = 1 then add 1 to DEP[J] and add AMT to CBAL[J]; if DEPWITH[J] = 2 then add 1 to WITH[J] and subtract AMT from CBAL[J].

A search algorithm similar to that of Section 2.2 will be used:

```
        (* PROCESS THE TRANSACTION JUST READ *)
          (* SEARCH FOR TRANSACTION ACCOUNT *)
             J := 1;
             WHILE ACCT[J] <> TACCT DO
(2.4h)          J := J + 1;
          IF DEPWITH = 1
             THEN BEGIN
                 DEP[J] := DEP[J] + 1;
                 CBAL[J] := CBAL[J] + AMT
               END
             ELSE BEGIN
                  WITHDR[J] := WITHDR[J] + 1;
                  CBAL[J] := CBAL[J] - AMT
               END
```

Note that (2.4h) assumes that the transaction is valid and does nothing to check this assumption. In general, it is highly unrealistic to assume that the data are in perfect form, and the program should check it in every way that is practical. For example, the program should provide for the possibility that the transaction account number is not valid -- that no such account will be found in the table. The program could include a check for this, similar to what was done in Section 2.2. There should also be a check to make sure that no value other than 1 or 2 is given as the action code. The obvious way to do this is with a conditional statement, but PASCAL provides an even better mechanism. DEPWITH can be declared to be a subrange of the integers 1..2, and PASCAL will automatically limit the values to this range and issue an error message if an attempt is made to assign some other value. It might be even better to use mnemonic values for the action code, such as DEP and WITH instead of 1 and 2. This suggests that DEPWITH should be declared a user-defined type with values DEP and WITH -- but unfortunately such values cannot be READ from data. DEPWITH could be a string variable, in which case an explicit test would have to be given to limit its values to the strings 'DEP' and 'WITH'. We will assume that the action code must remain 1,2 and will use a subrange declaration for DEPWITH.

Step 5. Refining "Print the results."

Statement 2a3 is the easiest to translate into PASCAL. Since an order was not specified by the problem description, we will print the accounts in the easiest order possible -- the order in which they were read in.

```
        (* PRINT THE RESULTS *)
           (* PRINT HEADING *)
             WRITE('1   ACCOUNT');
             WRITE('   PREVIOUS BALANCE    ');
             WRITE('WITHDRAWALS');
             WRITE(' DEPOSITS');
             WRITELN('    FINAL BALANCE     ');
(2.4i)       WRITELN;
           FOR I := 1 TO N DO
             WRITELN(' ', ACCT[I], IBAL[I], WITHDR[I],
                   DEP[I], CBAL[I])
```

The development tree now has become:

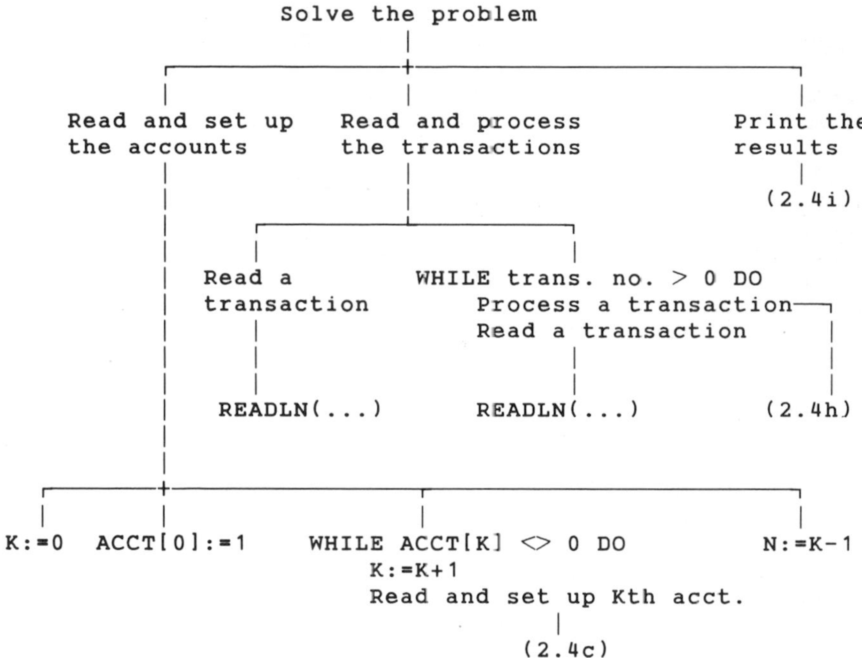

Step 6. Assembling the complete program.

The final task is to gather together the refinements for the three statements of (2.4a) into a PASCAL program. These refinements are (2.4d), (2.4g) with (2.4h) replacing the single English statement of (2.4g), and (2.4i). We also produce declarations from the descriptions of variables written in steps 2 and 4. We end up with the program below. It should be pointed out that this is not the only possible program. Just considering the same basic algorithm, there are many minor variations. For example, the statement "Read and set up the accounts" could have been written so that the array could be declared ACCT[1..200] instead of ACCT[1..201]. Many possibilities exist, and one cannot always say which is better.

```
(* SIMPLIFIED BANK ACCOUNTING PROGRAM *)
PROGRAM BANK(INPUT, OUTPUT);
VAR                         (* THE ACCOUNTS, IN ORDER READ: *)
    N: INTEGER;             (* THERE ARE N ACCOUNTS *)
    ACCT,                   (* THE ACCOUNT NUMBERS *)
    WITHDR,                 (* NUMBER OF WITHDRAWALS *)
    DEP:                    (* NUMBER OF DEPOSITS *)
         ARRAY[0..201] OF INTEGER;
    IBAL,                   (* THE INITIAL BALANCES *)
    CBAL:                   (* THE CURRENT BALANCES *)
         ARRAY[1..201] OF REAL;
                            (* CURRENT TRANSACTION: *)
    TACCT: INTEGER;         (* TRANSACTION ACCOUNT NUMBER *)
    DEPWITH: 1..2;          (* 1 = DEPOSIT, 2 = WITHDRAWAL *)
    AMT: REAL;              (* TRANSACTION AMOUNT *)
    I, J, K: INTEGER;       (* LOOP COUNTERS *)
BEGIN (* BANK *)
  (* READ AND SET UP THE ACCOUNTS *)
    K := 0;
    ACCT[0] := 1;
    WHILE ACCT[K] <> 0 DO
      BEGIN
        K := K + 1;
        READLN(ACCT[K], IBAL[K]);
        WITHDR[K] := 0;
        DEP[K] := 0;
        CBAL[K] := IBAL[K]
      END;
    N := K - 1;
```

```
  (* READ AND PROCESS THE TRANSACTIONS *)
    READLN(TACCT, DEPWITH, AMT); (* FIRST TRANSACTION *)
    WHILE TACCT <> 0 DO
      BEGIN (* TRAN LOOP *)
        (* PROCESS THE TRANSACTION JUST READ *)
          (* SEARCH FOR TRANSACTION ACCOUNT *)
            J := 1;
            WHILE ACCT[J] <> TACCT DO
              J := J + 1;
          IF DEPWITH = 1
            THEN BEGIN
                DEP[J] := DEP[J] + 1;
                CBAL[J] := CBAL[J] + AMT
              END
            ELSE BEGIN
                WITHDR[J] := WITHDR[J] + 1;
                CBAL[J] := CBAL[J] - AMT
              END;
        READLN(TACCT, DEPWITH, AMT)
      END; (* TRAN LOOP *)

  (* PRINT THE RESULTS *)
    (* PRINT HEADING *)
      WRITE('1   ACCOUNT');
      WRITE('   PREVIOUS BALANCE    ');
      WRITE('WITHDRAWALS');
      WRITE(' DEPOSITS');
      WRITELN('     FINAL BALANCE     ');
      WRITELN;
    FOR I := 1 TO N DO
      WRITELN(' ', ACCT[I], IBAL[I], WITHDR[I],
                   DEP[I], CBAL[I])
END. (* BANK *)
```

2.5 Scanning for Symbols

Many programs process "text". The PASCAL translator is such a program; this book was produced by a "text-editing program" (see Section 3.2.2). Such programs have the common sub-problem of reading lines of text and dividing them into separate "symbols". A "symbol", in this context, is simply a sequence of non-blank characters. For example, the line

THIS IS A SAMPLE LINE OF INPUT TEXT.

Contains eight separate symbols. The general algorithm for many text-processing programs is:

```
Repeat for all input text:
    Get next symbol;
    Process symbol.
```

"Process" might be as simple as "print, one symbol per line", or it could be a more complicated task such as "encrypt", "translate", or "tabulate frequency of usage". But here we are only concerned with the common sub-task to "get the next symbol".

The definition of a symbol makes the blank the key character. Any character (except blank) that follows a blank <u>begins a symbol</u>; any character (except blank) that a precedes a blank <u>ends a symbol</u>. We will assume that a symbol may be split over two lines. That is, it may run to the end of one line and continue at the beginning of the next line. Assume that the next symbol is to be assigned as value to a string variable named SYMBOL. Furthermore, let us assume that SYMBOL is long enough to accomodate the longest symbol that will be encountered in the text. An algorithm for "get next symbol" is simply:

S1: Find the first character of the next symbol.

S2: Copy of the characters of the symbol into SYMBOL.

For the time being, let us ignore the special problems that might arise with the <u>first</u> and the <u>last</u> symbols -- that is, we will postpone considering initialization and exit problems. We will first think about a routine that will work repeatedly, for the second to the second-last symbols. The routine will start knowing that the last character encountered was a blank (to terminate the previous symbol). The next character to be read may also be a blank, since there is nothing that specifies that symbols must be separated by exactly one blank. Hence S1 has be prepared to skip over any number of blanks looking for the first character of the symbol. S2 will also be looking for blanks, but not to skip over them. S2 must find a blank to know where the symbol ends. Note that the blank found by S2 <u>must not be copied into SYMBOL</u>, since it is not part of the symbol.

The implementation of S1 could be a WHILE loop that reads data characters into the first character of SYMBOL. It continues reading characters until a non-blank is found. Each character read by S1 replaces the last character read by S1 in the first position of SYMBOL, so that although blanks may be read into SYMBOL, they do not remain there since S1 will eventually replace the blank with a non-blank character.

```
(* FIND THE NEXT NON-BLANK CHARACTER *)
    READ(SYMBOL[1]);
    WHILE SYMBOL[1] = ' ' DO
         READ(SYMBOL[1])
```

This is an example of a situation where the REPEAT loop is preferable to the WHILE loop, since it tests the condition after the body of the loop, and no separate initialization is required:

```
(* FIND THE NEXT NON-BLANK CHARACTER *)
    REPEAT
         READ(SYMBOL[1])
      UNTIL SYMBOL[1] <> ' '
```

The implementation of S2 is a similar REPEAT loop, continuing until a blank is encountered:

```
(* COPY NON-BLANK CHARACTERS INTO SYMBOL *)
    I := 1;
    REPEAT
         I := I + 1;
         READ(SYMBOL[I])
      UNTIL SYMBOL[I] = '
```

There is a problem in this loop, since by the time it realizes it has found its terminating blank it has already copied that blank into SYMBOL. This can be easily solved by reporting the symbol length to be one character less than the number of characters copied.

The complete segment would be:

```
(* LOAD NEXT SYMBOL INTO SYMBOL *)
    (* FIND THE NEXT NON-BLANK CHARACTER *)
         REPEAT
              READ(SYMBOL[1])
           UNTIL SYMBOL[1] <> ' ';
    (* COPY NON-BLANK CHARACTERS INTO SYMBOL *)
         I := 1;
         REPEAT
              I := I + 1;
              READ(SYMBOL[I])
           UNTIL SYMBOL[I] = ' ';
         SYMLENGTH := I - 1
```

Now we must worry about some of the complications that we postponed. What happens in the case of the very first symbol? Does the segment depend upon the knowledge that the last character read was a blank? The answer is no, and the program as given will work as well for the first symbol as it does for subsequent symbols. However, it does need protection from running out of data, and both S1 and S2 should be revised to include EOF tests. The program should also detect and respond to the situation in which a symbol encountered in the data is longer than the variable SYMBOL. This is easily detected (by testing I in S2), but the interesting question is what action to take when the situation arises. You might also consider changing the definition of a symbol to allow it to be terminated by certain punctuation marks as well as blanks, and modify the program to implement such a definition. Also note that there is a peculiarity of the CDC operating system that affects programs of this type. See Appendix B.2.4.

We might note that of all the examples in the book, this one exhibits the most striking difference between the PASCAL version, shown above, and the PL/I version in the original _Primer_. The character-at-a-time READ of PASCAL is very natural for this task; the PL/I counterpart is much less convenient.

2.6 Interactive Computing Systems

This section is intended to give a brief glimpse of a different mode of computing. It is not immediately useful to PASCAL programmers since, to the best of our knowledge, there is not yet an interactive version of PASCAL. But it is nevertheless an important and growing aspect of computing, and you should be aware of its existence and understand how it is different. The examples given below assume the existence of an interactive PASCAL. A comparable system exists for PL/I and there is no technical reason why it cannot be done for PASCAL; it just hasn't been done yet.

The distinctive characteristic of an "interactive" computing system is, as the name implies, the opportunity for the user to interact with the program _during its execution_. He does this by supplying data to be read by the READ statements as they are executed in the program. The key point is that he _does not have to supply all the data at once and in advance_ of execution. Up to this point we have been describing computer systems where the data are prepared and submitted as a unit with the program for processing. When processing is completed all of the output is returned in one batch to the user. These are often called "batch" processing systems.

Now we are talking about a system in which the user employs a "terminal" -- usually a device like an electric typewriter, although sometimes equipped with a TV-like screen on which characters are displayed rather than a printing mechanism. The terminal is connected directly to the computer while the program is being executed. Execution output -- the result of executing WRITE statements -- appears on the terminal, and the data requested by the execution of READ statements is entered from the terminal. The crucial point is that the input and output are interleaved on this same device, corresponding to the order in which READs and WRITEs are encountered in execution of the program. This means that the data are not entered all at once, but just as needed for each execution of a READ statement. In deciding what data to supply in response to a particular request the user has before him all the execution output procuced up to that point in the program. The user interacts with the program by examining output and deciding on the basis of this information what data to supply in response to the next request. This in turn may influence the next output to appear, which affects future input, etc.

This mode of operation opens up some interesting new possibilities. The user and the program can cooperate or they can compete. For example, a problem could be attacked by a "trial and error" strategy in which the user supplies a trial value and the program obtains a solution based on this estimate and reports it to the terminal. The user then supplies the next trial value based somehow on the results of the previous trials. If the user can precisely describe the algorithm by which new trial values are determined from previous results then it can be incorporated into the program and the entire process can be run in the conventional batch mode. But there are some problems where the selection of new trial values is largely intuitive and the user cannot readily reduce his thought process to an algorithm. An interactive system allows some part of the process to remain intuitive while the rest is described algorithmically in the program. If done cleverly this makes it possible to combine the best features of human intelligence and computer processing, and allows an attack on problems that are not susceptible to a completely intuitive or completely algorithmic approach.

Another opportunity arises in programs in which the user is the adversary of the program. These are called "game-playing" problems, although the objective may in fact be serious business rather than pure entertainment. In such programs the user makes a "move" and describes it in input data to the program. The program operates on the data to determine its own "move", and reports this to the user. The program is usually performing two roles. It implements the mechanics of operating the game, as well as the implementation of the strategy of the opponent. (The user must trust that these roles are fairly separated and that his automated opponent is not in programmed collusion with the referee.)

In principal, an interactive system could be used for any problem a batch system could execute, in addition to those interactive problems for which it is uniquely qualified. However, interactive execution is generally more costly than batch execution, and the terminal is a relatively slow device for input and output. Hence programs with voluminous input and/or output may be painfully slow on an interactive system, and it may be somewhat extravagant to use an interactive system where its unique capabilities are not required. This issue is the subject of impassioned argument, with the apostles of interaction maintaining that a good, flexible interactive system is uniformly preferable and that eventually all computing will be done in this mode. Their arguments are quite persuasive.

2.6.1 Development of an Interactive Program

The development of a program to be used on an interactive system is not markedly different from that of a batch program. At the initial or highest levels of development one should essentially regard the user as part of the computing system, and his actions as part of the "program". For example, suppose we were developing a program to play a two-person game, such as Checkers. Our intention is to have the program represent one player, and keep track of the progress of the game, while a human user at a terminal represents the other player. The high-level comment outline for such a Checker-playing program might be something like the following:

```
(* PLAY CHECKERS *)
    (* INITIALIZATION *)
         (* OPTIONAL INSTRUCTIONS *)
              (* RULES OF CHECKERS *)
              (* CONVENTIONS OF THIS GAME *)
         (* INITIALIZE BOARD *)
         (* DETERMINE WHO PLAYS FIRST *)
    (* PLAY GAME: ALTERNATE MOVES -- USER & PROG *)
         (* DETERMINE MOVE *)
         (* UPDATE BOARD STATUS *)
         (* CHECK FOR TERMINATION *)
    (* REPORT OUTCOME *)
```

At this level the tasks are described in the same way -- regardless of whether they involve the user, the program or both. But as these tasks are further refined, the interactive nature of the process becomes apparent. Some tasks, such as "INITIALIZE BOARD", for example, are conventional programming tasks just like our previous examples, and they would be developed and programmed in the same way. But some tasks, like "OPTIONAL INSTRUCTIONS", would involve some interaction with the user at the terminal. This task would probably be refined into something like the following:

```
(* OPTIONAL INSTRUCTIONS *)
    WRITELN('0DO YOU WANT INSTRUCTIONS?',
             'YES OR NO');
    (* ACCEPT REPLY *)
         ANSWER := '   ';
         I := 1;
         WHILE NOT EOLN AND (I <= 3) DO
           BEGIN
              READ(ANSWER[I]);
              I := I + 1
           END;
         READLN;
         IF ANSWER = 'YES' THEN
              (* RULES OF CHECKERS *)
                   WRITELN(...
```

The "DETERMINE WHO PLAYS FIRST" task would similarly be refined to a user-program dialog.

Assuming the following declarations:

```
TYPE MOVER = (USER, PROG);
VAR  NEXTMOVE: MOVER
```

the "DETERMINE MOVE" task would be something like the following:

```
(* DETERMINE MOVE *)
    IF NEXTMOVE = USER
         THEN BEGIN
              (* GET USER MOVE *)
              NEXTMOVE := PROG
           END
         ELSE BEGIN
              (* DETERMINE PROGRAM MOVE *)
              NEXTMOVE := USER
           END
```

The refinement of "GET USER MOVE" would be a dialog with the user at the terminal; the "DETERMINE PROGRAM MOVE" would be an exceedingly complex (but non-interactive) program.

2.6.2 Programming for an Interactive System

The principal differences in programming technique appropriate for an interactive system are concerned with obtaining input from the terminal. There are two key issues: prompting and persistence in the face of errors.

Prompting is the process of providing instructions to the user at each point that input is required. Each READ in an interactive program will ordinarily be immediately preceded by a WRITELN which displays at the terminal sufficient instructions to tell the user what is expected of him. This is unique to an interactive system since in a batch system nothing printed by a particular execution of a program can be seen by the user in time to be of any help to him in preparing input. Once you understand the opportunity to prompt, and the need for it, it is not difficult to compose appropriate messages. However, unless your system uses a display screen you must remember that these messages will be printed on a printer that is painfully slow. It takes practice to develop skill in composing messages that are concise without being cryptic.

Long descriptive messages that are initially very helpful to the user will eventually become unnecessary, and finally become very annoying. It is often desirable to have several levels of prompting and to be able to switch to an abbreviated form as execution continues. For example, our Checker-playing program might initially prompt the user:

```
ENTER YOUR MOVE ON THE TERMINAL.  GIVE RANK  AND  FILE
OF  PIECE TO BE MOVED, AND THEN RANK AND FILE WHERE IT
IS TO BE MOVED.  THAT IS, GIVE MOVE AS 4 INTEGERS.
```

After the first move this could be reduced to:

```
YOUR MOVE.
```

An interactive program has the same responsibility as a batch program for testing its input for errors, but the interactive program can respond to errors in a very different way. Since the batch program cannot communicate with the user until after execution is completed it has only two options when an error is encountered: either <u>abort execution</u>, or effect some form of <u>repair</u> so execution can continue. The interactive program has the additional possibility of going back to the user and asking him to <u>try again</u>. This is so much more effective than either of the batch strategies that it is almost always used. The interactive program should <u>persistently return to the user</u> until it elicits the required input. For example, in Section 2.6.1 there was a subtask concerning instructions. This should actually be programmed as follows:

```
(* OPTIONAL INSTRUCTIONS *)
    WRITE('0DO YOU WANT INSTRUCTION?');
    ANSWER := '   ';
    WHILE (ANSWER <> 'YES') OR (ANSWER <> 'NO ') DO
      BEGIN (* ANSWER LOOP *)
         WRITELN('  ANSWER YES OR NO');
         ANSWER := '   ';
         I := 1;
         WHILE NOT EOLN AND (I <= 3) DO
           BEGIN
              READ(ANSWER[I]);
              I := I + 1
           END;
         READLN
      END; (* ANSWER LOOP *)
    IF ANSWER = 'YES' THEN
         (* RULES OF CHECKERS *)
             WRITELN(...
```

This segment simply will not terminate until a valid datum -- in this case either YES or NO -- is obtained from the terminal.

A segment such as this should be the standard technique for every request for input in an interactive system -- that is, a prompting message followed by a persistent loop that will not terminate until an acceptable response has been obtained.

A more sophisticated version of this approach would be to produce more detailed information as the user shows less ability to provide reasonable answers. A very short prompting message would be used initially, with provision for additional and more detailed information to be printed if the user does not respond successfully on his first try. Some interactive programs are written so they will accept some word such as "help" as input to any request -- and the program responds by describing what the user's options are at that point.

2.6.3 A Game-Playing Program

We will illustrate a complete program for an interactive system using a simple variation of a venerable game called NIM. This variation is just complex enough to be interesting, yet is simple enough to describe and program.

We call the game "Match-Snatch". There are two players. Our program will represent one player and the user at the terminal will be the other player, but we will initially describe the game as it would be played by two people.

Some number of matchsticks are placed in a pile between the two players. A "move" is for a player to remove some number of matches from those remaining in the pile. To be a valid move, he must take at least one match, and not more than some number agreed upon as a move-limit before the game begins. The players alternate moves and the object of the game is to avoid being the player who has to take the last match. (Obviously, without the move-limit the game would be trivial since faced with a pile of n matches the first player would immediately take n-1 and the second player would lose on his first move.) A typical game might start with a pile of fifteen matches and have a move-limit of three.

In the computer version of Match-Snatch there will, of course, not actually be any physical pile of matches. A variable, say MATCHES, will represent the number of matches in the imagined pile. The removal of matches from the pile will be simulated by announcing an integer representing the number to be removed. This number will be subtracted from MATCHES and the game will terminate when the value of MATCHES becomes zero.

There is an algorithm for playing this game which will allow the first player to assure himself victory <u>if he unfailingly follows the algorithm</u>. If he lapses on even one move, then this same algorithm becomes available to his opponent and allows him to guarantee victory -- if he is more careful. It is not difficult to discover what this algorithm is. Suppose the move-limit is k matches. If you can take enough matches to leave just one in the pile your opponent will lose on his next move. So obviously, if the pile presented to you on some move contains n matches, where 2 <= n <= k+1, you will simply take n-1 matches and leave your opponent with 1. But if n > k+1 it is not that simple since you cannot take enough matches to leave only 1. However, if you manage to leave k+2 matches in the pile after your move, no matter how many matches your opponent takes in his next move he cannot leave you with 1, and you will be able to leave him with 1 on your next move. By repeating this reasoning, you will discover that if you leave 2k+3 matches after some move you will surely be able to leave k+2 after the next move and leave 1 on the move after that. In general, if you can arrange to leave m(k+1)+1 matches in the pile after your move, for m=0,1,2,..., you will be able to win the game in m more moves. But if you ever fail to leave m(k+1)+1 matches after your move then your opponent can move to leave <u>you</u> m(k+1)+1 and he is in the driver's seat unless he gets careless (or unless he doesn't understand the game).

Our Match-Snatch program uses this algorithm for the computer's moves, so that if the user grants the computer the first move he will always lose, unless he has been clever and chosen initial values for the number of matches and the move-limit so that the number of matches is m(k+1)+1 when the program makes its first move. If the user claims the first move he <u>can</u> win, but if he slips up just once the computer will seize the opportunity and win.

In addition to acting as one player the Match-Snatch program also operates the game. It negotiates the initial conditions with the user, keeps track of the number of matches and announces the outcome. A high-level comment outline would look very much like that of the Checker program in Section 2.6.1:

```
(* MATCH-SNATCH GAME *)
    (* INITIALIZATION *)
         (* GET GAME PARAMETERS *)
         (* DETERMINE WHO MOVES FIRST *)
    (* ALTERNATE MOVES -- USER & PROGRAM *)
    (* REPORT OUTCOME *)
```

A complete program to play Match-Snatch on a hypothetical interactive PASCAL system is given below.

```
(* MATCH-SNATCH GAME *)
PROGRAM MATCHSNATCH(INPUT, OUTPUT);
TYPE MOVER = (USER, PROG);
VAR MATCHES,              (* NUMBER OF MATCHES LEFT *)
    MOVELIMIT: INTEGER;  (* LIMIT ON EACH MOVE *)
    WHOSEMOVE: ARRAY[1..3] OF CHAR;
                          (* 'YOU' = PROG; 'ME' = USER *)
    NEXTMOVE: MOVER;
    MOVE,                 (* CURRENT MOVE *)
    I: INTEGER;
BEGIN (* MATCHSNATCH *)
  (* INITIALIZATION *)
    (* GET GAME PARAMETERS *)
         WRITELN('0WELCOME TO MATCH-SNATCH');
         WRITELN;
         MATCHES := 0;
         WHILE MATCHES < 1 DO
           BEGIN
              WRITELN(' HOW MANY MATCHES TO START?');
              READLN(MATCHES);
              IF MATCHES < 1 THEN
                   WRITELN(' MUST BE AT LEAST 1')
           END;
         MOVELIMIT := 0;
         WHILE (MOVELIMIT < 2) OR (MOVELIMIT > MATCHES) DO
           BEGIN
              WRITELN(' HOW MANY IN 1 MOVE?');
              READLN(MOVELIMIT);
              IF MOVELIMIT < 1 THEN
                   WRITELN(' MUST BE AT LEAST 1');
              IF MOVELIMIT > MATCHES THEN
                   WRITELN(' NOT THAT MANY MATCHES')
           END;
    (* DETERMINE WHO MOVES FIRST *)
         WHOSEMOVE := '   ';
         WHILE (WHOSEMOVE <> 'ME ') AND
                   (WHOSEMOVE <> 'YOU') DO
```

```
            BEGIN (* FIRST LOOP *)
               WRITELN(' WHO MOVES FIRST --',
                    'YOU OR ME?');
               WHOSEMOVE := '   ';
               I := 1;
               WHILE NOT EOLN AND (I <= 3) DO
                 BEGIN
                    READ(WHOSEMOVE[I]);
                    I := I + 1
                 END;
               READLN
            END; (* FIRST LOOP *)
          WRITELN;
          IF WHOSEMOVE = 'YOU'
            THEN NEXTMOVE := PROG
            ELSE NEXTMOVE := USER;
   (* ALTERNATE MOVES -- USER AND PROGRAM *)
     WHILE MATCHES > 0 DO
       BEGIN (* MOVE LOOP *)
          IF NEXTMOVE = USER
            THEN BEGIN (* USER'S MOVE *)
               MOVE := 0;
               WHILE (MOVE < 1) OR (MOVE > MATCHES)
                         OR (MOVE > MOVELIMIT) DO
                 BEGIN
                    WRITELN(' HOW MANY DO YOU TAKE?');
                    READLN(MOVE);
                    IF MOVE < 1 THEN
                      WRITELN(' MUST TAKE AT LEAST 1');
                    IF MOVE > MOVELIMIT THEN
                      WRITELN(' THAT''S MORE THAN WE ',
                              'AGREED ON');
                    IF MOVE > MATCHES THEN
                      WRITELN(' THERE AREN''T THAT MANY')
                 END;
               MATCHES := MATCHES - MOVE;
               WRITELN(' THERE ARE', MATCHES, ' LEFT');
               NEXTMOVE := PROG
             END (* USER'S MOVE *)
            ELSE BEGIN (* PROGRAM'S MOVE *)
               MOVE := (MATCHES - 1) MOD (MOVELIMIT + 1);
               IF MOVE = 0 THEN MOVE := 1;
               WRITELN(' I TAKE', MOVE, ' MATCHES');
               MATCHES := MATCHES - MOVE;
               WRITELN(' THERE ARE', MATCHES, ' LEFT');
               NEXTMOVE := USER
             END (* PROGRAM'S MOVE *)
       END; (* MOVE LOOP *)
   (* REPORT OUTCOME *)
     (* PLAYER WHO MADE LAST MOVE LOST *)
       IF NEXTMOVE = USER
          THEN WRITELN('0YOU WON, NICE GOING.')
          ELSE WRITELN('0I WON, TOUGH LUCK.')
END.  (* MATCHSNATCH *)
```

If a game of Match-Snatch were played by executing this program on an interactive system the output would look roughly like the lines shown below. We have indented the lines that represent input from the terminal to distinguish them from lines of output printed by the program. We have also slightly modified the format of some of the output lines relative to what would actually be produced by the program as given above.

```
WELCOME TO MATCH-SNATCH

HOW MANY MATCHES TO START?
    10
HOW MANY IN 1 MOVE?
    0
MUST BE AT LEAST 1
HOW MANY IN 1 MOVE?
    15
NOT THAT MANY MATCHES
HOW MANY IN 1 MOVE?
    4
WHO MOVES FIRST -- YOU OR ME?
    I DO
WHO MOVES FIRST -- YOU OR ME?
    ME

HOW MANY DO YOU TAKE?
    9
THAT'S MORE THAN WE AGREED ON
HOW MANY DO YOU TAKE?
    2
THERE ARE 8 LEFT
I TAKE 2 MATCHES
THERE ARE 6 LEFT
HOW MANY DO YOU TAKE?
    2
THERE ARE 4 LEFT
I TAKE 3 MATCHES
THERE ARE 1 LEFT
HOW MANY DO YOU TAKE?
    0
MUST TAKE AT LEAST 1
HOW MANY DO YOU TAKE?
    2
THERE AREN'T THAT MANY
HOW MANY DO YOU TAKE?
    1
THERE ARE 0 LEFT

I WON, TOUGH LUCK.
```

Section 2 Exercises

Exercises 1 to 8 refer to the accounting problem of Section 2.4.

1. Why is ACCT declared as ACCT[0..201] instead of ACCT[0..200]?

2. For each of the 6 errors discussed in the first part of Section 2.4, indicate whether the program should stop or whether it may be reasonable to continue.

3. Change the program to consider these 6 errors. These changes should not be made by trying to revise the final program. Instead, go back to the proper step (3, 4, or 5) and perform the complete analysis and program creation once more, this time with the view of checking and documenting possible input errors.

4. Suppose the signal ending the accounts is a single 0 instead of two 0's. Change the program to reflect this. In making the changes, repeat the program analysis and development from the beginning; don't attempt to just change the final program. Which signal is better and why?

5. Suppose we wish to change the end-of-transaction signal to a single 0 instead of three. Change the program to reflect this.

6. Below are several problem statements. For each, develop an algorithm in English to solve it. This algorithm should contain no details about arrays used, variables used, etc. It should be only the first step toward a final program -- on the same level of detail as algorithm (2.4a). Note that the problem statements do not in fact give you exact details about the input. Compare your algorithms with each other and with (2.4a). Relate your algorithms to the program schemata of Section II.2.

   a) The input consists of two lists X and Y of numbers. Print out the number of times each number in list Y occurs in the first list X.

   b) The input consists of a list of bank accounts and transactions concerning these accounts. Print out the number of transactions for each account.

   c) The input consists of the text of a book, punched on cards, followed by a list of words. Print out the number of times each word on the list is used in the book.

   d) The input consists of a list of student records (name, address, grades in each course, etc.), followed by a list of a few student names. Find and print out the average, highest, and lowest grade point average for the students given in the second list.

7. In developing subalgorithm (2.4e), one problem was preventing the "Process transaction just read" statement from being executed if the transaction just read was the end-of-list

signal. Is there another way to write the loop without adding conditional statements? If you produce a different version, with or without conditional statements or GO TOs, is it more efficient? Easier to understand? Easier to modify?

8. Suppose the account numbers were limited to three digits. Can you think of a way to sort the accounts efficiently? What modifications would you have to make in the program? What are the relative merits of your solution and the one developed here in terms of time and space?

9. Below are several problem statements. For each, develop an algorithm, which shows the overall structure of the final program. Your algorithm should probably be along the lines of algorithm (2.4e).

a) The input consists of a list of integers. Print out all those integers which are even.

b) The input consists of a list of integers. Print out those integers which are prime. (An integer is prime if it is greater than 1 and evenly divisible only by 1 and itself. The integers 2, 3, 5, 7, 11, 59 are prime; the integers -2, 0, 1, 4, 9, 100 are not.)

c) The input consists of a list of names of people. Print out all the names that contain the letter A.

10. "Comment outlines" for the top level of development of several programs are given below. Complete the programs by adding the actual PASCAL statements that will perform what is specified by the heading comments. The problem requirements given in these comments are sketchy; assume whatever detail is necessary to write the programs. Document all such assumptions.

10a.
```
(* DETERMINE POSITIVE ROW AVERAGES, AND NBR ZEROS *)
PROGRAM POSROW(INPUT, OUTPUT);
VAR TAB: ARRAY[1..10,1..10] OF REAL;
              (* GIVEN ARRAY IS *)
    NR, NC: INTEGER; (* TAB[1..NR,1..NC] *)
    SUM, AVG: ARRAY[1..10] OF REAL;
              (* SUM[1..NR] ARE ROW SUMS OF TAB *)
              (* AVG[1..NR] ARE ROW AVERAGES OF TAB *)
    ZEROS: ARRAY[1..10] OF INTEGER;
              (* ZEROS[1..NR] ARE NBR OF ZEROS IN ROWS *)
    I, J: INTEGER;
BEGIN (* POSROW *)
 (* READ AND TEST: NR AND NC *)

 (* LOAD TAB IN ROW MAJOR ORDER *)

 (* REPLACE NEGATIVE ENTRIES WITH 0, AND *)
 (* COUNT ALL ZEROS IN EACH ROW *)

 (* COMPUTE ROW AVERAGES FOR NON-ZERO ENTRIES *)

 (* DISPLAY AVG AND NBR ZEROS FOR EACH ROW *)
END. (* POSROW *)
```

10b.
```
(* READ 7X9 ARRAY, INVERT ODD ROWS, *)
(* FIND COLUMN MAXIMA, AND DISPLAY *)
PROGRAM INVMAX(INPUT, OUTPUT);
VAR TAB: ARRAY[1..7,1..9] OF REAL;
    COLMAX: ARRAY[1..9] OF REAL;
                  (* COLUMN MAXIMA *)
    I, J: INTEGER;

BEGIN (* INVMAX *)
 (* LOAD ARRAY (ROW MAJOR ORDER) *)

 (* REVERSE ORDER OF ELEMENTS IN ODD-NUMBERED ROWS *)

 (* FIND MAXIMUM VALUE IN EACH COLUMN *)

 (* DISPLAY COLUMN MAXIMA *)

END.  (* INVMAX *)
```

10c.
```
(* REVERSE STRINGS AND TEST FOR "A" BEFORE "B" *)
PROGRAM REVTEST(INPUT, OUTPUT);
VAR STR: ARRAY[1..50,1..20] OF CHAR;
             (* TABLE OF STRINGS IS: *)
    N, L,         (* STR[1..N,1..L] *)
    I, J: INTEGER;

BEGIN (* REVTEST *)
 (* READ NBR AND LENGTH OF STRINGS FROM INITIAL DATA *)

 (* LOAD ARRAY OF STRINGS *)

 (* INVERT EACH STRING, *)
 (* CHARACTER BY CHARACTER, END FOR END *)

 (* PRINT A LIST OF INVERTED STRINGS IN WHICH AN "A" *)
 (* APPEARS TO THE LEFT OF THE FIRST "B" *)

END.  (* REVTEST *)
```

10d.
```
(* ROTATE SQUARE ARRAY QUARTER-TURN CLOCKWISE *)
PROGRAM ROTATE(INPUT, OUTPUT);
VAR AR, AR2: ARRAY[1..40,1..40] OF REAL;
             (* ARRAYS ARE *)
    N,            (* AR[1..N,1..N],AR2[1..N,1..N] *)
    I, J: INTEGER;

BEGIN (* ROTATE *)
 (* READ NBR OF ROWS, AND LOAD AR BY ROWS *)

 (* COPY EACH COLUMN OF AR, LEFT TO RIGHT, *)
 (* INTO ROW OF AR2, TOP TO BOTTOM *)

 (* DISPLAY ROTATED ARRAY AR2 BY ROWS, TOP TO BOTTOM *)

END.  (* ROTATE *)
```

11. For each of the following problems, develop a program to the point of having a "comment outline", such as those illustrated in Exercise 10.

11a. Given a list of non-zero numbers (with zero added to the end as a stopping flag) determine which numbers in the list are not unique (that is, which appear more than once). The list may be long but it will not contain more than 40 different numbers.

11b. Given a list of not more than 100 non-negative numbers either:

1. print a list of the numbers which are greater than the final value on the list and which are not repeated in the list, or
2. print a list of the numbers which are greater than the average of all the numbers on the original list.

Do 1 if there are more numbers on the list greater than the first value, than there are numbers less than the first value; otherwise do 2. There will be at least one value given. That is, the -1 stopping flag will not be the first value given.

11c. Given three lists of numbers, each n numbers long, produce another list called the "merged list" with the following properties:

1. It contains all the non-zero values from the 3 lists.
2. Values on the merged list are in the same order they appeared in the given lists.
3. If a value was in position i in one of the given lists, it will appear in the merged list before any number that was in a position later than i in any one of the given lists.

The 3 given lists are preceded by an integer n (less than 50) specifying the length of each of the 3 given lists. Print the merged list first, 3 values per line. Then print the given lists in 3 column format. For example, if the data are:

```
    4    7 0 3 9    0 4 5 0    1 2 0 0
```

the output would be:

```
MERGED LIST
  7   1   4
  2   3   5
  9

GIVEN LISTS
  7   0   1
  0   4   2
  3   5   0
  9   0   0
```

12. Rewrite the following program so that it has the same function but is properly structured and well-presented with appropriate labels, comments and indentation.

```
PROGRAM TEST(INPUT, OUTPUT);
LABEL 1, 2, 3, 4;
VAR J, N, K: INTEGER; LIM: REAL;
X: ARRAY[1..50] OF REAL;
BEGIN READLN(J, N, K, LIM);
J := 1;
1: IF J < N + 1 THEN GOTO 3;
J := 1;
2: IF J = K THEN GOTO 4;
IF X[J] < LIM THEN WRITELN(' ', J, X[J]);
J := J + 1;
GOTO 2;
3: READ(X[J]);
X[J] := X[J] + J;
J := J + 1;
GOTO 1;
4: END.
```

13. The game of NIM is similar to the Match-Snatch game described in Section 2.6.3. The differences are that there are several piles of matches in NIM instead of one, and in each move a player may take as many matches as he wishes (but at least one) but only from one pile. The object of NIM may be either to take the last match, or to avoid having to take the last match, at the option of the players and decided upon in advance.

Write an interactive program to play NIM. The parameters of the game are

1. How many piles there are;
2. How many matches there are in each pile;
3. Whether the winner takes the last match, or avoids doing so;
4. Who plays first.

As for Match-Snatch there is an algorithm for playing NIM such that the player to go first can win under all but some very special conditions. However it is not a trivial exercise to determine this algorithm. But even without an "optimal" algorithm you should be able to write a program that will be a "good" NIM player. In fact, if several students write NIM-playing programs, you could have a "NIM tournament"! This is actually done with programs that play Chess. Every year there is a tournament among the World's Chess-playing programs. Some of the programs play good Chess but so far they can all be beaten by any really excellent human Chess player.

Section 3 General Design Considerations

The preceding sections have described the basic idea of program development in several different ways:

1. Break a problem into a sequence of sub-problems.

2. Refine a statement into several finer statements with increasing detail.

3. Expand a statement of <u>what</u> has to be done into a specification of <u>how</u> it is to be done.

4. Expand "high-level" commands such as "solve", "find" or "compute" into lower-level statements of a programming language.

5. Translate a problem description from English to PASCAL.

These are different aspects of the same general process: the systematic transformation of a <u>statement of requirements in English</u> to a <u>detailed specification of actions in PASCAL</u>.

We outlined the phases of the process in Section 1 and gave examples in Section 2. In Section 3 we review the process and describe several of the key issues in more detail.

3.1 Top-Down Development

In general, development decisions should be made in "outside-in", "top-down" order -- in order of increasing detail. In the accounting problem of 2.4, initially there were a number of questions that could have been raised and answered -- how accounts should be stored, how the transactions should be processed, how the transactions should be stored, etc. Out of all these, we chose the one which helped determine the overall structure and which led to a correct program with just more detail: what were the main subproblems and in which order should they be executed?

This is not to say that your thoughts shouldn't skip to various parts of the program in varying amounts of detail. (They will whether you want them to or not.) There is nothing wrong in beginning by looking at various possibilities for the representation of data and subalgorithms to process them.

Sometimes this is necessary in order to obtain a better understanding of the problem and possible solutions. Sometimes this is necessary in order to come up with any idea at all. But this should just be considered a side trip. Any ideas discovered on it should not be accepted as final, and the main program development should then proceed top-down. It may be necessary to develop several alternatives to some depth before it is clear which one is best.

This top-down process is not as easy and straightforward as it may seem from the examples given in Section 2. Programming, like any problem solving, is a trial and error process. Mistakes will be made, or just the wrong avenue explored, which will cause the programmer to undo several levels of refinements (discarding several parts of the tree) and to repeat the process in a different manner. This "backing up" is discussed in more detail in Section 3.1.3.

Programming in top-down fashion may seem foreign and difficult, especially to beginners. Yet for most problems it is the best approach, because it will lead to efficient, understandable, and correct programs. Attempt right from the beginning to develop programs in a top-down, outside-in, general statement to fine detail, manner.

In programming in this fashion we attempt to make one clear decision at a time. A decision leads to a refinement of part of the program. The two types of refinement are:

1. A statement is refined.

2. The method of storing data is refined, by describing the variables used to store the data.

We discuss these separately in the next two subsections.

3.1.1 Refining a Statement

Concentrating on "What" rather than "How"

One of the advantages of top-down programming is that it helps us concentrate initially on what is to be done, and then systematically becomes concerned with how. For example, in developing the overall structure of the accounting problem in 2.4, we refined "Solve the problem" into algorithm (2.4a):

```
Read in and set up the accounts;
Read in and process the transactions;
Print the results;
```

Here, we were not primarily interested in how the accounts and transactions were to be stored or processed, but only in what was to be done, so that we could concentrate on the order in which the various functions were to be performed.

As another example, consider the sorting problem of 2.3. Sorting is refined in terms of

"move the maximum element to the end of the list".

This states what is to be done, but not how. There are several methods that could be used. "Move..." is refined into

"find the position of the maximum";
"interchange maximum and last".

This suggests what could be done to accomplish "move..." without specifying how either "find..." or "interchange..." will be performed.

Limiting Ourselves to Understandable Refinements

When refining a statement we replace a statement of what to do by an algorithm which indicates how to do it. In making such a refinement it is important to limit ourselves to refinements we can easily understand, and which we can easily communicate to others.

Given a statement, what possibilities exist? The most general possibility is a sequence of statements to be executed in order. Thus we should attempt to break the original statement into successive parts to be executed in order. Other possibilities for a refinement are:

1. Use a conditional statement to break the problem into two subcases.

2. Break it into several (instead of two) subcases.

3. Replace it by a loop (perhaps with initialization statements).

Faced with these limited possibilities for refining a statement, we can focus attention on the following questions:

1. How can it be broken up into successive parts?

2. Does it break up easily into two or more subcases?

3. Is it an iteration problem -- can a loop be used?

These methods of refinement lead naturally to the program units described in Section II.1.

Using Suitable Notation for Statements

Whatever language and notation suits the problem at hand should be used in order to aid in an orderly development and to make the final program as lucid as possible. Usually the initial notation consists of English commands like "Sort the list", "Process the transactions" and "Generate a value to ...". Any imperative statement can be used, provided its meaning is sufficiently clear.

In particular, it is often convenient to invent control mechanisms that do not exist in PASCAL (and perhaps not in any real programming language). One control mechanism we have been using all the time is the "exit statement", which we have had to write as a GOTO statement. As other examples, the meaning of the following two algorithms should be clear without any formal definition of how the "for each" statement is to be executed:

```
For each account in the list
   IF the account balance < 0 THEN Print a message

For each position of the chessboard
   IF the position is occupied by a white piece THEN
     BEGIN
          IF the white piece can capture the black king
             THEN Print "check";
          IF the white piece can capture the black queen
             THEN Print "watch out!"
     END
```

Using such statements helps postpone decisions about the order in which the accounts or positions on the chessboard should be processed. These can wait, and will probably depend on how the list and chessboard are stored as variables. Once we decide on an order, translating the "for each" loops into "WHILE loops" will not be difficult.

As another example, consider a program to simulate a baseball game. There would be variables to keep track of the score, the inning, the number of outs, men on base, etc. The heart of the program would be a section that determines the outcome of each pitch, and executes one particular routine for each outcome. The algorithm could be given as:

```
Determine outcome of pitch;
Execute one of following, depending on outcome:
    Strike routine;
    Ball routine;
    Foul ball routine;
    Struck batter routine;
    Bunt routine;
    Three-base hit routine;
         etc.
```

The best way to program this in PASCAL would be to use a user-defined type to record the outcome of the pitch, and the CASE statement to select the appropriate routine:

```
TYPE PITCHOUTCOME = (STRIKE, BALL, FOUL, STRUCK,
etc.);
VAR PITCH: PITCHOUTCOME;
    ...
    CASE PITCH OF
         STRIKE: ...
         BALL: ...
         FOUL: ...
              etc.
      END
```

If the programming language lacked the capability of defining new types you would have to encode the various outcomes using integer values:

value of PITCH	outcome
1	strike
2	ball
3	foul
etc.	

The CASE statement would still be used:

```
CASE PITCH OF
    (* STRIKE ROUTINE *)
         1: ...
    (* BALL ROUTINE *)
         2: ...
    etc.
```

However, most programming languages in general use today do not have either user-defined types or a CASE statement, so if you were not using PASCAL you would have to encode the outcome with integers and then use some other means to select one of the outcome routines -- perhaps a sequence of IF statements. Nevertheless, we could have developed the program in the same way, stating our requirement in the same English text, and only at the final stage of development succumb to the shortcomings of our particular programming language.

3.1.2 Refining a Data Description

Data refinements are just as important as statement refinements, but decisions about how to store the data should be postponed as long as possible, until no further statement refinements can be made without knowing more about the data structures used. You will gradually learn that there are many different ways of keeping data in variables. For example, the list of accounts in Section 2.4 can be kept in unsorted form in an array, or sorted in ascending or descending order. There are also more sophisticated storage structures such as hash tables, singly linked lists, doubly linked lists, circular lists, dequeues, stacks and trees. Each method has advantages and disadvantages, depending on the nature and form of the operations to be performed. In order to intelligently choose a method for data representation, it is necessary to wait until the operations to be performed on the data are well understood.

The method of storing transactions in the bank problem is a good illustration. We could have initially decided to use an array, since there were many transactions. But waiting and later deciding based on what was to be done with the transactions led to the discovery that only one transaction had to be stored at any time.

Whenever you decide upon variables, write down their names with their exact meanings immediately. Don't wait until you write the declaration for them. Every variable is important (or else it shouldn't be in the program) and you must know exactly why it is there. Don't trust these exact meanings to your memory; write them down.

A recent incident will illustrate the importance of this. A student came in with a two-page program, the relevant parts of which are given in (3.1.2a). The program was a simplified "text editor"; it read text -- a sequence of words interspersed with symbols for commands like "begin a new line" and "begin a new paragraph" -- and printed out the text as formatted by the commands. Each output line was "right justified", which means that not only were the left margins lined up, but also the right margins. (Right justification is performed by inserting extra blanks between words, as in the lines you are now reading.)

There was obviously an error, since occasionally a blank at the end of a word was missing -- "the big black fox" might come out as "thebig black fox". The problem was found by examining the exact role of the variables. Looking at the program, it was surmised that OUTLINE would contain the current line to be written out and LENGTHLINE would contain its length. The student was asked what N meant, since its meaning was not written down. After some uncertainty he said "Oh, it's just the length of the word being added to the current line OUTLINE." ("It's just" is used often when one doesn't really know. It seems to belittle the variable, making it all right not to know exactly why it is there.)

The program was then examined to find if N was always assigned and used in this way. The error was exposed when it was discovered that in one place, N was the length of the word, while in the other it was the length plus one, to take into account the blank character following it.

```
        ...
        IF ...
             THEN BEGIN
                  FOR I := M TO M+N DO
                       WORD[I-M+1] := LINE[I];
                  WORD[M+N+1] := ' '
               END
(3.1.2a)     ELSE BEGIN
                  WORD[N+1] := ' ';
                  N := N + 1
               END;
        ...
        LENGTHLINE := LENGTHLINE + M;
        OUTLINE := ...
        ...
```

The importance of clearly understanding and having an exact written description of each variable cannot be overemphasized.

Using Suitable Notation for Data

We used notation outside PASCAL in Section 2.4 during development of the accounting program, programming in terms of a "table of accounts" and a "transaction" as long as possible before describing how these quantities were to be represented in the PASCAL program. In effect, we talked as if the whole table of accounts were contained as a value in a variable. Data can often be represented using variables in many ways, and it is important to talk in general terms about the "list" or the "records" until more is known about the operations to be performed on them.

Using high-level notation for data structures is just as important as for processing actions. However it is difficult to give good examples of this until you have more programming experience and are familiar with a variety of different data structures. We leave this discussion to another book.

3.1.3 Backing Up

Program development is a trial and error process. We make refinements and try some subalgorithms, and if they don't serve our purpose we redo them. Redoing one subalgorithm may require us to change other parts of the algorithm, both in data structures and in statements, and it is important that all these changes be made in a systematic way. This should usually be done by "backing up" to a previous level of the algorithm which the changes don't affect, and then proceeding to redo all the top-down refinements taking the changes into account.

For example, suppose a top-down analysis has produced the tree of refinements (3.1.3a), where each Si is a statement and the lines leading down from a statement represent a sequence of statements to be executed from left to right, to replace that statement. Now suppose while attempting to refine statement S19 that we discover a mistake, or recognize that a change in data structures designed earlier will make S19 more efficient. In order to make the change, we must back up to a point where the change has no effect. Suppose this is S2 (see tree (3.1.3b)). Then we must proceed downward again, redoing all refinements (in the example, S4-S7, S11-S15, S18 and S19) to make sure that every refinement leads to a correct program.

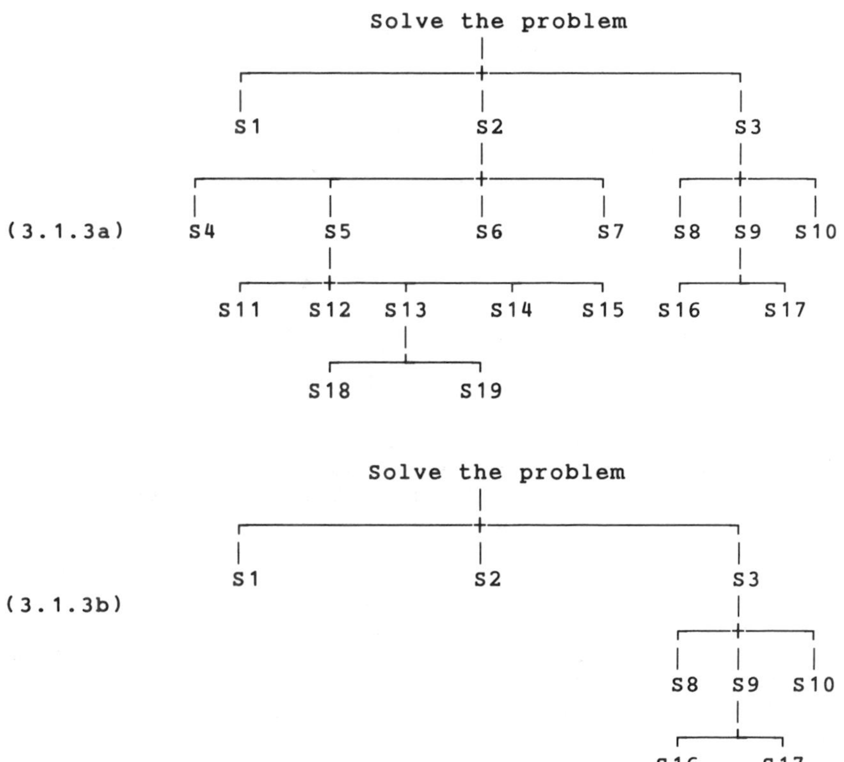

Backing up in this manner is extremely important if a correct program is desired. There is a limit to how much we can keep in our heads, and the only way to extend this limit is to keep things well organized on paper. The more complicated the program, the more important it is to back up systematically.

If instead of using such a systematic procedure, we just "looked around" and tried to figure out what to change, the chances are that we would miss at least one place to change or would change some segment incorrectly. Backing up with a tree as a guide indicates not only what has to be changed, but also what doesn't have to be changed. For example, in the above illustration, once we decide that the change affects only S2 and its refinements, we need not worry about changing anything else in the tree.

To illustrate this process on a real problem, consider again the sorting problem of 2.3. The algorithm used in (2.3e) is:

```
           (* SORT L[1..N] *)
               FOR M := N DOWNTO 2 DO
                 BEGIN (* SUBLIST LOOP *)
(3.1.3c)            Find position of maximum in L[1..M];
                    Interchange maximum and L[M]
                 END (* SUBLIST LOOP *)
```

Now consider a different way of performing the same task. Instead of finding the largest value and then making one interchange at the end, compare successive values and interchange immediately if out of order:

```
         (* SWAP VALUES OF L[1..M] TO PUT LARGEST IN L[M] *)
            FOR I := 2 TO M DO
(3.1.3d)       IF L[I-1] > L[I] THEN Swap L[I-1] and L[I]
```

This refinement has a property which may be of some use. Note that it looks at successive adjacent pairs of L[1..M] and swaps any pair that is out of order. If no swaps occur during an execution of this subalgorithm, then no adjacent pair is out of order and the array is already sorted. Hence, if no swaps occur the algorithm can be terminated.

How will we stop execution? We have a new idea now, but we must fit it in at the right program level. Part of the change must occur not only in (3.1.3d), but also in the higher level algorithm (3.1.3c) since it must terminate. Thus we should back up to the statement "Sort L[1..N]" and refine anew. This new refinement will be a modification of (3.1.3c).

Looking at (3.1.3c) we see that we now have <u>two</u> stopping conditions:

1. (M < 2), and

2. "no swaps performed during one execution of the loop body".

We introduce a new BOOLEAN variable SORTED which has the following meaning:

> Whenever the condition of the main loop is evaluated, SORTED is TRUE if the array is definitely known to be sorted, but SORTED is FALSE if we are not sure whether it is sorted or not.

Now modify (3.1.3c) into (3.1.3e):

```
          (* SORT L[1..N] *)
               SORTED := FALSE;
               M := N;
               WHILE NOT SORTED AND (M >= 2) DO
                 BEGIN (* BUBBLE LOOP *)
(3.3.3e)            Swap values of L[1..M] to put largest in
                      L[M], and also set SORTED as necessary;
                    M := M - 1
                 END (* BUBBLE LOOP *)
```

Now proceed down again to the next level, redoing the English substatement:

```
     (*  SWAP L[1..M] TO PUT LARGEST IN L[M] AND SET "SORTED" *)
         SORTED := TRUE; (* ASSUME L[1..M] IS SORTED *)
         FOR I := 2 TO M DO
           BEGIN (* SWAP LOOP *)
              IF L[I-1] > L[I] THEN
                BEGIN
                   Swap L[I-1] and L[I];
                   SORTED := FALSE
                END
           END (* SWAP LOOP *)
```

This yields the final program known as *bubble sort* (because it "bubbles" the largest value to the top of the list):

```
  (* SORT L[1..N] USING "BUBBLE SORT" ALGORITHM *)
    SORTED := FALSE;
    M := N;
    WHILE NOT SORTED AND (M >= 2) DO
      BEGIN (* BUBBLE LOOP *)
         (* SWAP L[1..M] TO PUT LARGEST IN L[M], SET "SORTED" *)
              SORTED := TRUE; (* ASSUME L IS SORTED *)
              FOR I := 2 TO M DO
(3.1.3f)        BEGIN (* SWAP LOOP *)
                   IF L[I-1] > L[I] THEN
                     BEGIN
                        T := L[I-1];
                        L[I-1] := L[I];
                        L[I] := T;
                        SORTED := FALSE
                     END
                END; (* SWAP LOOP *)
         M := M - 1
      END (* BUBBLE LOOP *)
```

The important point in the example is to note how we *backed up to a higher program level* in order to incorporate changes in a systematic manner. One *can* just look around and try to find all necessary places to change in a haphazard manner, but doing it in a systematic manner is actually easier and more reliable.

This systematic backing up process is particularly useful during testing. If an error is located during testing, it should be corrected by backing up as we have described here, and then proceeding down again, taking into account whatever changes are necessary. The discovery of an error during testing may well occur several days after that section of the program is written and your recollection may be less than perfect. Unless you proceed very systematically in the repair process there is a good chance you will introduce new errors while trying to eliminate old ones.

3.2 Sources of Ideas for Refinements

"How to invent something" is difficult to describe, and it is not clear that creativity can be effectively taught. Fortunately, the typical programmer is rarely asked to develop something radically different, and the type of creativity required is modest. Greater amounts of determination, logical thinking, hard work, attention to detail, and patience are involved. We attempt in this section to give some insight into how and where program ideas originate.

3.2.1 Sources of Ideas for Algorithms

A programmer has two main sources of ideas:

1. Programs previously written or studied;

2. Familiar algorithms from everyday life.

For the beginner, the first source is practically non-existent. One obvious way to expand this source is to read and study good programs written by others. Ask your instructor to provide examples of substantial and well-written programs. Try to reconstruct the algorithm and development tree that led to the program. Besides expanding your personal library of algorithms, studying other people's programs helps emphasize the importance of good style and programming practices. (You can't really appreciate the importance of these matters until you try and figure out a long program written by someone who doesn't believe in these things.)

The second source of ideas is almost unlimited. Every day we use algorithms or see others use them. Often, of course, they are informal and not too well defined, and describing them precisely may be difficult. But the ideas are there.

The accounting problem is a good example of this. How did we know what to do? Perhaps we imagined what a clerk would do to manually perform this task. In order to write a program for it, we needed only to be able to write down an exact description of the process the clerk performs, taking into account the format of the input (which the clerk need not worry about) and the fact that all data must be stored in variables. The top-down method of development was used only to aid us in writing the algorithm correctly and precisely.

As a second example, suppose we have an array B[1..N] whose values are in ascending order. We want to find the position J of another variable X in the list. That is, search B for X and store in variable J an integer such that B[J] = X. If no such integer exists, store 0 in J. If the list were not sorted we would use a simple search as in 2.2:

```
FOR J := 1 TO N DO
    IF B[J] = X THEN GOTO 9000;
J := 0;
9000:
```

However, the additional information that B is sorted may permit a more efficient algorithm.

Everyday situations in which something is sought in an ordered list are numerous, and in general a more efficient search method is used. A good example is looking for a name in the telephone book. To find a name, say "Smith", we look at some entry in the book rather randomly, but as near to the S's as we can get. The entry serves to divide the book into two parts -- "before" the entry and "after" the entry. If this entry is less than Smith (alphabetically), then Smith is located in the second part, after the entry. So we "discard" the first part and repeat the process using only the last part. If the entry is greater than Smith, we discard the second part and repeat the process using the first part.

Thus we can repeat a process over and over until we find the desired entry or until we have discarded the whole list (in which case the desired value is not in the list). This repetition suggests the use of a WHILE loop, and after some work we arrive at the following algorithm:

```
Let the list to be searched be B[1..N];
WHILE list to be searched is not empty DO
  BEGIN (* SEARCH LOOP *)
    K := index of some entry B[K] still in list, near X;
    IF B[K] = X THEN
       BEGIN
         J := K;
         GOTO 9000
       END;
    IF B[K] < X
         THEN discard first part of list, including B[K]
         ELSE discard second part of list, including B[K]
  END; (*SEARCH LOOP *)
J := 0; (* MEANS X IS NOT IN THE LIST *)
9000:
```

The statement

"K := index of some entry B[K] still in list, near X;"

is not precise enough. How do we compute "near"? To simplify this, let us just use

K = index of middle entry of the list;

which is easier to compute. It may not be as good an algorithm as we use with the telephone book, but this change does make it easier to program. When searching the telephone book, we have common sense information which is not ordinarily available to the program. For example, we know there are lots of S's and T's, but few V's and X's. This certainly affects the way we perform the search. The main problem in developing a program based on our experiences is to be able to formalize how we do something, to ferret out the essential details.

This is the beginning of the development of a well-known algorithm called "binary search". It is a vast improvement over the algorithm used in 2.2. For example, if there are 32,768 entries, the 2.2 algorithm may have to look at <u>all</u> the entries, while binary search will <u>never</u> have to look at more than 16 of them! The key point here is that the idea for this algorithm comes from the prosaic task of using a directory.

3.2.2 <u>Solving Simpler Problems</u>

Since we have not previously seen <u>every</u> problem we are asked to solve and program, somehow we must be able to find connections between the problems at hand and problems whose solutions we already know (or at least whose solutions are easier). Two obvious methods are to <u>simplify</u> the problem and to find <u>related problems</u>.

It is often useful to explore a problem similar in structure to the one assigned, but is simpler in detail. One can explore alternative strategies and algorithms in this simpler context, and chose which strategy to pursue for the real problem.

To illustrate consider the sorting problem again. We have all done this -- sorted mailing lists, books on shelves, and so on. The problem and its solution are not unfamiliar, but explaining <u>precisely</u> how to sort is not easy if we haven't seen an algorithm for it before. Let us attack the problem as if we had <u>not</u> seen it earlier, and look for simpler problems within the sort.

What must happen for the list L[1..N] to be sorted? For one thing, the largest value must eventually appear in L[N]. This is a simpler problem which we know how to handle (Section I.5, Exercise 4f).

```
            FOR I := 1 TO N-1 DO
(3.2.2a)          IF L[I] > L[N] THEN Swap L[I] and L[N]
```

What else must be done? The second largest value must appear in L[N-1]. If the largest has already been put into L[N] by the above algorithm, then this means we want to put the largest of L[1..N] into L[N-1]. This is roughly the same as (3.2.2a):

```
            FOR I := 1 TO N-2 DO
                  IF L[I] > L[N-1] THEN Swap L[I] and L[N-1]
```

Continuing, we should recognize that we are performing essentially the same process a number of times. Getting back to the original problem, we can write it as

```
             Swap values of L[1..N]   to put largest in L[N];
             Swap values of L[1..N-1] to put largest in L[N-1];
             Swap values of L[1..N-2] to put largest in L[N-2];
                                ...
             Swap values of L[1..2]   to put larger  in L[2]
```

or

```
            (* SORT L[1..N] BY "SUCCESSIVE MAXIMA" *)
               FOR M := N DOWNTO 2 DO
                 BEGIN (* SMAX LOOP *)
(3.2.2b)           Swap values of L[1..M] to put largest in L[M]
                 END (* SMAX LOOP *)
```

One way of refining the English substatement of (3.2.2b) is

```
            (* SWAP VALUES OF L[1..M] TO PUT LARGEST IN L[M] *)
               FOR I := 1 TO M-1 DO
                 BEGIN
(3.2.2c)           IF L[I] > L[M] THEN Swap L[I] and L[M]
                 END
```

Note that we got the idea for the program by tackling smaller simpler ones and noticing that we had to repeat essentially the same process many times. We then returned to the original level and wrote the program (3.2.2b). At this point, we <u>knew</u> how to write the segment for "Swap values of L[1..M] to put largest in L[M]", and yet we still wrote this statement in English in (3.2.2b). This was because we wanted to make <u>one</u> decision at a time, the decision turning out to be the order in which the values were placed in their final positions (first L[N], then L[N-1], and so on). <u>How</u> the values get in their positions is not a problem of (3.2.2b), but the order in which they get there is. We can even design different algorithms for swapping the values, different from the one in (3.2.2a) which helped us find the solution. Sometimes tackling a simpler problem or a subproblem is the only way we can proceed. But once the process of solving the simpler problem has led to an idea, set the solution to the simpler problem aside, at least temporarily, and concentrate again on the top-down analysis.

One way to <u>find</u> a simpler problem is to temporarily <u>make</u> the problem definition simpler. Set aside all inessential details (perhaps even some of the essential ones), until a simple, understandable problem emerges. Once this has been solved, the original problem can be attacked with more understanding. This deletion of material must of course be done with care to make sure that the remaining problem is instructive and not trivial.

To illustrate this, consider the following problem:

(3.2.2d) <u>A Text Editor</u>. Input to the program is to consist of normal words, on cards, each adjacent pair being separated by one or more blanks. A word may be split onto two cards (the end of one and the beginning of the next). The words are to be read in and written out in 60-character lines. Each line is to be both right and left justified (as are the lines of this book). A word may not be split onto two lines, unless it is more than 60 characters long or unless otherwise there will be only one word on a line (these are probably errors, but the program must handle them).

Interspersed between words (and separated from them by one or more blanks) may be <u>commands</u> to be executed by the program, at the time they are read. These are:

command	meaning
)L	Begin a new output line;
)P	Begin a new paragraph (indent 3 spaces);
)E	End of input.

When processing a command, if a partially filled line must be written out, do not right-justify that line. For example, the last line of a paragraph is never right-justified. Commands may not appear as words in the input; only as commands.

Below is some sample input, with the corresponding output shown at the right, using 14-character instead of 60-character lines to save space:

```
Sample input                        Sample output
)P One way to find a simpler        |   One  way  to
problem is to make the )L )L        |find a simpler
     problem                        |problem is  to
definition simpler.                 |make the
Throw out all                       |
inessential details.      )E        |problem defini
                                    |tion  simpler.
                                    |Throw  out all
                                    |inessential de
                                    |tails.
```

This description is full of details, and it is difficult to know where to start, so begin by temporarily setting details aside to make it simpler:

1. Any number of blanks may separate a pair of words, and a word can be split on two cards. This may be difficult, so initially consider the input to be just a series of words and commands. That seems to be the essential point.

2. Why are lines 60 characters, and not 61 or 62? Perhaps the line length should be part of the input to the program. For now, since we need some length, use 60.

3. Justifying a line looks relatively complicated, but does not seem important relative to the overall structure of the program. Set it aside.

4. The problem of words of 60 characters or more and the problem of only one word on the line do not seem essential. Set them aside.

5. The commands are essential, and yet probably difficult to work with. Try setting them aside, and if that doesn't work out, bring them back.

This leads to the following problem description:

(3.2.2e) Simplified Text Editor. Read in a sequence of "words" and print them out on 60-character lines. Put as many as possible on one line, but separate each pair by a blank. Don't split words across two lines.

This simpler problem is much easier to understand and work with. A variable L (say) will hold the line currently being built. It will be written out when the next word to be inserted causes it to be longer than 60 characters. The following algorithm could be designed fairly quickly:

```
          LINELENGTH  := 0; (* NOTHING IS IN THE CURRENT LINE *)
          WHILE there is another input word DO
            BEGIN (* WORD LOOP *)
              Read the next word into WORD and count its length;
(3.2.2f)      IF LINELENGTH + WORDLENGTH > 60 THEN
                BEGIN
                   Print L;
                   LINELENGTH := 0
                END;
              Add WORD onto L and add WORDLENGTH to
                                   LINELENGTH;
              IF LINELENGTH < 60 THEN
                   Add ƀ onto L and add 1 to LINELENGTH
            END; (* WORD LOOP *)
          Remove ƀ from end of L, if it has one and
                   subtract 1 from LINELENGTH;
          Print L
```

The most important part of the original problem left out of (3.2.2e) is the commands, so now reinsert them. This will complicate the algorithm (3.2.2f), so we first should hide some of its details. (3.2.2f) can be rewritten as

```
          LINELENGTH  := 0; (* NOTHING IS IN THE CURRENT LINE *)
          WHILE there is more input DO
            BEGIN (* WORD LOOP *)
(3.2.2g)      Read the next word into WORD and count its length;
              Process the word in WORD
            END; (* WORD LOOP *)
          Remove b̸ from end of L, if it has one and
                   subtract 1 from LINELENGTH;
          Print L
```

In adding commands, we see we must process either a word or command. We also know when to stop the loop -- when the command)E is read. Rewriting (3.2.2g) with this information yields

```
          LINELENGTH  := 0; (* NOTHING IS IN THE CURRENT LINE *)
          WORDLENGTH := 0; (* NO WORD OR COMMAND READ YET *)
          WHILE (WORD[1] <> ')') AND (WORD[2] <> 'E') DO
            BEGIN (* WORD LOOP *)
(3.2.2h)      Read the next word or command into WORD and
                        count its length;
              IF WORD[1] = ')'
                   THEN Process WORD as a command
                   ELSE Process WORD as text
            END; (* WORD LOOP *)
          Remove b̸ from end of L, if it has one and
                        subtract 1 from LINELENGTH;
          Print L
```

where "process WORD as text" is

```
          (* PROCESS WORD AS TEXT *)
              IF LINELENGTH + WORDLENGTH > 60 THEN
                   BEGIN
                        Print L;
                        LINELENGTH := 0
                   END;
              Add WORD onto L and add WORDLENGTH to
                             LINELENGTH;
              IF LINELENGTH < 60 THEN
                   Add b̸ onto L and add 1 to LINELENGTH
```

We now have a reasonable solution to the simpler problem (3.2.2e) plus commands. At this point the original problem should be reread and programmed in top-down fashion, using (3.2.2h) as a model.

On the text editor problem just described, the most common "mistake" is to write the main part of the program as a loop such as the following:

```
WHILE there exists a card DO
  BEGIN (* CARD LOOP *)
    Read a card;
    Process the card
  END (* CARD LOOP *)
```

This then requires a second loop in processing the card, and the whole program is unnecessarily complicated because a word could be split across card boundaries. If the problem is first simplified, we realize that the card boundary problem is just a detail to be handled at a later time, and is not an essential point in understanding the general flow of the program.

3.2.3 Solving Related Problems

Consider writing a program segment to sort an array C[1..N] in descending order: C[1] ≥ C[2] ≥ ... ≥ C[N]. You might recall having developed an ascending sort in the previous section (program (3.2.2b)). The new sorting program could just be a modification of the previous one.

Related problems, both in programming and in the everyday world, are a rich source of ideas. If we can find something related which we know how to handle, then the problem becomes much simpler.

In the previous section, we discussed solving simpler problems, which are of course related to the original problem. By a "related problem" in this section we mean one which is roughly the same order of magnitude in size or complexity. One which, with some work, can be transformed into the desired one. Everybody uses related problems all the time, and in effect we are just saying the obvious here. The point is that you should become aware of the fact that you are using related problems; this will increase your ability to find solutions and design programs. Learning consists not only of doing something, but also of learning why and how one does it.

In programming, related problems occur more often than one might think. For example, consider the four parts of Exercise 6 of Section 2. Although these look quite different, at the highest level they all have the same algorithmic solution:

```
Read in a list of values;
Read and process a second list of values;
Print results.
```

In fact, they are equivalent at this level to algorithm (2.4a) of the accounting problem of Section 2.4 and differ only in the meaning of "values", "read", "process", and "results". Similarly, all the problems of Exercise 9 of Section 2 have the solution

```
Read a value;
WHILE there exists input DO
  BEGIN (* INPUT LOOP *)
    Process the value read;
    Read the next value
  END (* INPUT LOOP *)
```

Each of these is an interpretation of schema (II.2b). In order to see that problems are related, we must be able to recognize the important elements of a problem. All four problems in Exercise 6 of Section 2 look different on first inspection, until we state them in a more general manner.

Most programs include a number of simple subalgorithms, many of which seem to occur over and over again (with perhaps slight variations). Examples are algorithms to:

Search a list.
Search a sorted list.
Find the position of a particular value on a list.
Find the maximum or the average of a set of values.
Delete duplicate values from a list.
Read in a list of values which ends with some signal.

Many of these will become part of your "repertoire of algorithms" and you will find that programming consists in part in determining how these standard subalgorithms should be combined into a larger program. In order to do this, however, you must be able to recognize familiar problems in the mass of detail of the overall problem, and work on modifying them to fit the current problem.

3.3 Handling Input Errors

Programs are written to be used in the real world -- which means that they must not assume that input data will always conform exactly to the problem specifications. In general, programs must check all input for errors, and when errors are detected provide informative output that will help the user to find and correct the mistake. When a data error is not detected, the best that can happen is that the program will "blow up" -- an infinite loop will be executed, in PASCAL an array subscript will be out of range, or some similar indication will be given. The worst that can happen is that the program processes the erroneous input as if it were correct, giving no indication that anything is wrong. If and when the error is eventually detected, it can be embarrassing and costly to correct.

Once you recognize the possibility that data errors can exist -- and in most situations are in fact likely to exist, you must decide what is the most reasonable response. For example, six alternative program segments are given in (3.3a) to (3.3f) below. Each is an interpretation of schema (II.2d); each is designed to perform the same task -- compute the sum of a set of integer data values. They differ only in the manner in which they react to a non-integer datum. In each case assume these segments are run in a program with the following declarations:

```
VAR SUM: REAL;
    INTG: INTEGER;
    N: INTEGER;
    NBR: REAL
```

To understand these segments, recall that the TRUNC built-in function (Section I.3.3) yields the integer value obtained by truncating the fractional part of a real argument. That is, TRUNC(3.5) is 3; TRUNC(-4.5) is -4.

```
(3.3a)   (* SUM N INTEGER DATA VALUES *)
             SUM := 0;
             READ(N);
             WHILE N > 0 DO
               BEGIN
                  READ(INTG);
                  SUM := SUM + INTG;
                  N := N - 1
               END
```

```
(3.3b)   (* SUM N INTEGER DATA VALUES *)
             SUM := 0;
             READ(N);
             WHILE N > 0 DO
               BEGIN
                  READ(NBR);
                  SUM := SUM + NBR;
                  N := N - 1
               END
```

```
(3.3c)   (* SUM N INTEGER DATA VALUES *)
             SUM := 0;
             READ(N);
             WHILE N > 0 DO
               BEGIN
                  READ(NBR);
                  IF NBR = TRUNC(NBR) THEN SUM := SUM + NBR;
                  N := N - 1
               END
```

```
(3.3d)   (* SUM N INTEGER DATA VALUES *)
              SUM := 0;
              READ(N);
              WHILE N > 0 DO
                BEGIN
                   READ(NBR);
                   IF NBR <> TRUNC(NBR) THEN
                        WRITELN('0NON-INTEGER VALUE:', NBR);
                   SUM := SUM + NBR;
                   N := N - 1
                END
```

```
(3.3e)   (* SUM N INTEGER DATA VALUES *)
              SUM := 0;
              READ(N);
              WHILE N > 0 DO
                BEGIN
                   READ(NBR);
                   IF NBR = TRUNC(NBR)
                        THEN SUM := SUM + NBR
                        ELSE WRITELN('0NON-INTEGER VALUE:',
                                  NBR);
                   N := N - 1
                END
```

```
(3.3f)   (* SUM N INTEGER DATA VALUES *)
              SUM := 0;
              READ(N);
              WHILE N > 0 DO
                BEGIN
                   READ(NBR);
                   IF NBR <> TRUNC(NBR) THEN GOTO 9077;
                   SUM := SUM + NBR;
                   N := N - 1
                END
              9077:
```

If the data happen to be perfect -- that is, N integers -- these six segments are equivalent. If one or more non-integers are present the segments behave quite differently:

(3.3a) causes execution of the program to stop with a PASCAL error message indicating non-integer data.

(3.3b) is not restricted to integers at all. It includes fractional portions of values in the sum. No indication of the presence of non-integers is given.

(3.3c) only includes integers in the sum. It rejects non-integers, not including them, but not reporting their presence.

(3.3d) reports the presence of non-integers, but includes them in the sum.

(3.3e) reports the presence of non-integers and does not include them in the sum.

(3.3f) terminates the process on encountering the first non-integer value, without including this value in the sum, and without reporting the premature termination. All subsequent values are left unread.

There are several other possibilities but these should serve to illustrate the point. One cannot say, in general, which is best. That depends upon the requirements of the particular problem. But one can say that it is generally necessary to admit the possibility of different types of errors, determine what response is appropriate, and write the program accordingly.

With some errors the program should stop and print a message. For example, in the accounting problem of Section 2.4 if the end-of-account signal is missing, then all transactions have been read as accounts, and there is no hope of proceeding usefully. With other errors the program should just print a message and continue. For example, if a transaction gives a non-existant account number, that transaction can be rejected and a message can be printed.

Many programs process data that actually consists of sections that are quite independent. For example, in Section 2.4 the data pertaining to each account is independent of the data preceding and following. An error in a particular item of data may well make processing for that account meaningless until the error is corrected, but it does not affect processing of the other accounts. This suggests that a well-designed program would reject the erroneous data with an informative error message, skip over that account, but resume processing with the next account. Error rates of several percent in hand-prepared data are not unusual and programs that have to process thousands of data cards are commonplace. If these programs were to stop as soon as any error is encountered and insist that it be repaired before proceding they would be impractical to use. On the other hand there are cases where the data are all logically related and the effects of errors are cumulative. In such cases it is pointless to continue processing. It requires both knowledge of the problem and good judgement to decide whether an error should terminate processing or whether there is some action that will permit continuation to be useful.

One could conceivably overdo error checking. The programmer must weigh each type of input error and the damage its occurrence might cause against the amount of programming necessary to detect it. But at least the programmer should <u>think</u> of all the possible errors and come to a rational decision on each one. If necessary the manager should be questioned about them. Very often the person in charge may not have thought about all the possibilities and will be delighted to hear they can be detected. On the other hand, he may be able to tell the programmer that a particular error will <u>never</u> occur because, for example, the data is produced by another program of known reliability.

In some cases error processing is so important that it dominates the program. For example, there are programs whose sole purpose is to screen data for errors so that these can be corrected prior to submitting the data for actual processing. In general, error processing should be considered an important and integral part of the problem. Error processing is usually more successful when it is developed along with other requirements rather than being added on after the program is otherwise finished.

Part II and Part III References

Aho, A. V., J. E. Hopcroft and J. D. Ullman, The Design and Analysis of Computer Algorithms, Addison-Wesley, 1974

Dahl, O. J., E. W. Dijkstra and C. A. R. Hoare, Structured Programming, Academic Press, 1972

Dijkstra, E. W., "GO TO Statement Considered Harmful", Communications of the ACM, March 1968

Dijkstra, E. W., A Short Introduction to the Art of Programming, Eindhoven University, 1971

Dijkstra, E. W., A Discipline of Programming, Prentice-Hall, 1976

Kernighan, B. W. and P. J. Plauger, Elements of Programming Style, McGraw-Hill, 1974

Kernighan, B. W. and P. J. Plauger, "Programming Style: Examples and Counterexamples", ACM Computing Surveys, December 1974

Knuth, D. E., "Structured Programming with GO TO Statements", ACM Computing Surveys, December 1974

McGowan, C. L. and J. R. Kelly, Top-Down Structured Programming Techniques, Petrocelli/Charter 1975

Mills, H., "Top Down Programming in Large Systems", in Rustin (ed.), Debugging Techniques in Large Systems, Prentice-Hall, 1971

Polya, G., How to Solve It, Princeton, 1945 (also excerpted in Newman, The World of Mathematics, Vol. 3, Simon & Schuster, 1956)

Van Tassel, D., Program Style, Design, Efficiency, Debugging and Testing, Prentice-Hall, 1974

Weinberg, G. M., The Psychology of Computer Programming, Van Nostrand, 1971

Wirth, N., "Program Development by Stepwise Refinement", _Communications of the ACM_, April 1971

Wirth, N., _Systematic Programming: An Introduction_, Prentice-Hall, 1973

Wirth, N., "On the Composition of Well-Structured Programs", _ACM Computing Surveys_, December 1974

Wirth, N., _Algorithms + Data Structures = Programs_, Prentice-Hall, 1976

Yohe, J. M., "An Overview of Programming Practices", _ACM Computing Surveys_, December 1974

Part IV
Independent Subprograms

Section 1 Procedures

The language features presented in Part I are adequate to write small programs, but something more is required if we are to effectively write and test significant programs. We need some means of organizing things so that

1. different sections of the program can be made relatively independent, so they can be written and tested separately;

2. program segments can be written in one place and executed "remotely" from some other point in the program;

3. program segments can be written so that they can be reused in different contexts without having to be rewritten; and

4. large programs can be easily constructed from smaller ones already written and checked out.

These capabilities are provided by "procedures" in PASCAL. One defines a procedure in one place in a program. This procedure can then be "called" or "invoked" into action from other places within the program. In executing the procedure, it behaves as if it were copied into each position from which it is invoked.

This technique is not peculiar to programming. For instance, when baking a cake we might be instructed to "make chocolate icing, page 56". The icing recipe is a separate procedure, with its own set of instructions. To execute this command, we postpone further action on the cake, turn to the icing recipe, and execute it. When finished, we return to the cake recipe and continue where we left off.

The following program is a simple example of the use of procedures. Its execution prints the following three lines:

```
FIRST LINE
SECOND LINE
FIRST LINE
```

The program is given below:

(1a)

```
(* PRINT 3 LINES *)
PROGRAM P3LINES(INPUT, OUTPUT);

(* PRINT "FIRST LINE" *)
PROCEDURE FIRST;
  BEGIN (* FIRST *)
    WRITELN(' FIRST LINE')
  END; (* FIRST *)

(* PRINT "SECOND LINE" *)
PROCEDURE SECOND;
  BEGIN (* SECOND *)
    WRITELN(' SECOND LINE')
  END; (* SECOND *)

BEGIN (* P3LINES *)
    FIRST;
    SECOND;
    FIRST
END.  (* P3LINES *)
```

While all of our previous programs have consisted of a single procedure, this program consists of <u>three separate procedures</u>:

> P3LINES is the <u>main procedure</u> because "PROGRAM" is given in its heading. A program <u>must have exactly one main procedure</u>.
>
> FIRST is a procedure defined within P3LINES. It is essentially an independent program that is executed by being invoked from the main procedure. When executed it causes the message "FIRST LINE" to be printed.
>
> SECOND is another procedure within P3LINES. When executed it causes the message "SECOND LINE" to be printed.

The execution of any PASCAL program always starts at the <u>first statement</u> of the <u>main procedure</u>, and continues until the main procedure is completed. In this case the first statement in P3LINES is the "procedure statement":

```
FIRST
```

The execution of a procedure statement is accomplished by <u>executing the procedure that it references</u> -- in this case, procedure FIRST. The execution of the main procedure is temporarily suspended while FIRST is executed, and then resumed when FIRST is completed. However, it is better to think of a procedure as adding a new operation to the language. The definition of the procedure specifies how the operation is to be performed. Once this has been done we can use the operation in different places, much as we use built-in functions like SQRT, without worrying about how it is performed.

P3LINES consists of three statements FIRST, SECOND and FIRST. Since there is no loop or condition its execution consists simply of the execution of these three statements in order. But effectively, this means execute procedure FIRST, then execute procedure SECOND, and then execute procedure FIRST again. It doesn't matter that the last statement requires the execution of a procedure that has already been executed once -- the same procedure can be executed any number of times in the course of executing a program.

Now consider in more detail what it means to execute procedure FIRST. Execution of FIRST means execution of the statements in its body -- which in this case happens to be a single statement. This means that the execution of the procedure statement FIRST in P3LINES is effectively the same as execution of the statement:

```
WRITELN(' FIRST LINE')
```

That is, the execution of the procedure statement FIRST causes the message "FIRST LINE" to be printed.

Overall, the result of executing P3LINES would be to produce the same printed output as the following program:

```
(* PROGRAM TO PRINT 3 SIMPLE LINES *)
PROGRAM PRINT3(INPUT, OUTPUT);

BEGIN (* PRINT3 *)
    WRITELN(' FIRST LINE');
    WRITELN(' SECOND LINE');
    WRITELN(' FIRST LINE')
END.  (* PRINT3 *)
```

This second form is obviously simpler and no one would actually use the first form -- but then no one would use a computer to write these three lines anyway. However, if the body of FIRST were a substantial program segment, it would be useful to be able to execute this segment from different points in the program just by writing the procedure statement FIRST at each point, rather than having to rewrite the body of FIRST each place its execution is required.

We will illustrate the idea of procedures by another example in Section 1.1, and then explore the definition and use of procedures in more detail in the following sections.

1.1 A Procedure to Interchange Values

Consider the task of exchanging the values of two variables X and Y. We can do this with the three assignment statements shown in (1.1a). These statements use a third variable T, in addition to X and Y.

```
(1.1a)   T := X;
         X := Y;
         Y := T
```

Alternatively, we can write a procedure to do this:

```
          (* SWAP VALUES OF X AND Y *)
          PROCEDURE SWAP(VAR X, Y: INTEGER);
            VAR T: INTEGER;
(1.1b)      BEGIN (* SWAP *)
              T := X;
              X := Y;
              Y := T
            END (* SWAP *)
```

This is the "definition" of the procedure SWAP. Such definitions are placed with the other definitions and declarations (LABEL, CONST, TYPE and VAR) at the beginning of the program. Procedure definitions come after the other definitions and declarations -- that is, they come just before the BEGIN that indicates the beginning of the body of the program.

In any program where the definition of SWAP has been included, the procedure statement SWAP(X, Y) can be used in the body of the program. Wherever you wanted to swap the values of X and Y, instead of writing the three statements of (1.1a) you would instead write the single statement SWAP(X, Y).

Executing this statement is equivalent to executing all of the statements in the body of the procedure SWAP.

For example, a complete program using the procedure SWAP of (1.1b) is given in (1.1c). During each repetition of the body of the loop in (1.1c) the READ statement obtains the next two values from the data list and assigns them to X and Y. Then if those values are out of order the procedure statement "passes" X and Y to the procedure SWAP. The next statement to be executed is the first assignment statement in SWAP, that is, T := X. That and the two following assignment statements interchange the values. The execution of the procedure SWAP is then completed, and hence the execution of the procedure statement SWAP(X, Y) in the main program is completed. The next statement executed is the WRITELN. This cycle is repeated N times, which completes the exection of the loop. A final WRITELN statement completes the execution of the main procedure ORDER2 so the execution of the program is finished. Note that execution of ORDER2 does not start with SWAP, just because SWAP appears at the beginning of

ORDER2. This is a declaration of SWAP as a procedure name, and the definition of what action SWAP represents. The procedure SWAP is executed only by execution of the procedure statement SWAP(X, Y).

(1.1c)

```
(* ORDER N DATA PAIRS *)
PROGRAM ORDER2(INPUT, OUTPUT);
VAR X, Y, I, N: INTEGER;
(* SWAP VALUES OF X AND Y *)
PROCEDURE SWAP(VAR X, Y: INTEGER);
  VAR T: INTEGER;
  BEGIN (* SWAP *)
    T := X;
    X := Y;
    Y := T
  END; (* SWAP *)
BEGIN (* ORDER2 *)
    WRITELN('0ORDERED PAIRS');
    WRITELN;
    READLN(N);
    FOR I := 1 TO N DO
      BEGIN
         READ(X, Y);
         IF X > Y THEN SWAP(X, Y);
         WRITELN(' ', X, Y);
      END;
    WRITELN('0END OF LIST')
END.  (* ORDER2 *)
    eor
3
9 8 5 0 1 15
```

Execution of (1.1c) with the data shown would print the following lines:

```
ORDERED PAIRS:

    8          9
    0          5
    1         15

END OF LIST
```

Now let's go one step further. Suppose we wanted to swap the values of some pair of variables whose names were not X and Y. It would be convenient not to have to have two different swap routines just because the variables to be swapped happened to have different names. For example, suppose there is a data list consisting of values in groups of three, and each group is to be rearranged so that its values are in non-decreasing order -- that is, a sort on lists of length 3. Each group could be assigned to a set of three variables, say A, B and C. Then by comparing A and B and swapping their values if they are out of order; comparing B and C and swapping their values if out of order; and finally comparing A and B again and swapping their values if out of order, the three values would be put in non-decreasing order. (This is just a special case of the sorting algorithm of Section III.2.3.) The point is that we would need to swap A and B, then B and C, and then A and B again. The SWAP procedure of (1.1b) is capable of doing this, without any change whatever. This is illustrated in (1.1d).

(1.1d)

```
(* ORDER N DATA TRIPLES *)
PROGRAM ORDER3(INPUT, OUTPUT);
VAR A, B, C, I, N: INTEGER;
(* SWAP VALUES OF X AND Y *)
PROCEDURE SWAP(VAR X, Y: INTEGER);
  VAR T: INTEGER;
  BEGIN (* SWAP *)
    T := X;
    X := Y;
    Y := T
  END; (* SWAP *)

BEGIN (* ORDER3 *)
    WRITELN('0ORDERED TRIPLES:');
    WRITELN;
    READLN(N);
    FOR I := 1 TO N DO
      BEGIN
         READ(A, B, C);
         IF A > B THEN SWAP(A, B);
         IF B > C THEN SWAP(B, C);
         IF A > B THEN SWAP(A, B);
         WRITELN(' ', A, B, C)
      END;
    WRITELN('0END OF LIST')
END.  (* ORDER3 *)
    eor
4
17 23 15
9 56 1
105 0 -2
42 43 44
```

Execution of (1.1d) with the data shown would print the following lines:

```
ORDERED TRIPLES:

   15          17          23
    1           9          56
   -2           0         105
   42          43          44

END OF LIST
```

In each repetition of the body of SWAP LOOP in (1.1d) the READ obtains the next three values from the data list and assigns them to A, B and C, respectively. If the values of A and B are out of order they need to be swapped. The procedure statement

```
SWAP(A, B)
```

executes the procedure SWAP to swap the values of A and B. The variable A takes the place of X in SWAP; the variable B takes the place of Y. The execution of this procedure statement is equivalent to executing SWAP as if its assignment statements had been written as

```
T := A;
A := B;
B := T
```

After the execution of procedure statement SWAP is completed, the next statement to be executed is another conditional statement. This time if the values of B and C are out of order SWAP(B,C) is executed. This time B takes the place of X in SWAP and C takes the place of Y. SWAP is now executed as if its assignment statements had been written as

```
T := B;
B := C;
C := T
```

The final conditional statement checks the ordering of A and B (which may have been upset by the interchange of B and C). After execution of these three conditional executions of SWAP the values of A, B and C will be in non-decreasing order.

Execution of SWAP(var1, var2) interchanges the values of whatever variables var1 and var2 are specified in the procedure statement. The fact that SWAP is written in terms of X and Y is immaterial. In fact, X and Y in SWAP are not variables at all -- they are parameters. A parameter is used in place of a variable in writing a procedure because it is not known until the procedure is executed what particular variable it will be. The specific variables to be used by the procedure are given in the procedure statement that causes the execution, and are known as the "arguments" of the procedure statement. A and B are the arguments of the first procedure statement SWAP in (1.1d); B and C are the arguments of the second procedure statement; and A and B are the arguments of the third procedure statement. Before executing the procedure body the parameters are replaced by the corresponding arguments of that particular procedure statement.

The replacement of parameters by arguments is exactly the same in (1.1c), but in that case the arguments happened to have the same names as the parameters -- which allowed us to postpone explaining what really happened until (1.1d). But actually, even in (1.1c) the parameter X in SWAP and the argument X in the procedure statement are different -- they just happen to have the same name. The execution of the procedure statement SWAP(X, Y) passes arguments X and Y to SWAP to have their values interchanged. The first parameter X of SWAP is replaced by the first argument X of the procedure statement; the second parameter Y by the second argument Y. It is just a coincidence that the names happen to be the same. Any pair of variables could be passed as arguments to SWAP to have their values interchanged.

However, the attributes of the arguments must exactly match those of the corresponding parameter. For example, if the variables A, B and C in (1.1d) had been declared to be REAL this program would not work properly, simply because the attributes of the arguments would not match the INTEGER attribute of the parameters of SWAP. So we must modify the previous claim, and state that SWAP of (1.1b) is capable of swapping any pair of INTEGER variables. If variables of some other type are to be swapped another procedure will have to be used. For example, if you needed to swap either REAL or INTEGER variables in a program, then two separate procedures could be defined:

```
(* SWAP INTEGERS X AND Y *)
PROCEDURE SWAPINT(VAR X, Y: INTEGER);
  VAR T: INTEGER;
  BEGIN (* SWAPINT *)
    T := X;
    X := Y;
    Y := T
  END; (* SWAPINT *)
(* SWAP REALS X AND Y *)
PROCEDURE SWAPREAL(VAR X, Y: REAL);
  VAR T: REAL;
  BEGIN (* SWAPREAL *)
    T := X;
    X := Y;
    Y := T
  END (* SWAPREAL *)
```

Note that exactly the same procedure SWAP is used in both (1.1c) and (1.1d). This reuse of a procedure is a common occurrence in programming. It means that after you have been programming awhile and have accumulated a repertoire of commonly used program segments you will not have to write each new program entirely from scratch. A procedure is a convenient way to add operations to a programming language to "personalize" it. You can develop your own library of procedures to perform operations peculiar to the type of problems you must program.

1.2 Definition of a Procedure

The general form of the definition of a procedure is:

```
(* Comment summarizing what the procedure does *)
PROCEDURE name(list of parameters and their types);
    Declarations & definitions for this procedure;
    BEGIN (* name *)
         Body of procedure
    END (* name *)
```

This definition is placed at the beginning of the program -- after other definitions and declarations, and before the BEGIN that denotes the beginning of the body of the program. The proper position is shown in (1.1c) and (1.1d).

The procedure-name is any identifier. This is the name by which the procedure will be referenced by a procedure statement. In effect, the definition of a procedure P in a program, creates a procedure statement P for that program. Procedure names should be chosen to suggest the action that the procedure performs, like SWAP in (1.1c). All procedure-names must be different. That is, you cannot have two procedures with the same name, and procedure-names must not be the same as the name of any variable in the program.

1.2.1 Parameter Declarations

The parameters of a procedure are declared by listing them, along with their types, within parentheses immediately after the procedure-name. There are two kinds of parameters in PASCAL, called "variable parameters" and "value parameters". The former are denoted by the presence of the keyword "VAR" in their declaration. Examples of both kinds of parameters are shown below:

```
PROCEDURE SOLVE(VAR X, Y, Z: REAL)

PROCEDURE FIND(N: INTEGER; VAR X: REAL)

PROCEDURE WRITE(STR: CHAR)
```

The form of the parameter declaration is very similar to that of the declaration of variables (except for the different role of the keyword "VAR".) Any of the standard types can be used, as well as any user-defined types which are defined in the program that uses the procedure. For example:

```
TYPE STRING80 = PACKED ARRAY[1..80] OF CHAR;
    ...
(* REVERSE LETTERS IN STR *)
PROCEDURE REVERSE(VAR STR: STRING80)
```

It is difficult to explain the distinction between variable parameters and value parameters until we have first explained in detail the way in which arguments are associated with parameters -- so that explanation is deferred to Section 1.3. However, we can note here that the distinction has to do with the role of the parameter in the procedure body. Some parameters serve as an output vehicle for the procedure -- they are the means by which the procedure communicates its result. Parameters that serve an output role must be declared as variable parameters. That is, they must have the keyword "VAR" in their declaration. On the other hand, some parameters serve only as input -- they deliver values to the procedure and are declared as value parameters. If a parameter serves for both input and output (a common occurrence) the output role demands that it be declared as a variable parameter. In summary, the rules are:

1. Output parameters must be variable parameters (declared VAR).

2. Input parameters should be value parameters.

3. Parameters that are both input and output must be variable parameters.

For example, in (1.1b) the parameters X and Y of SWAP are both input and output parameters, since each supplies a value to SWAP and is assigned a value by SWAP. Therefore, they have both been declared as variable parameters.

The names of the parameters of a procedure are "local" to that procedure. They have absolutely no connection with names used outside that procedure. It is immaterial whether or not they happen to be the same as some name outside the procedure. For example, in (1.1b) the names of the parameters of SWAP are X and Y. These names were chosen without any concern for where SWAP might be used and, in particular, whether the procedure that used SWAP might have its own use of the names X or Y. Indeed, in (1.1c) SWAP is used in a program ORDER2 that has its own X and Y. This is simply a coincidence; there is no conflict between the two different X's and the two different Y's. In (1.1d) SWAP is used in a procedure ORDER3 that does not happen to use the names X and Y. Note that SWAP is exactly the same in both (1.1c) and (1.1d), and the presence or absence of the names X and Y in the program using SWAP has no effect whatever on the way SWAP is defined or used.

Some procedures do not need any parameters. In such cases there are no parameter lists, and no declarations of parameters. Examples of such parameterless procedures are given in (1a) and (1.3a).

1.2.2 Other Definitions and Declarations in a Procedure

All the kinds of definitions and declarations that are used in the main program -- LABEL, CONST, TYPE and VAR -- can be given in a procedure. These definitions and declarations within a procedure define objects that are "local" to that procedure. They are undefined outside that procedure, and cannot be used outside the procedure. As in the case of parameter names, the names of these local objects are local to the procedure and have no connection with uses of the same name outside the procedure. For example:

```
(* SET Y TO ROOT OF CUBIC EQN *)
PROCEDURE CUBIC(C0, C1, C2, C3: REAL; VAR Y: REAL);
  LABEL 50, 9901;
  TYPE STRING50 = PACKED ARRAY[1..50] OF CHAR;
  VAR TEMP1, TEMP2: REAL; ERRMSG: STRING50;
    ...
```

50 and 9901 are labels in the body of CUBIC. There may or may not be labels 50 or 9901 in the main program or other procedures; it is immaterial to CUBIC. STRING50 is a user-defined type that is known only in CUBIC. Writing the declaration

```
VAR STR: STRING50
```

anywhere outside of CUBIC will be an error -- unless there is also another definition of a type named STRING50 outside of CUBIC.

The "scope" of an object is the section of the program in which that object is known and can be used. In PASCAL the scope of an object is simply the particular procedure in which the object was defined or declared. If the object is declared in the main procedure its scope is the entire program -- including procedures defined in the program. For example:

```
PROGRAM SOLVE(INPUT, OUTPUT);
VAR X: REAL;
  ...
PROCEDURE ROOT( ...
  VAR Y: REAL;
  ...
PROCEDURE FIND( ...
  VAR X: INTEGER;
  ...
```

The variable X is declared in the main procedure, so the scope of X is the entire program -- including the procedure ROOT. That means that statements in the body of ROOT can use variable X in exactly the same way as statements in the body of the main procedure. However, the procedure FIND has been deliberately excluded from the scope of X, by declaring the name X to have a local meaning in FIND. The rules are:

1. A local declaration always takes precedence over a "global" definition. That is, if there are two objects of the same name, a reference is always assumed to refer to the local object.

2. The declaration of a local object x in procedure p, automatically excludes p from the scope of any global object with the same name x.

This issue is discussed further in Sections 1.2.3 and 1.5.

Since any definition can be given in a procedure it follows that another procedure could be defined in a procedure. This is possible, and is commonly done in large programs, but we don't need this capability for our introductory purposes so we will not discuss the "nesting" of procedure definitions.

1.2.3 Statements in the Procedure Body

The procedure body consists of a sequence of statements which are executed whenever a procedure statement for that procedure is executed. Any statement may appear within the procedure body -- an assignment, conditional, READ, WRITE, compound statement, a loop, or a procedure statement for another procedure (as explained in Section 1.4). These statements can refer to

1. local objects declared in that procedure,

2. global objects not made inaccessible by a local declaration with the same name, and

3. objects supplied as arguments by the procedure statement.

When the objects are supplied as arguments by the procedure statement, the particular name may vary from one procedure statement to another. (Recall the use of SWAP in (1.1d).) You don't know as you write the statements of the procedure what the names of the argument objects will be -- but obviously <u>some name</u> must be given in the statement, and there must be a rule by which the procedure knows what that name means when it is executed. This is what parameters are all about. A parameter name is written in a statement <u>in place of the name of a variable</u>, because the name of the actual variable is not known at the time you write the statements. You may think of the parameters as variables as you write the statements, but you should understand that really they are just taking the place of variables whose names will be supplied later (during execution). In effect, the procedure is a way of describing a <u>specified action</u> on <u>unspecified variables</u>.

1.3 Procedure Statements

A procedure is executed by execution of a procedure statement with the same name. For example, in (1.1d)

```
SWAP(A, B)
```

causes the execution of the procedure SWAP. In particular, SWAP is executed with the argument variables A and B being used in the body of SWAP wherever the parameters X and Y appear. The procedure statement SWAP is said to "call" or "invoke" the procedure SWAP. The procedure statement "passes" its arguments to the procedure it invokes.

The only way a procedure can be executed is to be invoked by a procedure statement. It is not somehow automatically executed just because its definition is given. For example, consider the following trivial program:

```
          (* PRINT 2 LINES *)
          PROGRAM PRT2(INPUT, OUTPUT);
          (* PRINT "LINE 2" *)
          PROCEDURE L2;
            BEGIN (* L2 *)
              WRITELN(' LINE 2')
            END; (* L2 *)
(1.3a)
          BEGIN (* PRT2 *)
              WRITELN(' LINE 1');
              WRITELN(' LINE 3')
          END.  (* PRT2 *)
```

The execution output of (1.3a) would be

```
LINE 1
LINE 3
```

Note that "LINE 2" will never be printed because a procedure statement L2 is never executed.

Execution of a PASCAL program consists of one execution of the main procedure. In effect, PASCAL executes a single implied call (without arguments) of the main procedure. Execution of the program is finished whenever that single execution of the main procedure is completed -- regardless of whether or not other procedures defined in the program happen to have been invoked.

There are two forms of procedure statement:

procedure-name(list of arguments)

procedure-name

The procedure-name given in the statement must be the name of a procedure previously defined in this program. The second form (without arguments) is used for procedures that have been defined without parameters, as in (1.3a).

The arguments in the list are separated by commas. Each argument may be a reference to a variable or the name of an array (see Section 1.3.3). An individual element of an array, for example, X[I], can be given as an argument -- but not an element of a PACKED ARRAY. Under certain circumstances (Section 1.3.2) an argument can be an expression, rather than a variable.

The first argument corresponds to (replaces) the first parameter of the procedure, the second argument corresponds to the second parameter, and so on. The number of arguments given in the procedure statement must exactly match the number of parameters given in the definition of that procedure. Even if one of the arguments will not be used, some harmless argument must be given so that the proper number of arguments will be present.

A procedure statement is a normal PASCAL statement and can be used anywhere in a program that any other statement -- such as an assignment, a READ or a WRITE -- could be used. For example, it can be executed conditionally:

```
IF B < 0 THEN FIX(B)
```

It can be in the body of a loop:

```
WHILE X > 10E-5 DO
    NEXT(X)
```

Note that in this loop, unless the procedure NEXT eventually makes the value of X small enough this will be an infinite, never-ending loop.

A procedure statement can even appear within the body of another procedure, as will be explained in Section 1.4.

Execution of a procedure statement includes replacing parameters by arguments. We have described this replacement as a sort of "textual" substitution of one name for another. However, this replacement can be interpreted in several different ways, and we must therefore define more carefully what we mean by replacement, or parameter-argument correspondence. In order to do this, we must adopt a notation for describing which variables can be referenced at each point in a program.

Suppose we have a program with the procedures and declarations shown in (1.3b). We can show the variables and parameters of this program in boxes associated with their procedures as in (1.3c). This shows the variables that belong to each of the procedures, at some point during the execution of AXES. The array A and the variables I, J, X and T are declared in the main procedure, so they are shown in the box for that procedure. There is another variable T declared in SWAP and shown in the box for SWAP, but this variable has not yet been assigned a value. X and Y are declared as the parameters of SWAP and are shown in the box for SWAP, but note that they do not have lines for their values. Since X and Y are used for both input and output with regard to SWAP, they are declared as <u>variable parameters</u>. Variable parameters do not have values of their own, but when SWAP is called these parameters will be associated with some variables in the main procedure that are given as arguments of the call. This process is described in detail in Section 1.3.1.

```
        (* PROGRAM TO ROTATE AXES *)
        PROGRAM AXES(INPUT, OUTPUT);
        VAR A: ARRAY[1..2] OF INTEGER;
            I, J, X, T: INTEGER;
        (* SWAP VALUES OF X AND Y *)
        PROCEDURE SWAP(VAR X, Y: INTEGER);
          VAR T: INTEGER;
          BEGIN (* SWAP *)
            T := X;
            X := Y;
            Y := T
          END; (* SWAP *)
(1.3b)
        BEGIN (* AXES *)
            ...
            SWAP(I, J);
            ...
        END.  (* AXES *)
```

(1.3c)

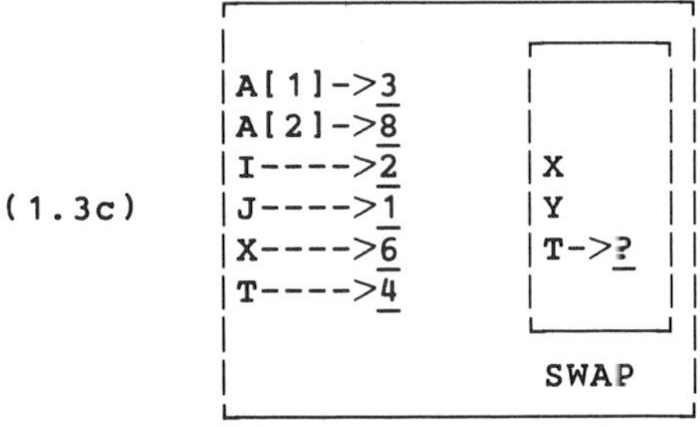

Note that we have drawn an arrow from each variable name to the line to which it is attached. Recall from Section I.2 that a name is attached by means of an arrow to a line; we omit the arrows only when the two are close enough. We will see that parameters are also attached to lines at the time parameter-argument correspondence is made. But in (1.3c) no arrows are attached to parameters X and Y because (1.3c) shows the situation while some statement in AXES other than SWAP(I, J) is being executed. That is, when SWAP is not being executed, local variable T has no value, and parameters X and Y are not associated with any arguments.

When executing a statement, to determine which variable a name references, we look _first_ in the box of variables for the procedure in which that statement occurs. If there is no variable of that name in the box for that procedure, we look _next_ for such a variable in the next larger box -- the box _containing_ the box for the procedure in question. For example, in (1.3b) there is a variable T declared both in AXES and in SWAP. Suppose a statement in SWAP references the name T. Looking in the box for SWAP, there is a T, so the statement references this T -- the one declared in SWAP. As long as there is a T declared in SWAP, no statement in SWAP can reference the T of the containing procedure AXES. On the other hand, suppose a statement in SWAP references A[1]. (There is no such statement in (1.3b) but there could be.) Since there is no A[1] in the box for SWAP, the A[1] referred to is that of the containing block AXES.

1.3.1 _Arguments and Variable Parameters_

Let us examine in detail how the execution of the statement SWAP(I, J) in the main procedure of (1.3b) actually works. Recall that the parameters X and Y in SWAP are _variable parameters_ since the keyword VAR is given when they they are declared in the definition of SWAP. They must be variable parameters in this case because they are used to _return a result_. T is a _local_ variable in SWAP. Execution of a procedure statement takes place as follows:

> Figure 1a shows the situation before the beginning of execution of SWAP(I, J). The box represents the main procedure AXES. Each of the six variables shown is declared in, and "belongs to" AXES.
>
> Figure 1b shows the beginning of execution of SWAP(I, J). A box is drawn to represent _this particular execution_ of the procedure SWAP.
>
> Figure 1c shows the establishment of the two parameters X and Y that were declared in the definition of SWAP. Since these are parameters, and _not variables_, no lines are drawn to receive values.
>
> Figure 1d shows the association of parameters and arguments. Each parameter of the called procedure is associated with an argument given in the call. This association is _by the order_ in which the parameters and arguments are given in their respective lists. The first parameter is associated with the first argument; the second parameter with the second argument, etc. The names of the parameters and arguments are immaterial in this association

-- it is strictly by their position in the lists. In this case, the first parameter X, is associated with the first argument I. The second parameter Y, is associated with the second argument J. The association is shown by drawing an arrow from X to the value of I. In effect, there are now two names for this one value. I is the original name, used in the procedure in which the variable was declared. X is another name for the same value, used in the procedure SWAP. Anything that can be done to the value by using the name I in AXES, can also be done in SWAP using the name X.

Figure 1e shows the creation of local variable T in AXES. Since T has been created, but not yet assigned a value, "?" is shown in place of its value.

Figure 1f shows the result of executing the first statement of SWAP, which is T := X. The value of X, which is 2, is assigned as value to the variable T.

Figure 1g shows the result of executing the second statement of SWAP, which is X := Y. The value of Y, which is 1, is assigned as value to X. Because of the association of Y with J, and X with I (as shown by the arrows), this actually means that the value of J is assigned to variable I.

Figure 1h shows the result of executing the third statement of SWAP, which is Y := T. The value of T, which is 2, is assigned as value to Y -- which is actually assigned to variable J. This is the last statement of SWAP, so the execution of SWAP(I, J) is completed.

Figure 1i shows the situation after the completion of execution of SWAP(I, J). The procedure SWAP no longer exists, and its box has been deleted to indicate this. Note, however, that the result of execution of SWAP(I, J) -- the interchange of the values of the arguments I and J -- does remain.

If the statement SWAP(I, J) were in a loop and was executed again, this process would take place all over again. That is, a box would be drawn for SWAP, the parameters of SWAP would be associated with the arguments, etc. If there was another call of SWAP, perhaps with different arguments, a similar process would take place, but the arrows from the parameters X and Y would be drawn to associate them with the appropriate arguments.

Study these steps carefully. Understanding this simple case of parameter-argument correspondence is necessary for understanding the more complicated situations that will arise later.

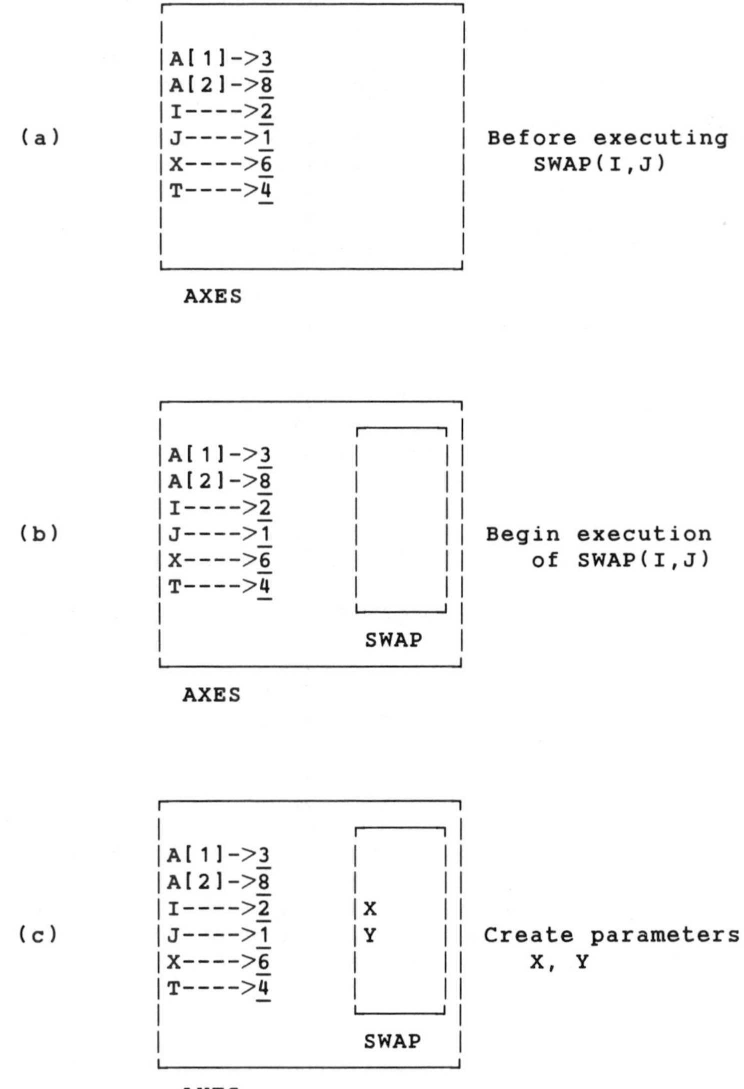

Figure 1. Example of Execution of a Procedure Statement

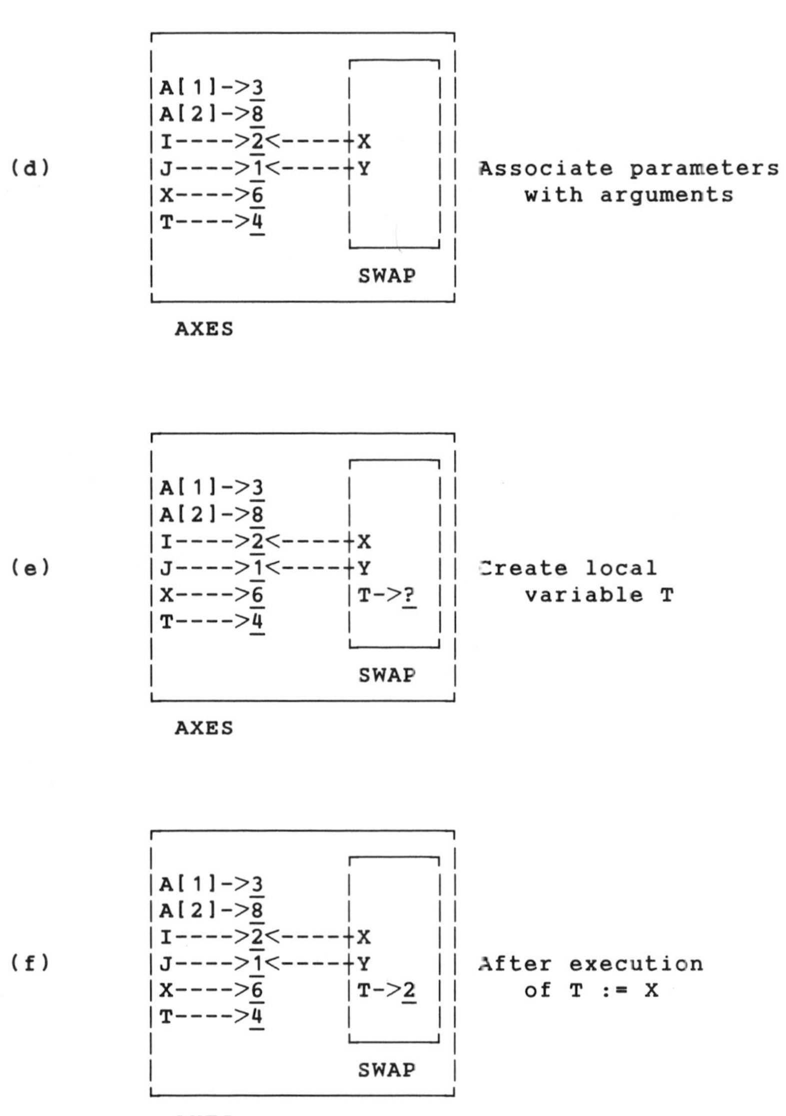

Figure 1. Execution of a Procedure Statement (continued)

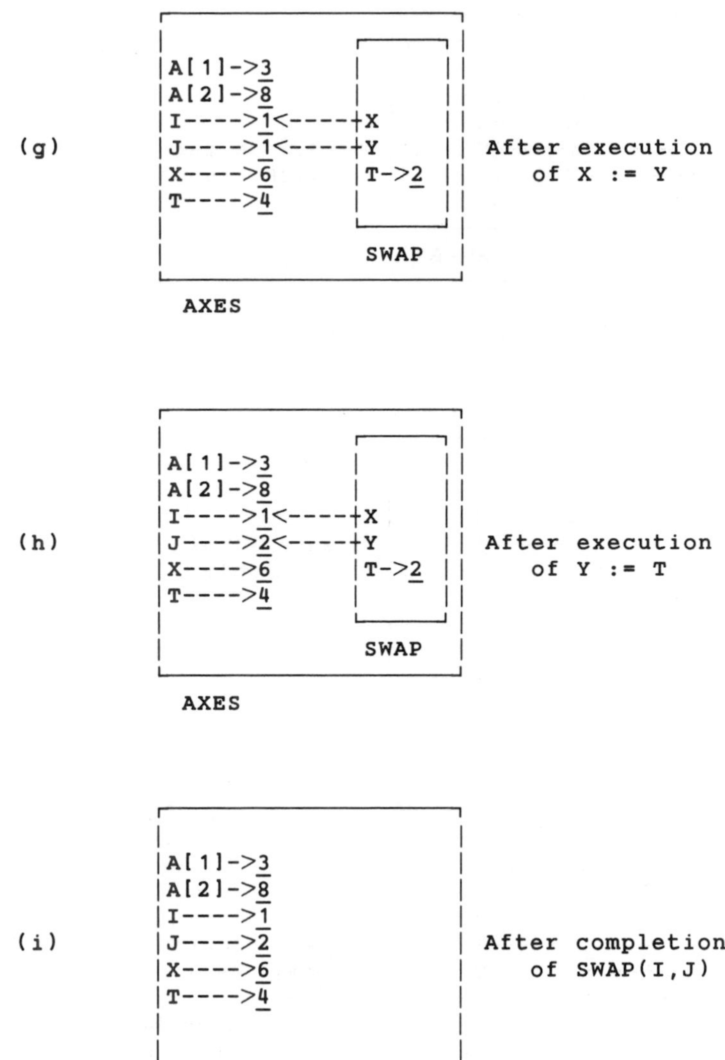

Figure 1. Execution of a Procedure Statement (continued)

Let us restate several important points concerning this process. First, the names declared in one procedure have nothing to do with names declared in others. In this case, both AXES and SWAP happen to have a variable named T, but these are two different variables. Any reference to T in AXES is assumed to mean the variable T declared in AXES; any reference to T in SWAP refers to the T declared in SWAP. You should not go out of your way to use common names like this, but on the other hand, there is no reason to avoid it. If T is the natural and suggestive name for the variable in both cases, then it should be used in both cases. PASCAL gives you the freedom to choose the best name for a variable in each procedure without worrying about whether that name happens to be used in another procedure.

Secondly, this fact that the names in each procedure are independent means that the names of parameters have nothing to do with the names of arguments. Arguments and parameters are matched strictly according to the order in which they appear in their respective lists -- their names are irrelevant in this matching. Figure 1 is drawn for the particular call shown in (1.3b), matching parameter X with argument I and parameter Y with argument J. Matching for various other possible calls is shown in Figure 2. (In Figures 2g, 2i and 2j the values for the subscripts I and J are taken from Figure 1a.)

	Call	Argument<----Parameter	
(a)	SWAP(J,I)	J<----X,	I<----Y
(b)	SWAP(X,J)	X<----X,	J<----Y
(c)	SWAP(J,X)	J<----X,	X<----Y
(d)	SWAP(T,X)	T<----X,	X<----Y
(e)	SWAP(A[1],J)	A[1]<----X,	J<----Y
(f)	SWAP(A[1],A[2])	A[1]<----X,	A[2]<----Y
(g)	SWAP(A[J],A[I])	A[1]<----X,	A[2]<----Y
(h)	SWAP(J,J)	J<----X,	J<----Y
(i)	SWAP(A[2],A[I])	A[2]<----X,	A[2]<----Y
(j)	SWAP(I,A[I])	I<----X,	A[2]<----Y

Figure 2. Matching Arguments and Parameters for (1.3b)

The correspondence between parameters and arguments is determined before execution of the body of the procedure begins, and is not changed throughout the particular execution. This means that if a subscripted variable is given as an argument, the subscript is evaluated before the execution of the procedure begins, and the correspondence between parameter and argument is based on this initial value. Although the value of the subscript may change during execution of the procedure the argument-parameter correspondence is not revised. For example, in Figure 2j, A[I] is given as the second argument. The value of I (from Figure 1a) is 2 so A[2] is associated with the second parameter Y. The value of I will be changed by SWAP, but this will not alter the association of Y with A[2]. Thus, according to the values in Figure 1a, after execution of SWAP(I,A[I]), I will be 8 and A[2] will be 2.

Several of the examples in Figure 2 show an element of an array being given as an argument. This can be done with ordinary arrays but not with PACKED arrays. Hence, since we are using PACKED arrays for strings of characters, an individual character of a string cannot be given as an argument of a procedure statement.

Finally, and most importantly, execution of a procedure call works as described above only if the attributes of each argument exactly match those of the parameter with which it is associated. That is, if a parameter X is declared REAL it must always be associated with an argument that has also been declared REAL. X can be associated with many different arguments, but every one of the arguments associated with X must be REAL.

1.3.2 Arguments and Value Parameters

For a value parameter, the corresponding argument is evaluated, and a separate copy of this value is associated with the parameter. The procedure operates on this new copy of the value. When the execution of the procedure is completed, this copy is deleted, along with all other traces of the procedure. The key point is that this secondary copy of the value is not copied back into the original argument value before the procedure is deleted. This means that for a value parameter, the procedure obtains a value from the argument, but is incapable of changing the value of that argument. This is the reason that a variable parameter, rather than a value parameter, must be used to return a result from a procedure.

For example, suppose the parameters of SWAP in (1.3b) had been declared:

```
PROCEDURE SWAP(X: INTEGER; VAR Y: INTEGER);
```

That is, X is a value parameter and Y is a variable parameter. Now consider the execution of SWAP(I, J) in contrast to the situation shown in Figure 1 where both X and Y were variable parameters. Figure 3 is the counterpart of Figure 1e. It shows the situation just before the execution of the first statement in SWAP. The parameters X and Y and the local variable T have all been created in the box representing this execution of SWAP. T has not yet been assigned a value, and "?" is shown in place of a value. Y is a variable parameter, as in Figure 1, and it has been associated with the second argument, J. This is indicated by an arrow from Y to the value of J. Y has no value of its own; it is simply another name for the value of J. The parameter X has been associated with the first argument I, just as in Figure 1. However, unlike Figure 1, X is now a value parameter, so the value of I is copied into the box for SWAP as a distinct value for X. This is denoted by a line from the value of I, through X, to the copy of the value. There is no arrow from X to the value of I, and X has no further access to that value. After the copy is made, the line from I to X can be erased. The only access to the value of the argument is to permit a copy to be made. The value of the argument cannot be changed.

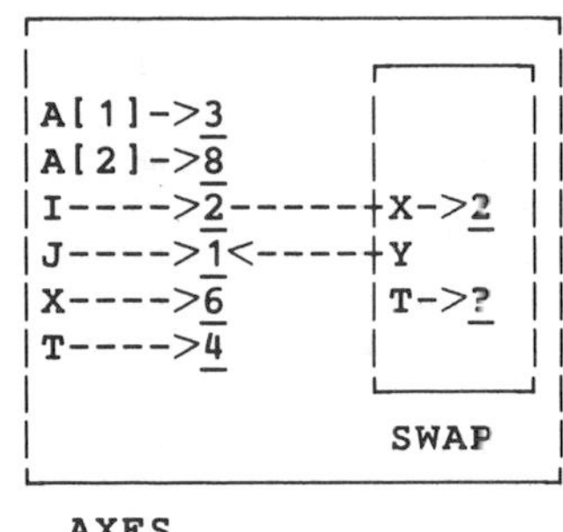

Figure 3. Value Parameter Counterpart of Figure 1e

Figure 4 shows the counterpart of Figure 1h -- the situation after executing the statements in the body of SWAP. The values of the parameters X and Y have apparently been interchanged, but only the value of the argument J, associated with the variable parameter Y, has been changed. The value of the value parameter X is a copy of the value of the argument I, and only that copy has been changed. Note that there is no longer any connection shown between parameter X and the argument I. The value of the argument I has not been affected by the action of SWAP. In effect, the result of executing SWAP, when its parameters are declared in this way, is to set the value of the second argument equal to the value of the first argument, rather than interchange the values.

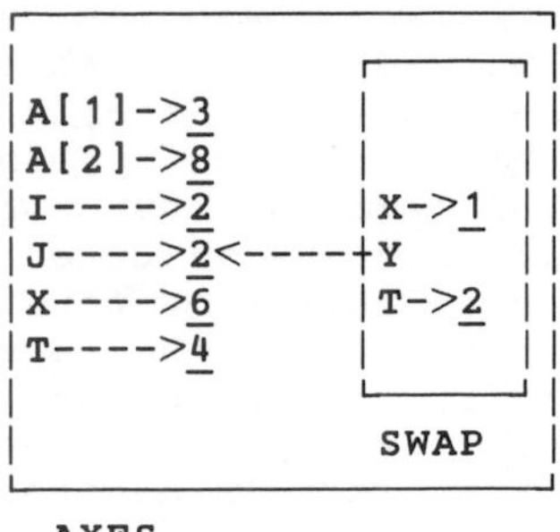

Figure 4. Value Parameter Counterpart of Figure 1h

This may seem complicated and confusing, and you might wonder why value parameters exist at all. The entire operation would be simpler to understand if all parameters were variable parameters. Indeed, most current programming languages -- PL/I, for example -- have no exact counterpart to PASCAL's value parameters. But this is an advantage of PASCAL, and once you understand their operation and significance, value parameters are well-worth the trouble they may cause a beginner. The key point is that they increase the independence between procedures. By permitting a variable given as an argument to be read but not changed, the calling procedure can be better-protected from possible errors in the called procedure. As programs become larger and more complicated, this becomes a significant virtue.

A further distinction between value and variable parameters is that value parameters permit an expression to be given as argument, whereas for a variable parameter only a variable can be given as argument. (A variable is just a special case of an expression -- so value parameters can have variables as arguments.) For example, this means that if SWAP is defined with X declared as a value parameter, as we have been assuming in this Section, then procedure statements such as the following could be used to call this procedure:

```
SWAP(7, J)

SWAP(X+T, J)

SWAP(TRUNC(X), J)
```

In each case, to execute the procedure the argument expression is evaluated to provide the initial value of the corresponding parameter.

1.3.3 Array Names as Arguments and Parameters

Individual elements of an array (but not of a PACKED array) may be passed as arguments to a procedure that is expecting to receive a simple variable, as for example in Figure 2. But it is often convenient to pass an entire array as a single argument. This can be done if

1. both the parameter and the argument are declared as arrays,

2. both have the same number of dimensions and the same number of elements in each dimension, and

3. both have the same type attributes (INTEGER, REAL, CHAR, BOOLEAN, PACKED).

To ensure this required compatibility PASCAL requires use of a TYPE definition. A TYPE definition given in the main procedure can be referenced in the declaration of the array that will be given as an argument, and again in the declaration of the parameter that will be associated with that argument. For example:

```
TYPE REAL50 = ARRAY[1..50] OF REAL;
    ...
PROCEDURE SEARCH(V:REAL; ROW:REAL50;
                 VAR RESULT:REAL)
```

A complete example is shown in (1.3.3a) where the type COLUMN is defined for the argument ITEM and the parameter VECT.

Note that the program SUMER in (1.3.3a) will accomodate lists of any length from 1 up to 50. The particular example shown in (1.3.3a) has a list of length 5, as specified by the first item of data. If the data list has more than 50 numbers, the program shown will not work. It would have to be changed to accomodate the greater length. Since the maximum length appears in several places in the program, a constant LENGTH is defined to represent the maximum length. This means that the change need be made in only one place, and it is then automatically reflected throughout the program. If it were not done this way, there would be considerable risk that you would miss some place where the length appears in the program.

```
(* PROGRAM TO SUM ITEMS OF A DATA LIST *)
PROGRAM SUMER(INPUT, OUTPUT);
CONST LENGTH = 50; (* MAXIMUM LENGTH OF LIST *)
TYPE COLUMN = ARRAY[1..LENGTH] OF REAL;
VAR ITEM: COLUMN;
    N: INTEGER; (* DATA LIST IS ITEM[1..N] *)
    SUM: REAL;
    I: 1..LENGTH;

(* SET SUM TO SUM OF VECT[1..M] *)
PROCEDURE COMPSUM(VECT: COLUMN;
                  M: INTEGER;
                  VAR SUM: REAL);
  VAR J: 1..LENGTH;
  BEGIN (* COMPSUM *)
    SUM := 0;
    FOR J := 1 TO M DO
         SUM := SUM + VECT[J]
  END; (* COMPSUM *)
```

(1.3.3a)

```
BEGIN (* SUMER *)
    READLN(N);
    IF (N < 1) OR (N > LENGTH) THEN
         WRITELN('0IMPROPER DATA LENGTH:', N);
    FOR I := 1 TO N DO
         READ(ITEM[I]);
    COMPSUM(ITEM, N, SUM);
    WRITELN('0SUM OF', N, ' ITEMS IS:', SUM)
END.  (* SUMER *)
    eor
5
49.3 4E2 -42 17 263.15
```

(1.3.3a) illustrates two unfortunate limitations of PASCAL. SUMER always deals with an array of maximum length (as specified by the constant LENGTH) regardless of the length actually required by the data. In (1.3.3a) an array of fifty elements is created, and passed to the procedure COMPSUM, even though only five elements are actually used. There is simply no way in PASCAL to have the number of elements of an array be determined from the data. This limitation was characteristic of early programming languages, such as FORTRAN, but facility to do this is present in ALGOL and PL/I, and its omission from PASCAL is surprising.

Even worse, since the array parameters of PASCAL procedures have a fixed number of elements, it is not possible to have different calls with arguments having different numbers of elements. For example, in ALGOL or PL/I you could have a procedure such as COMPSUM of (1.3.3a) that would compute the sum of the elements of an array of any size -- the number of elements is determined by the declaration of the argument and not the declaration of the parameter. But in PASCAL this is not possible. For example, if you have to compute the sum of an array of fifty elements, and also the sum of an array of forty elements, you would need two separate summing procedures. This is a serious limitation, and we understand that PASCAL is being changed to remedy it.

On the other hand, (1.3.3a) illustrates the proper use of a good feature of PASCAL -- value parameters, as described in Section 1.3.2. The procedure COMPSUM may or may not correctly compute the sum of the first N elements of the array ITEM, but at least it will not accidentally change these values, since the parameters with which these arguments are associated are declared to be <u>value parameters</u>. COMPSUM makes its own copy of these values, and works from this copy. (Unfortunately, this protection is not quite complete, since it only covers communication by means of parameters, and another communication path exists. For example, no reference to parameter M in COMPSUM can damage the value of the argument N, but an accidental reference to N in COMPSUM can alter the value of N directly, since there is no local declaration of N in COMPSUM.)

Another example in which an array is passed as an argument is shown in procedure SEARCH in (1.3.3b). SEARCH has four parameters:

Parameter 1: the array to be searched
Parameter 2: the index of the last element to be searched
Parameter 3: the value being searched for
Parameter 4: the index of the element found (or 0).

Assume SEARCH is to be defined in a main procedure CALP, that also includes the following definition and declarations:

```
PROGRAM CALP(INPUT, OUTPUT);
TYPE LIST = ARRAY[0..4] OF INTEGER;
VAR B: LIST;
    M, X, K: INTEGER
```

Then the definition of SEARCH is the following:

```
          (* SEARCH A[1..N] FOR VALUE X, SET J SO A[J] = X *)
          (* STORE 0 IN J IF NO SUCH INTEGER EXISTS *)
          PROCEDURE SEARCH(A: LIST;
                           N, X: INTEGER;
                           VAR J: INTEGER);
(1.3.3b)   LABEL 88;
            BEGIN (* SEARCH *)
              FOR J := 1 TO N DO
                   IF A[J] = X THEN GOTO 88;
              J := 0; (* INDICATES VALUE NOT FOUND *)
              88:;
            END (* SEARCH *)
```

Figure 5 illustrates execution of the procedure statement:

```
SEARCH(B, M, X, K)
```

Assume the values of the arguments before the call are as shown in Figure 5a. The parameter-argument correspondence is shown in Figure 5b. The result of execution is shown in Figure 5c. Note that parameter A refers to the whole array B[0..4], even though the procedure does not reference every element. Since M is 2, only B[1..2] is searched, and since this portion of the array does not contain a value 6, the result of execution is a 0 in K. Notice also that while the last element to be searched is specified by parameter N, the first element to be searched is always element 1. This is clearly specified in the heading comment of the procedure. Nevertheless, this is a source of potential trouble for the user. It would be easy to forget that SEARCH always starts with element 1, regardless of where the array starts. For example, CALP uses SEARCH for a [0..4] array. If the author of CALP really wanted to overlook the first element of B, then everything is fine. However, if he had simply forgotten that SEARCH always starts with 1, then there is trouble. PASCAL will not recognize this as an error, since everything is in legal form, and unless test data is carefully chosen, testing may not reveal the error either. Nevertheless, the error is present, and under certain circumstances the program will not give the required result. It would be better practice to have another parameter that would explicitly specify the first element to be searched.

Both of our examples (1.3.3a) and (1.3.3b) happen to involve an array value parameter -- a complete new copy of the array is created. Array parameters can also be variable parameters, in which case no copy is made and each element of the parameter array points to the corresponding element of the argument array. In this case the elements of the argument array can be changed by action of the procedure.

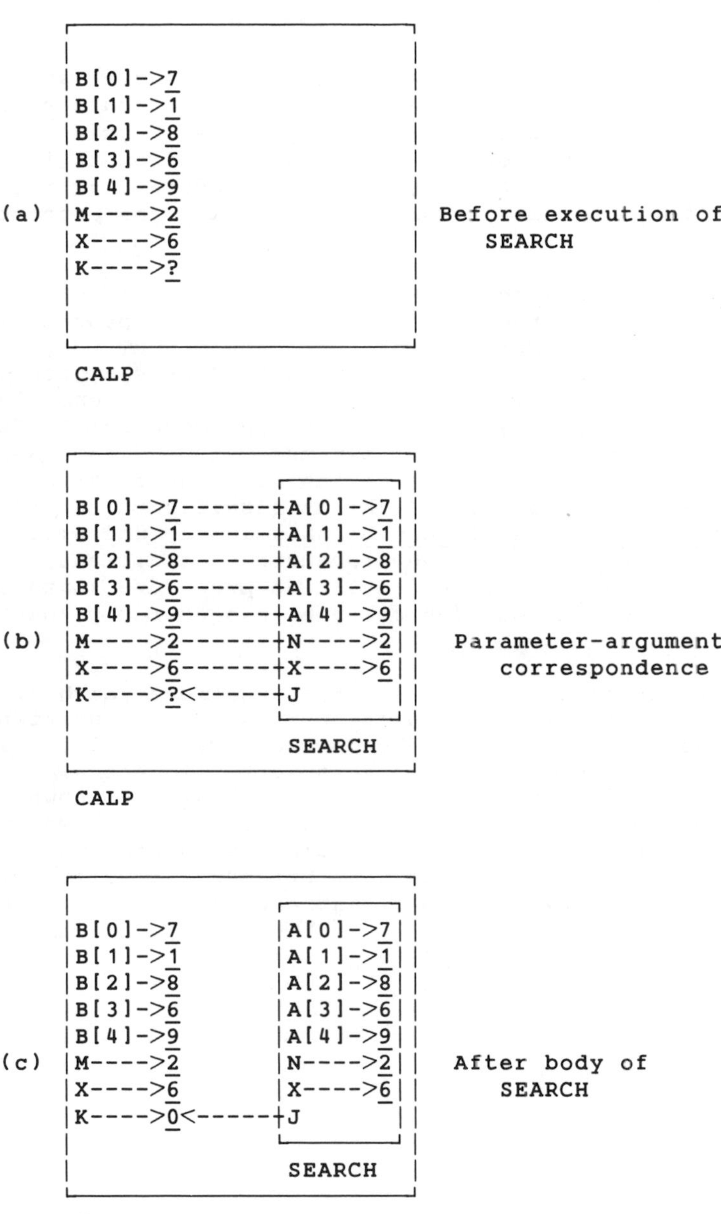

Figure 5. Execution of SEARCH(B, M, X, K)

1.4 Nested Procedure Statements

Thus far we have been considering only procedure statements in the main procedure. Actually, since a procedure statement may appear anywhere that a statement may appear, this includes the body of any procedure. A procedure statement is simply placed wherever the action of the procedure is required, specifying the particular arguments upon which the procedure is to be executed.

(1.4a) illustrates a complete program consisting of a main procedure and three other procedures. The main procedure SRTG reads in a list of integers, invokes procedure SORT to sort the list, and then prints the list. This SORT uses a successive-minima algorithm, a fairly obvious variation of the one used in Section III.2.3. It uses two other procedures: FINDMIN to determine the array element with minimum value, and SWAP to interchange the values of two variables. The ordering of the four procedure definitions in (1.4a) is significant; a procedure must be defined before it can be used in the definition of a subsequent procedure. Thus, the procedure definitions proceed from the most elementary (that contain no procedure statements), to the most complicated (which use procedures that use procedures, etc.)

The program consists of four separate sections, each of which performs some logically independent task, each written as a separate procedure. Each can be understood by itself, without having to understand how the others work. In actual practice one would rarely write such short procedures as are shown here; this program would have been just as readable had we written just a main program and a SORT procedure, performing the FINDMIN and SWAP operations within the sort procedure itself. We have written (1.4a) this way just to illustrate the use of nested procedure statements.

(1.4a)

```
(* READ IN 3 INTEGERS, PRINT IN SORTED ORDER *)
PROGRAM SRTG(INPUT, OUTPUT);
CONST N = 3;
TYPE SETOFN = ARRAY[1..N] OF INTEGER;
VAR A: SETOFN;
    I, M: INTEGER;

(* SORT ARRAY X[1..N] USING SUCCESSIVE MINIMA *)
PROCEDURE SORT(VAR X: SETOFN; N: INTEGER);
  VAR I, J: INTEGER;

  (* SET J TO INDEX OF MINIMUM OF X[I..N] *)
  PROCEDURE FINDMIN(X: SETOFN;
                    I, N: INTEGER;
                    VAR J: INTEGER);
    VAR K: INTEGER;
    BEGIN (* FINDMIN *)
         J := I;
         FOR K := I+1 TO N DO
              IF X[K] < X[J]
                   THEN J := K
    END; (* FINDMIN *)

  (* SWAP VALUES OF X AND Y *)
  PROCEDURE SWAP(VAR X, Y: INTEGER);
    VAR T: INTEGER;
    BEGIN (* SWAP *)
         T := X;
         X := Y;
         Y := T
    END; (* SWAP *)

  BEGIN (* SORT *)
    FOR I := 1 TO N-1 DO
      BEGIN
         (* PUT MINIMUM OF X[I..N] IN X[I] *)
              FINDMIN(X, I, N, J);
              SWAP(X[I], X[J])
      END
  END; (* SORT *)

BEGIN (* SRTG *)
    FOR I := 1 TO N DO
         READ(A[I]);
    M := N;
    SORT(A, M);
    FOR I := 1 TO N DO
         WRITELN(' ', A[I])
END.  (* SRTG *)
    eor
2 8 1
```

The procedure structure of (1.4a) is shown in Figure 6. The main procedure is SRTG. The definition of procedure SORT is nested within SRTG. The definitions of procedures FINDMIN and SWAP are both nested with SORT. SORT is called by procedure statements in the body of SRTG. Within the body of SORT are procedure statements calling FINDMIN and SWAP. In each case the definition of a procedure is given before a procedure statement that calls it.

```
PROGRAM SRTG
   |  PROCEDURE SORT
   |     |  PROCEDURE FINDMIN
   |     |     | ...
   |     |     END (* FINDMIN *)
   |     |  PROCEDURE SWAP
   |     |     | ...
   |     |     END (* SWAP *)
   |     |   ...
   |     |  FINDMIN(...)
   |     |  SWAP(...)
   |     |   ...
   |     END (* SORT *)
   |   ...
   |  SORT(...)
   |   ...
   END (* SRTG *)
```

Figure 6. Structure of (1.4a)

When a program has several procedure statements -- particularly nested procedure statements -- it can get complicated to remember what each parameter represents, and where to return to after completing execution of each procedure. In general, if you consider a procedure statement as an operation to be performed, and not worry about <u>how</u> it is performed, you should not have trouble. For example, in reading procedure SORT, simply accept FINDMIN and SWAP as operations to be performed. You can later read procedure FINDMIN to see how the operation is carried out, but don't interrupt your reading and understanding of SORT to study FINDMIN.

On the other hand, the actual exection of the program does involve the interruption of SORT to execute FINDMIN, and you should understand how this takes place. Figure 7 etc.

Figure 7 shows four of the key stages in the beginning of execution of (1.4a). Figure 7a shows the situation at BEGIN (* SORT *) during the first excution of SORT. The box for SORT has been created; the array variable parameter X has been associated, element by element with the array argument A; the value parameter N has been given a copy of the value of argument M; and the local variables I and J have been created, but not yet assigned a value. The execution of SORT then begins. On the first iteration of the loop, the index variable I is assigned value 1, and then the procedure FINDMIN is called.

This is the critical point for you to understand. During the execution of SORT, which was invoked from SRTG, the procedure FINDMIN is invoked from SORT. The execution of SORT is, in effect, suspended while FINDMIN is executed.

Figure 7b shows the situation at BEGIN (* FINDMIN *) during the first execution of FINDMIN, given during the first execution of SORT. The box for FINDMIN has been created. The array value parameter X has obtained copies of the values of the argument array X in procedure SORT. But the array X in SORT is a variable parameter, hence just another name for the argument array A of SRTG. So actually, the value paramter X of FINDMIN obtains copies of the values of array A in SRTG. The value parameter N has obtained a copy of the value of argument N of SORT. (It is a coincidence that the argument and parameter are both named N.) Similarly, the value parameter I obtains a copy of the value of argument I. The variable parameter J is associated with the argument J of SORT, which has not yet received a value. (The value of the argument J is the result of executing FINDMIN.) The local variable K of FINDMIN has been created, but not yet assigned a value.

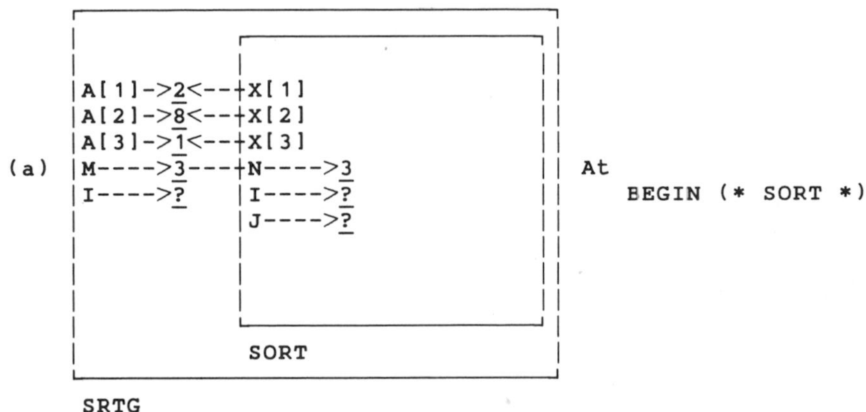

Figure 7. Execution of SORT(A, M) in (1.4a)

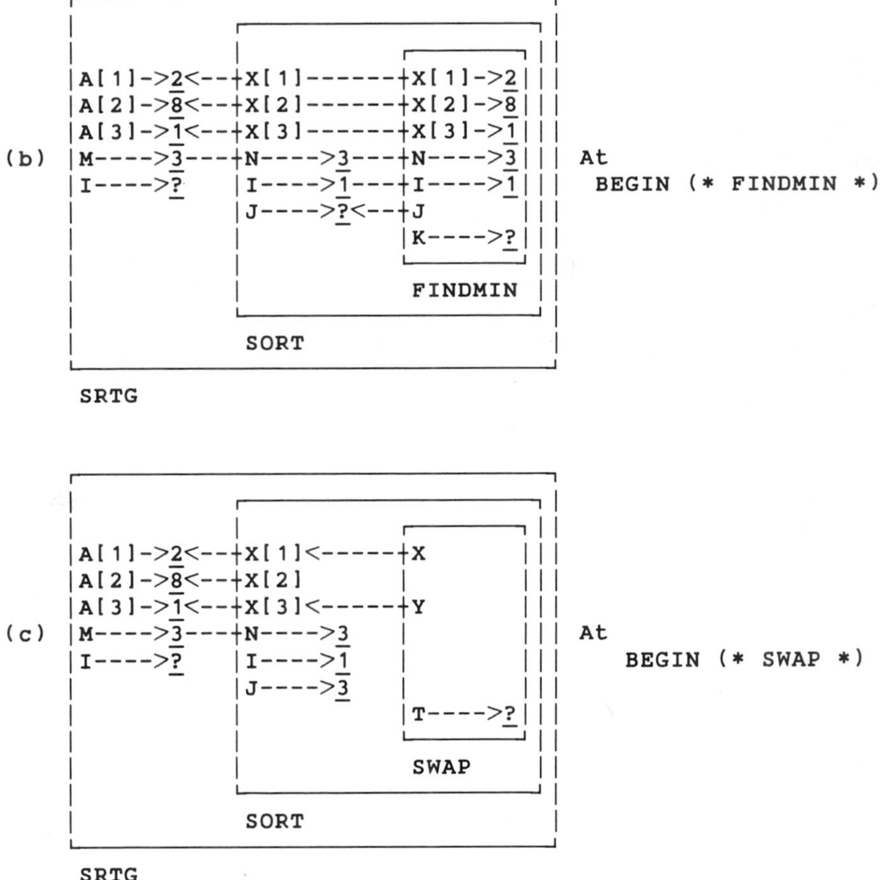

Figure 7. Execution of SORT(A, M) (continued)

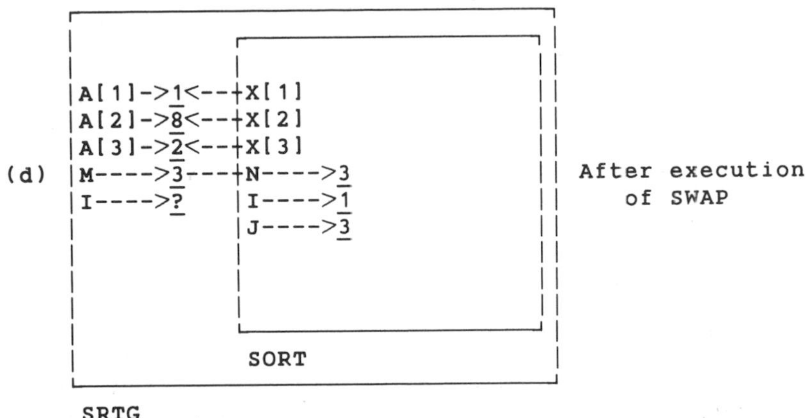

Figure 7. Execution of SORT(A, M) (continued)

Figure 7c shows the situation at BEGIN (* SWAP *) during the first execution of SWAP, given during the first execution of SORT. The execution of FINDMIN has been completed and the box for FINDMIN has been erased. The box for SWAP has been created in the same space that FINDMIN had previously occupied. The arguments are given as X[I] and X[J]. The value of I is 1 and the value of J is 3, so the arguments are actually X[1] and X[3] in SORT. These are variable parameters in SORT, associated with elements A[1] and A[3] in SRTG. Hence the variable parameters X and Y or SWAP are associated with the elements A[1] and A[3] in SRTG. The local variable T has been created in SWAP, but not yet assigned a value.

Figure 7d shows the situation after completion of execution of SWAP. The box for SWAP has been deleted, but the effects of its execution remain, in that the values of A[1] and A[3] have been interchanged.

The program would now continue with the second iteration of the loop in SORT. I in SORT would be assigned value 2, and FINDMIN would be executed again. FINDMIN would be created again, as in Figure 7b, but the values of the variables in SRTG and SORT would not be exactly like those shown in Figure 7b. After completion of FINDMIN, SWAP would be executed again, as in Figure 7c, but with different values.

Note that the whole purpose of FINDMIN is to set the value of J, which is then passed as an argument to SWAP to tell SWAP the location of the minimum value which is to be interchanged. Notice also the way in which value and variable parameters are used in the different procedures, depending upon whether or not the value of the argument has to be changed.

1.4.1 Recursion

You might wonder what would happen if a procedure "invoked itself". That is, what if P(...) is located in the body of procedure P?

```
PROCEDURE P(...)
  ...
  BEGIN (* P *)
    ...
    P(...)
    ...
  END (* P *)
```

In many programming languages this would be a serious error, but it is permitted in PASCAL, and in fact is very useful. (It is also permitted in ALGOL and PL/I, but not in FORTRAN or COBOL.) The process is called "recursion", or "recursive execution". However, we are not going to explain or use recursion in this *Primer*. If the idea seems intriguing, read Section VI.4 of our *Introduction to Programming*.

1.5 Permanent Variables

The figures in Section 1.3 and 1.4 show that a procedure is created each time it is called, and then deleted when that particular execution is completed. In particular the local variables, such as T in Figure 1, are *created as the procedure is entered* and *destroyed on return from the procedure*. This happens each time that the procedure is executed; during the intervals between executions the local variables simply do not exist. This process is called "dynamic storage management".

Dynamic storage management permits efficient use of storage space. Since variables are assigned storage space only when their procedures are being executed, the same space can be used at different times for different variables. For example, in Figure 7, FINDMIN and SWAP never exist at the same time. The space used for FINDMIN at one point in execution can be used for SWAP at another point. For the small problems used for instruction, space conservation is not a concern, but for serious production programs it can be important.

However, since the *value of local variables is not saved* from one execution of a procedure to the next, each execution of a procedure is completely independent of every other execution. Each execution has no recollection that the procedure was ever executed before, and is incapable of leaving any information that is available to future executions. For example, this means that a procedure is incapable of counting the number of times that it has been called. Suppose you were performing various tests on input data and wanted to have a procedure to write error messages like the following:

```
ERROR IN DATA:
     NEGATIVE VALUE
     ERRORS SO FAR: 14
```

What you would like would be to call the message procedure with the text of the message as an argument, and have the procedure print the message shown. Unfortunately, there is no way in PASCAL that the procedure, on its own, can keep track of the number of times it has been called, and be able to print the last line of the message.

In PASCAL, in order to save information from one execution of a procedure to the next, you must rely on some other procedure -- one that exists continuously throughout this interval. A variable, declared in some procedure that is relatively more permanent, must be used to save information. For example, in (1.4a), the procedure SORT is relatively permanent compared to procedures FINDMIN and SWAP which are repeatedly created and deleted during the lifetime of SORT. Hence SORT can be used to "save" information for either FINDMIN or SWAP. In fact, that is just what the variable J of SORT is for. J saves the result of the execution of FINDMIN so that it can be passed to SWAP. In a similar way, a variable of SORT could be used to save information from one execution of FINDMIN to the next. Referring again to the message-writing procedure, the variable that represented the cumulative number of errors so far would have to be declared in the procedure that called the message-writer, rather than in the message procedure itself. This count could be passed to the message procedure as an argument. (It would have to be associated with a variable parameter, since the message procedure needs to change its value.) Alternatively, if the message procedure avoided declaring its own variable with the same name, it could access this counting variable in the calling procedure without having it passed as an argument. The counting variable presumably would not be used in any way in the calling procedure, but would just be declared in the calling procedure because of its relatively longer life.

This is not an altogether attractive solution to the problem. It is inelegant, since the message procedure is not entirely self-contained. A variable which logically belongs to the message procedure must be declared somewhere else, just to circumvent a peculiarity of PASCAL. It is also dangerous, since there is nothing to prevent this variable from being accidentally used by the calling procedure, or some other procedure, where it should be the private property of the message procedure. Other programming languages, PL/I in particular, have better solutions to this problem.

If we want a variable to be really permanent -- that is, to exist throughout the execution of a program -- we declare it in the main procedure of the program since, by definition, the execution of a program consists of the execution of the main procedure. Variables declared in the main procedure for this purpose are said to be "global" since they are accessible everywhere. That is, any procedure defined in the main procedure, that does not declare a local variable of the same name, can access such a global variable.

As a specific example, procedure NEXTLET in (1.5a) serves to divide input words of ten characters each into individual letters. Each time NEXTLET is invoked it returns the next letter of the input data stream. On the first execution, and every tenth execution thereafter, NEXTLET obtains a new word from the external data list. The variable WORD, used in NEXTLET, must be global because it must get a value from the data list on the first execution and retain this value for nine more executions. If WORD were local to NEXTLET the value would be lost on return from the first execution. COUNT must also be global so that NEXTLET can keep track of the position in WORD of the "next" letter, and so it will know when the data word is exhausted and a new value must be obtained from the data list. COUNT must be assigned an initial value of 10 by the main procedure so that the first execution of NEXTLET will work properly.

(1.5a)

```
(* ...  *)
PROGRAM MAIN(INPUT, OUTPUT);
TYPE STRING10 = PACKED ARRAY[1..10] OF CHAR;
VAR WORD: STRING10;
    COUNT: INTEGER;
    S: CHAR;
...
(* SET L TO NEXT INPUT LETTER *)
PROCEDURE NEXTLET(VAR L: CHAR);
  VAR I: INTEGER;
  BEGIN (* NEXTLET *)
    (* GET NEW WORD (EVERY 10TH CALL) *)
         IF COUNT = 10 THEN
           BEGIN
              FOR I := 1 TO 10 DO
                   READ(WORD[I]);
              COUNT := 0
           END;
    (* PICK OUT NEXT LETTER *)
         COUNT := COUNT + 1;
         L := WORD[COUNT]
  END; (* NEXTLET *)

BEGIN (* MAIN *)
    COUNT := 10;
    ...
    NEXTLET(S);
    ...
END.  (* MAIN *)
```

Section 1 Summary

1. A procedure is a sub-program that performs some distinct, clearly specified task.

2. The definition (or declaration) of a procedure (excluding the main procedure) has the form:

```
(* Comment describing function of procedure *)
PROCEDURE name(declaration of parameters);
  Local declarations and definitions;
  BEGIN (* name *)
    Statements
  END (* name *)
```

3. Procedure definitions are placed immediately after the declaration of variables. The order of procedure definitions must be such that each is defined before it is used in a procedure statement.

4. Procedures are executed by executing the corresponding procedure statement. The execution of a procedure consists of the execution of the statements in its body. Upon completion of execution of the last statement of the body, execution of the calling procedure resumes with the statement following the call.

5. A procedure has its own declarations and definitions to create objects that are local to that procedure. These objects cannot be used outside the procedure in which they are declared.

6. Communication between procedures is primarily by means of the parameters of the procedure and the arguments of the corresponding procedure statement. Parameters and arguments are matched in the order listed (independent of their names). The attributes of parameters should exactly match those of the corresponding arguments.

7. Variable parameters become another name for the corresponding argument. This form of parameter must be used to return a result. A value parameter is provided with a copy of the value of the corresponding argument. This form of parameter cannot be used to alter the value of the corresponding argument -- hence cannot be used to return a result.

8. An alternative form of communication with a procedure is by means of "global" variables. A procedure can access a variable of the procedure in which it is defined, if there is no local variable of the same name.

9. Local variables of a procedure are created each time execution of the procedure begins, and destroyed when that execution terminates. To preserve information from one execution of a procedure to the next it is necessary to use a global variable.

Section 1 Exercises

1. For each sequence of statements below, write a procedure with that sequence as the body, complete with declarations. The parameters are those variables and arrays described in the comment. Other variables should be local to the procedure. All variables are INTEGER.

a)
```
(* STORE THE MAXIMUM OF A AND B IN C *)
    IF A >= B
         THEN C := A
         ELSE C := B
```

b)
```
(* SET SUM TO SUM OF ELEMENTS OF A[1..N] *)
    SUM := 0;
    FOR I := 1 TO N DO
      SUM := SUM + A[I]
```

c)
```
(* REVERSE THE ELEMENTS OF X[1..N] *)
    FIRST := 1;
    LAST := N;
    WHILE FIRST < LAST DO
      BEGIN
         T := X[FIRST];
         X[FIRST] := X[LAST];
         X[LAST] := T;
         FIRST := FIRST + 1;
         LAST := LAST - 1
      END
```

2. Make the program segments of Exercise 2, Section I.5, into procedures. Only the variables described in the comment of each program segment should be parameters.

3. Execute the following procedure calls by hand, drawing all necessary boxes. Procedure SWAP is given in (1.1b). Assume all variables are INTEGER.

a) SWAP(A,B)	where	A 5	B 6
b) SWAP(T,X)	where	T 3	X 4
c) SWAP(Y,X)	where	Y 1	X 8
d) SWAP(V,V)	where	V 3	

4. Write procedures for the program segments of Exercises 4, 5 and 6 of Section I.5.

5. Write a procedure MEAN which, given an array segment X[1..N]) calculates the mean of the values. The mean is the sum of the elements divided by N.

6. Execute the following procedure calls by hand, drawing all the boxes. Procedure SEARCH is given in (1.3.3c). The variables used are given below.

```
T[0] 6        N0 0        F 8
T[1] 8        N1 1        G 5
T[2] 4        N2 2        H 6
T[3] 9        N3 3        I 3
```

a) SEARCH(T, N0, H, I)
b) SEARCH(T, N1, H, I)
c) SEARCH(T, N3, H, I)
d) SEARCH(T, N3, G, I)
e) SEARCH(T, N3, F, I)

7. Write a procedure with five parameters that will set the fifth parameter equal to the sum of the first four.

8. Write a procedure MEDIAN which, given an array segment X[1..N] calculates the median of the values. The median is the value such that half the numbers are greater than that value and half are less. One way to do this is to first sort the array and then pick the middle value. If you use this method, use a previously written sort procedure to do the sorting. But be careful; MEDIAN should not change the order of the values in its argument array -- a procedure should never modify the arguments unless its specific task is to modify them.

9. Write a program to read a list of values and to print out the mean and the median. Your program should use the procedures written in Exercises 5 and 8.

10. Write a procedure which calculates sin(x) using the formula

$$\sin(x) = x/1! - x^3/3! + x^5/5! - x^7/7! + \ldots$$

The number of terms of the series to be used should be a parameter of the procedure. Next, write a program to compare the values of sin(x) calculated using the built-in SIN function against those values calculated by your procedure. Run the program with various values of x and various values of the number of terms used in the series.

11. Write a procedure to calculate the product of two n by n matrices A[1..N,1..N] and B[1..N,1..N]. Each element C[I,K] of the resulting matrix C[1..N,1..N] is defined as the sum of the values

A[I,J] * B[J,K]   for j = 1, ..., N.

12. Assume you are given the subroutine FLP shown below and told only that IN is an input parameter, OUT is an output parameter, and that the routine neither reads any data nor prints any lines. Write a program that will allow FLP to be tested by repeatedly calling it with different input values and displaying the results. Your program will include FLP but not change it in any way.

```
(* SET OUT TO ...   *)
PROCEDURE FLP(IN: PACKED ARRAY[1..100] OF CHAR;
              VAR OUT: INTEGER);
  ...
  BEGIN (* FLP *)
    ...
  END; (* FLP *)
```

13. What is the <u>execution</u> output from the program shown below:

```
(* SQUARE-DUPLICATE AND PRINT EACH OF J DATA PAIRS *)
PROGRAM LST(INPUT, OUTPUT);
TYPE STRING10 = PACKED ARRAY[1..10] OF CHAR;
VAR L: STRING10; (* INPUT STRING *)
    N,           (* INPUT NUMBER *)
    J,           (* NBR OF PAIRS *)
    K: INTEGER;
(* READ A STRING10 ENCLOSED IN QUOTES *)
PROCEDURE READ10(VAR STRING: STRING10);
  VAR CH: CHAR; (* INPUT CHARS *)
      K: INTEGER;
  BEGIN (* READ10 *)
    REPEAT
         READ(CH)
      UNTIL CH = '''';
    (* SET STRING TO ALL BLANKS INITIALLY *)
         FOR K := 1 TO 10 DO
              STRING[K] := ' ';
    (* READ THE DATA *)
         K := 1;
         READ(CH);
         WHILE CH <> '''' DO
           BEGIN
              STRING[K] := CH;
              K := K + 1;
              READ(CH)
           END
  END; (* READ10 *)
(* DUPLICATE FIRST CHARACTER OF STRING *)
PROCEDURE DUP(VAR STRING: STRING10);
  VAR I: INTEGER;
  BEGIN (* DUP *)
    FOR I := 10 DOWNTO 2 DO
         STRING[I] := STRING[I-1]
  END; (* DUP *)
```

```
(* SET VALUE = SQUARE OF VALUE *)
PROCEDURE SQUARE(VAR VALUE: INTEGER);
  BEGIN (* SQUARE *)
    VALUE := VALUE * VALUE
  END; (* SQUARE *)
(* SQUARE NBR; DUPLICATE FIRST CHAR OF CHR *)
PROCEDURE EDITOR(VAR NBR: INTEGER; VAR CHR: STRING10);
  BEGIN (* EDITOR *)
    IF NBR <> 0 THEN SQUARE(NBR);
    IF CHR <> ' ' THEN DUP(CHR)
  END; (* EDITOR *)

BEGIN (* LST *)
    READ(J);
    FOR K := 1 TO J DO
      BEGIN
         READ10(L);
         READ(N);
         EDITOR(N, L);
         WRITELN(' ', L, N)
      END
END.  (* LST *)
    eor
4 'X' 4 'YY' -3 'XYX' 0 '4'
4 'ABC' 567.9032
```

14. Write a procedure that will read a list of words whose lengths may be anywhere from 1 to 15 characters, and will print a list of any words that occur more than once in this data list. (Review Section III.2.5. A "word" here is equivalent to a "symbol" in that section.) The end of the data list is indicated by the string <*>, which is not itself considered an item on the list. Title the output appropriately.

15. Write a body for the procedure REPTEST, started below, so it will perform the task described in the heading comment. That is, it should check for repetitions of each character in the argument word. Any repetition of a character should be replaced by an asterisk. For example, 'AAABCDDBE' would become 'A**BCD**E'.

```
(* REPLACE ALL REPEATED OCCURRENCES (EXCEPT THE FIRST)
  OF ANY CHARACTERS IN WORD BY '*' *)
PROCEDURE REPTEST(VAR WORD: PACKED ARRAY[1..20] OF CHAR);
    ...
    BEGIN (* REPTEST *)
         ...
    END (* REPTEST *)
```

16. What is the execution output from the following program?

```
(* PROBLEM IV.1.16, PRIMER *)
PROGRAM PROB(INPUT, OUTPUT);
VAR M, N: INTEGER;
(* PRINT N AND M+2 *)
PROCEDURE SUB(VAR N: INTEGER);
    LABEL 55;
    VAR M: INTEGER;
    BEGIN (* SUB *)
         M := 5;
         M := M + 2;
         WRITELN(' INSIDE', M, N);
         GOTO 55;
         WRITELN(' STILL INSIDE', M, N);
         55:;
    END; (* SUB *)

BEGIN (* PROB *)
    N := 4;
    FOR M := 1 TO 3 DO
      BEGIN
         SUB(M);
         WRITELN(' RESULT IS:', M, N)
      END;
    WRITELN(' AFTER LAST CALL', M, N)
END.  (* PROB *)
```

17. Write a procedure DEBLANK to serve as a subroutine to eliminate all blanks from a character string given as argument.

18. Modify the subroutine DEBLANK of Exercise 17 so that it has a second parameter, which is fixed integer. If the second argument has a non-zero value then DEBLANK is to return as the value of the second argument the cumulative number of blanks that have been eliminated in all calls so far (including the current call). If the value of the second argument is zero then it is to remain unchanged by DEBLANK.

19. Complete the procedure FINDMAX started below. This is a procedure to receive positive numbers and report the greatest of the numbers received. Its action when called is the following:

-if ACT=1 the value given in VAL is to be saved -- that is, it is to be stored in some available slot in the array VALS. If this can be done indicate success by returning with RES=1; if no space is available indicate failure by returning with RES=0.
-if ACT=2 then the maximum of the values currently in VALS is to be returned in VAL. This maximum value is to be removed from VALS and the space it occupied made available for a new arrival. Indicate success by returning with RES=1 and failure (if VALS is empty) by returning with RES=0.

```
...
VAR VALS: ARRAY[1..5] OF REAL;
...
(* SAVE VAL IF ACT = 1; RETURN MAX VAL IF ACT = 2; *)
(* RES = 1,0 FOR SUCCESS, FAILURE *)
PROCEDURE FINDMAX(VAR VAL: REAL;
                ACT: INTEGER; VAR RES: INTEGER);
    ...
    END; (* FINDMAX *)

BEGIN (* MAIN PGM *)
    (* INITIALIZE VALS[1..5] TO -1 *)
    FOR I := 1 TO 5 DO
         VALS[I] := -1;
    ...
```

20. Write a procedure GETMAX(VAR VAL: REAL, ACT: INTEGER; VAR RES: INTEGER) that has exactly the same action from the caller's point-of-view as FINDMAX of Exercise 19. GETMAX is to work by calling FINDMAX, except that by keeping track of the kinds of calls GETMAX knows when FINDMAX would fail (return with RES=0) so in these cases GETMAX doesn't bother to call FINDMAX. It simulates FINDMAX's action and returns directly. Do not change FINDMAX.

21. Write a procedure that can be used to sum all the elements in a set of adjacent rows in a two-dimensional array. The parameters (all fixed decimal) are to be the following (in the order listed below):

Parameter 1: the array
Parameter 2: the number of columns in the array
Parameter 3: the first row to be included
Parameter 4: the last row to be included
Parameter 5: the sum of the required elements (the result).

22. Write a main procedure that can be used to test the summing procedure of Exercise 21. That is, this main procedure should

a) read a set of values that will serve as arguments
b) print the argument values (appropriately titled)
c) call the summing procedure
d) print the sum value returned.

Section 2 The Uses of Procedures

Procedures provide three different capabilities:

1. The ability to write a section of program in one place and have it executed as if it were written in another.

2. The ability to write a section in terms of parameters so that it can be used for different variables at different times. This is effectively defining a new operation to be used in a program, like SORT(A,N) or SWAP(X,Y).

3. The ability to create an independent environment whose names are distinct from those of the rest of the program, and for which the total communication is clearly and completely specified.

2.1 Subroutines

The term "subroutine" is often used in programming to identify some sequence of statements that is needed in more than one place in a program. It is convenient to be able to write the common statements only once and use them as often as and wherever necessary. If a subroutine is written in a general way, without commitment to particular variable names, its opportunity for use is clearly increased. This obvious use of procedures was suggested by the examples of the preceding sections.

There is generally a sense of both permanence and portability in subroutines. That is, they are written so that they can be used in more than one program. There are various "libraries" of subroutines that are quite permanent and widely used. In effect, the built-in functions of PASCAL -- SQRT, ABS, SIN, TRUNC, etc. -- constitute such a library.

Subroutines can be considered a means of extending a programming language; of adding whatever operators or statements the user needs that the language doesn't happen to offer. For example, in (1.1b) we developed a procedure to interchange the values of two variables. With this procedure appended to any program the "swap" operation is effectively added to the language. The procedure SEARCH in (1.3.3c) is another, more complex, example.

In Part III we often used a statement at a "higher level" than PASCAL, and then translated or expanded it into PASCAL terms. By writing a subroutine to perform that task we effectively add that high-level statement to the language (at least temporarily). For example, in Section III.2.3 we developed a program to order the elements of an array. If this were written as a procedure with the array as argument then one could regard

```
SORT(array)
```

as part of the language. Moreover, the procedure could be saved and reused in future programs whenever we had need of that particular function. For all practical purposes we could now think of "sort" as an operation available in our private, augmented-PASCAL. In the development of future programs, once we reached a point where the algorithm required "sort" we would not have to refine that particular branch of the tree any further.

Subroutines exploit all three capabilities of procedures. The first two are obvious, but it is the third -- the independent environment -- that allows a subroutine to be moved freely from one program to another without any concern for whether the variables in the subroutine happen to coincide with names in the host program.

2.2 Control Sections

Procedures can be used simply to improve the clarity and readability of programs. The techniques described in Part II, which make small programs clear and understandable, don't always work well when applied directly to large programs. For example, if the units at the highest level are so long that it is impossible to comprehend them as a single unit, then their role and relationship to other units is less clear. The indentation convention which makes vertical left-alignment significant in understanding a program clearly works best if successive statements with the same alignment appear on the same page. If the successor to a particular unit is several pages away vertical alignment is much less effective as a way of emphasizing the structure of a program.

Procedures can be used to alleviate all these problems by reducing the apparent size of programs. Simply take some convenient section of program, write it as a procedure, and provide a procedure statement in its original location. For example, suppose one has to perform some task on each element of a 3-dimensional array:

```
(* GRIMBLE THE ARRAY AR *)
    FOR I := 1 TO R DO
      BEGIN (* PLANE *)
         FOR J := 1 TO S DO
           BEGIN (* ROW *)
              FOR K := 1 TO T DO
                BEGIN
                   (* GRIMBLE AR[I,J,K] *)
                           ...
                END
           END (* ROW *)
      END (* PLANE *)
```

This unit is reasonably clear as long as the body of the "grimble" task is not too large. If it is large, or if it involves many levels of nesting, it is worthwhile writing it as a separate procedure:

```
...
(* PERFORM GRIMBLE PROCESS UPON G *)
PROCEDURE GRIMBLE(VAR G: REAL);
  ...
  END; (* GRIMBLE *)
...
    (* GRIMBLE THE ARRAY AR *)
         FOR I := 1 TO R DO
           BEGIN (* PLANE *)
              FOR J := 1 TO S DO
                BEGIN
                   FOR K := 1 TO T DO
                        GRIMBLE(AR[I,J,K])
                END
           END (* PLANE *)
```

Some reasonable rules-of-thumb for the size of individual units are:

1. The body of a unit should be no more than 50 lines (1 page) in length.

2. Nesting should not exceed 3 or at most 4 levels.

To maintain these limits, use procedures so that a procedure statement can replace some section of program, thereby reducing the size or apparent nesting level of the main program.

<u>Procedures should be routinely used in this way</u>. In fact, any program of more than one or two pages should be entirely written in this manner. At the highest level the program should consist of little more than procedure statements. The main procedure, doing nothing but invoking other procedures, serves as a <u>control section</u> of the program. It is short and shows clearly how the program is organized and the major steps in its action.

The sorting program in (1.4a) is written in this manner. The actual sorting is done by a procedure SORT invoked from the main procedure. This allows the main procedure to be very short and clear: it simply reads the data, executes SORT, and prints the sorted results. The details of how the sorting is actually done do not obscure the simple sequence of tasks in the main procedure.

The accounting problem of Section III.2.4 provides an even better example. This program has three sections:

```
(* READ AND SET UP THE ACCOUNTS.*)
(* READ AND PROCESS THE TRANSACTIONS.*)
(* PRINT THE RESULTS.*)
```

In the abbreviated form given in III.2.4 this all fits on one page and is not difficult to follow. A useful program for a realistic version of this problem, including adequate error checking, would be many pages long. It might still consist of three sections, but if each section were long and complicated the overall structure would not be clear to the reader. To preserve clarity of structure the main procedure of this program should be a control section, with each of the sub-tasks written as a separate procedure:

```
(* READ AND SET UP THE ACCOUNTS.*)
    ACCTRD(N, ACCT, WITH, DEP, IBAL, CBAL);
(* READ AND PROCESS THE TRANSACTIONS.*)
    PTRAN(N, ACCT, WITH, DEP, IBAL, CBAL);
(* PRINT THE RESULTS.*)
    PRINT(N, ACCT, WITH, DEP, IBAL, CBAL)
```

With this organization the accounts are declared in the main procedure and passed as arguments to each of the processing procedures. The extra variables needed to process the transactions -- TACCT, DEPWITH, AMT -- are needed only by PTRAN so they are declared in PTRAN rather than the main procedure.

As another example, the index for this book was produced by a sizable program. Nevertheless, its high level structure is clear from its control section:

```
(* PRIMER INDEX *)
PROGRAM INDEX(INPUT, OUTPUT);
TYPE STRING50 = PACKED ARRAY[1..50] OF CHAR;
VAR LN: ARRAY[1..3000] OF STRING50;
    TOPLINE: INTEGER; (* PTR TO TOP LINE IN LN *)
Procedure definitions;

BEGIN (* INDEX *)
    TOPLINE := 0;
    (* READ TOPIC/PG-NBR PAIRS INTO LN *)
         LOAD(LN, TOPLINE);
    (* SORT REFERENCES INTO ALPHABETICAL ORDER *)
         SORT(LN, TOPLINE);
    (* CONDENSE MULTIPLE REFERENCES TO A SINGLE LINE *)
         CONDENSE(LN, TOPLINE);
    (* CONVERT LINES TO FORMAT REQ'D BY TEXT-EDITOR *)
         CONVERT(LN, TOPLINE);
    (* PUNCH CARD FOR EACH LINE *)
         PUNCH(LN, TOPLINE)
END.  (* INDEX *)
```

These examples apparently violate the suggestion of Section II.1.6.1 that comments should not duplicate the program statements. In these cases the task of the procedure is sufficiently complex that it is not adequately implied by the procedure-name. Hence these comments give a more complete idea of the task performed by each procedure statement and are worth the extra trouble.

In general, a good way to organize and present a large program is to have four sections:

1. A block of comments that fully and precisely describe the function of the program.

2. A block of comments serving as a "table of contents" for the following procedures.

3. A set of procedures, invoked by the control section.

4. A control section of not more than one page that uses various other procedures to do the work.

Of course, some of the individual procedures may be so large that they would also benefit from the same treatment. Entry to such a procedure would encounter another control section, which would invoke other procedures. There is really no limit to how large a program can become, and still be understandable, if procedures are used to keep the apparent size down to where the techniques of Part II are effective.

2.3 Sectional Independence

A procedure is quite an independent section of a program, and this independence is very useful. Communication between procedures can be carefully controlled. It should primarily be by means of parameters and arguments, with limited use of global variables. Separate procedures have no other effects on each other. When reading a properly written program you can analyze each procedure separately, with confidence that no action (or mistake) elsewhere in the program will have the slightest effect on this procedure, except possibly in the way that it affects the inputs to this procedure -- the values of arguments and global variables. The modularity sought in the discussion of "program units" in Part II is provided automatically by procedures.

When writing a program section if you write it as a procedure you have less to worry about. You are entirely concerned with how to perform the required action. You have no concern that other sections of program will interfere with this one, or that this section may have unexpected side-effects elsewhere. You need not remember what variable names have been used elsewhere in the program; you can use whatever names are most natural for this local use. For example, you can use I as a subscript without wondering whether I is the index of some outer loop, and hence must not be disturbed. You can use SUM for a local variable without having to check to see whether that particular identifier is already in use. For example, compare the program segments given in (2.3a) and (2.3b).

(2.3a)

```
...
FOR I := 1 TO R DO
  BEGIN (* OUT LOOP *)
    ...
    SUM := TOTAL + NEWVAL[I];
    ...
    FOR J := 1 TO S DO
      BEGIN (* MID LOOP *)
        ...
        (* SET TRIAL[J] TO SUM OF X[1..T] *)
             SUM := 0;
             FOR I := 1 TO T DO
                  SUM := SUM + X[I];
             TRIAL[J] := SUM;
        ...
      END; (* MID LOOP *)
    ...
  END; (* OUT LOOP *)
...
```

(2.3b)
```
TYPE REALSZ = ARRAY[1..MAXSZ] OF REAL;
...
(* SET RESULT = SUM OF Y[1..N] *)
PROCEDURE INSUM(Y: REALSZ; N: INTEGER;
                VAR RESULT: REAL);
  VAR I: INTEGER; SUM: REAL;
  BEGIN (* INSUM *)
    SUM := 0;
    FOR I := 1 TO N DO
         SUM := SUM + Y[I];
    RESULT := SUM
  END; (* INSUM *)
...
    FOR I := 1 TO R DO
      BEGIN (* OUT LOOP *)
         ...
         SUM := TOTAL + NEWVAL[I];
         ...
         FOR J := 1 TO S DO
           BEGIN (* MID LOOP *)
              ...
              INSUM(X, T, TRIAL[J]);
              ...
           END; (* MID LOOP *)
         ...
      END; (* OUT LOOP *)
...
```

(2.3a) is incorrect because both the loop index I and the variable SUM are accidentally re-used. The error is obvious in this case because (2.3a) is short and most of the details have been omitted. However, if (2.3a) were several pages long so that the beginning of OUT LOOP was several pages away from the summing loop, and if the first part had been written several days earlier so that the details had been forgotten, then it would be very easy for such an error to occur. The risk would be reduced if the innermost summing task were written as a separate procedure, as in (2.3b). Then it is no longer necessary to check the rest of the program before choosing variable names for this task.

This independence of sections is particularly useful when a program is to be produced by a team of programmers. If each programmer (or group) is assigned a separate procedure the communication problems are minimized. Joint planning will concern only the function of each procedure, and its parameter communication. Given this "problem specification" the design and development of the procedure can proceed as described in Part III, just as if this were an independent problem. It should also be tested as if it were an independent problem. The procedures should be integrated into a final program only after there is great confidence in their individual performance.

For example, suppose a program is required to perform some task upon an array of words that are in alphabetical order.

Suppose that the input consists of lines in which the words are not in alphabetical order. Obviously the program will be required to scan lines and break them up into individual words, and then sort the resulting list of words into alphabetical order. It is useful to design a program with these "scan" and "sort" tasks as separate procedures. As far as the principal program is concerned all that has to be specified for these tasks is the action to be performed and the manner in which arguments are to be given. This specification is called the "interface" between the procedures. Once the interfaces have been specified the design, writing and testing of the scan procedure, the sort procedure and the rest of the program could proceed independently. All three could be done by one person (working in any order), by three separate programmers, or parts could be drawn from a library of existing subroutines. The programmers of the different procedures do not have to discuss with each other what local variables and labels they plan to use in their particular procedure.

One particularly important aspect of interface specification is the identifcation of each parameter as <u>input</u>, <u>output</u> , or <u>both</u> input and output. The independence of procedures protects the variables of one procedure from the actions of other procedures -- except for those variables that are given as arguments in the execution of another procedure. Arguments associated with value parameters are protected by PASCAL, so this form of parameter should be used whenever possible. Arguments associated with variable parameters are not protected, so the invoking and invoked procedure must have a clear understanding as to how each is to be treated. For example, if the invoking procedure regards a particular argument as providing only input to another procedure, the parameter of the invoked procedure must not be declared as a variable parameter (that is, VAR should not be given in the declaration). In any case, a procedure should change the value of the argument associated with a particular parameter <u>only if it is explicitly agreed that it is an output parameter</u>.

The interface specification must also include a precise description of which global variables can be accessed by the invoked procedure. Unfortunately, there is no way in PASCAL to automatically enforce this agreement (as can be done in PL/I, for example). If you forget to declare a variable that is used in the main procedure of a program, this is an error and PASCAL will warn you of the omission. However, if you forget to declare a variable used in another procedure, and <u>if there happens to be a variable of the same name</u> in the containing procedure, PASCAL does not consider this an error. The called procedure will simply use the variable of the containing procedure -- probably with disastrous effects for both procedures. This is a common, and often mystifying type of error. Watch out for it!

2.3.1 Separation of Action and Control

Recall the discussion in Section II.2 about the separation of action and control. Schema (2a) was used as an example:

```
(* Comment describing action of the unit *)
    i := 0;
    WHILE i < n DO
      BEGIN (* loop name *)
         i := i + 1;
         Body
      END (* loop name *)
```

We wanted to be able to state that this schema would repeat the body n times regardless of what the action of the body was. However, this statement is true only if the body is restricted:

1. it may not alter the values of i or n,

2. and it may not execute a GOTO.

Suppose the body is written as a separate procedure named TASK:

```
           (* Comment describing action of TASK *)
           PROCEDURE TASK(...   );
             VAR i, n: ...
               ...
             END; (* TASK *)
(2.3.1a)   ...
               (* Comment describing action of the unit *)
                    i := 0;
                    WHILE i < n DO
                      BEGIN
                         i := i + 1;
                         TASK(...   )
                      END
           ...
```

Now the body does not have access to the variables i and n of the invoking procedure (assuming that they are not given as arguments of the procedure statment) so it is not necessary to further restrict the body in this regard. Unfortunately, PASCAL does not prevent a GOTO from escaping from a procedure, so this problem still remains. <u>Using a GOTO to escape from a procedure is very bad practice</u> and should never be done. The target labels of whatever GOTOs are necessary in a procedure should always be local to that procedure. Hence there are only two things that have to be checked in a procedure:

1. The procedure must include declarations of all the variables it uses, so it cannot access variables of the containing procedure.

2. All GOTOs in a procedure must reference labels local to that procedure.

If these two restrictions are observed, this means that <u>any program</u> can be given as the body of TASK with <u>confidence that it will be repeated n times</u>.

However, there is one other aspect of the question that was neglected in II.2 but should be mentioned here. For example, suppose the following were given as the body of TASK:

```
WHILE TRUE DO
  BEGIN
  END
```

this loop will be repeatedly endlessly. The procedure will never terminate so the execution of its first call will never be completed. Therefore, it obviously will not be repeated n times. Hence we must modify our statement so that the guarantee of n repetitions only holds if the <u>program is finite</u> -- that is, if it will eventually terminate. For practical purposes, the guarantee only holds if the program will terminate in less than the time limit imposed. The loop shown here is obvious trouble, but there are many less obvious ways to make an error in a program and have the same effect on execution. For example

```
FOR I := 1 TO N DO
  BEGIN
    SUM := SUM + X[I];
    I := I - 1
  END
```

This loop never terminates because the body of the loop interferes with the loop index I so that its value never reaches the terminating value N.

There is also the opposite problem -- instead of running too long, the program might quit. An error in the body that caused termination of execution, would also cause the procedure to fail to be executed n times. For example

```
WHILE TRUE DO
  BEGIN
    SUM := SUM + X[I];
    I := I + 1
  END
```

No matter how many elements X has, the subscript I will eventually exceed the maximum permissible value. This will result in an error in each iteration of the loop, which will eventually exceed the error limit under which the program is run and cause execution to be terminated. The execution of the <u>entire program</u> is terminated and not just the execution of the faulty procedure.

Nevertheless these are local problems. They cannot affect what is done elsewhere in the program. If the procedure TASK in (2.3.1a) is <u>finite</u> and <u>executable</u>, then it is repeated n times.

Section 2 Examples

```
000006 (*DEMONSTRATE STRING OPERATIONS*)
000006 PROGRAM STRINGDEMO(INPUT,OUTPUT);
000464 CONST MAX = 50;
000464 TYPE STRING = ARRAY[0..MAX] OF INTEGER;
000464 VAR FST, SEC, THD, NXT, X:  STRING;
001063      N: INTEGER;
001064
001064 (*READ A STRING ENCLOSED IN QUOTES*)
001064 PROCEDURE GETSTRING(VAR STR: STRING);
000004      VAR CH: CHAR;
000005      BEGIN (*GETSTRING*)
000005           STR[0] := 0;
000007           (*SKIP BLANKS THRU A QUOTE*)
000007                REPEAT READ(CH) UNTIL CH = '''';
000016           (*READ THE CHARACTERS OF THE STRING*)
000016                READ(CH);
000023                WHILE CH <> '''' DO
000025                     BEGIN
000025                          STR[0] := STR[0] + 1;
000026                          STR[STR[0]] := ORD(CH);
000031                          READ(CH)
000035                     END
000035      END; (*GETSTRING*)
000044
000044 (* WRITE A STRING *)
000044 PROCEDURE PUTSTRING(VAR STR: STRING);
000004      VAR I: 1..MAX;
000005      BEGIN (*PUTSTRING*)
000005           WRITE(' ');      (*PAGE CONTROL*)
000011           FOR I := 1 TO STR[0] DO
000013                WRITE(CHR(STR[I]))
000025      END; (*PUTSTRING*)
000035
000035 (* CONCATENATE STRINGS A AND B TO FORM C *)
000035 PROCEDURE CONCAT(VAR A, B, C: STRING);
000006      VAR I: 1..MAX;
000007      BEGIN (*CONCAT*)
000007           FOR I := 1 TO A[0] DO
000011                C[I] := A[I];
000024           FOR I := 1 TO B[0] DO
000026                C[A[0] + I] := B[I];
000043           C[0] := A[0] + B[0]
000045      END; (*CONCAT*)
000053
000053 (*EXTRACT STRING OF LENGTH LEN STARTING AT*)
000053 (*POSITION POS IN STRING A TO FORM STRING B*)
000053 PROCEDURE SUBSTR(VAR A: STRING; POS, LEN: INTEGER;
000006                     VAR B: STRING);
000007      VAR I: 1..MAX;
000010      BEGIN (*SUBSTR*)
000010           IF (LEN + POS - 1 <= A[0]) AND (LEN > 0) AND (POS > 0)
000013                THEN BEGIN
000014                          FOR I := 1 TO LEN DO
000015                               B[I] := A[POS + I - 1];
000032                          B[0] := LEN
000033                     END
000034                ELSE B[0] := 0
000034      END; (*SUBSTR*)
000047
000047
000047
000047
```

```
000047
000047
000047
000047 (*REPLACE THE CHARACTERS IN STRING CNE STARTING*)
000047 (*AT POSITION M WITH THOSE FROM STRING TWO*)
000047 PROCEDURE PSUBST(VAR ONE, TWO: STRING; M: INTEGER;
000006                    VAR RESULT: STRING);
000007      VAR TEMP1, TEMP2: STRING;
000155          POS, K: 1..MAX;
000157      BEGIN (*PSUBST*)
000157          IF(0 < M) AND (M <= ONE[0])
000011              THEN BEGIN (*POSITION M IS WITHIN STRING ONE*)
000012                      (*EXTRACT FIRST M - 1 CHAR FROM ONE*)
000012                          SUBSTR(ONE,1,M-1,TEMP1);
000014                      (*CONCATENATE TEMP AND TWO*)
000014                          CONCAT(TEMP1,TWO,TEMP1);
000017                      (*EXTRACT REMAINING CHAR FROM ONE*)
000017                          K := M + TWC[0];
000024                          SUBSTR(ONE,K,ONE[0]-K+1,TEMP2);
000027                      (*CONCATENATE CURRENT RESULT AND TEMP*)
000027                          CONCAT(TEMP1,TEMP2,RESULT)
000031                   END
000032              ELSE RESULT := ONE (*POSITION M IS NOT IN STRING ONE*)
000033      END; (*PSUBST*)
000050
000050 (*LOCATE STARTING POSITION OF STRING B IN STRING A*)
000050 PROCEDURE INDEX(VAR A, B: STRING; VAR I: INTEGER);
000006      LABEL 85, 9006;
000006      VAR J: 1..MAX;
000007      BEGIN (*INDEX*)
000007          I := 1;
000010          IF A[0] >= B[0] THEN (*SEARCH*)
000012              REPEAT
000012                  (*TRY TO MATCH AT PCSITION I*)
000012                     FOR J := 1 TO B[0] DO
000014                         IF A[I+J-1] <> B[J] THEN GOTO 85;
000032                     GOTO 9006; (*MATCH FOUND*)
000033                     85:;
000033                     I := I + 1
000034                     UNTIL I > A[0] - B[0] + 1;
000037          I := 0;      (*MATCH NOT FOUND*)
000040          9006:;
000040      END; (*INDEX*)
000050
000050 BEGIN (*STRINGDEMO*)
000050      (*READ AND WRITE THREE INPUT STRINGS*)
000050          WRITELN('1');
000025          GETSTRING(FST);      PUTSTRING(FST);      WRITELN;
000032          GETSTRING(SEC);      PUTSTRING(SEC);      WRITELN;
000037          GETSTRING(THD);      PUTSTRING(THD);      WRITELN;
000044          WRITELN('0');
000047      (*DEMONSTRATE EACH OF THE STRING PROCEDURES*)
000047          CONCAT(FST,SEC,NXT);     PUTSTRING(NXT);      WRITELN;
000055          SUBSTR(FST,6,2,X);       PUTSTRING(X);        WRITELN;
000063          INDEX(NXT,THD,N);        WRITELN(N);
000073          INDEX(NXT,X,N);          WRITELN(N);
000103          PSUBST(NXT,THD,N,NXT);   PUTSTRING(NXT);      WRITELN
000110 END. (*STRINGDEMO*)
```

```
THIS IS
A STRING.
AT


THIS IS A STRING.
IS
         0
         3
THAT IS A STRING.
```

Section 2 Exercises

1. Suppose there were no ABS built-in function in PASCAL to find the absolute value of an argument. Design and write a procedure that would provide this "extension" to the language. (Note: The ABS built-in function does not change the value of its argument, so neither should your procedure. Use one parameter for input and a second parameter for output.)

2. Write a procedure to add two matrices, producing a third matrix. A matrix C is the sum of two matrices A and B if each element of C is the sum of the elements in the corresponding positions in A and B. That is

c(i,j) = a(i,j) + b(i,j)

All three matrices must have the same number of rows and columns. The procedure should have five parameters:
Parameter 1: first input matrix
Parameter 2: second input matrix
Parameter 3: output matrix
Parameter 4: number of rows in each matrix
Parameter 5: number of columns in each matrix.

3. Write a procedure to "rotate" a square matrix (one with the same number of rows as columns) 90^0 clockwise. That is, the element initially in the upper left corner will become the element in the upper right corner, etc. The procedure should have two parameters:
Parameter 1: matrix to be rotated
Parameter 2: number of rows (or columns).

4. Write a procedure to format print lines from individual words supplied as arguments. The procedure should have a single parameter which is a character string. On each call the procedure is presented with a "word". It builds a print line with these words, adding each new word to the right end of the line (with an intervening blank between words). The line length is at most 60 positions. When a new word cannot be added to the line without exceeding this length, the old line is printed and a new line is begun starting with the word that wouldn't fit on the old line.

5. Convert the final symbol-scanning program of Section III.2.5 into a procedure to deliver individual symbols when the input consists of test lines.

6. Write the programs described in Exercise 10 of Section III.2 in the form described in IV.2.2. That is, write them with a short control section invoking procedures to perform the actual subtasks.

Part V
Program Testing

Section 1 Errors, Testing and Correctness

Programming almost never results in an error-free program; it is just too complicated and detailed a process. If conducted by a careful and competent person the probability of each possible error is very small -- but there are so many opportunities that the probability of avoiding all errors is also very small. Prudence demands that we assume each new program is incorrect until we can demonstrate otherwise. We must accept the fact that testing is an integral part of the programming process -- and that a program is not really "finished" until we have demonstrated its correctness.

The magnitude of the testing effort required for large problems might surprise you. Often at least half of the manpower, cost and elapsed time of the total programming process is consumed in testing. In spite of this the results are often not always satisfactory. Computers are not publically regarded as reliable, when in fact they are exceedingly reliable machines -- handicapped by inadequately tested programs. However when the programming process is highly disciplined and when testing is <u>planned as the program is being created</u> rather than afterwards, testing is easier and the resulting programs are significantly more reliable.

Very few beginning programmers take the trouble to learn to test their programs efficiently. To plan testing in advance seems to be admitting failure in writing the program, so most beginners assume an ostrich-like, head-in-the-sand attitude, until the evidence that errors are present is unmistakable. Then testing proceeds in a manner that can charitably be called "random". This attitude winds up wasting a great deal of time, yet it is still the usual approach. Testing does not have to be nearly as time-consuming or as unpleasant as many beginners make it seem, but it must be taken seriously -- it is an art that must be studied and learned.

Before describing some techniques and tools that can be used to demonstrate that a program is correct, let us discuss the meaning of "correctness".

1.1 <u>The Meaning of Correctness</u>

"Program correctness" is not easily defined. The programmer and user of a program may discover they use quite different meanings of the word "correctness", and hence have quite different expectations of program performance. Consider the following possible interpretations of correctness -- listed in order of increasing difficulty of achievement:

1. The program contains no syntax errors that can be detected during translation by the language processor.

2. The program contains no errors, either of syntax or invalid operation, that can be automatically detected during translation or execution of the program.

3. There exists some set of test data for which the program will yield the correct answer.

4. For a typical (reasonable or random) set of test data the program will yield the correct answer.

5. For deliberately difficult sets of test data the program will yield the correct answers.

6. For all possible sets of data which are valid with respect to the problem specification, the program yields the correct answers.

7. For all possible sets of valid test data, and for all likely conditions of erroneous input, the program gives a correct (or at least reasonable) answer.

8. For all possible input, the program gives correct or reasonable answers.

In the early stages of your programming experience you will feel harassed by error messages during translation, and feel a sense of achievement when you have attained level 1 correctness. However, the absence of error messages is only a necessary and not a sufficient condition for reasonable correctness. You will eventually regard the detection of such errors as a helpful service, which unfortunately detects only the easiest of errors.

Some students never mature beyond level 3 for an interpretation of correctness. We are regularly involved in arguments challenging the grade assigned to a problem on grounds that it "worked" on the student's own data, hence must be correct. In effect, the student is arguing that level 3 is adequate. Considering higher levels (say 4, 5 or 6) it is clear that satisfactory performance on any single set of test data is not sufficient grounds for an assertion of correctness, but failure on a single test is sufficient to demonstrate that the program is not correct. <u>No matter how many tests the program may have passed successfully, just one test on which it fails is</u>

<u>enough to show that it is not correct</u>. This is not inherently a democratic process, and a program that works "most of the time" is a dangerous tool.

From the "customer's" point of view a reasonable definition of correctness is certainly not less than level 6. Level 7 is better and level 8 is what he would really like. The programmer may maintain that a literal interpretation of problem specifications cannot demand more than level 6, while the customer will maintain that certain implied requirements do not have to be explicitly stated. In effect, this corresponds to the "implied warranty of merchantability" that accompanies a manufactured product. A consumer is entitled to assume that a product is "suitable for the purpose for which it is intended". A car buyer, for example, can rightfully assume that all the wheels will remain firmly attached to the car, without having to obtain a written guarantee from the dealer. In the same way, much is assumed about a computer program, without its having been explicitly detailed in the problem requirements. The user of a program is entitled to consider it incorrect if it fails to satisfy implicit as well as explicit requirements.

Unfortunately this often leads to heated discussions between programmer and user, the object being to assign blame for a program belatedly found to be incorrect. The programmer takes the position that there is no such thing as implicit requirements; the user maintains that, in retrospect, anything he neglected to specify is covered by implicit commonsense requirements. Both parties should realize that implicit requirements are an inherent part of most problem descriptions, and that it is a <u>mutual</u> responsibility to explore this subject to ensure mutual understanding of context of use, nature of errors, appropriate reactions and communications.

The <u>primary responsibility rests with the programmer</u>. A program is <u>incorrect if it does not serve the user's purposes</u>. This may occur because the programmer failed to elicit an adequate description, because he failed to recognize implicit requirements, or because he made mistakes in designing or translating the algorithm into a programming language. Most programmers admit responsibility for only the last two sources of error, but the distinction between different types of failure is not interesting to a user with an unsolved problem.

In summary, the situation is the following. The user would like to have level 8 correctness -- but this is usually impossible, and he might as well get used to that fact. Level 7 is a reasonable compromise, which is obviously going to lead to arguments since it leaves critical questions open to varying interpretations. The programmer's dilemma is that level 5 is the highest that can be achieved by purely empirical means -- by running the program on test cases -- so he must thoughtfully design test cases while writing the program that will permit a plausible assertion that level 6 has been achieved. To achieve level 7 the programmer must know enough about the intended use of the program to estimate what errors are likely to be encountered, and what response is appropriate.

1.2 Types of Errors

There are four distinct types of errors:

1. Errors in understanding the problem requirements.

2. Errors in understanding the programming language. For example, errors could result from not understanding PASCAL's use of the semi-colon.

3. Failure of the algorithm underlying the program.

4. Accidents. Errors where you knew better but simply slipped up.

Errors in understanding the problem description will no doubt increase as the problems you work on become larger, more varied, and less precisely stated. Although one can learn from experience, human communication is difficult at best; English is surprisingly ambiguous; and programming demands an unfailing precision. Some errors of this type seem inevitable. Caution and more and more communication with the user will tend to keep these errors to a minimum.

Errors in understanding the programming language will diminish in frequency with experience, and fortunately PASCAL has relatively few curious or unexpected properties, so the opportunities for this type of error are not numerous. The best antidote is to stick to the simple, well-thought-out language features, and to leave the vague, tricky ones alone. For example, avoid reading mixed numeric and character data from cards.

The third type of error is greatly reduced in frequency by systematic development and careful structuring of programs. Errors that remain are in fairly predictable places -- often just entry and exit problems -- and can be systematically sought using the diagnostic tools described in the following sections. These kinds of errors <u>must</u> be kept to a minimum if you want to be known as a good programmer. They are the hardest to correct later on. One main purpose of a programming course is to get you to think carefully, methodically, completely, and in a structured manner so that these kinds of errors don't often occur.

Accidents occur everywhere in the process, to experienced as well as beginning programmers. They range from syntax errors detected by the translator to subtle errors with intermittent effect that elude competent and persistent testing. The only general defense is a skeptical attitude that regards every program segment as a potential haven for accidental errors.

It somehow can be very difficult to spot our own mistakes. We will go over a troublesome section of program many times and be unable to spot an obvious error. Often a fresh view will help to find an error quickly. A colleague or programming consultant can spot an error not because he knows more, but because he has no preconceptions about what the program is supposed to do. He reads what _is_ there, and not what he wants to be there. Quite often we ourselves will see the error while explaining the program to a friend or consultant. Programming _should_ be more of a group process, with at least two people reading and understanding each program segment.

You _must_ accept the fact that _all_ errors in the program are your responsibility. Too much time is wasted trying to blame the _computer_, the _programming language_, or the _problem description_. In Section 1.1 we asserted that the programmer must accept responsibility for clarification of problem requirements; now we exonerate the computer and the language.

True machine errors are exceedingly rare, so every time you become convinced a machine error has happened, you are just postponing the eventual necessity of discovering what really happened. Blaming errors on the programming language is a similar delusion. Every programming language has its surprises -- things that are done in an unexpected way. While the language may be unreasonable, it is _not wrong_. For example, what is the value of I printed by the following program segment?

```
...
FOR I := 1 TO 45 DO
  BEGIN
    ...
  END;
WRITELN(I)
...
```

Whether or not it seems reasonable to you, the value 45 is printed. (The comparable result in PL/I would be 46.) It is your responsibility to learn what the language actually means, and what execution will actually do, rather than assume it means whatever you think is reasonable.

In this connection you might as well learn to distrust every source of assistance in the programming process, except the computer. Both programming language reference manuals and textbooks (including this one) contain errors. Each teacher, and each programming consultant at your computing center has his own misconceptions about certain programming language features. Again, the best way to guard against such misunderstandings is to use only the simple, well-used features of the language. When learning a new programming language feature, _always_ use it in several small examples, to learn how it really works, before using it in a large program.

Section 2 The Design of Test Cases

It is reasonable to initially test a new program on easy test cases. However, satisfactory execution for such test cases only demonstrates "level 3 correctness" (see Section 1.1) and this is not sufficient. Further test cases must be used to attain levels 4 or 5. You must not be satisfied that your program is correct as soon as it will successfully run some single set of test data.

Contriving difficult test cases is an art that has to be learned. It draws upon your knowledge of programming and experience with the kinds of errors likely to occur. For example, having experienced difficulty before with declarations, conditions, and entry and exit from repetitions, you should contrive test cases that exhibit the following properties:

a. Extremes of volume: the legal minimum and maximum, as well as too little and too much.

b. Extreme values: the legal minimum and maximum as well as excessive values -- too big, too small, too negative.

c. Special values: zero, blank, one, etc., depending on the problem.

d. Non-integer values, where allowed.

e. Values falling on and near stated limits.

f. Repeated values and ties of various sorts.

Unfortunately, even the most persistent, perceptive and malicious testing campaign cannot demonstrate more than level 5 correctness, and yet level 6 is the minimum reasonable standard. We cannot ever (well, hardly ever) demonstrate level 6 experimentally, since we cannot run a program for all possible sets of input. We can try difficult cases, and infer from success on these that many other cases, somehow "bracketed" by the hard ones, will be handled properly. But the precise meaning of "bracket" and the rules of inference are not clear. No matter how many tests have been run successfully we cannot absolutely state that level 6 has been achieved -- that the program would yield the correct answer for all possible valid input. On the other hand, to disprove correctness we only have to find <u>one</u> test case on which the program fails.

The situation can be summarized as follows. Testing a program can never prove its correctness (at level 6 or higher); it can only fail to disprove its correctness. Based on the effort and ingenuity expended in failing to disprove correctness we can acquire increasing confidence in a program's reliability, but this can never reach the level of absolute proof.

Testing in which one examines only the input and output of a program without studying its internal construction is sometimes called "black-box testing". It is not a bad way to start testing, but at some point an examination of the internal construction must be used to contrive adequately difficult test cases. Furthermore, any hope of asserting correctness beyond level 5 is beyond the ability of experimental testing, and will have to depend upon the examination of the program itself and not just its external actions.

2.1 Testing the Program of I.1.1e

To illustrate the limits of experimental, black-box testing, suppose that example (2.1a) is submitted as a solution to the "find maximum" problem of Section I.1.1. (2.1a) is absurd, but the point is to see what prospects there are of discovering all its absurdities solely by running it with various sets of test data.

(2.1a)

```
     (* COMPUTE THE MAXIMUM OF NON-NEGATIVE NUMBERS *)
     (* DUMMY -1 ADDED FOR STOPPING TEST *)
     PROGRAM FINDMAX(INPUT, OUTPUT);
     VAR NUMBER,    (* THE CURRENT NUMBER *)
         MAXNBR,    (* MAXIMUM NUMBER SO FAR *)
         COUNT:     (* NUMBER OF NUMBERS SO FAR *)
                 INTEGER;

     BEGIN (* FINDMAX *)
         MAXNBR := 2; (* INITIAL VALUE < POSSIBLE DATA VALUES *)
         COUNT := 1;
         READ(NUMBER, NUMBER);
         WHILE NUMBER <> -1 DO
           BEGIN
              COUNT := COUNT + 1;
              IF NUMBER = 63 THEN NUMBER := -3;
              IF NUMBER = MAXNBR THEN MAXNBR := MAXNBR + 1;
              IF NUMBER > MAXNBR THEN MAXNBR := NUMBER;
              READ(NUMBER)
           END;
         MAXNBR := 12;
         WRITE(' NUMBER OF VALUES =', COUNT);
         WRITELN(' MAXIMUM VALUE =', MAXNBR)
     END.  (* FINDMAX *)
         eor
     3 7 12 2 6 -1
```

(2.1a) actually provides the correct answer <u>for the data given</u>, so it is "correct" at level 3 (according to Section 1.1). If the ever-optimistic programmer accepts this as confirmation of correctness, he will have declared an incredibly bad program "correct".

This program actually produces correct answers for many sets of data: any set for which the maximum value is 12. Only if data with a maximum other than 12 is used will an error be discovered.

Assuming the strange preference for 12 is detected, and "MAXNBR := 12" is removed, the program will give correct answers for even more sets of test data. But it will still have difficulty in the situations below. Good test cases would detect a, b, c, f and g, and might detect d, but discovering e is just a matter of luck.

a. The maximum value happens to be the first value.
b. The maximum value appears two or more times in the set.
c. The maximum value is not an integer (it has significant digits to the right of the decimal point).
d. The maximum value is less than 2.
e. The maximum value happens to be 63.
f. No input is provided.
g. No -1 stopping value is supplied.

2.2 Multiple Test Cases

To allow running several tests in one computer run, we must be able to repeat execution of a program with different sets of data. This is easily done just by changing the "main" procedure to an ordinary procedure, changing the period after its end to a semi-colon, and placing the procedure to be tested inside a new main procedure used to control the repetition. For example, suppose (2.2a) is some program that processes data until a stopping flag of -1 is encountered. (2.2b) illustrates a simple "test control" procedure that will cause (2.2a) to be repeated N times, where N is given as the first item of data. When testing is complete the program must of course be restored to its original form by removing the test control procedure and replacing the original PROGRAM card. Note also that the main procedure TSC can be used to test <u>any</u> such program, as long as its name is EPD. We need not write a different test control main procedure for each different program.

(2.2a)

```
(* EDIT POSITIVE DATA; STOP ON -1 *)
PROGRAM EPD(INPUT, OUTPUT);
    ...
END.  (* EPD *)
    eor
23 74 56.1 423.19 -1
```

(2.2b)

```
(* TEST CONTROL FOR EDP ROUTINE *)
PROGRAM TSC(INPUT, OUTPUT);
VAR N,                   (* TOTAL NUMBER OF TESTS *)
    NSOFAR: INTEGER; (* NUMBER PERFORMED SO FAR *)

(* EDIT POSITIVE DATA; STOP ON -1 *)
PROCEDURE EPD;
    ...
END; (* EPD *)

BEGIN (* TSC *)
    READLN(N);
    WRITELN('1', N, ' CONSECUTIVE TESTS OF EPD');
    (* REPEAT EPD N TIMES *)
         NSOFAR := 0;
         REPEAT
              NSOFAR := NSOFAR + 1;
              WRITELN('0EPD TEST NUMBER', NSOFAR);
              EPD
           UNTIL NSOFAR >= N
END.  (* TSC *)
    eor
3
23 74 56.1 423.19 -1
0 1 1 0 -1
9999 0.01 0.001 0 0 -1
```

Section 2 Examples

```
000006 (*TEST MEAN-MAX-MIN PROGRAM*)
000006 PROGRAM TESTM(INPUT,OUTPUT);
000464 VAR NBRTESTS,       (*NUMBER OF SEPARATE TESTS*)
000464     TESTNBR:  INTEGER;
000466
000466 (*COMPUTE MEAN, MAX AND MIN OF DATA*)
000466 (*STOP WHENEVER A VALUE OCCURS TWICE IN SUCCESSION*)
000466 PROCEDURE MMM;
000003 VAR LAST, CURRENT,       (*VALUES READ FROM DATA*)
000003     MAXVAL, MINVAL,
000003     SUM, MEAN:  REAL;
000011     COUNT:  INTEGER;     (*NUMBER OF VALUES READ*)
000012 BEGIN (*MMM*)
000012     (*INITIALIZE*)
000012         READ(LAST);
000011         COUNT := 1;
000012         MAXVAL := LAST;
000013         MINVAL := LAST;
000013         SUM := LAST;
000014         READ(CURRENT);
000017     WHILE CURRENT <> LAST DO
000021         BEGIN
000021             COUNT := COUNT + 1;
000022             SUM := SUM + CURRENT;
000023             IF CURRENT > MAXVAL THEN MAXVAL := CURRENT;
000025             IF CURRENT < MINVAL THEN MINVAL := CURRENT;
000030             LAST := CURRENT;
000031             READ(CURRENT)
000034         END;
000035     (*PRINT RESULTS*)
000035         WRITELN('0RESULTS OF MEAN-MIN-MAX PROGRAM');
000043         WRITELN('0', COUNT, ' VALUES READ');
000057         MEAN := SUM / COUNT;
000063         WRITELN(' MEAN IS', MEAN);
000075         WRITELN(' MAXIMUM IS', MAXVAL);
000107         WRITELN(' MINIMUM IS', MINVAL);
000121 END; (*MMM*)
000156
000156 BEGIN (*TESTM*)
000156     TESTNBR := 0;
000023     READ(NBRTESTS);
000026     WHILE NBRTESTS > 0 DO
000030         BEGIN
000030             TESTNBR := TESTNBR + 1;
000031             WRITELN('-TEST NUMBER', TESTNBR);
000043             WRITELN('0');
000046             MMM;
000047             NBRTESTS := NBRTESTS - 1
000047         END;
000051     WRITELN('-END OF TESTS')
000056 END. (*TESTM*)
```

```
000006 (*TEST SIMULTANEOUS EQUATION SOLVER*)
000006 PROGRAM TESTSIMUL(INPUT,OUTPUT);
000464 VAR TEST: PACKED ARRAY[1..4] OF CHAR;
000465     TESTNBR, I: INTEGER;
000467
000467 (*SOLVE A SIMULTANEOUS EQUATION*)
000467 PROCEDURE SIMUL;
000003 VAR A, B, C, D, E, F,          (* INPUT COEFFICIENTS *)
000003     DENOM,                     (* DENOMINATOR = A*E - B*D *)
000003     X, Y:  REAL;               (* SOLUTION *)
000014
000014 BEGIN (*SIMUL*)
000014     READLN(A,B,C,D,E,F);
000031     WRITELN('   A =', A, '   B =', B, '   C =', C);
000065     WRITELN('   D =', D, '   E =', E, '   F =', F);
000121     DENOM := A*E - B*D;
000124     IF DENOM <> 0
000124         THEN BEGIN
000127                 X := (C*E - B*F) / DENOM;
000131                 Y := (A*F - C*D) / DENOM;
000133                 WRITELN('0  SOLUTION:  X=', X, '   Y =', Y)
000155             END
000156         ELSE WRITELN('0  NO SOLUTION');
000165     WRITELN('0')
000167 END; (*SIMUL*)
000231
000231 BEGIN (*TESTSIMUL*)
000231     FOR I := 1 TO 4 DO
000023         READ(TEST[I]);
000041     WHILE TEST = 'TEST' DO
000044         BEGIN
000044             READ(TESTNBR);
000047             WRITELN('-  TEST NUMBER', TESTNBR);
000061             WRITELN('0');
000064             SIMUL;
000065             FOR I := 1 TO 4 DO
000066                 READ(TEST[I])
000102         END;
000105     WRITELN('-  END OF TESTS')
000112 END.  (*TESTSIMUL*)
```

Section 2 Exercises

1. Consider the "list-inquiry" program developed in Section III.2.2.

   a. Make a list of the potential problems, special cases, extreme values, etc. that ought to be tested before this program is pronounced "correct".

   b. Devise a set of test data that will reveal a flaw (if one exists) for each of the problems listed in 1.a.

   c. Devise a test procedure for "list-inquiry", such as the one shown in (2.2b), so that several of the test cases produced in 1.b can be combined in a single run.

2. Repeat exercise 1 for the sorting program developed in Section III.2.3.

3. Repeat exercise 1 for the symbol-scanning program developed in Section III.2.5.

Section 3 Automatic Diagnostic Services

A limited amount of diagnostic information is provided automatically for the programmer, as syntactic mistakes are detected or when invalid actions are to be performed. This information is especially helpful to beginners, since they tend to make many errors of this type. But as programmers gain experience, such errors become relatively less frequent and significant, and their elimination is only a prelude to serious testing. These syntactic slips and keypunch mistakes must be eliminated before the demonstration of correctness can begin.

These automatic services help reveal some "accidents" (see Section 1.2) and occasionally a language or algorithm error. When a program runs without any diagnostic messages, correctness only at level 2 (as defined in Section 1.1) has been achieved.

3.1 Detection of Errors

Only two types of errors are automatically detected: syntax errors are detected during loading and reported on the source listing, and requests to perform invalid actions are detected during execution and reported in the execution output. These are discussed in Sections 3.1.1 and 3.1.2.

3.1.1 Syntax Errors

Regardless of what programming language is used, every violation of the syntax rules of the language should be detected by the computer during loading of the program. The manner in which detection is announced and the amount of explanation provided depends upon the language used. In many cases the flaw is obvious and the correction is straightforward. However, in some situations the actual error may be far removed from the statement where its presence was detected. In these cases the messages provided are not always helpful. For example

```
Y := X[I]
```

might be flagged as erroneous not because it is improperly formed, but because a missing or faulty declaration has failed to declare X as an array. However mystifying the error messages may be, they are neither spontaneous nor random. There is something in your program that is wrong, or at least suspicious, and you must find out what it is. However elusive the cause, every syntax error must be tracked down.

Unfortunately, many mistakes are not recognizable as such by PASCAL. For example, suppose an assignment statement should be given as

```
COUNT := COUNT + 1
```

Suppose that variables I, U and COUNTT have been declared as well as COUNT. Each of the following variations might somehow appear in place of the correct statement:

```
a.  COUNT := COUNT + .1
b.  COUNT := COUNT - 1
c.  COUNT := COUNT + I
d.  COUNT := COUNT + U
e.  COUNT = COUNT + 1
f.  COUNTT := COUNT + 1
```

None of these alternatives is correct, but only the missing colon in e will be recognized as a syntax error. Each of the others is syntactically but not functionally correct in this program. (Alternatives c and d might be detected as execution errors if no value had been assigned to I or U.) Alternatives c, d and f probably are just errors in keypunching, but are not detected because we assumed that variables I, U and COUNTT had been declared. More realistically, most keypunch errors will not happen to coincide with other variables, so PASCAL will recognize that something is wrong. It will report the problem as a missing declaration, rather than as a misspelling of a declared variable, but at least it draws your attention to the problem. (In some languages complete declaration is not required, so a keypunch mistake "implicitly declares" a new variable.)

The example above should suggest that some care in the choice of variable names will make your program less susceptible to keypunch errors. For example, it is not a good idea to have variables named COUNT and COUNTT in the same program. Their spelling is too similar and it is too easy to write or punch one when you should have the other. A common mistake on a keypunch is the transposition of adjacent characters -- to punch NXET when you meant NEXT. Recognizing the likelihood of such errors, you should try to avoid having variable names whose spelling differs only by a transposition. That is, don't deliberately have two variables such as TEMP and TMEP, or X12 and X21, in the same program. Another common error is a alphabetic-numeric shift failure. That is, you get the alphabetic character from a key when you wanted the numeric character, or vice-versa. It is asking for trouble to have two variables X4 and XJ in the same program. Alternative d above is an example of this, since U is on the same key as 1. In fact, this particular error is so common that U ought to be avoided as a variable name. Of course, I and J are similarly handicapped, but they are everybody's favorite subscript variables, so it would be unrealistic to suggest avoiding them.

Syntax errors in declarations and definitions are particularly serious since failure of a declaration will cause subsequent statements to be considered incorrect. This produces many error messages from one little mistake. For example:

```
000006 (*SOLVE SIMULTANEOUS EQUATIONS*)
000006 PROGRAM SIMUL(INPUT, OUTPUT);
000464 VAR A, B, C: D, E, F,          (*INPUT COEFFICIENTS*)
******                  ^104^6
000464      DENOM,
000464      X, Y: REAL;
000464
000464 BEGIN  (*SIMUL*)
000464      WHILE NOT EOF DO
000023           BEGIN (*READ AND SOLVE LOOP*)
000023                READLN(A,B,C,D,E,F);
******                               ^104^104^104
000032                WRITELN(' A=', A, ' B=', B, ' C=', C);
000055                WRITELN(' D=', D, ' E=', E, ' F=', F);
******                                 ^104        ^104        ^104
000100                DENOM := A*E - B*D;
******                     ^104  ^104  ^104
000100                IF DENOM <> 0
******                      ^104
000100                   THEN BEGIN
000100                             X := (C*E - B*F)/DENOM;
******                             ^104    ^104  ^104   ^104
000100                             Y := (A*F / C*D)/DENOM;
******                             ^104    ^104  ^104   ^104
000100                             WRITELN('0SOLUTION: X=', X, ' Y=', Y)
******                                                         ^104       ^104
000114                         END
000115                   ELSE WRITELN('0NO SOLUTION');
000124                WRITELN('0');
000127                WRITELN('0')
000131           END (*READ AND SOLVE LOOP*)
000132 END.  (*SIMUL*)
```

The only real mistake in this program is a colon instead of a comma after C in the declaration of variables, but this terminated the declaration, so D, E, F, DENOM, X and Y were not declared. Everytime one of these names is used in the program, PASCAL reports an undeclared variable.

When there is an error in a declaration or definition it is difficult to decide just how much of the faulty declaration has been accepted. This in turn makes it difficult to understand which error messages in the rest of the program are a consequence of the failure in the declaration. Unfortunately, the Control Data implementation of PASCAL does not provide a summary list of variables and their types, from which you could see precisely what was created. With this implementation, you essentially have to eliminate all errors in declarations and definitions before you can even begin to look for, and understand errors in the body of the program.

3.1.2 Invalid Operations

There is another type of error that can be automatically detected. Even though all the declarations and statements of your program are in syntactically correct form, it may be that in their execution they direct PASCAL to perform some invalid operation. Just what constitutes an invalid operation depends on the language and computer being used. Generally these include such operations as:

a. dividing by zero,
b. taking the square root of a negative number, or
c. adding two numbers whose sum exceeds the largest number the computer can handle

The error message will be given when the invalid operation is actually attempted, but usually the problem lies somewhere else. Usually some previous combination of actions has led to conditions that make this operation invalid. For example, suppose statement 000067 includes the operation of obtaining the square-root of a variable X. If X has a negative value when statement 67 is executed, the SQRT built-in function will give an error message blaming statement 67. Of course, the problem is not in 67 but in the statement that assigned the negative value to X, or in some earlier statement that produced one of the values used in this assignment to X. In general, execution error messages simply announce the point at which the result of an error causes an invalid operation to be requested, and unfortunately they rarely can give much hint as to what actually caused the error.

Some languages are more helpful than others in this regard. For example, if an array has been declared AMT[1..5], PASCAL will object to executing the statement

```
SUM := SUM + AMT[6]
```

but many languages find no fault in this statement. They will execute this statement, obtain some extraneous value for AMT[6], and provide no warning that anything irregular has occurred. On the other hand, other languages are better than PASCAL in warning you about the use of "uninitialized" variables. For example:

```
(* SET TOTAL TO SUM OF A[1..N] *)
    FOR I := 1 TO N DO
         TOTAL := TOTAL + A[I]
```

This is incorrect, because TOTAL was not initialized to 0 before entering the loop. The program should be:

```
(* SET TOTAL TO SUM OF A[1..N] *)
    TOTAL := 0;
    FOR I := 1 TO N DO
         TOTAL := TOTAL + A[I]
```

Some languages -- PL/C, for example -- would recognize that the first version is incorrect, because on the first iteration of the loop TOTAL is asked to provide a value before it has ever been assigned a value. An error message would be given. Since PASCAL does not consider the use of a non-existent value an error, the first version will run, and will produce an improper answer with no warning that it is wrong.

3.2 Automatic Repair of Errors

PASCAL, or at least the Control Data version of PASCAL, does not attempt to correct errors. Some years ago this was to be expected, but by now many languages attempt at least some repair of minor errors. The extreme example of this is PL/C -- which attempts to repair *every* error. After reporting an error to the user, PL/C makes some repair and continues. It would be nice to make a *correction*, but all PL/C provides is a *repair*. Sometimes a repair happens to be a correction; it achieves what the programmer intended. While this occurs fairly often, the real purpose of the repair is simply to permit continuation of execution. The objective is to *obtain as much information as possible from each attempt to process a program*.

There is nothing inherent in the PASCAL language that makes automatic error repair impossible or impractical. Hopefully, some day PASCAL will be more helpful in this regard.

3.3 The Post-Mortem Dump

If execution of a program is termined because of an execution error detected by PASCAL, a "post-mortem dump" is provided. (You can ensure appearance of the dump, regardless of whether or not an error is found, by ending your program with execution of the built-in procedure HALT.)

The dump was introduced in Section I.7.2.2 and examples are given there. The dump provides a considerable amount of useful information. The display of final values of variables often helps by showing values of variables that you did not expect to be interested in, and hence did not bother to display. It also reveals variables created but never used -- often due to a keypunch error, or a faulty declaration. Although the dump is produced automatically, there are some actions on your part that will increase the usefulness of the information it provides. For example, avoid the reuse of variables -- even temporary utility variables, such as subscripts. Since the dump reports only the final value of each variable, each time you reuse a variable you are throwing away potentially useful information about the early portions of the program. (Our examples do not generally follow this suggestion, but it is nevertheless a good idea.) For example, suppose a program contains the following segment:

```
...
FOR ITEST := 1 TO N DO
  BEGIN (* TEST LOOP *)
    ...
    IF X < Y THEN GOTO 9070;
    ...
  END; (* TEST LOOP *)
9070:;
...
```

In analyzing the results of test execution of this program you may need to know whether TEST LOOP ran to normal completion (N iterations), or whether it was terminated prematurely by the GOTO exit. If neither N nor ITEST was used subsequently in execution their final values, as displayed in the dump, will indicate how TEST LOOP terminated. On the other hand, if you routinely use I for the index of TEST LOOP and most other loops in your program the value of I will have been changed by some later loop and the dump will not tell you how TEST LOOP terminated. You would have to rerun the program with a temporary output statement such as

```
WRITELN('0FINAL I,N AFTER TEST LOOP:', I, N)
```

placed after the label 9070.

Section 3 Examples

```
000006 (* PRINT A TABLE OF BASE-10 LOGARITHMS *)
000006 PROGRAM PLOG10(INPUT,OUTPUT);
000464
000464 CONST N = 50;
000464 VAR X, Y,           (* Y = LOG10(X) $)
000464     LOGE10:  REAL;  (* LN(10) *)
000464     I :  1..N;
000467
000467 BEGIN (*PLOG10*)
000467     LOGE10 := -LN(10);
******         ^104
000030     WRITELN('1      TABLE OF LOGARITHMS');
000036     WRITELN('0S);
******                ^202
000036     FOR I = 0 TO N DO;
******       ^4,14^51
000053         BEGIN
000053             X := I DIV 10;
000065             WRITE(' ', X)
000073             Y := X * LOGE10
******             ^6
000073             WRITELN('B', Y)
000073         END;
000073 END    (*PLOG10*)
000073
****** EOF ENCOUNTERED
```

```
000006 (* PRINT A TABLE OF BASE-10 LOGARITHMS *)
000006 PROGRAM PLOG10(INPUT,OUTPUT);
000464
000464 CONST N = 50;
000464 VAR X, Y,             (* Y = LOG10(X) *)
000464     LOGE10:  REAL; (* LN(10) *)
000467     I :  1..N;
000470
000470 BEGIN (*PLOG10*)
000470     LOGE10 := -LN(10);
000031     WRITELN('1       TABLE OF LOGARITHMS');
000037     WRITELN('0');
000042     FOR I := 0 TO N DO;
000051         BEGIN
000051             X := I DIV 10;
000062             WRITE(' ', X);
000070             Y := X * LOGE10;
000072             WRITELN(' ', Y)
000100         END;
000101 END.  (*PLOG10*)
```

```
     TABLE OF LOGARITHMS




  PROGRAM TERMINATED AT% 000044 IN PLOG10


PLOG10

  I            =          0
  LOGE10       =  -2.3025850929941E+000
  Y            =   0.0000000000000E-295
  X            =   0.0000000000000E-295




20.55.18.* VALUE OUT OF RANGE
20.55.18.* AT ADDR 000044 IN PROCEDURE PLOG10
```

Section 4 Explicit Diagnostic Facilities

It is generally difficult to ascertain correctness by using only results displayed as part of the problem requirements. Some temporary provision must be made to obtain additional printed output during testing.

The additional information needed to establish the correctness of a section of program is most easily identified while that section is being written; hence the temporary testing facilities should be designed and included as the program is being written. Unfortunately, many programmers will not admit that extra output is always required, and make no provision to obtain it until after the program has been completed and test runs show something to be wrong.

The basic diagnostic tool in any programming language is the ordinary output statement. If you learn where to position temporary output statements and what information to display, you can test any program. The following sections suggest different ways in which PASCAL's output statement can be used to produce diagnostic information.

Some languages include special facilities for printing diagnostic information, but unfortunately PASCAL does not. However, such facilities are only a convenience, since nothing is provided that could not be obtained with other elements of the language, but they are nevertheless very helpful. As an example of facilities provided by other languages, see Part V of our Introduction to Programming.

4.1 Flow Tracing

In Section I.4.1.2 and I.4.5 we referred to the hand execution of programs as "tracing". The same word is used to describe computer execution when detailed information about the flow of execution is obtained. This can be done by placing output statements at strategic points in the program.

One type of statement reports the value of some key variable each time the value is changed. The output statement must of course also identify the position in the program at which the assignment is made -- the value alone will not be very helpful. For example:

```
(* COMPUTE THE QUADRATIC SUM OF DATA *)
PROGRAM QUADSUMMER(INPUT, OUTPUT);
...
    READLN(POINT);
    WRITELN(' 1. POINT =', POINT);
    QUADSUM := 0;
    FOR IQSUM := 1 TO POINT DO
      BEGIN (* QSUM LOOP *)
         WRITELN(' 2. IQSUM =', IQSUM);
         ...
         WRITELN(' 3. QUADSUM =', QUADSUM);
         ...
      END; (* QSUM LOOP *)
    WRITELN(' 8. IQSUM =', IQSUM);
    ...
END.  (*QUADSUMMER *)
```

Another use of a diagnostic output statement is just to report the arrival at some particular point in the program. For example:

```
PROGRAM SOLVE(INPUT, OUTPUT);
...
    WRITELN(' ENCOUNTER MAIN LOOP');
    WHILE ...
      BEGIN (* MAIN LOOP *)
         WRITELN(' ENTER MAIN LOOP');
         ...
      END; (* MAIN LOOP *)
    WRITELN(' PAST MAIN LOOP');
    ...
```

Similar messages should report each entry to a procedure, displaying the values of the arguments, and the return from a procedure, displaying the results of the procedure's execution. For example:

```
(* ...
PROCEDURE FIND(A, B, C: REAL; VAR ANS: REAL);
  BEGIN (* FIND *)
    WRITELN(' ENTER PROCEDURE FIND');
    WRITELN(' INPUTS ARE:', A, B, C);
    ...
    WRITELN(' LEAVE PROCEDURE FIND');
    WRITELN(' RESULT IS:', ANS)
  END; (* FIND *)
```

4.2 The Memory Dump

An alternative to continuous tracing is to periodically display the values of key variables. This is called "dumping memory". It does not provide as complete information, but for just that reason it is useful in a preliminary search to determine the neighborhood of an error. By displaying values at different key points (usually section interfaces) during execution, one can determine which intervals need to be traced in detail.

PASCAL lacks special facilities for dumping, so the ordinary output statements must be used. It is important that each dump include sufficient identification to relate it both to its position in the text of the program and to a point in the execution of the program. For example, a report

```
3
7
9
```

is not particularly helpful. It does not stand out from the normal output; the variables are not identified, nor is the point in execution when these values exist. A more helpful display would be:

```
DUMP AT END OF MAIN LOOP
    ITERATION NUMBER          8
    X:          3
    Y:          7
    Z:          9
```

This should be separated by at least one blank line from the output that precedes and follows it.

The key idea about dumping is to be periodic and selective rather than continuous and exhaustive. Hence the dump will often be made conditional. For example:

```
(* DUMP RESULTS EVERY 10TH ITERATION *)
    IF DUMPCOUNT <> 10
         THEN DUMPCOUNT := DUMPCOUNT + 1
         ELSE BEGIN
              WRITELN('0DUMP IN FIND LOOP');
              WRITELN(' ITERATION:', INDEX);
              ...
              WRITELN;
              DUMPCOUNT := 0
           END
```

DUMPCOUNT would have to be initialized to 0 before entering FIND LOOP.

Another possibility would be to produce the dump only when something has gone wrong:

```
(* DUMP ON FAILURE TO FIND VALUE *)
    IF ANS = 0 THEN
      BEGIN
         WRITELN('0TROUBLE IN FIND LOOP');
         WRITELN(' ITERATION:', INDEX);
         WRITELN(' INPUTS ARE:', X, Y);
         WRITELN(' SEARCH ARGUMENT IS:', TEMP);
         ...
         WRITELN
      END
```

A dump may require the display of an array or a string, in which case the dump will require a loop of its own. For example:

```
(* DUMP LIST IF SEARCH FAILS *)
    IF LOCN = 0 THEN
      BEGIN
         WRITELN('0DUMP POINT 3; VALUES OF LIST:');
         FOR IDUMP := 1 TO N DO
              WRITELN(LIST[IDUMP]);
         WRITELN(' END OF LIST')
      END
```

A dump loop such as this can be inserted anywhere in a program, without its presence affecting the execution of the rest of the program, provided the <u>index variable</u> (which is the only variable changed by the loop) <u>is not the same</u> as some other variable in the procedure.

4.2.1 Data Display

In analyzing test output it is essential that you be able to know with absolute certainty just what data values were obtained by each execution of a READ statement. The only sure way of knowing is to print the values out immediately after they are read in. For example, suppose a program contained the following segment to load an array:

```
(* LOAD A[1..N] FROM DATA *)
    READLN(N);
    FOR I := 1 TO N DO
         READ(A[I])
```

In testing form, this segment might look like the following:

```
(* LOAD A[1..N] FROM DATA *)
    READLN(N);
    WRITELN('0LOAD LOOP.  N=', N);
    WRITELN(' VALUES OF A[1..N]:');
    FOR I := 1 TO N DO
      BEGIN
         READ(A[I]);
         WRITE(A[I]);
         (* PRINT 5 VALUES PER LINE *)
              IF I MOD 5 = 0
                   THEN WRITELN
      END;
    WRITELN('0')
```

Section 4 Summary

Actions that can be taken by the programmer to increase the amount of diagnostic information produced during execution of a program are:

1. Place a "HALT statement" at the end of your program to ensure the production of the post-mortem dump. Increase the useful information in the dump but not reusing the same variable for different purposes in the program. This applies even to index variables.

2. Insert additional, temporary output statements at various points in your program to:

   a. report the value assigned to a key variable,

   b. report a data value read in,

   c. report the arrival at a certain point, particularly conditional sections, loops and procedures,

   d. report the input arguments passed to a procedure,

   e. report the results returned from a procedure.

These output statements can provide a continuous "trace" of the execution of the program, or a periodic and selective "dump" of various intermediate results.

Section 4 <u>Examples</u>

```
000006 (*PRINT A TABLE OF BASE-10 LOGARITHMS*)
000006 PROGRAM PLOG10(INPUT,OUTPUT);
000464
000464 CONST N = 5;
000464 VAR X, Y,              (*Y = LOG10(X)*)
000464 LOGE10:  REAL;         (*LN(10)*)
000467     I:  1..N;
000470
000470 BEGIN (*PLOG10*)
000470     LOGE10 := LN(10);
000030     WRITELN('1    TABLE OF LOGARITHMS');
000036     WRITELN('0');
000041     FOR I := 1 TO N DO
000042         BEGIN
000046
000046             (*1*) WRITELN(' 1  I =', I);
000060             X := I / 10;
000066             (*2*) WRITELN(' 2  X =', X);
000100             Y := LN(X) / LOGE10;
000105             (*3*) WRITELN(' 3  Y =', Y);  WRITELN;
000120             WRITELN(' ', X, Y);
000133         END;
000135     HALT
000135 END. (*PLOG10*)
```

```
    TABLE OF LOGARITHMS


1  I =          1
2  X =  1.0000000000000E-001
3  Y = -1.0000000000000E+000

  1.0000000000000E-001 -1.0000000000000E+000
1  I =          2
2  X =  2.0000000000000E-001
3  Y = -6.9897000433601E-001

  2.0000000000000E-001 -6.9897000433601E-001
1  I =          3
2  X =  3.0000000000000E-001
3  Y = -5.2287874528034E-001

  3.0000000000000E-001 -5.2287874528034E-001
1  I =          4
2  X =  4.0000000000000E-001
3  Y = -3.9794000867204E-001

  4.0000000000000E-001 -3.9794000867204E-001
1  I =          5
2  X =  5.0000000000000E-001
3  Y = -3.0102999566398E-001

  5.0000000000000E-001 -3.0102999566398E-001
```

```
  PROGRAM TERMINATED AT% 000135 IN PLOG10


PLOG10

  I              =          5
  LOGE10         =    2.3025850929941E+000
  Y              =   -3.0102999566398E-001
  X              =    5.0000000000000E-001





  73B   04/14/76  SCOPE 3.4.4 BMI 414 CYBER 73  R.D 10.03
20.54.36.CARL03H  FROM    /AD
20.54.36.IP  00000256 WORDS - FILE INPUT  , DC 00
20.54.36.CARL,CM57000,P10,T10.
20.54.36.PROJECT,A3019.AEFACT320A.  ZIMMERMAN
20.54.36.MAP(OFF)
20.54.36.ATTACH,BCLLIB.
20.54.36.PFN IS
20.54.36.BCLLIB
20.54.37.PF CYCLE NO. = 008
20.54.37.LIBRARY,BCLLIB.
20.54.37.PASCAL.
20.55.01.- LOAD FL 043704
20.55.02.LGO.
20.55.04.- LOAD FL 004474
20.55.04.* AT ADDR 000135 IN PROCEDURE PLOG10
20.55.04.* HALT
20.55.04.OP  00000384 WORDS - FILE OUTPUT , PR 40
20.55.04.MS     3584  WORDS  (    7168 MAX USED)
20.55.04.MM  057000B WORDS MAX CM FL
20.55.04.CP        2.180 SEC.
20.55.05.IO         .567 SEC.
20.55.05.CM         .324 SEC.
20.55.05.SS        4.000 SEC.
20.55.05.EJ  END OF JOB, AD
```

Section 4 Exercises

1. Rewrite the program given in (I.1.1e) as it should be for an initial testing run

   a) using additional WRITE statements,

   b) with a test control procedure similar to (V.2.2b) that permits the program to be repeated with several data sets.

2. What execution output is produced by the program shown below?

```
(* MOVE MINIMUM TO HEAD OF LIST *)
PROGRAM MINMOVE(INPUT, OUTPUT);
LABEL 9000;
VAR L: ARRAY[1..50] OF REAL;
    MINVAL: REAL; (* MIN VALUE SO FAR *)
    MINPOS,       (* POSITION OF MINVAL IN LIST *)
    N,            (* EFFECTIVE LENGTH OF LIST *)
    I: INTEGER;

BEGIN (* MINMOVE *)
    (* LOAD L[1..N] FROM DATA *)
         READ(N);
         IF (N < 1) OR (N > 50) THEN
           BEGIN
              WRITELN('0IMPROPER LENGTH; N=', N);
              GOTO 9000
           END;
         FOR I := 1 TO N DO
              READ(L[I]);
    (* MIN MINVAL TO MINIMUM OF L[1..N]
      AND SET MINPOS TO INDEX OF MINVAL IN L *)
         MINVAL := L[1];
         MINPOS := 1;
         WRITELN(' 1 MINPOS=', MINPOS);
         FOR I := 2 TO N DO
           BEGIN (* LOC LOOP *)
              IF L[I] < MINVAL THEN
                BEGIN
                   MINVAL := L[I];
                   MINPOS := I;
                   IF I <= 4 THEN
                        WRITELN(' 2 MINPOS=', MINPOS)
                END
           END; (* LOC LOOP *)
    (* SWAP MIN L[I] WITH L[1] AND REPORT *)
         L[MINPOS] := L[1];
         L[1] := MINVAL;
         WRITELN(' MIN VALUE IS', L[1]);
         WRITELN(' ORIG INDEX OF MIN IS', MINPOS);
    9000:;
END.  (* MINMOVE *)
    eor
8 7 6 9 8 5 4 6 4 3
```

3. Rewrite the following program to report each time a value is assigned to LOW, HIGH, INT or SUM.

```
(* COMPUTE BOUNDED INTEGER SUMS *)
PROGRAM SUMER(INPUT, OUTPUT);
VAR LOW, HIGH,    (* RANGE LIMITS *)
    INT,          (* CURRENT INTEGER *)
    SUM: INTEGER; (* SUM OF INTEGERS *)

BEGIN (* SUMER *)
    READLN(LOW, HIGH);
    IF LOW > HIGH THEN
        WRITELN('0IMPROPER BOUNDS');
    (* SET SUM TO SUM OF INTEGERS FROM LOW TO HIGH *)
        SUM := 0;
        FOR INT := LOW TO HIGH DO
            SUM := SUM + INT;
    WRITELN('0', LOW, HIGH, SUM)
END.  (* SUMER *)
```

4. Rewrite the following program segment to report the arrival at labels 1, 2 and 3.

```
PROCEDURE X(...
LABEL 1, 2, 3;
...
1: IF X + Y < Z
    THEN 2: Y := 2 * Z
    ELSE 3: Y := 0;
...
```

5. How many lines of <u>execution</u> output would be produced by the following program:

```
(* COUNT OCCURRENCES OF SPECIFIED CHARACTER *)
PROGRAM CTCHAR(INPUT, OUTPUT);
LABEL 10;
VAR TESTCHAR,      (* CHAR TO BE COUNTED *)
    INCHAR: CHAR;  (* CHAR TO BE TESTED *)
    NBR,           (* NO.  OF OCCURRENCES *)
    WORDNUM: INTEGER;
    NEWWORD: BOOLEAN; (* NEW WORD SWITCH *)
```

```
BEGIN (* CTCHAR *)
    NEWWORD := TRUE;
    WRITELN(' NEWWORD=', NEWWORD);
    NBR := 0;
    WORDNUM := 0;
    WRITELN(' WORDNUM=', WORDNUM);
    READLN(TESTCHAR);
    (* PROCESS EACH INPUT CHARACTER UNTIL EOF *)
         WHILE NOT(EOF) DO
           BEGIN (* CHAR LOOP *)
              IF INCHAR = ' '
                THEN BEGIN
                   NEWWORD := TRUE;
                   WRITELN(' NEWWORD=', NEWWORD);
                   GOTO 10
                 END
                ELSE BEGIN (* NON-BLANK *)
                   IF NEWWORD THEN
                     BEGIN
                        WORDNUM := WORDNUM + 1;
                        WRITELN(' WORDNUM=', WORDNUM);
                        NEWWORD := FALSE;
                        WRITELN(' NEWWORD=', NEWWORD)
                     END;
                   IF INCHAR = TESTCHAR THEN
                        NBR := NBR + 1
                 END; (* NON-BLANK *)
              10:;
              READ(INCHAR)
           END; (* CHAR LOOP *)
    (* DISPLAY RESULTS *)
         WRITELN('0TEST CHAR IS:  ', TESTCHAR);
         WRITELN(' TOTAL OCCURRENCES :', NBR);
         WRITELN(' NBR WORDS TESTED:', WORDNUM)
END.  (* CTCHAR *)
    eor
P
1P2P3P4P5P6P7P 123P123P123P
PPPPPPP M MP 12345678P
```

6. Rewrite the program given below so that its action is unchanged except that it will print additional diagnostic information. This information should include

a) an announcement of the beginning of each pass,

b) the details of each interchange.

```
(* SORT LIST INTO ASCENDING ORDER *)
PROGRAM SORT(INPUT, OUTPUT);
VAR L: ARRAY[1..50] OF REAL; (* LIST TO BE SORTED *)
    N: INTEGER; (* EFFECTIVE LENGTH OF L *)
    TEMP: REAL;
    I, J: INTEGER;
```

```
BEGIN (* SORT *)
    (* LOAD L[1..N] FROM DATA *)
        READLN(N);
        IF N > 50 THEN
            WRITELN('0LIST TOO LONG');
        FOR I := 1 TO N DO
            READ(L[I]);
    (* SORT L[1..N] BY 'BUBBLE SORT', *)
    (* BRINGING LARGEST TO TOP ON EACH PASS *)
        FOR J := N DOWNTO 2 DO
          BEGIN (* BUBBLE LOOP *)
             (* CARRY MAX VALUE TO END OF L[1..J] *)
                 FOR I := 1 TO J-1 DO
                   BEGIN (* MAX LOOP *)
                      (* INTERCHANGE IF OUT OF ORDER *)
                           IF L[I] > L[I+1] THEN
                             BEGIN
                                TEMP := L[I];
                                L[I] := L[I+1];
                                L[I+1] := TEMP
                             END
                   END (* MAX LOOP *)
          END; (* BUBBLE LOOP *)
    (* DISPLAY L[1..N] IN SORTED ORDER *)
        WRITELN('0   SORTED LIST');
        WRITELN('0');
        FOR I := 1 TO N DO
            WRITELN(' ', L[I])
END.  (* SORT *)
```

Section 5 Modular Testing

5.1 Bottom-Up Testing

It is essentially impossible to test large programs -- there are just too many combinations of things to be tested. Really all we can do is thoroughly test small segments of programs and then construct a large program from these components. The testing of a program should be based on the tree that was constructed during the development of the program. During development the tree is constructed in a generally top-down direction, as the problem statement is successively refined into program units. Testing can follow the tree from the bottom-up, as the correctness of components is used to assert the correctness of a compound unit. At any point, the development tree illustrates how a particular task is decomposed into a sequence of subtasks. Equivalently, it shows the sequence of subtasks, each of whose correctness is necessary to assert the correctness of the task.

The lowest level of the tree should be program units whose structure and function are sufficiently simple that they can be clearly understood and exhaustively tested. One can then understand and test at the next level up, in terms of these proven components.

5.2 Independent Test of Procedures

Testing should take advantage of the procedural structure of a program. Each major subroutine should be tested separately. This requires the construction of a "driver routine" -- a program whose sole purpose is to call the procedure to be tested, supply it with arguments and display its results. The idea is essentially the same as the control procedure in Section 2.2 except that the procedure being tested usually has parameters. There is undeniably some extra effort required to write such drivers but it is comparatively modest once you have written one or two of them and the effort is generously rewarded by a reduction of test time when you put the program together.

For example, suppose a program must be protected against a number of special conditions that might occur in its data. The testing provisions might usefully be isolated as a separate procedure:

```
(* DETECT AND CORRECT EACH CATACHRESIS IN A[1..N] *)
PROCEDURE DATATEST(VAR A: REALIST; N: INTEGER);
    ...
  END; (* DATA TEST *)
```

This subroutine can be tested by the following type of driving routine:

```
(* TEST DRIVER FOR DATATEST *)
PROGRAM DTDRIVER(INPUT, OUTPUT);
CONST MXSZ = 10;
TYPE REALIST = ARRAY[1..MXSZ] OF REAL;
VAR X: REALIST;
    N:, I: INTEGER;

(* DETECT AND CORRECT EACH CATACHRESIS IN A[1..N] *)
PROCEDURE DATATEST(...
    ...
  END; (* DATATEST *)

BEGIN (* DTDRIVER *)
    (* LOAD AND PRINT X[1..N] *)
         N := 10;
         WRITELN('0ARRAY SIZE IS', N);
         FOR I := 1 TO N DO
           BEGIN
              READ(X[I]);
              WRITELN(' ', X[I])
           END;
    DATATEST(X, N);
    WRITELN('0CORRECTED ARRAY AFTER DATATEST');
    FOR I:= 1 TO N DO
         WRITELN(' ', X[I])
END.  (* DTDRIVER *)
```

5.2.1 Testing with Dummy Procedures

It is often useful to replace actual procedures with highly simplified versions during program development and testing. The simplest replacement is just a dummy procedure that returns immediately upon entry without doing anything at all. This strategy can allow the testing of the calling procedure before the called procedure has been written, or before the called procedure has been thoroughly tested. It can also be used to shortcut the action of a fully-tested procedure just to reduce the cost (or printing volume) of testing the calling procedure.

For example, in Section 5.2 certain error-checking provisions of a program are isolated in a procedure DATATEST. For initial testing of the main program, using carefully prepared, error-free data, these provisions are not needed and the program could be run with the following version of DATATEST:

```
(* DUMMY VERSION OF INPUT ERROR-CHECKING ROUTINE *)
PROCEDURE DATATEST(VAR A: REALIST; N: INTEGER);
    BEGIN (* DATATEST *)
    END (* DATATEST *)
```

This dummy version of DATATEST looks like the real DATATEST to the calling procedure. As far as the calling procedure knows, the real DATATEST is present performing the required checking -- but never discovering anything wrong. The dummy and real versions of DATATEST can be interchanged repeatedly as program testing proceeds. (Such dummy procedures are also sometimes called "stub" procedures.)

Sometimes it is desirable to have the dummy procedure report each time it is called and display the values of the arguments given in the call. A dummy version of DATATEST that would report in this way is shown below.

```
(* DUMMY VERSION OF INPUT ERROR-CHECKING ROUTINE *)
PROCEDURE DATATEST(VAR A: REALIST; N: INTEGER);
    VAR I: INTEGER;
    BEGIN (* DATATEST *)
         WRITELN('0DATATEST CALLED.',
              '  VALUES OF A[1..N] ARE:');
         FOR I := 1 TO N DO
              WRITELN(' ', A[I]);
         WRITELN
    END (* DATATEST *)
```

Section 5 Examples

```
000006 (*CALCULATOR PROGRAM*)
000006      (*DATA IS "+" OR "*", FOLLOWED BY 2 NUMBERS*)
000006      (*ALL SEPARATED BY ONE OR MORE BLANKS*)
000006      (*REPEAT UNTIL "F"*)
000006 (*TEST OF MAIN CONTROL SECTION*)
000006 PROGRAM CALC(INPUT,OUTPUT);
000464 VAR X, Y:  REAL;    (*OPERANDS*)
000466      OPERATION:  CHAR;
000467
000467 (*ADDITION SUBROUTINE*)
000467 PROCEDURE ADDR(VAL1, VAL2: REAL);
000005      BEGIN (*ADDR*)
000005           WRITELN('0ADDR CALLED WITH', VAL1, VAL2)
000024      END; (*ADDR*)
000037
000037 (*MULTIPLICATION SUBROUTINE*)
000037 PROCEDURE MULT(VAL1, VAL2: REAL);
000005      BEGIN (*MULT*)
000005           WRITELN('0MULT CALLED WITH', VAL1, VAL2)
000024      END; (*MULT*)
000037
000037 BEGIN (*CALC*)
000037      READ(OPERATION);
000027      WHILE OPERATION <> 'F' DO
000031           BEGIN (*OP LOOP*)
000031                READLN(X, Y);
000040                (*PERFORM OPERATION*)
000040                     IF (OPERATION = '+') OR (OPERATION = '*')
000042                          THEN CASE OPERATION OF
000051                                    '+':     ADDR(X, Y);
000054                                    '*':     MULT(X, Y)
000055                                  END
000062                          ELSE WRITELN('0UNKNOWN OPERATION');
000071                READ(OPERATION)
000076           END (*OP LOOP*)
000076 END. (*CALC*)
```

```
000006 (*CALCULATOR PROGRAM*)
000006 (*TEST OF ADDITION SUBROUTINE*)
000006 PROGRAM TESTAD(INPUT,OUTPUT):
000464 TYPE OPNAME = PACKED ARRAY[1..10] OF CHAR;
000464 VAR T1, T2: REAL;
000466     NBRTESTS: INTEGER;
000467
000467 (*PRINTING ROUTINE*)
000467 PROCEDURE RESULT(OPERN: OPNAME; FIRST, SECOND, ANS: REAL);
000007     BEGIN (*RESULT*)
000007         WRITELN('0RESULT CALLED WITH');
000016         WRITELN(' ', OPERN, FIRST, SECOND, ANS)
000041     END; (*RESULT*)
000056
000056 (*ADDITION SUBROUTINE*)
000056 PROCEDURE ADDR(VAL1, VAL2: REAL);
000005     VAR SUM: REAL;
000006         MESSAGE: OPNAME;
000007     BEGIN (*ADDR*)
000007         MESSAGE := '   ADD    ';
000011         SUM := VAL1 + VAL2;
000012         RESULT(MESSAGE, VAL1, VAL2, SUM)
000013     END; (*ADDR*)
000027
000027 BEGIN (*TESTAD*)
000027     READ(NBRTESTS);
000025     WHILE NBRTESTS > 0 DO
000027         BEGIN
000027             READ(T1, T2);
000035             WRITELN('-NEWTEST');
000043             WRITELN(' ', T1, T2);
000056             WRITELN;
000057             ADDR(T1, T2);
000062             NBRTESTS := NBRTESTS - 1
000062         END;
000064     WRITELN('-END OF TESTS')
000071 END. (*TESTAD*)
```

```
000006 (*CALCULATOR PROGRAM*)
000006     (*DATA IS "+" OR "*", FOLLOWED BY 2 NUMBERS*)
000006     (*ALL SEPARATED BY ONE OR MORE BLANKS*)
000006     (*REPEAT UNTIL "F"*)
000006 PROGRAM CALC(INPUT,OUTPUT);
000464 TYPE OPNAME = PACKED ARRAY[1..10] OF CHAR;
000464 VAR X, Y:  REAL;    (*OPERANDS*)
000466     OPERATION:  CHAR;
000467     OPNBR: INTEGER;
000470
000470 (*PRINTING ROUTINE*)
000470 PROCEDURE RESULT(OPERN: OPNAME; FIRST, SECOND, ANS: REAL);
000007     BEGIN (*RESULT*)
000007         OPNBR := OPNBR + 1;
000012         WRITELN('0OPERATION NUMBER', OPNBR);
000024         WRITELN(' ', OPERN, FIRST, ' AND', SECOND);
000051         WRITELN(' RESULT IS:', ANS)
000062     END; (*RESULT*)
000102
000102 (*ADDITION SUBROUTINE*)
000102 PROCEDURE ADDR(VAL1, VAL2: REAL);
000005     VAR SUM: REAL;
000006         MESSAGE: OPNAME;
000007     BEGIN (*ADDR*)
000007         MESSAGE := '   ADD    ';
000011         SUM := VAL1 + VAL2;
000012         RESULT(MESSAGE, VAL1, VAL2, SUM)
000013     END; (*ADDR*)
000027 (*MULTIPLICATION SUBROUTINE*)
000027 PROCEDURE MULT(VAL1, VAL2: REAL);
000005     VAR PRODUCT: REAL;
000006         MESSAGE: OPNAME;
000007     BEGIN (*MULT*)
000007         MESSAGE := ' MULTIPLY ';
000011         PRODUCT := VAL1 * VAL2;
000011         RESULT(MESSAGE, VAL1, VAL2, PRODUCT)
000013     END; (*MULT*)
000027
000027 BEGIN (*CALC*)
000027     OPNBR := 0;
000023     READ(OPERATION);
000027     WHILE OPERATION <> 'F' DO
000031         BEGIN (*OP LOOP*)
000031             READLN(X, Y);
000040             (*PERFORM OPERATION*)
000040                 IF (OPERATION = '+') OR (OPERATION = '*')
000042                     THEN CASE OPERATION OF
000051                             '+':    ADDR(X, Y);
000054                             '*':    MULT(X, Y)
000055                            END
000062                     ELSE WRITELN('0UNKNOWN OPERATION');
000071             READ(OPERATION)
000076         END (*OP LOOP*)
000076 END. (*CALC*)
```

Section 5 Exercises

1. Write a dummy version of the "list-inquiry" program developed in Section III.2.2 that could be used to test a larger program of which list-inquiry was to be a part.

2. Repeat exercise 1 for the sorting program developed in Section III.2.3.

3. Consider the procedure SORT in (IV.1.4a).

   a. Make a list of the potential problems, special cases, extreme values, etc. that ought to be tested before this procedure is pronounced "correct".

   b. Devise a set of test data that will reveal a flaw (if one exists) for each of the problems listed in 3.a.

   c. Devise a "test driver" that will allow the SORT procedure to be tested independently of the test of (IV.1.4a). The driver should permit several of the test cases developed in 3.b to be combined in a single run.

   d. Devise a dummy version of SORT that will allow the main procedure SRTG of (IV.1.4a) to be tested without using the actual SORT procedure.

Section 6 Testing Habits and Error Patterns

Testing a non-trivial program is a difficult task, probably requiring as much time, effort and knowledge as the construction of the program in the first place. In testing you are effectively looking for an unknown number of needles in a haystack. Yet too often this search is not conducted in a systematic and intelligent manner. Consequently testing takes longer than it should, and is less likely to reveal all of the errors present. The preceding sections of Part V have described the particular tools available in PASCAL and have given suggestions and examples of their use. But it will require both thought and practice to learn to use these tools effectively.

It is helpful to critically analyze your own testing habits by reviewing the course of the battle after testing is completed. For example, how many times have you written a program that ran perfectly on the first try? How many times have you submitted a new program for its first run just to see if it might happen to "work", before giving serious thought to the information you will need to find out why it doesn't work? Once in a great while you may be lucky, but the odds are that you consistently waste the first few computer runs just discovering that something is wrong.

After you have finally tracked down an error, review the strategy of your attack. Knowing what the error is, and where it is, determine what sort of attack would have been most effective. Evaluate each test run to see which runs actually provided useful information. The next error will, of course, be different, but in the long run a pattern will emerge. You will learn what sort of information is generally useful, at what points in a program to seek information, and how to systematically eliminate possibilities. It is good practice to save every output until testing is completed. Then go back and see which runs were wasted and why, and see which errors should have been detected several runs earlier.

Admittedly it is very difficult to force yourself to do this. By the time you finish testing a program you are usually thoroughly sick of looking at it and thinking about it. But unless you learn from this experience you are doomed to repeat it -- and as your assignments become more complex the burden of testing will become overwhelming.

6.1 The Complete Development and Testing Process

The development process described in Part III and the testing process of Part V should be closely interwoven. The steps that should be followed in the development and testing of a significant program are outlined below. Although the steps occur roughly in the order shown, in practice there is a good deal of overlap and backtracking.

1. Clarify the problem requirements (Section III.1.1).

2. Design a program strategy (Section III.1.2), producing a development tree (III.1.2.2) and a comment outline (III.1.2.3).

3. Specify critical data structures (Section III.1.3).

4. Determine the procedure structure of the program (Section IV.2) to suit the higher level of the development tree.

5. Develop the program and test data for each procedure independently.

    5.1 Clarify the functional requirements of the procedure.

    5.2 Clarify the communications interface for the procedure -- the number and types of parameters.

    5.3 Write a dummy version of the procedure (Section 5.2.1) that will serve in place of this procedure in testing other parts of the program.

    5.4 Design an internal strategy for the procedure, producing a development tree and comment outline. (If the procedure is large, repeat the entire process from step 4 at this level.)

    5.5 Write the program -- that is, write the actual program statements to perform tasks described in the comment outline.

    5.6 Verify the program against the algorithm. In particular, check the role of each variable, and the entry and exit conditions for each loop.

    5.7 Add diagnostic facilities -- temporary statements, prefixes, etc. to provide tracing and intermediate results during testing.

    5.8 Design a sequence of test cases, ranging from trivial to maliciously difficult.

    5.9 Write a driving program (Section 5.2) that will permit the procedure to be run independent of the rest of the program. It should permit multiple tests in a single run (Section 2.2).

6. Perform a sequence of diagnostic runs of each procedure separately. When errors are revealed make the necessary corrections. If the error is superficial you can make a correction and continue the process. If the problem is more deeply rooted it may be necessary to abandon testing and return to the development process. That is, if you find a statement is wrong -- fix it; but if you find that the algorithm is inadequate -- start over. Don't apply band-aids to a procedure that needs major surgery.

6.1 The first run should provide enough information to eliminate all syntax and keypunch errors. Follow up each error message until you understand why it was given. Check every line in the program listing to make sure each variable in the program was explicitly declared and has the proper attributes. It may take more than one run to reveal all errors of this sort, since one error can sometimes mask another -- but don't get in the "one bug per run" habit.

6.2 On each run compare the results produced with what you expected (which implies that you know in advance what the answers should be). This comparison involves

a. tracing messages and statement frequency counts to make sure the flow-of-control in execution was as expected, and

b. intermediate as well as final results.

6.3 When the most difficult test cases have passed examination without any surprises, remove the temporary diagnostic provisions for the procedure. (Save a listing that shows these provisions in place so that if it turns out their removal was premature, they can be restored with a minimum of difficulty.)

7. Replace the dummy procedures with real procedures and make final test runs that concentrate on testing the interfaces and communication between procedures. If the program is a large one this should not happen all at once. Insert real procedures one at a time and test after each insertion.

This seems like a very involved process. It is -- because the production of correct programs for substantial problems is a demanding task. Various shortcuts are obviously appropriate for small problems -- but unfortunately the techniques that are tolerable on small problems are too often extended to larger problems. It is essentially impossible to test a medium-sized program (say, 100 statements or more) all at once without any special diagnostic provisions and carefully designed test data. Yet neophyte programmers regularly attempt this impossible task. They spend seemingly endless hours in the battle, and conclude that programming is something to be avoided if possible and otherwise endured. The brief moment of elation when a program finally "runs" is not adequate compensation for the hours of frustration, and is forgotten altogether when the program subsequently fails on the instructor's set of test data.

Large programs can be written to perform interesting and useful tasks. It is a practical and creative process that can yield considerable satisfaction -- and remunerative employment. But the production of reliable programs is a complex and demanding art, which requires time and effort to learn.

Appendices

Appendix A The PASCAL Language

Appendix A.1 The Primer Subset

The following is a summary of the subset of the PASCAL language that is used in this *Primer* (which does not coincide with the "official" PASCAL-S subset). For a description of the full PASCAL language, see Jensen and Wirth, *The PASCAL User Manual and Report*.

This Appendix simply indicates what elements of the language are included in the subset. It shows the general form of each construction included, but does not explain what it does or how it should be used. To find the appropriate explanation in the body of the text, look up the keywords of these constructions in the Index.

Declarations and Definitions

```
LABEL integer1, integer2, ... ;

CONST name1 = value1; name2 = value2; ... ;

TYPE name1 = type1;
     name2 = (name3, name4, ... );
     name5 = value1..value2;
     ... ;

VAR name1, name2, ... : type;
    name3, name4, ... : value1..value2;
    ... ;

PROCEDURE name(list of parameters and their types);
     local declarations and definitions;
     BEGIN (* name *)
          statements of the body
     END; (* name *)
```

Types

```
REAL
INTEGER
BOOLEAN
CHAR
Subrange
User-defined types
ARRAY[subrange] OF type
PACKED ARRAY[subrange] OF CHAR
```

Statements

```
WHILE condition DO
    statement

REPEAT
    statement
  UNTIL condition

FOR variable := expr1 TO expr2 DO
    statement

FOR variable := expr1 DOWNTO expr2 DO
    statement

IF condition
    THEN statement

IF condition
    THEN statement1
    ELSE statement2

CASE expression OF
    case-label1: statement1;
    case-label2: statement2;
          ...
  END
```

Note: in each of the above, "statement" can be a compound statement of the form:

```
BEGIN
     sequence of statements
END
```

```
variable := expression

procedure-name

procedure-name(list of arguments)

READ(list of variables)

READLN(list of variables)

READLN

WRITE(list of variables and literals)

WRITELN(list of variables and literals)

WRITELN

GOTO label

label:
```

Operators

\+ - * / DIV MOD

Relations

= <> > >= < <=

Boolean Operators

AND OR NOT

Constants

integers

decimal and exponential numbers

characters and strings of characters (in quotes)

TRUE and FALSE

values of user-defined types

Built-in Functions

ABS(x)
ARCTAN(x)
CHR(x)
COS(x)
EOF(x) or EOF
EOLN(x) or EOLN
EXP(x)
LN(x)
ODD(x)
ORD(x)
PRED(x)
ROUND(x)
SIN(x)
SQR(x)
SQRT(x)
SUCC(x)
TRUNC(x)

A.2 Other PASCAL Features

In this Appendix we attempt to give a brief glimpse of three topics that are likely to be the next things you will need beyond the features in the Primer subset. For further explanation of these topics, and for a description of the other features of PASCAL, see Jensen and Wirth.

A.2.1 Output Format Control

In the body of the text we have always used the standard or default format for printed output. This is the easiest to use, but if you want to specify your own output format you can do so.

In the text, each element in the list of a WRITE or WRITELN statement was a variable or a literal. In fact, each item can be a pair of expressions:

```
expr1 : expr2
```

Expr1 specifies the *value* to be displayed. Variables and literals are special cases of expressions, but more general expressions involving operators can be given. The value specified by the expression can be of type INTEGER, REAL, BOOLEAN, or CHAR, or it may be a character string in PACKED ARRAY[...] OF CHAR form. Expr2 specifies the *format* for the value. Expr2 may be omitted, in which case the standard or default format is used. (If expr2 is omitted, the colon is also.)

If expr2 is given, it must be an INTEGER-valued expression, whose value specifies the *minimum field width* the value will occupy. That is, X:6 means print the value of variable X in a field of at least 6 spaces. If the field width specified by expr2 is not sufficient to accomodate the actual value provided by expr1, then the field width is automatically increased. That is, expr2 specifies the *minimum* field width, not necessarily the actual width that will be used.

For example, suppose there were variables and values as follows:

```
IP   8731 [integer]
IM  -8731 [integer]
B   FALSE [Boolean]
RP   12.677 [real]
RM  -12.677 [real]
S   EXITƀƀƀ [string7]
```

Then the results of various output expressions would be as shown below:

WRITE(IP) gives b̸b̸b̸b̸b̸b̸8731

WRITE(IP:4) gives 8731

WRITE(IP:5) gives b̸8731

WRITE(IM:5) gives -8731

WRITE(IP:2) gives 8731

WRITE(IM:2) gives -8731

Note that in the last two examples, the field specified is inadequate, so it is automatically increased.

Examples of the display of a BOOLEAN value are:

WRITE(B) gives b̸b̸b̸b̸b̸FALSE

WRITE(B:5) gives FALSE

WRITE(B:3) gives FALSE

WRITE(B:8) gives b̸b̸b̸FALSE

Display of string values differs slightly in that if the field width is inadequate, the field width is <u>not</u> increased -- the string is <u>truncated</u> from the right:

WRITE(S:7) gives EXITb̸b̸b̸

WRITE(S) gives EXITb̸b̸b̸

WRITE(S:12) gives b̸b̸b̸b̸b̸EXITb̸b̸b̸

WRITE(S:5) gives EXITb̸

WRITE(S:2) gives EX

The display of a REAL value is more complicated. The display field is always at least 10 positions:

b̸sd.dEsddd

where "s" is a sign and "d" is a digit. The field always starts with a blank. The second position is the sign, but a blank is given instead of a +. The number of digits to the right of the decimal point is always at least one, and increases as the field width specified increases above 10. For example:

```
WRITE(RP:10) gives ƀƀ1.2E+001

WRITE(RP:11) gives ƀƀ1.27E+001

WRITE(RP:12) gives ƀƀ1.268E+001

WRITE(RP:13) gives ƀƀ1.2677E+001

WRITE(RP:15) gives ƀƀ1.267700E+001

WRITE(RM:13) gives ƀ-1.2677E+001
```

Alternatively, a REAL value can be displayed in <u>decimal</u> rather than exponential form. To do so, three expressions are given:

```
expr1 : expr2 : expr3
```

Expr1 and expr2 are as before. Expr3 is an INTEGER-valued expression than specifies the number of digits to the right of the decimal point. For example:

```
WRITE(RP:5:1)  gives ƀ12.7

WRITE(RP:7:3)  gives ƀ12.677

WRITE(RP:8:4)  gives ƀ12.6770

WRITE(RP:8:3)  gives ƀƀ12.677

WRITE(RM:8:3)  gives ƀ-12.677
```

Note that in this decimal form the values are right-justified, and the field is filled on the left with blanks.

A.2.2 Functions

In addition to the type of procedure described in Part IV, there is a different form called a "function procedure", or just a "function". These are used just like the built-in functions (such as SQRT and TRUNC) that are included in PASCAL. That is, the result of executing the function is a value that is assigned to the function name itself. For example, recall that for the built-in function SQRT(x), the value of SQRT(x) is the square root of the argument expression x. The function SQRT(x) can be used as a term in an arithmetic expression. In effect, SQRT(x) can appear in place of x wherever you need the square root of x rather than x itself.

Function procedures provide a mechanism by which you can add other functions to be used the same way. For example, if F(x) is defined as a function, the value of F(x) is the result of performing some action (specified in the definition of F) upon the argument x. F(x) can be used as a term in an expression. This is significantly different from the procedures described in Part IV, which must be used by executing a procedure statement. That is, if P(x) is defined as a PROCEDURE, it is invoked by the procedure statement P(argument). P(argument) cannot be used as a term in an expression, because P itself has no value. The action of P might well assign a new value to the argument (assuming it is declared as a VAR parameter), but P itself has no value.

The definition of a function is in most respects analogous to the definition of a procedure, as described in Section IV.1.2. However, there are three essential differences:

1. The keyword FUNCTION is used (instead of PROCEDURE).

2. The function heading must specify the type of the function value. This is done by adding a type specification after the parameter list:

```
FUNCTION name(list of parameters
                  and their types) : function-type
```

Function-type must be a scalar -- REAL, INTEGER, BOOLEAN, CHAR, a user-defined scalar, or a subrange. It cannot be an array or a packed array. For example:

```
FUNCTION CUBE(X : REAL) : REAL
```

3. The body of the function must cause at least one assignment to be executed in which a value of appropriate type is assigned to the function name itself. For example:

```
CUBE := X * SQR(X)
```

One particularly important use of functions is to segregate some set of tests, and have the function return a BOOLEAN value as a result of the tests. For example, suppose a problem required each datum to be subjected to extensive validity checks before it is accepted and processed. These checks could be written in a function DATACHECK, whose type is BOOLEAN:

```
FUNCTION DATACHECK(DATUM:REAL):BOOLEAN
```

The body of this function could be written so that DATACHECK is assigned the value TRUE if the datum passed all of the checks, and assigned the value FALSE if it fails any one of the checks. Then the main processing loop could be written as follows:

```
READ(X);
WHILE NOT EOF DO
  BEGIN (* READ LOOP *)
    IF DATACHECK(X) THEN
      BEGIN
         ...  Processing routine
      END;
    READ(X)
  END (* READ LOOP *)
```

A.2.3 Additional Files

An input file is a source of input data for READ and READLN statements. An output file is a destination or target for information delivered by WRITE or WRITELN statements. Our examples have involved only one of each -- the standard input file named INPUT, and the standard output file named OUTPUT. But as problems become larger and more complicated it is often convenient to have several distinct sources of data, and/or several distinct destinations for output. Hence PASCAL provides a means of using input and output files in addition to the standard INPUT and OUTPUT files.

There are several aspects to using such files:

1. The names of files must be declared. This involves three different parts of the program:

1.a The additional file-names must be included in the VAR declaration, specifying the standard type TEXT. For example:

```
VAR X, Y: REAL;
    ALTINP, ALTOUTP: TEXT;
```

This declaration applies only to additional files -- INPUT and OUTPUT cannot be included in the VAR declaration.

1.b The additional file-names must be listed in the program heading after the standard files. For example:

```
PROGRAM MULTILIST(INPUT,OUTPUT,ALTINP,ALTOUTP)
```

The standard files must come first; the order of listing the additional file-names is not critical.

1.c An expanded form of LGO control card must be used, on which all the file-names are listed. For example:

```
LGO(INPUT,OUTPUT,ALTINP,ALTOUTP)
```

The order of file-names on the LGO card must match the order in the PROGRAM heading.

2. Each READ, READLN, WRITE and WRITELN statement must specify which file it uses. This is done by giving the file-name as the first element on the list, whenever the name is something other than INPUT or OUTPUT. For example:

```
READ(ALTINP, X)
```

obtains the next value from input file ALTINP and assigns it to variable X.

```
WRITE(ALTOUTP, X)
```

writes the current value of X onto the output file ALTOUTP. The standard file-names INPUT and OUTPUT need not be given on the list when the standard files are used.

3. Files other than INPUT and OUTPUT must be initialized before they can be used. Two built-in functions are used for this purpose:

> RESET(file-name) initializes an input file, and must be executed before anything can be READ from that file.
>
> REWRITE(file-name) initializes an output file, and must be executed before the first WRITE or WRITELN statement for that file. Any information that may be in an output file is deleted when REWRITE is executed for that file.

These functions cannot be applied to the standard INPUT or OUTPUT files.

4. The EOF(file-name) and EOLN(file-name) built-in functions can be used for any file. The standard file INPUT can be given as an argument, but when INPUT is intended, the function is usually given without an argument, as we have done in our examples. When an input file f is RESET, EOF(f) becomes FALSE, unless f is completely empty.

A.3 Syntax of the Full PASCAL Language

This Appendix is copied from Appendix D, pages 116-118, of Jensen and Wirth, PASCAL User Manual and Report (2nd ed), Springer-Verlag, 1975.

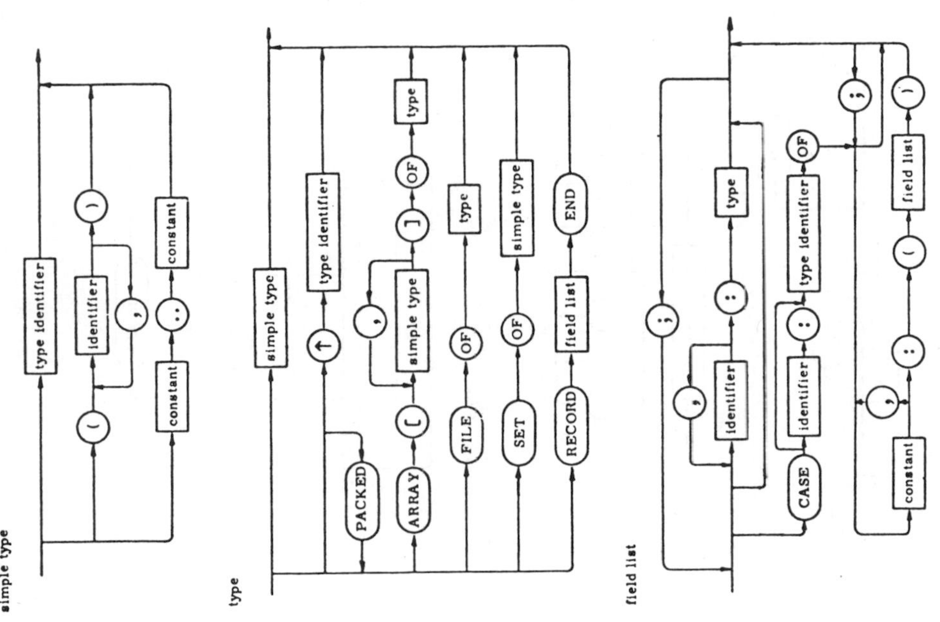

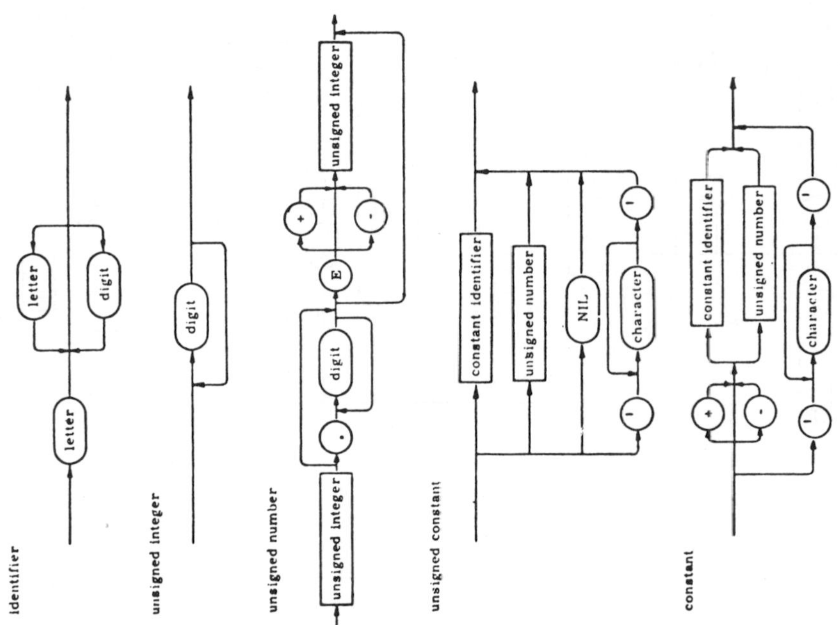

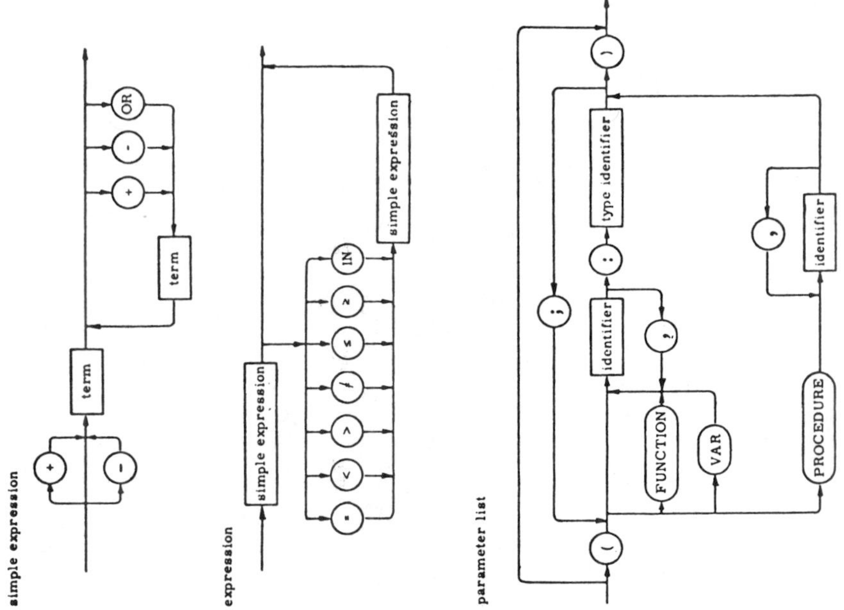
simple expression
+
-
term
term
+
-
OR
expression
simple expression
=
<
>
≠
≤
≥
IN
simple expression
parameter list
(
FUNCTION
VAR
identifier
,
:
type identifier
;
)
PROCEDURE
identifier
,

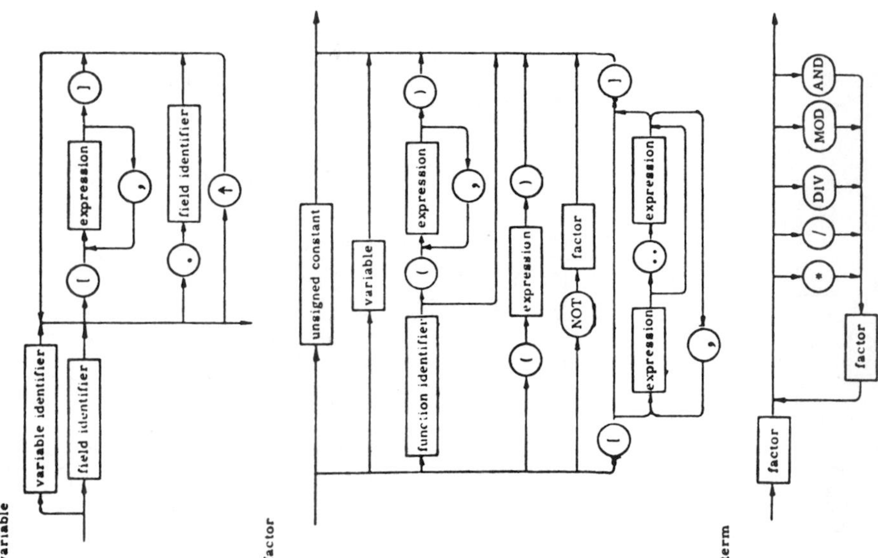
variable
variable identifier
field identifier
[
expression
,
]
.
field identifier
↑
factor
unsigned constant
variable
function identifier
(
expression
,
)
(
expression
)
NOT
factor
[
expression
..
expression
,
]
term
factor
*
/
DIV
MOD
AND
factor

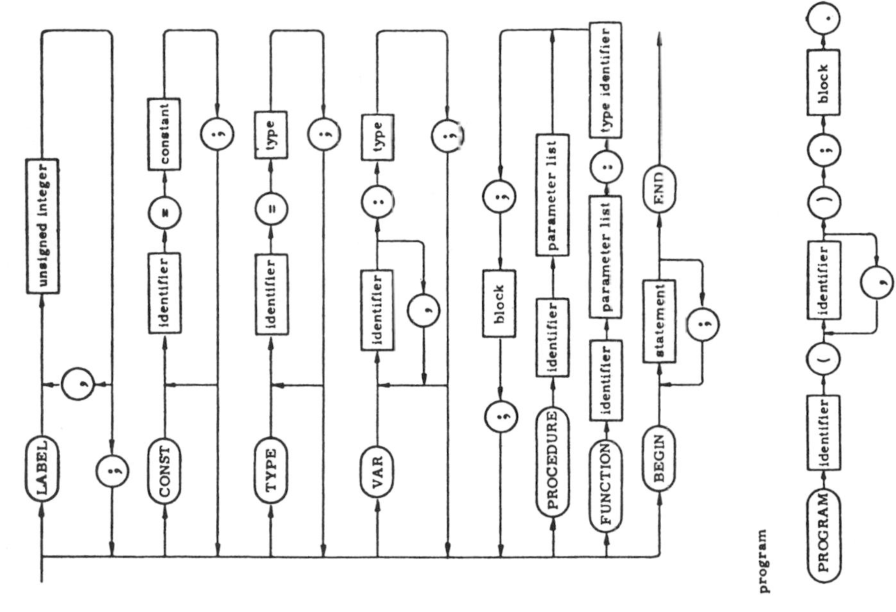
block
LABEL
unsigned integer
,
;
CONST
identifier
=
constant
TYPE
type
VAR
:
block
PROCEDURE
parameter list
FUNCTION
type identifier
BEGIN
statement
END
program
PROGRAM
(
)
.

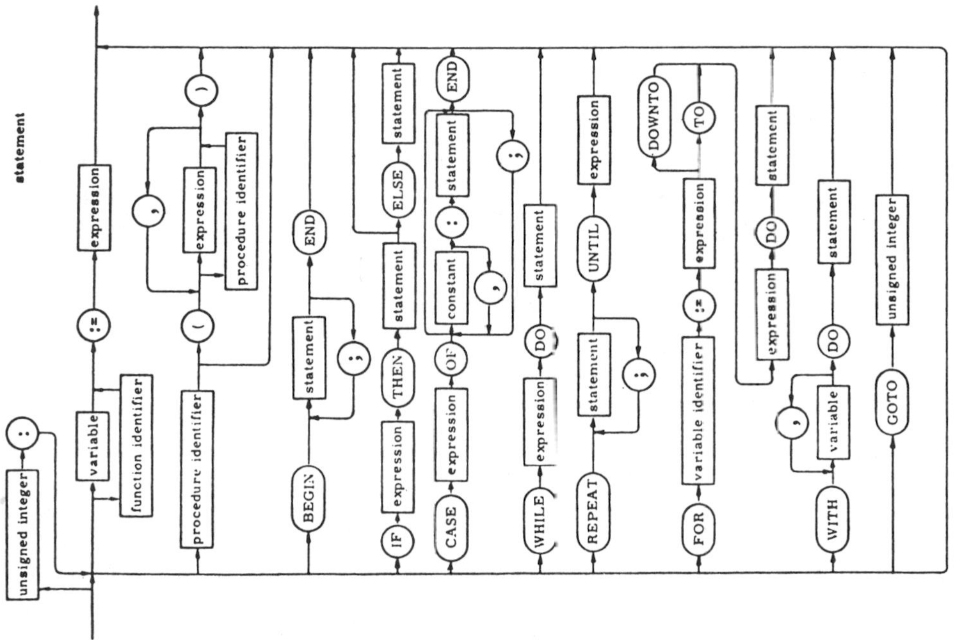
statement
unsigned integer
:
variable
function identifier
:=
expression
procedure identifier
(
,
)
BEGIN
statement
;
END
IF
THEN
ELSE
CASE
OF
constant
WHILE
DO
REPEAT
UNTIL
FOR
variable identifier
TO
DOWNTO
WITH
GOTO

Appendix B The CDC Implementation of PASCAL

B.1 Operating Instructions

B.1.1 Program Deck Structure

The deck structure for a PASCAL program with input data is the following:

```
Local control cards
PASCAL.
LGO.
    end-of-record card
Source program cards
    end-of-record card
Data cards
    end-of-job card
```

For a program without input data the structure is:

```
Local control cards
PASCAL.
LGO.
    end-of-record card
Source program cards
    end-of-job card
```

The format of control cards, program cards and data cards is shown in Appendix B.1.3. The structure of the source program itself is shown in Section I.4.1 in the body of the text.

The "local control cards" are peculiar to each individual computer installation. Get local instructions from your instructor or computer center.

B.1.2 Compiler Options

Options are specified to the CDC compiler by a special form of comment -- one in which the first character is a dollar sign:

```
(*$ ... *)
```

Such comments can be inserted anywhere in the source program, so the options in effect can be changed at different points in the program.

We will only describe four of the CDC options; for a complete list, see Jensen and Wirth. In each case the option is designated by its identifying letter L, U, T or P), followed by a plus or minus to indicate whether the option is to be turned on or off. For example, the option comment

```
(*$L+,U-,T+,P+*)
```

turns options L, T and P on, and option U off. This particular example describes the default options -- those that will be in effect unless you change them.

The options are the following:

L The L option controls the listing of the program. L+ causes the listing to be printed; L- causes the listing to be suppressed. The default is L+. This option affects only the source listing -- it has no effect on the execution output produced by execution of WRITE and WRITELN statements.

U The U option controls the portion of the card that will be scanned by the compiler. U- causes the entire card to be scanned; U+ causes only columns 1 to 72 to be scanned. (Columns 72 to 80 are often used for card identification and numbering.) The default is U-. Note that this option applies only to program cards; it has no effect on data cards read during the execution of the program.

T The T option controls the performance of various automatic tests. These are tests to ensure that:

1. The subscripts of arrays are valid -- that they yield values within the declared array bounds.

2. Assignments to variables of subrange types are valid -- values to be assigned are within the defined range. (The test is performed before the assignment.)

3. Divisors are not of value zero.

4. Conversions from REAL to INTEGER are possible -- that is, ABS(integer) < 2^{48}. (Jensen and Wirth apparently has this backwards.)

5. The value of CASE expressions are valid -- it corresponds to one of the specified case labels.

T+ specifies that the tests are to be performed; T- specifies that they are to be omitted. The default is T+.

Note that this option controls whether or not these tests are inserted as the program is translated. It does not turn the tests on or off during execution of the program. For example, if T+ is in effect during translation of procedure P, the tests will be inserted in appropriate places in P and will be executed whenever P is executed.

P The P option controls generation of the program needed to produce the post-mortem dump. P+ specifies that the program should be provided; P- specifies that it should be omitted. The default is P+. This option does not ensure that a post-mortem dump will be produced; it only makes it possible for the dump to be produced if the program is stopped by executing HALT or by encountering an execution error.

Many other systems provide options to limit the amount of computer time that can be consumed by a program, and the amount of printed output that it can produce. CDC PASCAL provides this capability only indirectly, through use of the CLOCK function and the LINELIMIT procedure. To limit the execution time of your program, insert a statement such as

```
IF CLOCK > limit THEN HALT
```

where "limit" gives the maximum number of milliseconds the program is to run. Make sure that this statement is inserted in a position where it will be encountered, so the test will be performed.

To set a limit on the number of lines of printed output, execute the procedure statement

```
LINELIMIT(OUTPUT, integer)
```

where "integer" gives the maximum allowable lines of output. The limit can subsequently be changed just by executing LINELIMIT again with a different limiting value.

B.1.3 Card Formats

Control Cards

An end-of-record card is multiple-punched with 7, 8 and 9, all in column 1. To do this, hold down the MULT PCH key (upper left corner of the keyboard) while punching 7, 8 and 9. Columns 2 and 3 may require special characters, or they may be blank -- get local instructions. The rest of the card -- columns 4 through 80 -- is ignored. In effect, it is a comment, and may be left blank or used for identification purposes.

An end-of-job card is similar to end-of-record, but has 6, 7, 8 and 9 multiple-punched in column 1. Columns 2 and 3 may be significant -- get local instructions. Columns 4 through 80 are a comment.

The PASCAL card normally has PASCAL. punched in the first 7 columns. However, if your installation does not use the standard file names this may be different and you may need local instructions.

The LGO card normally has LGO. punched in the first 4 columns. If your installation does not use the standard file names this may be different and you may need local instructions.

If your program uses files in addition to the standard INPUT and OUTPUT files (see Appendix A.2.3) you will have to use a different form of LGO card:

```
LGO(INPUT, OUTPUT, list of file-names)
```

The file-names on the LGO card must match the file-names given in the PROGRAM heading. The order of names on the two lists is critical.

Program Cards

The default format for program cards is to use the entire card. The position of program elements on the card is <u>not significant</u> to PASCAL. Hence you should take advantage of this indifference and position the lines so they will be easier for a human reader to understand, and so they will clearly exhibit the nesting structure of the program.

A blank is assumed to separate column 80 on one card and column 1 on the next card, so you <u>cannot divide a single symbol</u> over two cards. For example, in a long procedure heading, if you are punching INTEGER and reach column 80 after INT, you cannot just continue with EGER on the next card. Each individual symbol (keyword, identifier, number) must be contained on a single card.

The U+ option causes the compiler to scan only columns 1 to 72 of program cards. The contents of columns 73 to 80 are considered to be a comment. These rightmost columns are often used to identify and number the cards of the program. A four-character abbreviation of the program name can be punched in columns 73 to 76, and automatically duplicated from one card to the next (see Format Control on the Keypunch, below). Cards should be serially numbered in columns 77 to 80, with initial numbers in intervals of ten or more to leave room for later insertions. For example, a sorting program might be identified and initially numbered:

```
SORT0010
SORT0020
SORT0030
...
```

This card numbering and identification will probably seem like a waste of time -- until the first time you or the computer operator drops one of your decks.

Data Cards

The full card is always read for data cards -- the U option does not apply to data cards.

Data cards are considered to be a continuous stream of characters, with a blank assumed between column 80 of one card and column 1 of the next.

See Sections I.3.4.1, I.9.2.2, I.9.2.2.1 and I.9.2.2.2 in the text for discussion of the format of values on the data cards.

Also see Appendix B.2.4 concerning the CDC operating system's truncation of trailing blanks.

Format Control on the Keypunch

The use of program format to emphasize the structure of a program requires a convenient means of indenting. The keypunch offers a facility comparable to the "tab stops" on a typewriter for this purpose. The "stops" are set by a control card which is placed around a drum in the upper center of the IBM 029 keypunch. When the "star wheels" are lowered onto the face of this drum (by depressing the left side of the toggle switch just below the drum), pushing the SKIP key on the keyboard will cause the card to advance to the next "stop" position, as specified by a field-starting punch as shown below.

The drum control card also controls automatic skipping, automatic duplication (copying from one card to the next), and the alpha/numeric shift of the keyboard. Consider the control card to be divided into sets of adjacent columns called "fields". One character is used to start a field (in the left-most column of the field), and another character is used to continue the field:

Type of field:	To start:	To continue:
alpha shift	1	A
numeric shift	blank	+
automatic skip	-	+
automatic duplicate	/	A

The alpha/numeric shift in the control card can be overridden by the ALPHA and NUMERIC keys on the keyboard. For the automatic skip and automatic duplicate to be effective the AUTO SKIP DUP switch at the left top of the keyboard must be ON (in the "up" position).

The following is a typical card layout for program cards:

Column 1; automatic skip
Columns 2-5, 6-9, 10-13, ...; alpha fields with stops every four columns
Columns 73-76; automatic duplicate (for program identification)
Columns 77-80; numeric (for card serial number)

The drum control card for this layout would be punched as follows:

```
                    1         2         3         4
columns   1234567890123456789012345678901234567890
cont.char -1AAA1AAA1AAA1AAA1AAA1AAA1AAA1AAA1AAA1AA

          4         5         6         7         8
columns   1234567890123456789012345678901234567890
cont.char AAAAAAAAAAAAAAAAAAAAAAAAAAAAAAAA/AAA +++
```

If you do not want to use columns 73-80 for card identification, columns 73-80 of the control card should be punched as follows, to automatically release the card as soon as column 72 is punched, and feed a new card:

```
              7      8
columns    34567890
cont.char  -+++++++
```

If you are using the complete card for program text (option U- is in effect) then columns 73-80 of the control card should contain A's.

B.2 CDC Dependencies in the Primer

B.2.1 CDC Character Set

The situation with respect to the set of characters used in PASCAL is unbelievably confused. There are at least the following different possibilities:

1. The CDC Scientific 64 character set.
2. The CDC Scientific 63 character set.
3. The ASCII 64 character set.
4. The ASCII 64 character set, modified by CDC ordering.
5. The PASCAL-Report character set.

What actually determines the character set used at a particular computer installation is the particular printer employed -- and this may well not exactly correspond to any of the above.

All of these character sets are similar -- they just differ with respect to some of the special characters. For programming at the level represented by this *Primer*, this should not really be a problem, but it does mean you will see some PASCAL publications, and possibly some computer output, that don't look quite like what we have shown.

The disparities between character sets are most evident with respect to four special characters: the colon, the single quote (apostrophe), and the curly brackets that delimit comments. The colon and quote are shown in the *Primer* as they are used in the PASCAL Report (see Jensen and Wirth). But some printers lack these characters and some other special character will take their place. The PASCAL Report uses curly brackets { and } to delimit a comment, but few computer printers include these characters. The usual substitution involves the double characters (* and *), as we have shown in the *Primer*.

The examples in the *Primer* were run on a CDC 1700 printer, whose character set, shown at the beginning of Section I.9, doesn't coincide exactly with any of the standard sets listed above.

B.2.2 CDC Printing Format

The standard or default field widths for display of values on printed output depends upon the particular implementation, and can be altered by a particular computer installation. We have used the standard CDC values (see Section I.6.1):

REAL	22 positions
INTEGER	10 positions
BOOLEAN	10 positions

but these may have been changed at your installation. See Appendix A.2.1 for a description of the means to override these default field widths.

B.2.3 CDC File Names

PASCAL requires that the heading of a program be of the form:

```
PROGRAM program-name(list of file-names)
```

The particular files-names, INPUT and OUTPUT, shown in the text are peculiar to the CDC implementation. Even some CDC installations may use other names, so you should check with your local installation. The first name on the list designates the input file -- the source of data for READ and READLN statements. The second name designates the output file -- the target of WRITE and WRITELN statements. If you use additional files (see Appendix A.2.3) these file-names will follow on the list. In this case, the file-names will also have to be given on the LGO card (see Appendix B.1.3), and the lists on the LGO card and in the PROGRAM heading must agree. CDC requires that all file-names be identifiers with 7 or fewer characters.

B.2.4 CDC Truncation of Trailing Blanks

The CDC operating system has a peculiar way of treating trailing blanks when reading cards. (Trailing blanks are the blanks to the right of the last non-blank character on the card.) It takes the liberty of deleting some or all of such trailing blanks, and hence presenting PASCAL with a truncated image of the actual card. What is worse, the amount of truncation is, for all practical purposes, unpredictable.

This means that the number of characters received by PASCAL is not always exactly 80 per card, and your programs must be prepared for this. There is no problem on program cards, or on data cards that contain only numeric data. But data cards containing character data must be handled very carefully. A blank is a significant character to PASCAL -- it is treated just like any other character. But the operating system that actually reads the cards and presents the contents to PASCAL does not respect blanks if they are trailing. Hence if a data card has trailing blanks it may be truncated, and when PASCAL reaches the end of this truncated card it will go on to the next card. For example, if STR80 is an 80-character string (PACKED ARRAY[1..80] OF CHAR) consider the following read loop:

```
FOR I := 1 TO 80 DO
    READ(STR80[I])
```

There is just no way for the programmer to know exactly how many data cards will be read by this segment in order to supply 80 characters to STR80.

As another example, suppose you have 50 strings, each 20 characters long, and punch them into columns 1 to 20 of 50 cards. Say you want to load these into an array NAME: ARRAY[1..50] OF STRING20 (as in example I.9.3a). The obvious program segment to do this would be:

```
FOR I := 1 TO 50 DO
  BEGIN
    FOR J := 1 TO 20 DO
         READ(NAME[I,J]);
    READLN
  END
```

This segment is correct PASCAL, but it won't necessarily work in the CDC version, since if some of the strings have trailing blanks this loop can get out of synchronization with the cards. The following is a less attractive version, but it will work in spite of CDC:

```
FOR I := 1 TO 50 DO
  BEGIN (* READ LOOP *)
    J := 1;
    WHILE NOT EOLN AND (J <= 20) DO
      BEGIN
         READ(NAME[I,J]);
         J := J + 1
      END;
    READLN;
    FOR K := J TO 20 DO
         NAME[I,K] := ' '
  END (* READ LOOP *)
```

Note that the EOLN function becomes TRUE when PASCAL reaches the end of the line -- that is, when it reaches the end of the truncated card received from the operating system.

B.3 CDC Additions to PASCAL

The following built-in functions and procedures, not part of standard PASCAL, are available in the CDC compiler.

Functions

CLOCK -- Function has no argument. The result (INTEGER) is the computer time, in milliseconds (thousandths of a second), since the start of the job. Successive uses of CLOCK might be used, for example, to measure the amount of time required to perform some action to measure the length of time required to execute some portion of a program. It can also be used to limit the total time taken for the program; see Appendix B.1.2 on Options.

EXPO(x) -- The result (INTEGER) is the exponent of the argument x, where x is a REAL valued expression.

UNDEFINED(x) -- The result (BOOLEAN) is TRUE if x (a REAL valued expression) is "out of range" or "indefinite". Otherwise, the result is FALSE.

Procedures

DATE(s) -- The argument s is a string of length 10 (PACKED ARRAY[1..10] OF CHAR). The result of calling DATE is to assign the current calendar date to string s, in the form ƀMM/DD/YYƀ, where MM is the month, DD is the day, and YY is the year.

HALT -- Calling HALT terminates execution of the program, and causes a post-mortem dump to be printed.

LINELIMIT(OUTPUT,n) -- Calling LINELIMIT will limit the total number of lines that can be printed by the program to the value given by the INTEGER argument n.

TIME(s) -- The argument s is a string of length 10 (PACKED ARRAY[1..10] OF CHAR). The result of calling TIME is to assign the current time of day to the string s. The form is ƀHH.MM.SSƀ, where HH is the hour (24 hour clock), MM is the minute, and SS is the second.

B.4 PASCAL Error Number Summary

1: error in simple type
2: identifier expected
3: 'program' expected
4: ')' expected
5: ':' expected
6: illegal symbol
7: error in parameter list
8: 'of' expected
9: '(' expected
10: error in type
11: '[' expected
12: ']' expected
13: 'end' expected
14: ';' expected
15: integer expected
16: '=' expected
17: 'begin' expected
18: error in declaration part
19: error in field-list
20: ',' expected
21: '*' expected

50: error in constant
51: ':=' expected
52: 'then' expected
53: 'until' expected
54: 'do' expected
55: 'to'/'downto' expected
56: 'if' expected
57: 'file' expected
58: error in factor
59: error in variable

101: identifier declared twice
102: low bound exceeds highbound
103: identifier is not of appropriate class
104: identifier not declared
105: sign not allowed
106: number expected
107: incompatible subrange types
108: file not allowed here
109: type must not be real
110: tagfield type must be scalar or subrange
111: incompatible with tagfield type
112: index type must not be real
113: index type must be scalar or subrange
114: base type must not be real
115: base type must be scalar or subrange
116: error in type of standard procedure parameter

117: unsatisfied forward reference
118: forward reference type identifier in variable declaration
119: forward declared; repetition of parameter list not allowed
120: function result type must be scalar, subrange or pointer
121: file value parameter not allowed
122: forward declared function; repetition of result type not allowed
123: missing result type in function declaration
124: F-format for real only
125: error in type of standard function parameter
126: number of parameters does not agree with declaration
127: illegal parameter substitution
128: result type of parameter function does not agree with declaration
129: type conflict of operands
130: expression is not of set type
131: tests on equality allowed only
132: strict inclusion not allowed
133: file comparison not allowed
134: illegal type of operand(s)
135: type of operand must be Boolean
136: set element type must be scalar or subrange
137: set element types not compatible
138: type of variable is not array
139: index type is not compatible with declaration
140: type of variable is not record
141: type of variable must be file or pointer
142: illegal parameter substitution
143: illegal type of loop control variable
144: illegal type of expression
145: type conflict
146: assignment of files not allowed
147: label type incompatible with selecting expression
148: subrange bounds must be scalar
149: index type must not be integer
150: assignment to standard function is not allowed
151: assignment to formal function is not allowed
152: no such field in this record
153: type error in read
154: actual parameter must be a variable
155: control variable must not be formal
156: multidefined case label
157: too many cases in case statement
158: missing corresponding variant declaration
159: real or string tagfields not allowed
160: previous declaration was not forward
161: again forward declared
162: parameter size must be constant
163: missing variant in declaration
164: substitution of standard proc/func not allowed
165: multidefined label
166: multideclared label
167: undeclared label
168: undefined label

169: error in base set
170: value parameter expected
171: standard file was redeclared
172: undeclared external file
173: Fortran procedure or function expected
174: Pascal procedure or function expected
175: missing file "input" in program heading
176: missing file "output" in program heading

201: error in real constant: digit expected
202: string constant must not exceed source line
203: integer constant exceeds range
204: 8 or 9 in octal number

250: too many nested scopes of identifiers
251: too many nested procedures and/or functions
252: too many forward references of procedure entries
253: procedure too long
254: too many long constants in this procedure
255: too many errors on this source line
256: too many external references
257: too many externals
258: too many local files
259: expression too complicated

300: division by zero
301: no case provided for this value
302: index expression out of bounds
303: value to be assigned is out of bounds
304: element expression out of range

398: implementation restriction
399: variable dimension arrays not implemented

References

Jensen, K. and Niklaus Wirth, PASCAL User Manual and Report (2nd ed), Springer-Verlag, 1975.

Richmond, George H. (editor), PASCAL Newsletter, No. 1 (March, 1974), No. 2 (May, 1974), No. 3 (February, 1975), Computing Center, University of Colorado.

Mickel, A. (editor), PASCAL Newsletter, Computer Center, University of Minnesota. (This replaces the earlier Newsletter from Colorado.)

Wirth, Niklaus, "The Programming Language PASCAL", Acta Informatica, 1, 35-63, 1971.

Wirth, Niklaus, Systematic Programming: An Introduction, Prentice-Hall, 1973.

Hoare, C. A. R. and and Niklaus Wirth, "An Axiomatic Definition of the Programming Language PASCAL", Acta Informatica, 2, 335-355, 1973.

Index